D0775477

Patrick Brontë

Patrick Brontë

FATHER OF GENIUS

DUDLEY GREEN

For my sister Rosemary, my brother Stephen,
and
in memory of
my father
the Revd Edgar Green,
Incumbent of St James' Church, Ryde, Isle of Wight,
1934–1974,
my mother Isobel,
and my brother Hugh

First published by Nonsuch Publishing (an imprint of The History Press) 2008
This edition published 2010

The History Press
The Mill, Brimscombe Port,
Stroud, Gloucestershire, GL5 2QG
www.thehistorypress.co.uk

British Library Cataloguing in Publication Data.
A catalogue record for this book is available from the British Library

ISBN 978 0 7524 5445 0

Typesetting and origination by The History Press
Manufacturing managed by Jellyfish Print Solutions Ltd
Printed and bound in India by Replika Press Pvt. Ltd.

Contents

PART FOUR: Grief and Determination, 1847–1861

APPENDICES

Foreword by the Archbishop of Canterbury

The Most Revd and Rt Hon. Dr Rowan Williams

Thanks to Mrs Gaskell, the world still has a vivid but pretty misleading picture of Haworth parsonage and its incumbent. This excellent biography, making use of extensive archival material and written by a scholar who has already produced a first-class edition of Patrick Brontë's correspondence, gives us for the first time a really three-dimensional portrait of a man remarkable in his own right as well as remarkable for being the parent of one of the most gifted families in the history of English literature, a man whose gifts took him from early poverty to acquaintance with some of the leading figures of his generation.

We learn in these pages something that is often forgotten: that the difficulties of travel in the early nineteenth century did not in the least prevent people from enjoying a cosmopolitan experience and perspective. The Brontës were never prisoners in remote Yorkshire, but shared in the intellectual and imaginative currents of the day; they may have been in important senses 'local' voices, giving unforgettable shape to a particular landscape. But they were also Europeans, absorbing the challenge of a wider world.

We see also, though, what the conditions of life were in rural Yorkshire at the time, what kinds of poverty and vulnerability to disease were the daily accompaniments of life, not only for the poor but for the professional classes, too. This book shows us not just a remarkable man in the setting of his remarkable family, but an ordinary, devoted parish priest, at the service of a community, struggling with their irregularities, ministering in their needs and taking responsibility for their education, painfully conscious of and angry about the practical help that was denied them in times of economic hardship or epidemic. Here is early nineteenth-century rural society in miniature, neither romanticised nor made impossibly remote from us.

This is a very welcome book indeed, which will illuminate the background of that endlessly fascinating family, but will also tell us all sorts of things we did not know about Church and society in a period of dramatic change, the period of a life spanning the long Hanoverian afternoon, the French wars and the beginnings of the Victorian age. It is a study full of detail, energy and insight, and it is a delight to be able to commend it to the reader.

✝ Rowan Cantuar:

Preface

Patrick Brontë was a clergyman of the Church of England for fifty-five years. His career is remarkable, both for his emergence from a poor and humble background in the north of Ireland to take his degree at St John's College, Cambridge, and proceed to ordination, and also for his long clerical ministry, forty years of which were spent in Yorkshire as the incumbent of Haworth during a period of great social and ecclesiastical change in the country. As the son and grandson of clergymen my interest in the Brontë family has always centred on Patrick and on the details of his clerical life. When I retired from teaching in 1995, in an effort to discover more about his ministry, I decided to make a collection of his letters. During the next ten years I managed to identify around 250 letters. These showed a wide variety of content. Some were personal, relating to the members of his family and to the sad bereavements which he suffered. Others dealt with the many concerns of a busy incumbent in his parish. A significant number were written to the local press and showed his interest in the wider issues of the day, while others revealed him to be a resolute campaigner on a variety of local matters. My edition of *The Letters of Patrick Brontë* was published in 2005.

It is unfortunate that, in the century and a half since Mrs Gaskell published her famous *Life of Charlotte Brontë* in 1857, Patrick Brontë has been a much maligned man. In an effort to clear Charlotte and her sisters of the charges of coarseness and insensitivity in their novels, Mrs Gaskell portrayed them as living in a wild and remote area cut off from the normal decencies of civilised society, and their family background as lonely and austere. She also depicted Patrick as a remote father given to eccentric behaviour and strange fits of passion. The justifiably great success of her biography has meant that her unfavourable portrait of him has remained etched in the public mind ever since. In this, the first biography of Patrick to be published for over forty years, I have made an attempt to redress the balance. It has been my aim to present a fair and accurate account of Patrick's life and ministry, based on the considerable documentary evidence which is available. I hope that the picture here presented reveals a kindly and loving father who took a keen interest in his children's development and an able and faithful clergyman, who was ever sensitive to the pastoral needs of his parishioners.

Dudley Green
Clitheroe
January 2008

Acknowledgements and Thanks

I should like to express my thanks to Dr Rowan Williams for the honour he has done me by writing the Foreword to this work. In the midst of the very busy schedule of a Lambeth Conference year it was an act of kindness which I deeply appreciate. I think his action would have brought great pleasure to Patrick Brontë. For much of Patrick's time at Haworth his diocesan was Dr Charles Longley, the first Bishop of Ripon, who later became Archbishop of Canterbury and founded the Lambeth Conference. Among the new items in my book is a moving letter from Patrick Brontë thanking Dr Longley for his expression of sympathy at the time of Charlotte's death. This letter has only recently been discovered among the Longley Papers in Lambeth Palace Library. I am very grateful to the Right Rev'd George Cassidy, Bishop of Southwell & Nottingham, for putting me in touch with Dr Williams, and for the kind assistance given to me by members of the Lambeth Palace staff, especially by Jana Edmunds.

In my edition of *The Letters of Patrick Brontë* I expressed my gratitude to those who had assisted me in my research during the previous ten years. I should again like to thank Robert and Louise Barnard for their continued support and encouragement and for making available information from their *Brontë Encyclopaedia* prior to its publication last year. Robert also read my MS in draft form and made many helpful suggestions. A great debt is also due to my brother Stephen who has once again proved to be a mine of information on ecclesiastical matters and, although not an inveterate Brontë lover, read my draft MS through on two occasions and gave much useful advice. I am grateful to Wendy Smith for kindly reading through my proofs. My thanks are due to Ann Dinsdale for her expert help and advice and for the warm welcome which I received on my visits to the library at the Brontë Parsonage Museum. I am also grateful to Sarah Laycock for her work on the illustrations.

Once again I acknowledge my great debt to Juliet Barker's *The Brontës*, a monumental work which, with its detailed notes of reference, is an indispensable aid to all those who engage in research on the Brontë family. I have also made frequent use of Margaret Smith's meticulous three-volume edition of *The Letters of Charlotte Bronte* and I have gained much information from *A Man of Sorrow* by John Lock and W.T. Dixon, who had access to some details about the life of Patrick which sadly have since been lost.

I am grateful to my friends in the Irish Section of the Brontë Society for their help over the details of Patrick's childhood and youth: to Margaret Livingston for arranging my visits to Northern Ireland, to Ivan and Roberta McAulay for kindly providing hospitality and to Finny O'Sullivan for reading my Irish chapter and giving me historical advice. I should like to thank Malcolm Underwood, the Archivist of St John's College, Cambridge, for his assistance over the details of Patrick's scholarships at the college. I am grateful to Richard Middleton, the Archivist of the Minster Church of All Saints, Dewsbury, for supplying me with his history of the church, to Robin Greenwood for once again allowing me to profit from his detailed knowledge of the nineteenth-century history of Haworth and to Ruth Battye for her kind hospitality on my visits there. I am indebted to Mr W. R. Mitchell for his permission to use the photograph of Dr William Cartman, his great-great-grandfather and Patrick's life-long friend. I am grateful to the late Geoffrey Sharps for his assistance over the date of the third edition of Mrs Gaskell's *Life of Charlotte Brontë* and for sharing with me his knowledge of the background to the article on Charlotte Brontë in *Sharpe's London Magazine*. I also wish to thank Brian Wilks for informing me of the recently discovered letter which Patrick wrote to the Bishop of Ripon after Charlotte's death. I am grateful to Andrew McCarthy for his information on publicity and to Joan Leach, Professor John Chapple and Alan Shelston for their assistance and encouragement.

I should like to record my particular thanks to Simon Hamlet of Nonsuch Publishing for his constant support and encouragement. He has been patient in dealing with my many queries and I am grateful for all his help and advice. I should also like to thank his editorial assistant, Joanna Howe.

Finally, I wish to pay tribute to the memory of three friends in the Brontë Society who have greatly influenced me in my knowledge and understanding of Patrick Brontë's the life and ministry: Chris Sumner, for many years Chairman of the Membership Committee who inspired all who knew her with her enthusiasm for the study of the Brontës; Muriel Greene, formerly the Secretary of the Irish Section, who was the first to take me round the places associated with Patrick's early life in County Down; and Charles Lemon, member of Council and editor of *Transactions*, whose record of seventy years unbroken membership of the Society was an indication of his life-long devotion to the Brontë family.

Format and Conventions

Quotations in the text

The MS spelling and punctuation has been followed in all cases. Obvious misspellings have been left without comment, less obvious ones are marked [*sic*]. For greater clarity, authorial deletions have been omitted except where they are relevant to the subject-matter.

Rendering of the name Brontë

Although Patrick Brontë almost invariably accentuated the final syllable of his surname, he was not consistent in his method. The first appearance of the diaeresis in his surname was on the title page of *The Cottage in the Wood*, published in 1815. Since Patrick did not use it at this time in his signatures on letters and in the church registers, it seems that this was a printer's error. It was not until December 1849 that he began to use the diaeresis in his letters. Prior to that date he usually signed himself *Brontë* or *Bronté*. For the sake of consistency, in this work his name is always written *Brontë*.

Symbols used in quotations from original MSS

| |	denotes later additions to the text by the writer
< >	denotes deletions by the writer
[ ]	denotes an editorial insertion

Illustrations

All of the illustrations, with the exceptions of numbers 6, 27 and 41, are courtesy of the Brontë Society

I have no objection whatever to your representing me as a <u>Little</u> eccentric, since you and your learned friends would have it so; only don't set me on in my fury to burning hearthrugs, sawing the backs off chairs, and tearing my wife's silk gowns ... Had I been numbered amongst the calm, <u>concentric</u> men of the world, I should not have been as I now am, and I should in all probability never have had such children as mine have been.

Patrick Brontë to Mrs Gaskell, 30 July 1857

I have not the honour of knowing you personally, and yet I have a feeling of profound admiration for you, for in judging the father of a family by his children one cannot be mistaken and in this respect the education and sentiments that we have found in your daughters can only give us a very high idea of your worth and of your character.

Monsieur Heger to Patrick Brontë, 5 November 1842

PART ONE

From Ireland to Haworth, 1777–1820

I

'Ireland … Ah! "Dulce Domum"'
1777–1802

I had a letter lately from Ireland, They are all well. Have you heard, since I saw you, from America? And how are your relations there? Ah! "Dulce Domum".[1]

Patrick Brontë to the Rev'd John Campbell,[2] 12 November 1808

'My father's name was Hugh Brontë. He was a native of the south of Ireland.' So wrote the seventy-eight-year-old Patrick Brontë to the novelist Mrs Gaskell on 20 June 1855, eleven weeks after the death of his daughter, Charlotte. After hearing that Mrs Gaskell was agreeable to his request that she should write an account of his daughter's 'life and works'[3] and, feeling that it would be necessary to gratify curiosity about Charlotte's family background, he proceeded to give her some further information about his father and about his own early life in Ireland:

He was left an orphan at an early age. It was said that he was of ancient family. Whether this was or was not so I never gave myself the trouble to inquire, since his lot in life as well as mine depended, under providence, not on family descent but our own exertions. He came to the north of Ireland and made an early but suitable marriage. His pecuniary means were small – but renting a few acres of land, he and my mother by dint of application and industry managed to bring up a family of ten children in a respectable manner. I shew'd an early fondness for books, and continued at school for several years. At the age of sixteen – knowing that my father could afford me no pecuniary aid – I began to think of doing something for myself. I therefore opened a public school – and in this line I continued five or six years. I was then a tutor in a gentleman's family – From which situation I removed to Cambridge and enter'd St John's College.[4]

This statement, tantalisingly brief though it is, represents the only account we have in Patrick's own words of his Irish origins. It may be regarded as the irreducible minimum of what is known of his boyhood and early life.

The only other account of Patrick's Irish background to be given in any detail during his lifetime was in an article which appeared in the *Belfast Mercury* under the heading 'Currer Bell' a few weeks after Charlotte's death:

> We recently quoted from the *Daily News* an interesting article on this gifted authoress, or rather on the person known to the reading public by that pseudonym. We have since learnt some particulars respecting her father's family which will be more especially interesting to our readers, when they learn, probably for the first time, that they were natives of the county Down. The father of the authoress was Mr Patrick Prunty, of the parish of Ahaderg, near Loughbrickland. His parents were of humble origin, but their large family were remarkable for physical strength and personal beauty. The natural quickness and intelligence of Patrick Prunty attracted the attention of the Rev Mr Tighe, rector of Drumgooland parish, who gave him a good education in England and finally procured him a curacy in —. In his new sphere he was not unmindful of the family claims, for he settled £20 per annum on his mother.[5]

The publication of Mrs Gaskell's *Life of Charlotte Brontë* in March 1857 focused attention on the lives and background of the Brontë family, and after Patrick's death in March 1861 this interest continued to grow. In 1893 the Revd Dr William Wright (a native of Finard, near Rathfriland, County Down, and a former Presbyterian missionary with the British and Foreign Bible Society in Damascus) published an exhaustive study of the Brontë family's Irish background. Based on his interest in the family from his student days at Queen's College, Belfast, in the 1850s, and also on several visits to Ireland after his return from the Middle East in 1875, it is at once a fascinating but also an exasperating work.[6]

Many of Dr Wright's informants were able men of integrity, who had a good knowledge of the Brontë homeland in the 1840s and whose family connections went back to the time of Patrick Brontë's boyhood. Chief among them was the Presbyterian minister of Finard, the Revd William McAlister, who had been Wright's classics master in the 1850s. He told Wright that Patrick's father, Hugh, had a considerable local reputation as a storyteller. He said that as a child he had heard his father's account of Hugh Brontë's fireside tales, and he even claimed to have heard the aged Hugh himself. In his tuition of the young Wright, McAlister had shown himself to be an imaginative teacher. He had sometimes given his pupil the plot of a Greek play and left him to fill in the details in his own words, and occasionally he had treated the stories told by Hugh in the same way. This creative method of teaching may be admirable for developing a pupil's imagination, but it is hardly calculated to produce a desire for scholarly precision. Much of Wright's account of the Brontë family is couched in this folk-tale style of writing, where the essential feature seems to be the quality of the story rather than the accuracy of the facts.

The uniformly Presbyterian connection of Wright's informants has given rise in the minds of some critics to the suspicion that it was one of Dr Wright's aims to stress the influence of Presbyterianism on the Brontë family. It was also his declared intention to emphasise the hitherto-neglected Irish contribution to the Brontë story. We have, therefore, to be on our guard when we see claims for an Irish origin for the plot of *Wuthering Heights*, and an Irish venue cited for Patrick's famous encounter with a drunken bully on the Sunday School walk.[7] We also have to remember that Wright's book was published over ninety years after Patrick left Ireland, at a time when myths about the Brontë family were proliferating. The comprehensive nature of Wright's study, however, makes it the only source available for much of his narrative. There are very few written sources for that time in Ireland and verification of Wright's account is in most cases not possible. Moreover, it was an age when oral tradition was seriously regarded and any attempt to provide a narrative of Patrick's early life must take account of Wright's work, although we have to realise that for much of the time we are not in the field of serious historical writing.

Patrick Brontë was born on 17 March 1777 (St Patrick's Day), the eldest of the ten children of Hugh and Alice Brontë'. At the time of his birth his parents were living in a small two-roomed cottage at Emdale in the parish of Drumballyroney. While Patrick's own description of his father's origins in his letter to Mrs Gaskell was excessively brief, Wright gives an elaborate account of Hugh Brontë's family background and of the struggles of his early life. Hugh's grandfather is said to have been a prosperous farmer on the banks of the River Boyne, near Drogheda in the south of Ireland. In the course of his work he made frequent voyages to Liverpool to sell cattle. After one of these journeys, he agreed, on the promptings of his wife, to adopt a strange child who had been found abandoned on the ship after its return to Ireland. The adopted child, who was given the name of Welsh, soon became Mr Brontë's favourite in the family. Welsh took a great interest in the cattle-dealing business and Mr Brontë came to depend on him. This aroused the jealousy of the rest of the family and, after Mr Brontë's death, Welsh was thrown out of the house. He later got his revenge. After securing the post of sub-agent of the estate, he deceived and married Mary, one of the Brontë daughters, and, after evicting the family from their holding, he took possession of the farm himself. But he then suffered a change of fortune. A fire destroyed the farmhouse and he fell into poverty. Having no son and heir, he went to visit one of his wife's brothers, now a prosperous farmer in a distant part of Ireland. After expressing penitence for the wrongs he had brought on the family and a desire to make amends, Welsh persuaded his brother-in-law to agree that he should adopt one of his sons, named Hugh. The young boy, aged seven or eight at the time, was taken on a long and exhausting journey to the old Brontë farm on the banks of the River Boyne. Here he was brought up in appalling conditions. He received cruel treatment from his uncle and was expected to work all day on the farm. Several years passed until eventually, at the age of fifteen, Hugh managed to escape and make his way north.

The links between Wright's account and the story of *Wuthering Heights* are obvious. Even some of the details are similar. Welsh had a sanctimonious servant called Gallagher who reported on Hugh's shortcomings and gloated over his sufferings. It should also be noted that the dog which befriended the young Hugh on Welsh's farm was called Keeper.[8] Wright's account is said to be based on the story Hugh himself told of his early life, but it must be remembered that it first appeared in print over forty years after the publication of *Wuthering Heights*. We have to take seriously the possibility that it may reflect a desire to show an Irish origin for the structure of Emily's plot. None of the participants in this strange story were alive at the time of Wright's investigations and it is not possible to check the authenticity of his account. Moreover, he tells the story in a highly dramatic manner and in a style which seems more appropriate to a folk-tale. Edward Chitham, who in his examination of Wright's account shows himself to be the most sympathetic of his critics, is forced to conclude:

> We do not find in Wright's record any intense or close study of a scholarly kind: his method used intuition, charm, lengthy and capacious but perhaps inaccurate memory, and elegant language.[9]

In his description of the circumstances leading to Hugh Brontë's marriage, Wright seems to be on slightly firmer ground. After travelling north from the Boyne, Hugh secured work at some lime-kilns at Mount Pleasant, near Dundalk in County Louth. He did so well there that he was promoted to be overseer. His work eventually brought him into contact with Paddy McClory, a red-haired Catholic youth, who regularly came south from Ballynaskeagh in County Down to obtain lime. A friendship developed between the two young men and Hugh was invited to visit the McClory household, where he rapidly fell in love with Paddy's sister, Alice (who seems also to have been known as Eleanor). As a Catholic family, however, the McClorys strongly opposed any possibility of Alice entering into a marriage with the Protestant Hugh Brontë. Plans were made for her to marry a Catholic farmer who lived nearby, but on the day appointed for the wedding Alice eloped with Hugh. After their marriage in Magherally parish church, near Banbridge, they set up home in a small cottage in Emdale in Drumballyroney parish. Patrick Brontë was born in the following year. Although once again the details of this account cannot be substantiated, there is nothing in the essentials of Wright's story that runs contrary to Patrick's own laconic statements about his father. The places mentioned may still be visited today, and Catholic descendants of the McClory family still live in the neighbourhood of Emdale.

The early days of Hugh and Alice's married life must have been very difficult. The small cottage had two rooms. At the back was their bedroom and the front room served as a kitchen and as a reception room. It also seems to have been used as a primitive sort of kiln, so that Hugh could earn a living by drying his neighbours' corn. He is later said to have been a ditcher and maker of fences and, according to Patrick, he rented a few acres of land. Hugh must have prospered to some extent, however, for the baptismal record of his third son, also called Hugh, shows that by May 1781 he had moved his family to a more substantial house in nearby Lisnacreevy. By the time of the birth of his last daughter, Alice, the family had moved again to a large house at Ballynaskeagh, just uphill from the McClory cottage where Hugh had first set eyes on his future wife.

Hugh Brontë's greatest claim to fame in his locality, according to Wright, was as a storyteller in the old Irish tradition, a role similar to that of the Homeric bard. During long winter nights he would sit beside the fire telling stories to an audience of rapt visitors. He only learned to read late in life and his favourite books were the Bible, *The Pilgrim's Progress* and the poems of Robert Burns. He also had a reputation as a passionate supporter of the rights of tenant farmers against their unscrupulous landlords. The only first-hand account we have of him was given by Patrick's sister Alice a few days before her death in 1891 at the age of ninety-five. Speaking to the Revd J. B. Lusk, the Presbyterian minister at Glascar, she said:

> My father came originally from Drogheda. He was not very tall, but purty [*sic*] stout; he was sandy-haired, and my mother fair-haired. He was very fond of his children and worked to the last for them.[10]

No baptismal records were kept in the parish of Drumballyroney until after 1778, when the Revd Thomas Tighe became the vicar, so there is no record of Patrick's baptism in the parish register. When, in 1806, at the time of his ordination, Patrick needed to prove his age, he had to ask his father to sign a certificate. The signature 'Hugh Brontë' on the document which was then drawn up is the only written record we have of Patrick's father.[11]

By his own account the young Patrick showed an early interest in books. We have no knowledge of the school he attended, although the account of his sister Alice's funeral in the *Banbridge Chronicle* in January 1891 stated that he 'was educated at a school near Glascar'. It seems that as a lad he frequented the blacksmith's forge in Emdale and at some stage received training in weaving. According to Wright's account the critical moment in his intellectual development occurred when the Revd Andrew Harshaw, a Presbyterian minister who ran a small school at nearby Ballynafern, overheard Patrick reading aloud from Milton's *Paradise Lost*. Realising the young man's intellectual potential, Harshaw agreed to give him free tuition in the early hours of the morning, leaving him free to continue his weaving during the daytime.

Eventually, through Harshaw's influence, Patrick was appointed schoolmaster of the Glascar Hill Presbyterian church school. Here he showed himself to be an enlightened teacher, carefully matching his pupils' tasks to their intellectual capabilities. During the summer holidays he also took parties of senior pupils on walking expeditions in the Mourne mountains. In support of his account, Wright cites the evidence of the Revd John McCracken, minister of Ballyeaston Presbyterian church, Belfast. McCracken had been baptised at Glascar in January 1836 and he had often heard his mother tell how, as a very young girl, she had been a pupil at the school in Patrick's time. Wright also claims that it was at this time that Patrick started writing poetry. He even goes so far as to say that most of the poems published in 1811 in Patrick's collection of *Cottage Poems* were written during his time at Glascar.[12]

Patrick's appointment as schoolmaster at Glascar Hill came to an abrupt end when he was detected among the corn-stacks kissing one of his older pupils, a red-haired girl called Helen. She was the daughter of a prosperous farmer who was also a senior officer of the Glascar Presbyterian church. The family were outraged and Patrick was dismissed from his post, and it seems that the school was disbanded. After an interval of some months, again through the influence of Andrew Harshaw, Patrick secured the post of teacher at the Drumballyroney parish school and also tutor to the children of the vicar, the Revd Thomas Tighe.

Any assessment of Wright's description of Patrick's time at Glascar has to take into account the two tendencies which are inherent throughout Wright's work. The first is to stress the influence of the Presbyterian Church over the early years of Patrick's life, seen here in the advice given him by the Revd Andrew Harshaw.[13] The second, even more prevalent, is Wright's frequent claim to have discovered an Irish origin for the flowering of the Brontë genius, here seen in his assertion that much of Patrick's poetry was written during his time as schoolmaster at Glascar.

In his own brief description of his time as a teacher, Patrick told Mrs Gaskell:

> At the age of sixteen … I opened a public school – and in this line I continued for five or six years; I was then a tutor in a gentleman's family.[14]

If Wright's account is authentic, Patrick's statement must refer to his time at Glascar Hill school, but there are difficulties in accepting this. By an odd quirk of historical fate, Patrick's statement is supported by a piece of documentary evidence. In a letter to the *Belfast Newsletter* of 23 February 1937, a local historian, C. Johnston Robb, revealed the existence of an account book belonging to John Lindsay of Bangrove, a large house near Hilltown. In this book there is an intriguing entry:

> November 1793 Paid Pat Prunty, one pound, David's school bill.[15]

Patrick Brontë was sixteen in 1793 and by his own account this was the year he opened a public school. The schoolboy David Lindsay must have been about fourteen at the time, for he was commissioned in the Royal Downshire Militia in 1796. He later served in the 18th Regiment of Foot and died in the West Indies. David's father would clearly have been a member of the minor gentry and it is hard to reconcile his paying a considerable sum of money and sending his son some eight miles to be educated by Patrick Brontë with Wright's account of Patrick teaching the children of farmers and labourers in a village school. Unfortunately, the brevity of Patrick's reference to his time as a teacher and the absence of any evidence to support Wright's account mean that the details of Patrick's first teaching post can not be established with any certainty.[16]

According to Patrick's statement to Mrs Gaskell, it was in 1798 or 1799 that he took up his post at Drumballyroney. The year 1798 was a significant one in Irish history. Spurred on by the example of the French Revolution, the movement of the United Irishmen, led by Theobald Wolfe Tone, sought to break Ireland's connection with England and to establish a republic on similar principles. When the government responded with a policy of repression, open rebellion broke out. In the north, County Down was the main centre of rebellion and the revolt was supported by many Presbyterians. Several thousand men gathered on Windmill Hill, Ballynahinch, and in the battle which took place on 12–13 June they were defeated by government forces. One of those who took part was Patrick's brother William, aged nineteen at the time. William later told his grandchildren how he fled for his life after the battle, taking refuge in County Armagh before making his way home. Government reprisals were savage and William was lucky to escape with his life. Patrick does not appear to have taken any active part in the rebellion. Although in later life he was always fervent in his opposition to any instance of injustice, he had a constant horror of revolution and was a strong supporter of Ireland's union with England. Many years later, in a letter written to the *Halifax Guardian* in July 1843, he referred to 'the insane but fearful project of the repeal of the Union, in the Emerald Isle'.[17] And, in a letter to his brother Hugh in November that year, he wrote:

As I learn from the newspapers, Ireland, is at present, in a very precarious situation, and circumstances there must, I should think – lead to civil war – Which in its consequences, is the worst of all wars … But, whatever … be done, should be in strict accordance with the Laws.[18]

The exact nature of Patrick's teaching position at Drumballyroney is hard to define. He himself told Mrs Gaskell that he was 'a tutor in a gentleman's family', but there seems some doubt over whether he was appointed to be a tutor to the vicar's sons or as a teacher in the parish school. A great-nephew of Thomas Tighe, writing in 1879, recalled hearing one of Tighe's sons claim that 'Paddy Prunty had a school in one of my father's parishes', and that his father had recognised Patrick's ability and had taken great pains to teach him, although he denied that Patrick had ever been a tutor to the family.[19] The church at Drumballyroney was rebuilt in 1800 and it seems that the school was renovated at the same time. It may be that, while he was himself receiving instruction from Thomas Tighe, Patrick was employed by him to teach the country children in the church school. Whatever the nature of Patrick's appointment at Drumballyroney, however, the friendship and patronage of Mr Tighe was to change the whole course of his life.

The Revd Thomas Tighe was a Justice of the Peace and a man of considerable ability and influence. The fourth son in a rich Irish family, he had been educated at Harrow and St John's College, Cambridge. After graduating in 1775, he had been a fellow of Peterhouse for three years before returning to Ireland in 1778 to take up the appointment of vicar of Drumballyroney and rector of Drumgooland. He served in this united parish for forty-three years. Tighe was a committed evangelical and his family had entertained John Wesley at their home at Rosanna in County Wicklow during Wesley's last visit to Ireland in June 1789. As his vicar, Thomas Tighe must have known the young Patrick well, and it seems that he came to recognise his potential as a future minister of the church.

If Patrick was to offer himself as a candidate for ordination, it would be necessary for him to graduate from one of the three Anglican universities of that time: Oxford, Cambridge or Trinity College, Dublin. For university entrance he would need a thorough grounding in Greek and Latin and it is probable that Thomas Tighe provided the necessary tuition. When he had made sufficient progress to be able to consider university entrance it must have seemed obvious that he should apply to St John's College, Cambridge. Not only was it Tighe's own college, but it was where other members of his family had been educated. St John's was also well known for its close connections with the evangelical movement in the Church of England. Moreover, for a man in Patrick's straitened financial circumstances, it had the added advantage of possessing the largest funds of any Cambridge college for assisting poor but able men to gain a university education. In 1802, on Thomas Tighe's recommendation, Patrick Brontë, at the age of twenty-five, was admitted to a place at St John's. In July that year he took the momentous step of leaving his home in County Down and sailing to England to start a new career at Cambridge.

'I have been educated at Cambridge'
1802–1806

'I have been educated at Cambridge, and taken my degree at that first of Universities.'

Patrick Brontë to Stephen Taylor, 8 July 1819

Patrick arrived in England several weeks before the start of the university term. In a footnote to his letter to Mrs Gaskell of 20 June 1855 he said that he entered St John's College in July 1802. His early arrival in Cambridge is supported by a letter to William Wilberforce, the anti-slavery campaigner and a Yorkshire M.P., written some eighteen months later by Henry Martyn, a fellow of St John's. Thanking Wilberforce for his offer to give financial assistance to Patrick, Martyn told him:

> He left his native Ireland at the age of 22 [*sic*] with seven pounds, having been able to lay by no more after superintending a school some years. He reached Cambridge before that was expended, and then received an unexpected supply of £5 from a distant friend. On this he subsisted some weeks before entering St John's.[1]

Presumably Patrick occupied this time in reading to prepare himself for his degree course. The identity of the 'distant', presumably Irish, friend who sent him £5 is not known.

Patrick was formally admitted to St John's College on 1 October 1802 at the age of twenty-five. The Admissions Register of the college has the following entry for that date:

1235   Patrick Branty   Ireland   Sizar   Tutors: Wood & Smith[2]

It seems that in his case the college was content with the minimum of information. The columns for *Father's name and address, Mother's, Birthplace, Age* and *School or Schoolmaster* are left blank. The mistake over his surname was presumably due to his strong Irish accent. When he took up residence two days later, his surname was again

written as 'Branty', but this time Patrick took pains to have the entry amended to read:
'Patrick <Branty> Bronte'.[3]

Patrick's status is recorded as that of a sizar. Undergraduates at that time were classified
in three groups: fellow commoners, pensioners and sizars. Fellow commoners were
noblemen, of whom there were seven entering St John's that year. They dined separately
with the fellows of the college. Pensioners consisted of the younger sons of the arist-
ocracy, and also the sons of gentlemen and the professional classes: thirty-four of them
entered the college in 1802. Patrick was one of four sizars. Sizars were undergraduates
who received financial assistance from the college in the form of a reduction of expenses
and the provision of rooms free of charge. In return, he was expected to do some form
of domestic service and to undertake certain duties, one of which was to record the
names of those who failed to attend the compulsory university sermon.

Life at St John's must have presented Patrick with many financial problems, despite
the assistance he received from his status as a sizar. On entry to the college he would
be required to pay the sizar's reduced admission fee of £10 and thereafter 6/4d (32p) a
quarter. In addition, there were fees to be paid to the university on matriculation and
graduation. He would also be responsible for providing wood and coals to heat his
rooms and candles for lighting. An interesting commentary on Patrick's situation is
provided by the evidence of Henry Kirke White, later well known as the author of the
hymn 'Oft in danger, oft in woe'. He was admitted as a sizar to St John's in April 1804.
He was the son of a Nottingham butcher and while at Cambridge had many financial
problems. In a letter to his mother of 26 October 1805 he expressed his admiration for
the way in which Patrick was coping:

> I have got the bills of Mr — [Bronte], a Sizar of this college, now before me, and from them
> and his own account, I will give you a statement of what my college bills will amount to …
> 12£ or 15£ a-year at the most … The Mr [Bronte] whose bills I have borrowed, has been at
> college three years. He came over from [Ireland], with 10£ in his pocket, and has no friends
> or income or emolument whatever, except what he receives from his Sizarship; yet he does
> support himself, and that, too, very genteelly.

All the sizars dined in hall, where as White explained, the provision of food was generous:

> Our dinners and suppers cost us nothing; and if a man chooses to eat milk-breakfasts, and
> go without tea, he may live absolutely for nothing; for his college emoluments will cover the
> rest of his expenses. Tea is indeed almost superfluous, since we do not rise from dinner until
> half-past three, and the supper-bell rings a quarter before nine. Our mode of living is not to
> be complained of, for the table is covered with all possible variety; and on feast-days, which
> our fellows take care are pretty frequent, we have wine.[4]

One wonders what Patrick's feelings were as he regularly passed through the great Tudor gateway of St John's. Fifteen years earlier William Wordsworth had entered the college. He was well aware of its distinguished history and looking back on his experience a few years later he wrote in *The Prelude*:

> I could not print Ground where the grass had yielded to the steps of generations of illustrious men,
> Unmoved.

And yet he did not take advantage of his time at St John's. It was not a formative period in his life.

> From the first crude days of settling time in this untried abode,
> I was disturbed at times by a strangeness in the mind,
> A feeling that I was not for that hour,
> Nor for that place.[5]

For Patrick Brontë the opposite was true. He knew that his time at Cambridge provided him with an exceptional opportunity for advancement and he was determined to make the most of his chances. He was fortunate in having an outstanding tutor in James Wood. Wood came from Bury in Lancashire and was the son of a weaver. He had entered the college as a sizar in 1778, and in his early days as a student had known great poverty. Unable to afford the cost of lighting, he had studied by the light of the rush candles on the staircase to his rooms, keeping himself warm by wrapping his feet in straw. He was an able mathematician who later became a Fellow of the Royal Society and a Doctor of Divinity. In 1815 he was elected Master of St John's and in the following year served as Vice-Chancellor of the University. As a sizar who himself had made the most of his opportunities, he clearly gave great encouragement to Patrick, who devoted himself to his studies with resolute determination.

In December 1802 the half-yearly class lists based on college examinations contain twenty-one names in the first class, followed by four other names, the last of which is that of Patrick Brontë, prefaced by the comment: 'Inferior to the above but entitled to prizes if in the 1st class at the next examination.'[6]

In June 1803 Patrick's name was one of nineteen listed in the first class and he maintained this position for the rest of his time at Cambridge. He was one of only five in his year to achieve this distinction. Those placed in the first class in both annual examinations were entitled to prizes. Two of the books which were awarded to Patrick are now in the Brontë Parsonage Museum.[7] One is a copy of *The Works of Horace* edited by Richard Bentley, 1728, with Patrick's fly leaf entry: 'Prize obtained by the Rev. Patrick

Bronte, St John's College.' The other, *Homer's Iliad* edited by Samuel Clark, 1729, bears the proud inscription:

> My prize book for having always kept in the <u>first class</u>, at St John's College – Cambridge – P
> Bronte, A.B. To be retained semper- [7]

There were several awards available at St John's for able scholars of limited means. At Christmas 1802 Patrick's hard work and dedication was rewarded by his election to a Robson Exhibition. William Robson was a citizen of London who had left a benefaction to be awarded to two sizars, who were to be chosen in their first year and to retain their exhibition until they took their degree. Under this award Patrick received a half-yearly payment at midsummer and in December of £2-10-0 (£2.50), a valuable source of additional income. In February 1803 he was also awarded a Hare Exhibition, which he continued to hold until March 1806. This award, endowed by Sir Ralph Hare, was valued at £64 a year, the income of the rectory of Cherry Marham in Norfolk. It was intended for 'the maintenance of 30 of the poorest and best disposed scholars of the foundation' and was worth about £2 to each exhibitioner. At Christmas 1803 Patrick was also elected to a Suffolk Exhibition. This was a benefaction endowed by the Dowager Duchess of Suffolk for the assistance of four poor scholars. It gave Patrick a half-yearly payment of 16/8 (about 83p), which he continued to receive for the rest of his time at Cambridge. In midsummer 1805 he was also elected for one half-year to a Goodman Exhibition, which provided him with 14/- (70p). The Goodman Exhibition arose from a benefaction of lands and money endowed in 1579 for the benefit of two scholars by a former Dean of Westminster. These awards gave Patrick an income of between £6 and £7 a year for most of his time at Cambridge.[8] He also seems to have earned a little money by tutoring other students. Amongst his books at the Brontë Parsonage Museum there is a copy of Lempriere's *Bibliotheca Classica* which bears the inscription: 'The gift of Mr Toulmen pupil – Cambridge. Price 12s/. [60p].'[9]

Despite all his efforts at stringent economy, however, Patrick found it very difficult to make ends meet. It seems that he had already taken the decision to be ordained and early in 1804 he approached Henry Martyn, a fellow of the college and a leading evangelical, and asked him whether he knew of any sources of financial assistance for those intending to enter the ordained ministry. Martyn wrote to an evangelical friend of his, the Revd John Sargent, the vicar of Graffham in Sussex:

> An Irishman, of the name of Bronte entered St John's a year & a half ago as a sizar. During
> this time he has received no assistance from his friends who are incapable of affording him
> any – Yet he has been able to get on pretty well by help of Exhibitions &c which are given to
> our sizars. Now however, he finds himself reduced to great straits & applied to me just before

I left Cambridge to know if assistance could be procured for him from any of those societies, whose object is to maintain pious young men designed for the ministry.[10]

On receipt of this letter Sargent contacted Henry Thornton, M.P., a banker and a member of the famous evangelical group known as the Clapham Sect. Thornton was the treasurer of the recently founded Church Missionary Society and also a cousin of William Wilberforce, another member of the Clapham Sect and a former student at St John's. Wilberforce and Thornton agreed to supplement Patrick's income for the rest of his time at Cambridge. On 14 February 1804 Martyn wrote to Wilberforce thanking him for his offer of assistance:

I availed myself as soon as possible of your generous offer to Mr Bronte and left it without hesitation to himself to fix the limits … There is reason to hope that he will be an instrument of good to the church, as a desire for usefulness in the ministry seems to have influenced him hitherto in no small degree. I desire to unite with him in thanks to yourself and the directors of the Society.[11]

This letter is endorsed in Wilberforce's hand: 'Marytn abt Mr Bronte Henry & I to allow him 10L each anny'. It says much for Patrick Brontë's commitment and dedication that men of the calibre of Henry Martyn, Henry Thornton and William Wilberforce were prepared to support him financially during his time at St John's.

Cambridge was a stronghold of the growing evangelical movement in the Church of England. One of its foremost leaders was Charles Simeon, a fellow of King's College and the incumbent of Holy Trinity church, Cambridge. He had been one of the founders of the Church Missionary Society in 1799 and he was also a prominent supporter of the British and Foreign Bible Society. He exercised a strong influence in the university and there were regular gatherings of students in his rooms. One of his aims was to recruit dedicated young men for service in the mission field. During his brilliant academic career at St John's, Henry Martyn had come under Simeon's influence and, after his ordination in 1803, he served as Simeon's curate at Holy Trinity church before going to India in 1805 as a chaplain to the East India Company.

Patrick seems to have attached himself to this evangelical circle and may have attended the student gatherings in Simeon's rooms. When over forty years later his daughter Charlotte wrote to her friend Ellen Nussey thanking her for her offer of a recently published life of Simeon, she told her:

Your offer of Simeon's 'Life' is a very kind one, and I thank you for it. I dare say papa would like to see the work very much, as he knew Mr Simeon.

Three months later she wrote again:

> Papa has been very much interested in reading the book. There is frequent mention made in
> it of persons and places formerly well known to him; he thanks you for lending it.[12]

Apart from his academic work very little is known of the way in which Patrick spent
his time at Cambridge. A close friend was a fellow sizar, John Nunn. They entered the
college in the same year and may have shared rooms. We know few details of their
friendship at Cambridge but years later Nunn's niece, while staying at her uncle's rectory
at Thorndon in Suffolk, heard him say of Patrick: 'He was once my greatest friend.'[13]

Patrick's first years at Cambridge coincided with renewed fears of a French invasion of
England. Napoleon's Grand Army was drawn up across the Channel waiting for France
to gain control of the sea. Volunteers were recruited for the local militia and by December
1803 over 460,000 men had enrolled. At Cambridge a separate university volunteer corps
was formed, which by February 1804 had 154 members, and the university authorities
reluctantly gave permission for all lay members of the university to be allowed one hour
a day for military drill. The students paraded in the market place and were instructed
in the use of arms by Captain Bircham of the 30th Regiment. The St John's contingent,
which was led by the eighteen-year old John Henry Temple, later better known as Lord
Palmerston, numbered thirty-five and included Patrick Brontë and John Nunn in
its ranks. For the rest of his life Patrick remained proud of his military association at
Cambridge with Lord Palmerston, who was destined for an outstanding political career
in the highest offices of state. In her *Life of Charlotte Brontë* Mrs Gaskell noted:

> I have heard him allude, in late years, to Lord Palmerston as one who had often been
> associated with him in the mimic military duties which they had to perform.[14]

Towards the end of 1805 Patrick took the decision to proceed to his degree after the
minimum residence qualification of four years. Since he was unable to submit the
required baptism certificate, he secured a statement from his old mentor, Thomas
Tighe, certifying his age:

> I hereby certify that by the Registers of this Parish it appears that William Bronte, Son of
> Hugh and Elinor Bronte, was baptized on 16th March 1779 – & I further certify that Patrick
> Bronte, now of St John's College, Cambridge, is the elder brother of the said William – &
> that no Register was kept of Baptisms in this Parish from time immemorial till after Sept 1778
> – when I became minister. –
> 30 Decr 1805
>
>   T. Tighe
>   Minister of Drumballeyroney[15]

Patrick also obtained a certificate from Dr Fawcett, the Norrington Professor of Divinity, stating that he had attended forty-seven of his lectures. He had missed only three, 'one omission was occasioned by indisposition, two by necessary business in the country'.[16] Patrick graduated Bachelor of Arts on 23 April 1806 at the age of twenty-nine. It was the custom of St John's to give £4 to all students on obtaining their degree. Patrick must have thought the occasion worthy of a special celebration for he bought a copy of Walter Scott's *Lay of the Last Minstrel* which had been published that year. On the flyleaf he proudly wrote: 'P Bronte. B.A. St John's College.'[17] Oddly enough, Patrick left his name on the college books for two years after taking his degree, despite the fact that this would make him liable for various fees and college bills. It seems that for a time he entertained the faint hope that he might become a fellow of the college.

Patrick now turned his attention to preparations for his ordination as deacon. His friends in the evangelical world clearly gave him support. By 28 June he had secured the nomination of the Revd Dr Joseph Jowett, Regius Professor of Civil Law at Cambridge and vicar of Wethersfield in Essex, to be his curate at a salary of £60 a year.[18] Joseph Jowett, who was a fellow of Trinity Hall, the patron of the living of Wethersfield, was a friend of Charles Simeon and a leading evangelical. His sermons at St Edward's church, Cambridge, drew large congregations and his appointment of Patrick Brontë as his curate was a sign of Patrick's good standing in evangelical circles.

On 29 June the curate of All Saints' church, Cambridge, publicly gave notice: 'that Mr Patrick Bronte intended to offer himself a Candidate for Holy Orders'.[19] Three days later the Master and senior fellows of St John's College signed Letters Testimonial to the fact that:

> the said Patrick Bronte hath behaved himself studiously & regularly during the time of his residence amongst us. ... Nor do we know that he hath believed or maintained any opinion contrary to the doctrine or discipline of the Church of England.[20]

Patrick sent these documents to the Secretary of the Bishop of London on 4 July, together with an accompanying letter:

> I beg leave to offer myself a candidate for Holy Orders, at his Lordship's next Ordination. If I be admitted by his Lordship, be so kind as to let me know as soon as convenient, when and where his Lordship will hold his Ordination; and (if customary) what books I shall be examined in; with whatever directions you may judge necessary.[21]

He was ordained deacon on 10 August by the bishop, Dr Beilby Porteous, in his chapel at Fulham Palace.

Since Dr Jowett would reside in the parish and perform all the duties during the long vacation, Patrick was not required to take up his curacy in Wethersfield until the beginning of October. It seems that he used this time to pay his first visit back to Ireland. In her old age Alice Brontë, Patrick's youngest sister, told the Revd J. B. Lusk that Patrick returned to Ireland shortly after his ordination and preached at Drumballyroney church:

> Patrick came home after he was ordained, and preached in Ballyroney. All our friends and neighbours were there, and the church was very full. ... He preached a gran' sermon, and never had anything in his han' the whole time.[22]

Such a visit would seem an appropriate act of gratitude in return for all the help and advice that Thomas Tighe had given him. After an absence of four years Patrick would also no doubt wish to see his family again. It is significant that his sister stressed his preaching without a note in his hand. With a few isolated exceptions, extempore preaching was to remain a leading feature of his long ministry.

It was probably during this visit to Ireland that he secured from his father two copies of a formal letter certifying his age. Since he had no baptism certificate he would need such a document for his ordination as priest in the following year. It is notable that his age was wrongly stated to be twenty-eight. He was in fact twenty-nine.

County of Down
Ireland

I Hugh Bronte of Ballinaskeigh Parish of Ahaderg, in the said County, do swear, that my son Patrick Bronte late of St Johns College Cambridge England, is twenty eight years of age.

Hugh Bronte

Sworn before me,
This 25th of septr. 1806

John Fury[23]

The text is written in a formal hand but the letter is personally signed by Hugh Brontë. It provides a unique and authentic link with Patrick's Irish childhood.

3

'Two Curacies in the South'
1806–1809

After nearly four years' residence, I took the Degree of Bachelor of Arts – and was soon after ordain'd to a Curacy in the South of England. Having officiated in two Curacies in the South, I came to Yorkshire.

Patrick Brontë to Mrs Gaskell, 20 June 1855

Wethersfield was a small village in Essex set in rich arable country some thirty-five miles to the south-east of Cambridge. It consisted of a small cluster of mainly seventeenth- and eighteenth-century half-timbered houses beside the village green and was an attractive place for Patrick to begin his ministry. It had a population of just over 1,300, most of whom were employed on the land. The parish church was dedicated to St Mary Magdalene and after Patrick's time was extensively restored in the 1870s. The oldest parts of the building are the tower and the nave, both of which date back to the twelfth century and there are some fine fifteenth-century effigies in the chancel.

Much of our information about the parish comes from the return made by Patrick's vicar for the Bishop of London's visitation in 1810, a couple of years after Patrick had given up his curacy.[1] Dr Jowett stated that the parish was comprised of three villages: Wethersfield, Blackmore End and Beazeley End. At least half of his parishioners were Dissenters, who had their own resident minister. Services were held in the parish church twice every Sunday and communion was celebrated at least five times a year, with the usual number of communicants varying between twenty and thirty. The collections taken at these services were distributed amongst the poor by the curate. There had been a Sunday school in the parish for many years. Dr Jowett said that he provided a resident curate in the parish, since for most of the year he was in Cambridge. It seems from the registers that he normally officiated at services from the end of July to the beginning of October each year and that the curate was left in charge for the remaining nine months. To a young curate about to embark on his first curacy this must have seemed a daunting and rather lonely prospect.

Facing the village green there is a Congregational chapel built in 1707, with a large manse adjoining it. Unlike the Methodists, who were still in communion with the established Church, the Congregationalists were fiercely independent and had no love for the Church of England. In 1806 the minister was the Revd Thomas Mark. The presence of a strong group of Dissenters in the parish dated back to the time of the Reformation and there had been an independent chapel in the village for many years. John Cole, the incumbent of the parish from 1655 to 1660 during the Commonwealth, had been removed from the living at the time of the Restoration because he refused to take the Oath of Uniformity which required him to use the Book of Common Prayer. After being imprisoned for eight years he had started the custom of holding services in his own house.

On his arrival Patrick took up residence at St George's House, an eighteenth-century building opposite the church owned by an elderly spinster, Miss Margaret Davy. Patrick performed his first duty in the parish on 12 October 1806, taking a marriage and a baptism. His work load was not heavy. Marriages averaged about one a month, with two baptisms, usually performed during Sunday services, in the same period. There was a considerable variation in the number of burials. At first these averaged three a month, but in December an outbreak of typhus fever raised the total to eight. Patrick's conscientious approach to his duties would have led him to visit the sick regularly and to comfort the dying. He probably taught the Scriptures at the local charity school, founded by Dorothy Mott, where it was a requirement of the foundation that the girls should learn their catechism and attend regularly at the parish church. He may also have been responsible for distributing to the poor on 21 December each year the excess funds from Dorothy Mott's foundation, although the vicar and churchwardens took all the necessary decisions. There seems to have been little opportunity for Patrick to make his mark and years later the village doctor, a Nonconformist who had shared his lodgings at St George's House, when asked for his view of Patrick, gave the jaundiced comment: 'I had no acquaintance with him or notice from him, and nobody took any notice of him.'[2]

After he had served in the parish for nine months Patrick began to make preparations for his ordination as priest. On 1 July 1807 he wrote to the Bishop of London's secretary asking when the next ordination would be held and what papers he was required to submit. A few days later, taking advantage of Dr Jowett's return to the parish for his usual summer residence, Patrick went to Colchester, where he stayed for some weeks. His next letter to the bishop's secretary (dated 20 July 1807) was written from there:

> Agreeably to your orders I have sent all my papers except my Si Quis,[3] which I cannot possibly get before the next Sunday, at which time I shall send it, hoping that his Lordship will excuse my not sending it sooner. By addressing a few lines to me at Colchester (as I shall reside here for a few weeks) mentioning the time of the Ordination, and his Lordship's pleasure respecting my papers, you will very much oblige.

One motive for Patrick wishing to spend time in Colchester was that the family of his Cambridge friend, John Nunn, lived there. It must have given him great pleasure to renew this friendship and to talk over old times. A second reason was that St Peter's church, Colchester, had a great reputation. The vicar, Robert Storry, was known as a staunch evangelical and one of the trustees of the church was Charles Simeon. Patrick became friendly with Robert Storry, who was exercising a very active ministry and was trying to attract Methodists to his church. It may be that Patrick was interested in the possibility of securing a curacy with him and that he took the opportunity of his visit to discuss the matter.

On his return to Wethersfield Patrick took the final steps for his ordination as priest. His notice of candidature had been signed by Dr Jowett and the two church wardens of Wethersfield. He now submitted letters testimonial signed by three local clergy:

> To the Right Reverend Father in God, Beilby, by divine permission, Lord Bishop of London, Greeting.
>
> Whereas our well beloved in Christ, Patrick Bronte Bachelor of Arts, hath declared to us his intention of offering himself a candidate for the sacred office of a Priest, and for that end hath requested of us letters testimonial of his learning and good behaviour: we therefore, whose names are hereunto subscribed, do testify, that the said Patrick Bronte having been personally known to us, during his residence at Weathersfield [sic], which was nine months; hath during that time liv'd piously, soberly, and honestly, and diligently applied himself to his studies; nor hath he at any time (as far as we know or have heard) maintained or written any thing contrary to the doctrine or discipline of the Church of England; and moreover we think him a person worthy to be admitted to the Sacred Order of Priests.
>
> In witness wereof [sic] we subscribe our names.
>
> > Thomas Stevens, Rector of Panfield
> > John Thurlow, Vicar of Gosfield
> > Thomas Jee, Vicar of Thaxted[4]

Patrick was ordained priest on 21 December 1807 by the Bishop of Salisbury (the Rt Rev'd John Fisher) in the Chapel Royal at St James's Palace. It was quite common for a priest to be ordained by a bishop who was not his diocesan but was holding an ordination on a convenient date.

A regular visitor to St George's House was the eighteen-year-old Mary Burder, Miss Davy's niece. Mary was the eldest of four children of a local farmer who had recently died. She lived with her mother, two brothers and a sister at The Broad, a large farm, a mile away across the fields. On her father's death her uncle who lived at nearby Great Yeldham assumed responsibility for the family. Mary often came to visit her aunt and the young Patrick rapidly fell in love with her. According to Mrs Lowe, Mary's daughter, who later gave an account of the affair to Augustine

Birrell when he was writing his life of Charlotte Brontë, they first met in Miss Davy's kitchen when Mary had brought a present of game for her aunt.[5] As their affection grew Mary made more frequent visits and Patrick regularly walked back with her to The Broad. They shared a common interest in books and fifteen years later Patrick remembered her as 'affectionate, kind, and forgiving, agreeable in person, and still more agreeable in mind'.[6] The only drawback to their relationship was that Mary worshipped at the Congregational chapel and was not a member of the Church of England. Patrick's courtship of her seems undoubtedly to have led to an engagement which was subsequently terminated.

Fifteen years later, after the death of his wife Maria, Patrick, desperately seeking someone who would provide a mother for his six children, got in touch with Mary again. The three letters that he wrote in 1823, two to Mary and one to her mother, together with her bitter reply, provide our only authentic information about their relationship. It seems clear that they had been engaged. In his letter to Mary of 28 July 1823 Patrick wrote:

> You were the first whose hand I solicited, and no doubt I was the first to whom you promised to give that hand. I am sure you once loved me with an unaffected innocent love.

The reasons for the breakdown of their engagement are not clear. According to the version given by Augustine Birrell in 1887 Mary's uncle intervened and insisted that Mary broke off the relationship. Patrick's Irish origins and uncertain future prospects were cited against him.[7] Mary was taken from her home to her uncle's house where she stayed until Patrick ended his curacy at Wethersfield in January 1809. Patrick's letters were intercepted and destroyed and he was forced to return all her letters to him. He is said to have enclosed a small card with them bearing his likeness in profile and the words 'Mary you have torn the heart, spare the face.' When she heard no more from Patrick Mary came to accept that the engagement was at an end.[8]

It is clear, however, that Patrick's letters were, in fact, not intercepted and destroyed. When Patrick contacted her again in 1823, Mary wrote a bitter rejoinder to his overtures in which she referred to her:

> recent perusal of many letters of yours bearing date eighteen hundred and eight, nine and ten addressed to myself and my dear departed Aunt.

It is apparent from this that Patrick had continued to write to her after his departure from Wethersfield (January 1809) and that she had carefully kept his letters. Mary was clearly very bitter over the way in which she had been treated. She said that she was grateful to that Providence:

which then watched over me for good and withheld me from forming in very early life an indissoluble engagement with one whom I cannot think was altogether clear of duplicity. A union with you under then existing circumstances must have embittered my future days.[9]

The evidence suggests that it was Patrick who broke the engagement rather than Mary's family, although her relations do seem to have opposed the union. It appears that in 1808 he may have been contemplating marriage. On 26 May he took his name off the books of St John's College.[10] This indicates that he had given up the possibility of being elected a fellow of the college. At that time only unmarried men could hold fellowships. Mary was under the legal age when she could marry without her guardian's consent and the bitterness of her letter suggests that she thought that Patrick would wait until she was free to marry him.

Patrick's position in Wethersfield was now an embarrassing one and it was necessary for him to look for another post. Sometime in late September or early October 1808 he travelled to Glenfield, a small parish on the outskirts of Leicester. Both the vicar, Robert Cox, and the curate, John Campbell, had been contemporaries of his at Cambridge. Patrick obviously discussed with these friends his situation over Mary Burder and Robert Cox offered him a curacy at Glenfield. After returning to Wethersfield Patrick wrote to John Campbell on 12 November, saying that he had decided not to accept the curacy. His letter seems to reveal the reason why he had broken off the engagement:

> I will be much oblige[d] to you ... to tell Mr Cox, that I shall not return to Glenfield, if therefore, he wishes to get rid of that Curacy ... Let him keep it only a quarter of a year from this date. ... Had I not been circumstanced as I am, I should have kept the Glenfield Curacy, for a year or two at least. ... The Lady I mentioned, is always in exile; her Guardians can scarcely believe me that I have given the affair entirely up for ever. All along, I violated both the dictates of my conscience and my judgment. "Be not unequally yoked," says the Apostle. But Virgil was not far wrong, when he said, "Omnia vincit Amor";[11] & no one can deny Solomons [sic] Authority, who tells us that "Love is stronger than Death". But for Christs [sic] sake we are, to cut off a right hand, or to pluck out a right eye, if requisite. May he by his grace enable me always to conform to his will.

The quotation from St Paul refers to marriage between Christians and non-Christians. Patrick is clearly not referring to the social gulf between him and Mary Burder, nor to any lack of Christian belief on her part. The insuperable obstacle appears to be the fact that she was a Congregationalist, an ardent Nonconformist. If Patrick married her he might well jeopardise his future promotion in the Church of England. This fact would seem to explain one of Mary's sarcastic comments in her letter to him:

> Happily for me I have not been the ascribed cause of hindering your promotion, of preventing any brilliant alliance, nor have those great and affluent friends that you used to write and

speak of withheld their patronage on my account, young, inexperienced, unsuspecting, and ignorant as I then was of what I had a right to look forward to.

It is clear that Patrick had been very much in love with Mary and had asked her to marry him. When her family opposed their marriage he seems to have seen this obstacle as divine intervention. He gradually came to feel that he had allowed his heart to rule his head and that, however much he loved her, his service to God came first. But it was no easy decision for him to make. His letter to John Campbell concerning the Glenfield curacy shows that he had agonised over the choice between his love and his duty:

> Who is he who can say he has not a wish unfulfilled? Oh! that I could make my God and Saviour, my home, my Father, my All! But this happy state is reserved for better men than I ... but God's will be done; in due time he may bring me nearer to himself, & consequently nearer to heaven and happiness.

The tragedy of the situation was that his decision caused great suffering to Mary as well. Fifteen years later she was still bitter over the way Patrick had treated her. In 1824, the year after Patrick sought to renew contact with her, she married the Revd Peter Sibtree, the Dissenting minister of Wethersfield.

Patrick also wrote letters at this time to John Nunn, in which he expressed the anguish and spiritual turmoil which he was suffering. In 1857, when John Nunn's niece, Maria Tipton, was staying with her uncle she made a reference to the recently published *Life of Charlotte Brontë* by Mrs Gaskell which she was reading, and Mr Nunn told her that Patrick Brontë was once his greatest friend. On the next morning he brought down a bundle of letters which he had received from Patrick, which he said referred to his spiritual state. He said that he had read them again and was going to destroy them.[12]

John Nunn was now a curate at Shrewsbury and it may have been with his assistance that Patrick secured a curacy at nearby Wellington in Shropshire under the Rev'd John Eyrton. On 22 December 1808 he took his last burial service at Wethersfield and he left the village at the end of the year. He had served in the parish for two years and three months.

Wellington was a prosperous and busy town of 8,000 inhabitants situated in the midst of the industrial heartland of England. It had a rapidly growing trade in coal and iron and the population had been increased in recent years by labourers seeking employment in the local mines and foundries. There had been a weekly market since the thirteenth century and there were regular coaches every day to Shrewsbury and London. All Saints' church faced a small green near the town centre. It was a new building, constructed in 1790 to replace an earlier medieval church. Built in the classical style, with a grey stone façade and rectangular windows, it has the appearance of an elegant chapel. Its most distinctive feature is a large clock and bell tower. The interior is pleasantly light and airy. On three sides there is a gallery supported on iron pillars cast at nearby Coalbrookdale. Also in the parish was the little red-brick church of St Catherine at Eyton, which lay a couple of miles outside the town and served the needs of 400 parishioners.

The vicar of All Saints' in 1809 was the Revd John Eyton, the third son of the local squire, Thomas Eyton. Like Patrick he was a graduate of St John's, Cambridge (although they were not contemporaries) and had come under the evangelical influence of Charles Simeon. John Eyton had been appointed vicar of All Saints' by his father, the patron of the parish, in 1802, and had rapidly established a reputation as a powerful preacher and a conscientious pastor. He was a regular visitor of the poor and the sick, and also took a keen interest in the running of the Wellington Free School.

According to local tradition Patrick had lodgings in the splendid Georgian vicarage. There were many duties for him to perform and his share of these was increased by the fact that his vicar's health was beginning to break down. Although Mr Eyton employed two curates to assist him the senior one seems to have been fully occupied performing the duties at St Catherine's. During the year Patrick spent at Wellington there were 164 burials and 271 baptisms. It is not clear how many of these were performed by Patrick, since the parish clerk did not enter the name of the officiating minister. The marriage register, however, which was completed by the minister himself, indicates that Patrick took nearly half of the fifty marriages performed in 1809. A manuscript preserved at St Catherine's church also shows that on 5 May Patrick, together with the churchwarden and overseer of the poor, made and signed an assessment for the relief of the poor in the parish.

Apart from the registers there is little record of the eleven months which Patrick spent at Wellington. He would have been involved in the special services which were held in the parish during 1809. The concern felt in England over Napoleon's Spanish campaign was heightened by the death of Sir John Moore at Corunna on 16 January 1809. As was customary at times of national crisis a day of national fasting and humiliation was called on 8 February. On 11 June the annual services for the benefit of the Wellington Sunday schools were held, at which the Rev'd John Waltham, the evangelical vicar of Darlaston in Staffordshire, preached and a large collection of £72 was raised. Patrick would also have assisted in the organisation of an important meeting held in Wellington on 1 June, which was attended by all the contributors to the fund for the relief of clergymen's widows and orphans in the archdeaconry of Salop.

The most memorable event of the year, however, was the celebration on 25 October of the fiftieth anniversary of George III's accession. Every house in Wellington was brilliantly illuminated. The squire, Thomas Eyton, supplied the poorer inhabitants with candles so that they could take part. His own house was lit with lamps forming the motto 'Fear God Honor [sic] the King'. Bonfires were lit on the Wrekin and other surrounding hills and at a civic service in Shrewsbury John Nunn preached on the text 'Let the king live for ever'.

During his leisure time Patrick no doubt made frequent ascents of the Wrekin (1,335 feet), the hill which dominated the town a couple of miles to the south west. He also took advantage of the opportunity to make contact with fellow evangelical clergy in the neighbourhood. John Nunn was the curate at St Chad's church, Shrewsbury, just ten miles away, and Patrick must have paid him frequent visits to talk over old times and to share their experience of the ordained ministry. While he was in Shrewsbury Patrick became friendly with Nunn's vicar, Thomas Stedman, an Oxford man who had rebuilt St Chad's after the tower had collapsed and destroyed the nave. Stedman had employed as architect George Steuart, the man who had built All Saints', Wellington, and the two churches are very similar in style. Stedman was an able preacher and the author of several tracts and sermons. Patrick also made the acquaintance of Charles Hulbert, an antiquarian who enjoyed a local reputation as the historian of Shropshire. In addition to his literary activities Hulbert had set up the first cotton factory in Shrewsbury in 1803. As a Methodist circuit steward his preaching duties would have regularly brought him to Wellington. Another Methodist who became a friend was John Fennell, the master of the Wellington day school. He was later to have a considerable influence on Patrick's life and to be ordained into the Church of England.

The closest friend Patrick made during his time at Wellington, however, was his fellow curate at All Saints', William Morgan. Mr Morgan was a rotund Welshman five years younger than Patrick. He had been in Wellington since 1806 and he shared Patrick's evangelical fervour and also his ambition to play an active role in the life of the church. Both were shortly to move to clerical positions in Yorkshire and he was to be Patrick's friend for many years and to provide him with support at some of the saddest moments of his life.

It was through William Morgan that Patrick was introduced to an important circle of evangelical friends who used to gather in the neighbouring parish of Madeley, six miles to the south of Wellington. Through the outstanding ministry of John Fletcher, the vicar of the parish from 1760 until his death in 1785, Madeley had become a great centre for evangelical clergy. John Fletcher had been an able preacher, laying great stress on the need for conversion and rejecting the Calvinist doctrine of election. He had also written numerous books and tracts. He had travelled widely and had been a close friend of both John and Charles Wesley. At one time John Wesley had wanted to name him as his successor, but Fletcher's love of his parish work at Madeley led him to refuse the offer. His ministry had exerted an enormous influence on evangelicals and on the Methodists, and he had become the model and inspiration for many young clergymen.

After John Fletcher's death in 1785 his widow Mary continued to live in the vicarage at Madeley, where she sought to continue her husband's work by keeping open house for evangelicals in the area. Before her marriage she had lived for several years in Yorkshire and she was aware that the growth in population in the industrial north had created a pressing need for faithful clergymen to minister in that area. She used her extensive contacts to secure appointments for committed evangelicals in the northern counties of England, and especially in Yorkshire. It was not long before Patrick became a regular member of the group which met there. His vicar, John Eyton, was a frequent visitor and others who gathered there included Samuel Walter, Patrick's predecessor as curate and now the vicar of Madeley, John Fennell, the Wellington schoolmaster, who was himself Fletcher's godson, and Joshua Gilpin, the vicar of nearby Wrockwardine, who had been a devoted follower of Fletcher and had written a short account of his life.

After all the mental and spiritual turmoil which Patrick had gone through as a result of his relationship with Mary Burder, it must have been a great relief for him to be able to consult such a wise and dedicated counsellor as Mary Fletcher. He was clearly influenced by her devotion to the evangelical cause and he rapidly came to the decision to play his part in the great missionary campaign which she outlined. It is quite likely that among the clergy paying visits to Madeley at this time was John Crosse, who had been the vicar of Bradford in the West Riding of Yorkshire from 1784. He had been a friend of Mary Fletcher for many years. When Crosse died in June 1816 Patrick told William Morgan, who was writing Crosse's biography, that he considered 'Mr C[rosse] and Mrs F[letcher] as very similar to each other in their Christian simplicity, zeal, and manner of speaking to their friends, on the leading subjects of religion.'[13]

From his contacts at Madeley Patrick learnt that Bradford was one of the fastest growing parishes in the country and that the surrounding area was desperately short of clergy. When he heard that John Buckworth, the vicar of Dewsbury, an industrial town a few miles from Bradford, was looking for an evangelical curate to assist him in his work, Patrick thought that this was the opportunity for which he had been waiting. He was still considering the matter, however, when early in November 1809 he received a letter from James Wood, his former tutor at St John's, offering him the position of chaplain to the Governor of Martinique in the West Indies. This island had recently been captured by the British in the war against Napoleon and the position of chaplain there must have seemed an exciting and unusual one which would provide the opportunity for a useful ministry. Patrick wrote to Mr Wood asking whether the post was likely to be permanent and whether he would receive any advance of his salary to enable him to meet the expenses of the voyage.[14] It is not known what reply he received, but by the end of November he had accepted the position of curate to Mr Buckworth at Dewsbury.

Patrick conducted his last wedding at Wellington on 18 November 1809 and set off for Yorkshire on 4 December. He took with him a leather-bound volume entitled *Sermons or Homilies appointed to be read in churches*, a gift from his colleague William Morgan who had written on the flyleaf:

The Reverend P. Bronte's book – Presented to him by his friend W:Morgan as a Memorial of the pleasant and agreeable friendship, which subsisted between them at Wellington, – & as a Token of the same Friendship, which it is hoped, will continue for ever. By this shall all men know that ye are my disciples, if ye love one another – Jesus Christ.

Let brotherly love continue. St Paul.[15]

'I came to Yorkshire'
1809–1811

Having officiated in two Curacies in the South, I came to Yorkshire.

Patrick Brontë to Mrs Gaskell, 20 June 1855

Dewsbury was a small town beside the River Calder in the West Riding of Yorkshire. It was proud of its ancient past, having been first mentioned in the Domesday Book. Although in modern times the town has been swallowed up by an encroaching urban sprawl, in 1809 it was surrounded by fields and woods and had a distinct identity of its own, separate from the many small villages on the surrounding hilltops. Dewsbury was a centre of the wool trade and there had been mills in the town since the 1780s, although many of the inhabitants still produced cloth on hand looms in their own homes. With the spread of industrialisation the population was steadily growing and by 1811 had reached 5,059.

According to tradition, the parish church of All Saints' had been founded by Paulinus in 627. He had been sent by Pope Gregory the Great as an assistant to St Augustine and, after working as a missionary in Kent, he was on his way north to Northumbria when he founded a monastery on the site. Most traces of this settlement had disappeared by the time of the Norman Conquest, although fragments of ninth- and tenth-century stone crosses and gravestones were still preserved in Patrick's time. As a minster church, Dewsbury had sent out priests to serve the outlying communities and many West Riding churches, including Bradford and Huddersfield, still paid tithes to the vicar. The parish also included the villages of Sorthill, Ossett, and Hartshead-cum-Clifton, whose 7,539 inhabitants were served by their own clergymen, under the jurisdiction of the vicar of Dewsbury. The medieval parish church had been rebuilt in the eighteenth century, and the tower built in 1767 still remains, although there have subsequently been many changes to the building which Patrick knew.

There was a strong Methodist presence in Dewsbury. John Wesley and his brother Charles had been regular visitors to the town and the Methodists had established their own meeting place in 1764, although they maintained good relations with the vicar and his congregation. There were also several settlements of the Moravian Church, a small Protestant body which had originated in what is now the Czech Republic.

The vicar, John Buckworth, had spent all his ordained ministry in the parish. His education at St Edmund Hall, Oxford had been paid for by evangelical patrons and after his ordination in 1804 he had come to Dewsbury as a curate. On the death of the incumbent two years later he had been appointed vicar. He was a talented preacher and widely respected for his deep personal faith and great humility. He was also renowned for the pastoral concern which he showed for his parishioners.

Much of our information about Patrick's time there is derived from a book written in 1897 by a local journalist, Mr W.W. Yates, under the title *The Father of the Brontës: His Life and Work at Dewsbury and Hartshead*. Mr Yates was keenly interested in the Brontë family and was one of the founders of the Brontë Society when it was established in 1893. His account of Patrick's ministry is mainly based on the childhood memories of older people in the town who had known Patrick during his time there as curate.

Patrick arrived in the parish on 5 December 1809 and for the first few months of his curacy had lodgings in the vicarage. He was given a separate room for use as a study and often took his meals there. He seems to have fed himself chiefly on oatmeal. Mr and Mrs Buckworth regularly urged him to keep a better table but he declined to change his habits, although he regularly dined with the family on Sundays. A few months after his arrival, he left the vicarage and took up lodgings in the Ancient Well House in Priest Lane. His landlord was a man called Elliot Carrett. His daughter, a Mrs Jackson, told Mr Yates that her father considered Patrick Brontë to be 'clever and good-hearted, but hot-tempered, and in fact a little queer.'[1] A former mayor of Dewsbury said that his grandfather 'always spoke of Mr Brontë as a very earnest man, but a little peculiar in his manner.'[2] Patrick regularly carried a stout stick with him as he walked round the parish and came to be known to his fellow clergy as 'Old Staff'.

Patrick soon found that his clerical duties kept him fully occupied. Mr Buckworth expected his curate to perform most of the routine work of the parish in order that he himself could concentrate on his preaching and pastoral ministry. In the sixteen months of his curacy Patrick performed nearly 130 marriages. During the same period 426 baptisms were carried out, usually during the normal services or on church festivals, but the name of the officiating minister was not recorded. During Patrick's first ten months in the parish there was an average of twenty burials a month. Between October 1810 and February 1811 this number rose to over fifty, with a peak of seventy-three in November. It seems likely that during this period there was an outbreak of typhus or influenza. It was also a time of great hardship in the parish. The failure of the harvest that year had increased the ongoing problems of unemployment caused by the industrial depression.

Mr Buckworth also expected his curate to take a leading role in the running of the Dewsbury Sunday school, which, when it was established in 1783, was the earliest Sunday school in Yorkshire. Patrick was required to conduct the classes which were held each week. He opened the meetings with prayers and the singing of a hymn before he gave an address to the whole school. Afterwards he inspected the pupils and gave religious instruction. He also taught the basic skills of reading and writing. Mr Yates records meeting an old Dewsbury man named Senior:

> Mr Senior stated that he himself was one of the scholars of the Sunday School and was regularly taught both to read and to write – secular as well as religious knowledge being imparted to the children in those comparatively dark days – and that Mr Brontë was frequently one of his instructors.

When asked what sort of a teacher Mr Brontë was, Mr Senior replied:

> I can hardly say, I was but a little lad. He was resolute about being obeyed, but was very kind, and we always liked him.[3]

Patrick was probably also expected to attend the evening meetings which Mr Buckworth held twice a week at the vicarage in support of the recently founded Church Missionary Society. The aim of these gatherings was to instruct and prepare young men for ordination, by teaching them theology and the rudiments of Greek and Latin. Patrick, who came from a similar background to these students, would seem to have been eminently suited for this work.

Several dramatic stories were told by Mr Yates of Patrick's time at Dewsbury. One concerned the rescue of a boy who had fallen in the river. Throughout his life Patrick enjoyed walking in the countryside and a regular outing of his was along the banks of the River Calder, which flowed just behind the church. One day during the winter of 1809–1810 he passed a group of boys playing on the river bank. They were amusing themselves trying to recover some pieces of wood from the flooded stream. Patrick had not gone far before he heard the sound of screaming and looking back he noticed that one of them, an older, rather simple-minded boy, had fallen into the swiftly flowing river and was in danger of being carried away by the current. He immediately ran back, plunged in and with some difficulty managed to rescue the boy. Mr Yates told the story as he heard it from the son of one of the boys who had been in the group:

> A tall gentleman came up and passed, but took little if any notice of the youthful party. He had, however, not got more than ten or a dozen yards away before one of the lads – "I believe it was my father," said our informant – gave a rather hard push to the weak-headed boy, who to the horror of all, fell into the water and was instantly battling for life. They screamed, and the gentleman, turning, ran back, and plunged into the flooded and swiftly-flowing river, and succeeded, though with evident difficulty, in reaching the drowning boy and bringing him to the bank. He then … carried him to the cottage of his mother, a poor widow at Dawgreen

– then a suburb, and now a part of the town of Dewsbury – one of the unfortunate lad's companions showing the way, and the others staying at some distance.

Mr Bronte stayed a short time in the cottage … and then set off for the vicarage. The other lads, frightened at what had occurred, and reluctant to go to their several homes, had loitered near and were met by him. … They now recognised him as the curate of the Parish Church. Mr Brontë was plainly shivering, yet he stopped in his hurried walk, having recognised them, to lecture the party on their conduct, and especially the chief offender. This lad excused himself by saying, "I only picked (pushed) him, to make him wet his shoon," whereupon the parson's stern expression of face relaxed, and, smiling, he bade them go to the widow's cottage to ask her pardon and that of her unfortunate son. They eagerly promised to do so, and then he strode off, changed his walk to a run, and was soon out of sight.[4]

At Whitsun it was the custom of all the scholars and teachers of the Sunday school to walk in procession through Dewsbury to the nearby village of Earlsheaton. The procession was normally led by the vicar, but in 1810 he was away in Oxford taking his M.A. degree, so the leading role fell to Patrick. As the march was in progress a drunken man stepped into the road, threatened them and refused to let them pass. Patrick hastily came forward and, when his remonstrances proved to be of no avail, seized the man by the collar, threw him to the side of the road and instructed the procession to move on. The intruder was heard to mutter that on the return journey he 'would hev it aat w't parson', but in the event the Sunday school party had a safe return.

In his account of this incident Mr Yates again drew on the memory of old Mr Senior who had been a Sunday school scholar in the procession.

The bully, he said, belonged to Gawthorpe, a hamlet in the township of Ossett, and was a notorious cockfighter and boxer, and much addicted to drinking. The old man was asked, did he see the actual flinging of the Gawthorpe man across the road, and he replied, "No, I was lower down in the procession, the girls being first; but what happened was soon known by all of us … and we talked about it for many a Sunday."[5]

Yates also quotes the evidence of another Dewsbury resident, a Mr Wilson Hemingway:

My mother, then a Miss Wilson, and the daughter of a manufacturer at Dawgreen, was one of the processionists, and an eyewitness of what took place. She was a girl of eleven years of age at the time, and the occurrence made a deep impression on her mind. … My mother often talked to me and the rest of the children about the Revd. Patrick Brontë, and told us more than once of the big rough man that would not let the procession of scholars pass, and that the revd. Gentleman coming hastily up, flung him to the side of the road.[6]

Charlotte Brontë, who doubtless heard of this incident from her father, made good use of it in *Shirley*, where Mr Helstone took firm action to enable the Sunday school march to continue, when it was confronted by a rival procession of 'the Dissenting and Methodist schools, the Baptists, Independents and Wesleyans, joined in unholy alliance'. After the singing of 'a dolorous canticle' by the opposition had been met by a firm rendition of 'Rule Britannia', the Sunday school party marched boldly forward along their route causing their opponents to give way.

Patrick, like his vicar, was a strict keeper of the Sabbath. One Sunday, when he was in temporary charge of the parish while the vicar was away, after conducting the evening service and returning to his lodging, he was very surprised to hear the bells ring out again. A bell-ringing contest with men from neighbouring towns was to take place on the next day and the ringers had thought they would take advantage of the vicar's absence to have a practice peal undisturbed. The parish clerk had connived at their suggestion that he should lock them in the church tower. But they had not reckoned with the diligence of the curate:

> He soon let them know somebody was in charge. Seizing his favourite stick, an Irish shillelagh, he darted out of the room, made for the house of Thomas Smith, the parish clerk, and enquiring why the bells were being rung, was told of the forthcoming competition. The news incensed Mr Brontë very greatly. Ringing the bells for such a purpose was a desecration of the Sabbath, and that he would not permit any longer. He accordingly obtained the keys, ran to the church, hastily ascended the winding steps of the tower, and brandishing his weapon, stopped the astonished ringers, and drove them out, giving all a stern admonition, which they would interpret as "dare to do the like again."[7]

By the next morning the ringers had recovered their courage and they came round to call on Patrick. They explained that a series of bell-ringing contests was about to start and said that they were not fully prepared. Since the evening service was over and they had performed all their duties, they could not see why they might not have an hour's practice. Patrick, however, remained adamant and spoke so severely to them that one ringer stated that he would never enter the tower again until Mr Brontë apologised, and he apparently kept his word, never being seen in the ringing chamber again.

Mr Yates also tells a rather strange story of an altercation between Patrick Brontë and his vicar's father-in-law, John Halliley. Neighbouring clergy, including Patrick, had regularly been giving assistance to William Lucas, the perpetual curate of Hartshead, who had been in poor health for some time. One Sunday Patrick agreed to go to Hartshead to take the morning and afternoon services. On such occasions his duties at Dewsbury would normally have been limited to reading some of the prayers at the evening service. On this Sunday, however, his vicar had told him that he would like Patrick to take the entire service as he wished to spend the evening with his wife's relatives, the Halliley family, who lived at a house called the Aldams. John Halliley was the owner of the largest mill in Dewsbury and was known locally as the 'King of Dewsbury'. On the appointed Sunday Patrick set out for Hartshead accompanied by Joseph Tolson, a young man with whom he had become friendly and who occasionally acted as the parish clerk. On their return journey they were caught in a thunderstorm and became drenched to the skin:

> Mr Brontë, instead of going to his rooms to effect a change of clothing, made speed for the Aldams. ... On arriving he was met by Mr Halliley, senr., to whom he explained that according to an arrangement made between himself and the Vicar he was to take the entire service, and that being wet to the skin, he wished Mr Buckworth to officiate instead. On hearing this Mr Halliley exclaimed, and very likely in jest, "What! Keep a dog and bark himself." Mr Brontë saw no fun in the remark, but taking it to be a deliberate insult, was highly incensed. He, however, said not a word, but turning off abruptly left Mr Halliley.

The young Joseph Tolson, who had overheard this exchange, made sure that he was present at the evening service in the parish church to see how Patrick would react:

> Mr Brontë was already there, and seemingly quite cool and collected. Prayers were gone through, the psalms said or sung, and the lessons read. Then in due course, and whilst a hymn was being rendered, Mr Brontë ascended the higher stairs of the "three-decker" to deliver his sermon. If the congregation were at all sleepy that evening they must soon have been aroused, for he announced that it was not his intention to preach again after that evening, giving as his reason that he had been most grievously insulted. ... Mr Brontë then gave out his text and preached a sermon of considerable power, but made no allusion in it to what had occurred but a short hour or so before at the Aldhams. The extraordinary incident formed the theme of conversation when service was over and the congregation dispersing. Mr Brontë was as good as his word. That was his last discourse in Dewsbury Parish Church.[8]

There are several oddities in this account and it would appear to be an exaggerated version of what may have occurred. Patrick could not have withdrawn from his preaching duties at Dewsbury and continued to serve as Mr Buckworth's curate. Nor in such circumstances would Mr Buckworth have subsequently promoted him to the perpetual curacy of Hartshead, an office which lay in his gift as vicar of the parish. From all that we know of Patrick Brontë, it is most likely that he would have taken offence at such a jocular remark made in such circumstances, and that in the heat of the moment he may well have threatened never to preach at Dewsbury again. Moreover, Joseph Tolson may have interpreted his subsequent move to Hartshead as being a fulfilment of this threat.

The most famous incident during Patrick's curacy at Dewsbury concerned a young man named William Nowell. On 25 September 1810 Nowell, who lived at Daw Green, a suburb of the town, was arrested as a deserter from the army. He was taken from his home and committed to Wakefield prison. The only prosecution witness against him was a soldier named James Thackray, who said that he had enlisted William Nowell eight days earlier at Lee Fair, one of several annual fairs in the Dewsbury area. In Nowell's defence it was stated that, although his parents had been to Lee Fair, he had stayed behind in Dewsbury and that he had several witnesses who would testify to the truth of this statement. Mr Dawson, the magistrate presiding over the committal hearing at Wakefield, refused to accept the evidence of these witnesses and also would not allow time for more witnesses to be found. He committed Nowell to prison as a deserter.

The case attracted considerable attention in Dewsbury and there was an immediate outcry. It is clear that Patrick took a leading part in the events which followed. He was one of four gentlemen from Dewsbury who went to Wakefield a few days later to see Mr Dawson. They were accompanied by two witnesses who swore that on the day of the fair they had been with James Thackray all afternoon and that he had not enlisted any recruits at Lee Fair. Mr Dawson, however, refused to examine these new witnesses. Patrick, together with the churchwardens and principal inhabitants of Dewsbury, was also one of the signatories to a memorial which was sent to the Commander-in-Chief of the Army and then referred to the Secretary at War, Lord Palmerston. A reply was received from the Secretary at War asking 'The Clergyman' whether the facts were true to his own knowledge, or whether he only believed them to be true. In response to this query Patrick called a vestry meeting at which he took signed depositions from all the witnesses and sent them to Lord Palmerston, who replied that he could not interfere in the decision of a civil magistrate.

Nowell's supporters then decided to write to William Wilberforce, who was one of the two M.P.s for the West Riding of Yorkshire. Their letter was delivered by the vicar's father-in-law, John Halliley, who happened to be in London at the time. Wilberforce and Halliley went round to the office of the Secretary at War but Palmerston was out of town. Wilberforce then requested Mr Dawson to re-examine the evidence, but he refused. Those working on Nowell's behalf then urged Wilberforce to seek an urgent interview with Lord Palmerston. This he did, with the result that an 'imperative order' was sent to Dawson to review the case.

A hearing was arranged for 2 November 1810. Patrick went to Wakefield accompanied by Mr Hague, a Dewsbury banker, Mr Rylah, a local attorney, and John Halliley's son. They brought with them fifteen witnesses, including a Wakefield hairdresser who swore that Thackray had told him that his story was a pack of lies. When the magistrate remarked that 'they might have bought off the youth for £25', he was told that 'they were not going to buy justice on those terms'. After the hearing, the evidence was sent to London and five days later William Nowell was released from prison. He had been in jail for ten weeks.

The whole story was printed in the *Leeds Mercury* of 15 December 1810 in a letter written under the pseudonym 'Sydney'. It has often been assumed that this letter was written by Patrick himself, but this seems unlikely. The text of a letter which Lord Palmerston wrote to Patrick is printed in the paper immediately below the letter from 'Sydney', thus rendering the use of a pseudonym completely pointless if Patrick was the author. The 'Sydney' letter also contains the phrase 'we Englishmen', an expression unlikely to be used by Patrick who was always proud of his Irish ancestry.

It must have given Patrick great satisfaction at the conclusion of the affair to receive a letter from the Secretary at War himself. He was proud of the fact that Lord Palmerston had been his contemporary at St John's College, Cambridge, and had commanded the college corps in which he had served when fears of a French invasion were high. Palmerston's letter showed that, now that the facts of the matter had been clearly established, he felt very strongly about the injustice which had been done to William Nowell:

War Office
5th Dec. 1810

No. 22,429.

SIR

Referring to the correspondence relative to William Nowell, I am to acquaint you, that I feel so strongly the injury that is likely to arise to the service from an unfair mode of recruiting, that if by the indictment that the lad's friends are about to prefer against James Th[r]ackray they shall establish the fact of his having been guilty of perjury, I shall be ready to indemnify them for the reasonable and proper expences [sic] which they shall incur on the occasion.

I am, Sir, Yours, &c.
PALMERSTON.

The Rev. P. Brontë,

Dewsbury, near Leeds.[9]

On 7 December 1811 James Thrackray was found guilty of wilful and corrupt perjury at York Assizes and was sentenced to transportation for seven years.

It is likely that Patrick's appointment to Dewsbury was always intended to be a short-term affair. When in 1809 Mr Buckworth invited him to come to Yorkshire to serve as his curate, it is probable that he also offered him the attractive prospect of shortly being appointed to the perpetual curacy of Hartshead, which lay within his gift. Patrick had only been in Dewsbury six months when, on 6 June 1810, he wrote to the Archbishop of York's secretary discussing his move to Hartshead and indicating that his present position was somewhat anomalous:

I thank you for your information – I have got certificates for three years of my ministry, reckoning back from this period. The living of Hartshett [sic] is small: salary only 62£ a year. I am not at present licensed to the curacy of Dewsbury. Will you have the goodness, Sir, to inform me, whether I can get Licensed to this curacy, be inducted into Hartsheath [sic] Living,

and obtain License [sic] for non-residence, in time, to give a title to a Gentleman, who intends
to offer himself a candidate for Holy Orders, at his Graces [sic] next ordination? ... Be so kind
Sir, as to inform me what steps I am to take, and to excuse the trouble I have given you.

It may be that Patrick's lack of a licence to the curacy of Dewsbury was caused by the
fact that he had expected, almost immediately after his arrival there, to be appointed
to the living of Hartshead, whose present incumbent, William Lucas, had been ill for
some time and whose resignation must have seemed imminent. The situation was
complicated by the fact that, although Mr Buckworth had the right of appointment
to Hartshead, as a perpetual curate Mr Lucas had security of tenure and could only be
removed by resignation or by death.

Patrick's request to the Archbishop for a licence for non-residence indicates that, after
being inducted to Hartshead, he did not intend to move into the parish in the immediate
future. At the end of June he sent to the Archbishop his Letters Testimonial, signed by
fellow clergy who had known him in Essex, Shropshire and Yorkshire. Mr Lucas resigned
from the living shortly afterwards and on 19 July 1810 Mr Buckworth nominated:

> the Revd : Patrick Brontë Clerk B.A. of St John's College Cambridge to ... the Parochial
> Chapelry of Hartshead cum Clifton ... now void by the resignation of Willm. Hanwell
> Lucas, the last Incumbent there'.[10]

On the following day the Archbishop licensed Patrick to the living.

Patrick's appointment to Hartshead might now appear to be settled, but it is clear
that some anomalies remained. For the next eight months, most of the duties there were
taken by the Revd David Jenkins, the curate appointed to succeed him in Dewsbury.
Mr Jenkins performed nine marriages at Hartshead between 9 August 1810 and 28
March 1811. Moreover, Patrick continued to sign the registers at Dewsbury as 'curate'
and not as 'officiating minister' which he was now entitled to do. He also did not sign
the Hartshead registers as 'minister' until the end of March 1811. It seems that from July
1810 until March 1811 Patrick continued to live in Dewsbury and to perform the duties
of curate to Mr Buckworth. Lord Palmerston's letter on the William Nowell affair, dated
5 December 1810, was addressed to 'The Revd P Brontë, Dewsbury, near Leeds'.

Patrick had reason to be grateful to John Buckworth, both for his wise and inspiring
leadership, and also for giving him his first independent living. On his departure from
Dewsbury Mr Buckworth presented Patrick with a volume of his latest sermons, in which
he had written 'Revd P Brontë, 1811. A testimony of sincere esteem from the Author.'[11]

In later years Patrick maintained his friendship with the Buckworth family. A
revealing indication of their close relationship is seen in a poem which Patrick wrote
a few months after taking up residence in Hartshead. It was dated 11 June 1811 and
was addressed to Mrs Buckworth, who was away from home at the time. The poem is

written in the persona of the Buckworth's dog, Tweed, and expresses Tweed's sorrow in the continuing absence of his mistress:

Ah! Mistress, dear,
    Pray lend an ear,
To simple Robin Tweed:
    I've been to you,
    Both kind and true,
In every time of need.

    I have no claim,
        To rank or name,
Amongst the barking gentry;
    No spaniel neat,
    Nor greyhound fleet,
To grace the street or entry.

    But then you know,
        I still can shew,
A bonny spotted skin:
    Can watch the house,
    Kill rat or mouse,
And give you "welcome in".

    How oft have I,
        With wishful eye,
And fondly wagging tail,
    And bark, and whine,
    And frisk so fine,
Said, "Mistress dear, all hail."

    Rap! At the door –
        I soiled the floor,
With capering, and with jumping,
    Whilst on my back,
    With lusty thwack,
Fierce Esther was a thumping!

    My love for you,
        Still bore me through,

Whatever my disaster;
   If you said "Tweed"! –
And stroked my head,
Each wound had then a plaster.

   Each night I lie,
      With sleepless eye,
And longing wait the morrow;
   And poke my nose,
   And smell your clothes,
And howl aloud for sorrow!

   The other night,
      By clear fire light,
I saw your gown a drying,
   So, on the stones,
   I stretched my bones,
And spent the night in sighing!

   But all in vain!
      I thus complain,
Alas! There's none to heed me,
   You have not sent,
   As you were went,
To Esther for to feed me.

   Hard is my lot!
      Since I'm forgot,
By one I'll love for ever! –
   But mankind change,
   As round they range, –
A dog, he changes, never!

   A long farewell! –
      The gloomy Knell,
Will soon inform the neighbours,
   That Tweed is dead,
   And has got rid,
Of all his cares and labours!

Your kind, trusty,
   And humble Dog, Robin Tweed,
At my kennel near the Vicarage,
   Dewsbury, this 11th June 1811.[12]

'My dear saucy Pat'
1811–1815

My dear saucy Pat ... Both the Dr and his lady[1] very much wish to know what kind of address we make use of in our letters to each other – I think they would scarcely hit on this!!

Maria Branwell to Patrick Brontë, 18 November 1812

The ancient parish church of St Peter's, Hartshead, stands in an isolated position high on a moorland ridge about five miles to the west of Dewsbury. The parish of Hartshead-cum-Clifton included both the small village of Hartshead, just a cluster of farmhouses a mile to the south, and the slightly larger settlement of Clifton, a mile and a half to the west. The neighbouring areas of Hightown and Roberttown also lay within the parish. The parishioners had a variety of occupations. Many worked in the cottage woollen industry or in the mills in neighbouring towns, while others were engaged in open-cast coal mining and stone-hewing. Between Hartshead and Clifton lay Kirklees Hall, the seventeenth-century mansion of Sir George Armitage. In the grounds of this estate stood the ruins of Kirklees Priory, a Benedictine nunnery founded in the reign of Henry II. The priory grounds were renowned for allegedly containing the grave of Robin Hood. St Peter's church is of Saxon origin and traces of the original foundation may still be seen in the low, castellated tower, the south door, and the chancel arch. At the time of Patrick's arrival there were high box pews, a double-decker pulpit for the preacher and the parish clerk, and a gallery at the west end for musicians and singers, but the building was in a dilapidated condition.

Patrick's appointment to Hartshead represented an important promotion for him. Although the living lay in the gift of the vicar of Dewsbury, as a perpetual curate Patrick was free to run the parish as he wished and, once appointed, could not be removed by the vicar. As there was no parsonage house he took lodgings at Thorn Bush Farm, then known as Lousy Thorn Farm, just opposite the church. It was rented by a Mr and Mrs Bedford, who had previously been the lodge-keepers at Kirklees Hall.

Patrick signed the register at Hartshead for the first time as minister at the end of March 1811. His duties there were comparatively light compared with Dewsbury.

There were on average eleven or twelve marriages a year, about ninety baptisms, almost always undertaken during public worship on Sundays, and between fifty and sixty burials. During 1811 Patrick sought to extend the range of his evangelistic ministry by publishing a collection of twelve poems which he described as intended 'for the unlearned and poor' under the title of *Cottage Poems*.[2] He also continued to assist his former Dewsbury colleagues by occasionally taking a marriage service at the parish church. The esteem in which he had been held in Dewsbury is shown by the fact that some of the youths he had taught in the Sunday school walked over to Hartshead on several occasions, a return trip of ten miles, in order to attend his services there.[3]

As he settled in his new parish Patrick struck up good relations with the surrounding clergy. One friendship he established was with Hammond Roberson, a notable evangelical who had preceded Patrick both as a curate at Dewsbury and as the incumbent of Hartshead. Hammond Roberson had been ordained in 1779 and had resigned from his curacy at Dewsbury to found a boys' school on Dewsbury Moor. In 1795 he had transferred this school to Healds Hall, Liversedge, where he had combined the running of the school with the incumbency of Hartshead. At the time of Patrick's appointment, Mr Roberson was planning to build a church at Liversedge, of which he subsequently became the incumbent. He was an able preacher and was renowned locally as a strong and forceful personality. Patrick also became friendly with David Jenkins, who had succeeded him as a curate of Dewsbury. His closest relationship, however, was with William Morgan, the Welshman who had been a fellow curate at Wellington. Mr Morgan had recently moved to Yorkshire as a curate to John Crosse at Bradford parish church and he also served as the minister of Bierley chapel, Bradford.

At the end of July 1811 Patrick suddenly made the disturbing discovery that, since his arrival in the parish three months earlier, he had not on two successive Sundays publicly made the formal declarations of Assent to the Thirty-Nine Articles of the Church of England and to the Book of Common Prayer, which were legally required for him to become the minister of the parish. In some panic he wrote to the secretary to the Archbishop of York:

> For want of proper information on the subject, I neglected, reading myself in, in due time, in consequence of which I find that I am not lawfully possessed of this Living. I therefore take the liberty of requesting that you will be so kind as to inform me how I am to proceed, in order to regain right and lawful possession. …
>
> Will it be necessary that I should get another presentation and by his Grace's permission, be reinducted? Or will it do, if, through your mediation, I be licensed anew?[4]

Eventually, after obtaining a new set of letters testimonial from the local clergy of Dewsbury and a second nomination to the perpetual curacy of Hartshead-cum-Clifton from John Buckworth, Patrick was relicensed to the living at the end of August.[5]

This time he ensured that he read himself in properly and that he was legally the incumbent of the parish.

As Patrick settled into his work at Hartshead, he became aware that the West Riding of Yorkshire was threatened by very serious industrial unrest and that his parish lay in the centre of the affected area. The long war with France was causing great economic suffering. Supplies of wool and cotton were disrupted and markets for finished cloth and textiles were cut off. Unemployment, which was already high, now rose further and those in work were forced to accept a reduction in wages. An additional threat was presented by the introduction of new, more efficient, machines in the mills. These produced better cloth, at a greatly reduced cost, than was possible in the old cottage-based industries which were now being forced out of production. There was already great poverty among the working classes and, as conditions became more desperate, working men began to meet in secret to formulate plans to destroy the new machinery. They adopted the name of Luddites, after a young Leicestershire stocking-knitter, Ned Ludd, who in 1782 was said in a fit of temper to have smashed the machine on which he was working. In March 1811 gangs of men calling themselves Luddites caused havoc in the Nottingham area as they went round smashing the machines of those employers who had earned their hostility.

It was not long before the West Riding of Yorkshire was affected by this violence. In February 1812 a band of local Luddites attacked a consignment of cropping machines as it was crossing Hartshead moor on the way to Rawfolds Mill near Cleckheaton. William Cartwright, the owner of Rawfolds Mill, had taken a leading role in the introduction of new machinery and had publicly declared his defiance of the Luddites. Guessing that his mill might be the object of attack, he took careful precautions to defend it. He slept there every night, along with four trusted employees and five soldiers.

In the following weeks several attacks were made on mills in the Huddersfield area. On the night of 11 April a large force of men, mainly drawn from Hartshead, Clifton, Roberttown and Hightown (all of which lay in Patrick's parish), gathered at the Dumb Steeple, an obelisk marking a crossroads on Hartshead Moor, intending to mount an attack on Rawfold's Mill. As they made their way in organised groups across the moor their route took them past Hartshead church and Patrick's lodgings at Lousy Thorn Farm. On reaching the mill they broke through the gates and battered on the door, but were unable to gain entry. The defenders fired on them from the first floor and the mill bell was rung to summon reinforcements. A supporting group of Luddites from Leeds heard the opening volley of shots and turned away and fled. Despite all their efforts the attackers could not gain entry to the mill and many were wounded by the constant gunfire. Eventually they turned tail and fled, leaving behind two of their number who had been mortally wounded and could not walk. As soon as the attackers had dispersed many local people appeared on the scene with offers of assistance, including Hammond Roberson, who is said to have turned up with a drawn sword in his hand. Mr Roberson was renowned for his hatred of the Luddites and had offered his house as a billet for the soldiers who had been brought into the area to guard against trouble. Patrick's daughter Charlotte later portrayed him as the militant clergyman, Matthewson Helstone, in her novel *Shirley*.

A week later an attempt was made on the life of William Cartwright as he was returning home from Huddersfield, but he escaped unhurt. On 28 April William Horsfall, a woollen manufacturer from Marsden who had taken a leading role in defying the Luddites, was ambushed and shot as he was returning from Huddersfield market. His murder, however, marked the virtual end of Luddite activity in Yorkshire. Under a special commission, sixty-six Luddites were put on trial at York and seventeen were executed, including five for the attack on Rawfolds Mill and three for the murder of William Horsfall. Six other men were transported for seven years.

Patrick's parish lay at the centre of this violent activity. From all we know of him, it would seem probable that he supported the authorities and disapproved of the violent methods used by the rioters. He did not, however, turn up at the mill after the attack and he did not share the militant sentiments of his friend Hammond Roberson. Acquaintance with poverty in his native Ireland had made him sympathetic to those in need, and he would have been well aware of the sufferings of his parishioners. He might also have feared reprisals against himself, since there was a strong feeling in favour of the Luddites in his parish. It is not known whether he signed the testimonial, whose twenty-five signatures are now illegible, which was presented to William Cartwright, together with a subscription of £3,000, in recognition of his doughty defence of the mill. It was probably from this time that Patrick acquired his habit of keeping a loaded pistol in the house at night, which he discharged out of the window each morning.[6]

In his account of Patrick's ministry at Hartshead, Mr Yates relates a strange story of some secret burials in the churchyard. Yates heard the story from a Mrs Hirst, who for many years had worked as a servant for Thomas Atkinson, Patrick's successor as incumbent of Hartshead. According to Mrs Hirst, who heard the details from Mr Atkinson himself, after the execution of the Luddites at York some of the bodies were brought back to Hartshead and secretly buried in the churchyard at dead of night. Patrick, noticing the disturbance in the churchyard, realised what had happened but let it pass without any comment. In its details the story is, as Yates himself points out, clearly inaccurate. After the executions there was no need for secrecy and several of the men were given public burials. It is far more likely that some of those injured in the attack on Rawfolds Mill later died of their wounds and were secretly interred by night in Hartshead churchyard. The fact that this story was current in Hartshead in 1897, when Yates was writing his account, reveals a lingering local belief that Patrick was not without sympathy for the suffering of the Luddites.

In July 1812 Patrick was asked by John Fennell, the headmaster of the newly founded Woodhouse Grove School at Rawdon, near Leeds, to visit the school to examine the boys in the classics. It had been opened in January that year by Wesleyan Methodists to provide an education for the sons of their ministers and preachers. John Fennell was known to Patrick from the time of his curacy in Wellington, where Fennell had been the schoolmaster, and on Patrick's arrival in Yorkshire, the two friends had renewed contact. As the first headmaster Fennell was anxious to provide assurance to the board of governors about the quality of teaching in the school. Patrick's appointment was as 'examiner in classical learning'.[7] In his report he commented unfavourably on the teaching of the subject and as a result the classics master, a Mr Burgess, was dismissed.

While he was staying at Woodhouse Grove Patrick came into contact with the headmaster's niece, Maria Branwell, who was assisting her aunt Jane on the domestic side of the school. When John Fennell had been appointed headmaster it had been arranged that his wife Jane would act as the matron and housekeeper. The school rapidly expanded and Jane soon secured the assistance of her niece, Maria, to help with the housekeeping. Maria Branwell was at the time aged twenty-nine and had been living at the family home in Penzance with her two unmarried sisters, Elizabeth and Charlotte.[8] The Branwell family were prominent members of the strong Wesleyan Methodist community in the town. Maria's aunt, Jane, had married John Fennell in 1790. He had been a Methodist local preacher and class leader there, before his move to Wellington. Maria's father, Thomas Branwell, a successful grocer and tea-merchant and a leading member of Penzance Town Council, had died in 1808, and her mother had died in the following year. The ownership of the family home, 25 Chapel Street, had passed to her uncle Richard, but after his death in 1811 the family circle was broken up. Elizabeth continued to reside in the town, probably living with her married sister Jane. Charlotte accepted the offer of marriage from her cousin Joseph, and Maria moved to Yorkshire to assist her aunt at Woodhouse Grove School.

Patrick's duties as examiner required him to pay regular visits to Woodhouse Grove and he and Maria Branwell soon fell in love. Patrick was regarded as an old and trusted friend by John Fennell and he was readily accepted into the family circle. He was also the closest friend of his old Wellington colleague, William Morgan, who was busily courting the headmaster's daughter Jane, Maria's cousin. Patrick's visits to the school now became more frequent. Sometimes he walked the twelve miles in each direction in a day and on other occasions he stayed overnight at the school.

Patrick and Maria regularly wrote to each other during their rapid courtship in the summer of 1812. Although his own side of the correspondence is lost, Patrick carefully preserved Maria's letters to him and the text of nine of her letters has survived.[9] They reveal a moving and intimate relationship between the two lovers and are important for giving us virtually the only knowledge we have of the mother of the Brontë children.

Maria's first letter is dated 26 August 1812. It seems that at their previous meeting she had accepted Patrick's proposal of marriage. Addressed to 'My dear Friend' she wrote:

I do indeed consider you as my <u>friend</u> yet, when I consider how short a time I have had the pleasure of knowing you, I start at my own rashness. … Do not think that I am so wavering as to repent of what I have already said.

On 5 September she wrote again:

My dearest Friend,
I have just received your affectionate and very welcome letter. In all my addresses to the throne of grace I never ask a blessing for myself but I beg the same for you, and considering the important station which you are called to fill, my prayers are proportionately fervent that you may be favoured with all the gifts and graces requisite for such a calling. O my dear friend, let us pray much that we may live lives holy and useful to each other and all around us! … I pitied you in your solitude, and felt sorry it was not in my power to enliven it.

She went on to express concern that he had told some of his friends of their engagement:

Have you not been too hasty in informing your friends of a certain event? Why did you not leave them to guess a little longer? I shrink from the idea of its being known to everybody.

And then, with a jocular touch, she added:

I do, indeed, <u>sometimes</u> think of you, but I will not say how often, lest I raise your vanity.

Her next letter, dated 11 September, gives an insight into her lively and spirited character and also provides a flavour of the happy days they were spending together that summer. In her correspondence Maria frequently referred to William Morgan, who was also a regular visitor to the school as he courted her cousin, Jane. He is often jocularly referred to as 'the Doctor':

You surely do not think you trouble me by writing? … Be assured your letters are and I hope always will be received with extreme pleasure and read with delight.
Jane had a note from Mr Morgan last evening. … You may expect frowns and hard words from her when you make your appearance here again, for, if you recollect, she gave you a note to carry to the Doctor, and he has never received it. What have you done with it? If you can give a good account of it you may come to see us as soon as you please, and be sure of a hearty welcome from all parties. Next Wednesday we have some thoughts, if the weather be fine, of going to Kirkstall Abbey once more, and I suppose your presence will not make the walk less agreeable to any of us.

A week later she told him:

> I believe a kind Providence has intended that I shall find in you every earthly friend united;
> nor do I fear to trust myself under your protection, or shrink from your control. It is pleasant
> to be subject to those we love.

Again he came in for criticism, however, for his absentmindedness. It seems that he had
made an arrangement with Mr and Mrs Bedford, his landlords at Lousy Thorn Farm,
that they should come to Woodhouse Grove to discuss an order for supplying blankets
to the school. When they arrived, however, the Bedfords had found no one in, because
Patrick had failed to forewarn the Fennells. John Fennell's comment was that Patrick
ought to be sent to the lunatic asylum at York:

> I do not know whether you dare show your face here again or not after the blunder you have
> committed. When we got to the house on Thursday evening, even before we were within
> the doors, we found that Mr and Mrs Bedford had been there, and that they had requested
> you to mention their intention of coming – a single hint of which you never gave. ... They
> all agreed that I was the cause of it. Mr Fennell said you were certainly <u>mazed</u> and talked
> of sending you to York. ... Even I begin to think that <u>this</u> bears some mark of <u>insanity</u>!
> However, I shall suspend my judgement until I hear what excuse you can make for yourself. I
> suppose you will be quite ready to make one of some kind or another.

On 23 September she wrote expressing agreement with his plan that they should
continue to live for the time being in his present lodgings at Lousy Thorn Farm. She
went on to express her deep feelings for him:

> Your joys and sorrows must be mine. Thus shall the one be increased, and the other diminished.
> ... And may we feel every trial and distress, for such must be our lot at times, bind us nearer
> to God and to each other! My heart earnestly joins in your comprehensive prayers. I trust they
> will unitedly ascend to a throne of grace, and through the Redeemer's merits procure for us
> peace and happiness here and a life of eternal felicity hereafter. Oh, what sacred pleasure there
> is in the idea of spending an eternity together in perfect and uninterrupted bliss!

A few days later she chided him on his failure to write to her:

> How could my dear friend so cruelly disappoint me? Had he known how much I had set
> my heart on having a letter this afternoon, and how greatly I felt the disappointment when
> the bag arrived and I found there was nothing for me, I am sure that he would not have
> permitted a little matter to hinder him. But whatever was the reason for your not writing,
> I cannot believe it to have been neglect or unkindness, therefore I do not in the least blame

you. I only beg that in future you will judge of my feelings by your own, and if possible
never let me expect a letter without receiving one. You know in my last which I sent you at
Bradford, I ... begged I might be favoured with hearing from you on Saturday.

On 21 October she again expressed her deep feelings for him and her longing to share
her life with him:

Unless my love for you were very great how could I so contentedly give up my home and
all my friends – a home I love so much that I have often thought nothing could bribe me
to renounce it for any great length of time together, and friends with whom I have so long
accustomed to share all the vicissitudes of joy and sorrow? Yet these have lost their weight,
and though I cannot always think of them without a sigh, yet the anticipation of sharing
with you all the pleasures and pains, the cares and anxieties of life, of contributing to your
comfort and becoming the companion of your pilgrimage, is more delightful to me than any
other prospect which this world can possibly present.

Her next letter, written nearly a month later, provides a further indication of her lively
personality and of the depth of her affection for Patrick:

My dear saucy Pat,
    Now don't you think you deserve this epithet, far more, than I do that which you have
given me? I really know not what to make of the beginning of your last; the winds, waves and
rocks almost stunned me. I thought you were giving me the account of some terrible dream
... having no idea that your lively imagination could make so much of the slight reproof
conveyed in my last. What will you say then when you get a <u>real</u>, <u>downright</u> <u>scolding</u>? ...
I firmly believe the Almighty has set us apart for each other; may we by earnest, frequent
prayer, & every possible exertion, endeavour to fulfil His will in all things! I do not, cannot,
doubt your love, & here, I freely declare, I love you above all the world besides!

She went on to report an unfortunate accident which had occurred:

I suppose you never expected to be much the richer for me, but I am sorry to inform you that
I am still poorer than I thought myself. – I mentioned having sent for my books, clothes etc.
On Saturday evg about the time when you were writing the description of your imaginary
shipwreck, I was reading and feeling the effects of a real one, having then received a letter
from my sister giving me an account of the vessel in which she had sent my box, being
stranded on the coast of Devonshire, in consequence of which the box was dashed to pieces
with the violence of the sea & all my little property, with the exception of a very few articles,
swallowed up in the mighty deep.

She concluded the letter with a postscript:

> Both the Dr and his lady very much wish to know what kind of address we make use of in
> our letters to each other – I think they would scarcely hit on this!!

Maria's last surviving letter to Patrick, written on 5 December, included plans for the wedding celebrations:

> We intend to set about making the cakes here next week, but as fifteen or twenty persons
> whom you mention live probably in your neighbourhood, I think it will be most convenient
> for Mrs B[edford] to make a small one for the purpose of distributing there, which will save
> us the difficulty of sending so far.

Patrick and Maria were married on 29 December 1812 in Guiseley parish church, in a joint wedding ceremony with William Morgan and Jane Fennell. Both brides were given away by John Fennell and each acted as bridesmaid for the other. The two young curates performed the ceremonies for each other. On the same day, over 400 miles away in Penzance, Maria's sister, Charlotte, was married to her cousin Joseph Branwell at Madron church. Patrick and Maria seem at first to have taken up residence at Lousy Thorn Farm, Patrick's previous lodgings, but soon afterwards they moved to Clough House at Hightown. Clough House was a stone-built house standing opposite the top of Clough Lane. It had three living rooms and five bedrooms and lay about a mile from Hartshead Church.

For some time now Patrick had been trying to secure the building of a parsonage house for Hartshead. He had first raised the matter a year earlier and he returned to the subject again in the autumn of 1812, at the time of his courtship of Maria. On 5 October 1812 he wrote to John Paterson, the Treasurer to the Governors of Queen Anne's Bounty, a charitable fund which had been established in 1704 to augment the livings of poorer Anglican clergy. He stated that:

> the small living of Hartshead-Cum-Clifton, though of very ancient standing, is without any
> parsonage-House. This serious inconvenience, together with a very small salary, has prevented
> Ministers, from being able to stay long in the place in consequence of which ... the Parish
> has suffered much injury. ... I write therefore to solicit the attention of the Governors and
> to beg, that you will inform me, as soon as you conveniently can, what they will give toward
> building a House.

He said that the cost would probably be about £400 but, unless the Governors provided the whole of this expense, the poverty of the local people would prevent the plan from going ahead. He added that the matter was urgent since he had heard that:

there is a piece of land, (and perhaps the only piece, that can be had) about to be sold, at a little distance from the Church, and conveniently situated, for ready water, prospect &c.

In response, Patrick received a letter from the Secretary, Richard Burn, stating that the only money appropriated to the parish of Hartshead amounted to £200 and that the Governors 'are not authorized to advance more, for ye purpose you mention.' In the following April Patrick wrote again saying that he thought that the Governors' failure to augment the living of Hartshead might be due to their ignorance of the correct rate of his salary. He said that with fees this amounted on average to £64:13:0 (£64.65), from which £15 to £20 must be deducted for the rent of a parsonage house, making his actual salary not more than £50.

Two months later he contacted the Secretary again, informing him that a gentleman was willing to make available a piece of land for the building of a parsonage:

He proposes selling it for £50. May I beg leave to ask, will the Governors, advance this sum, and bear the expense of writings &c? And in case they should do this, will they give as much at least, towards building the parsonage, as can be raised by voluntary contribution, amongst the Inhabitants?

This scheme also came to nothing and the Governors refused Patrick's request to defray the expenses he had incurred, saying that: 'It was the duty of the … Vendor to furnish you with a correct Abstract of the Title at his own expense.'

Although Patrick's salary was small, and it must have needed considerable thrift for him to live in a style appropriate to his calling, the early years of his marriage to Maria seem to have been a very happy period. Some indication of this may be seen in a poem which he wrote entitled 'Lines addressed to a Lady on her Birthday'. This appeared in a second collection of poems which he published in September 1813, nine months after their marriage, under the title *The Rural Minstrel*. It is addressed to Maria on her thirtieth birthday and reveals the depth of his love for her:[10]

Maria, let us walk, and breathe, the morning air,
   And hear the cuckoo sing, –
And every tuneful bird, that woos the gentle spring,
   Throughout the budding grove,
   Softly coos the turtle-dove.
      The primrose pale,
      Perfumes the gale,
The modest daisy and the violet blue,
Inviting spread their charms for you.

How much enhanced is all this bliss to me,
Since it is shared, in mutual joy with thee!
And should our vernal sky with clouds o'ercast,
Be rent by whirlwinds, and the sleeping blast;
    Should thunders roll,
    From pole to pole,
  And shake the fearful world;
E'en then, thy sweet society would cheer the gloom,
    And light a ray of hope,
    And bear my spirits up,
    ...
    Whilst thou dost love, and still art kind,
No gloomy changes can my peace destroy.

The Rural Minstrel contained eleven poems, including one entitled 'Kirkstall Abbey', in which the setting was the medieval Cistercian abbey on the banks of the River Aire near Leeds. Patrick and Maria had come there on several occasions with family gatherings from Woodhouse Grove and it is said that this was the scene of Patrick's proposal of marriage to Maria.

In October 1813 Patrick was present at the inaugural meeting in Bradford of a local Association of the Church Missionary Society, an evangelical body which had been established in 1799 with the aim of sending out missionaries to Africa and the East. John Crosse, the vicar of Bradford, and Patrick's friend, William Morgan, were among the co-founders of this local auxiliary. Patrick showed his support for the cause in a practical way by taking out a subscription of ten shillings and sixpence (52½p) to support the funds, and by inviting his former vicar, John Buckworth, to give a sermon on behalf of the Church Missionary Society at Hartshead on 25 September 1814. On 15 October that year Patrick gave the address at the anniversary meeting of the Bradford branch of the British and Foreign Bible Society and he also assisted in the formation of a Dewsbury auxiliary.

After decades of constant warfare, the abdication of Napoleon in April 1814 and the subsequent Peace of Paris brought the return of some prosperity to the country. It is probable that Patrick took some of his Sunday school pupils to Dewsbury to join a gathering of over 1,000 children in a huge celebration commemorating the peace on 7 July 1814. Earlier in the year Patrick and Maria had had their own personal cause for rejoicing in the birth of their first child, a daughter whom they named Maria. The date of her birth is not precisely known, but she was baptised in Hartshead church by William Morgan on 23 April 1814. A year later, on 8 February 1815, a second daughter, Elizabeth, was born.

It was probably the expense of maintaining his growing family which made Patrick responsive to a suggestion from a neighbouring clergyman that he should consider moving from Hartshead. Early in 1815 he was approached by the Revd Thomas Atkinson, the perpetual curate of Thornton, near Bradford, with the proposal that they should exchange livings. Mr Atkinson was a graduate of Magdalene College, Cambridge, and had been the perpetual curate of Thornton since his ordination in 1804. It seems that he was anxious to win the hand of Frances Walker of Lascelles Hall, near Huddersfield, and that he considered he would more easily achieve his objective if he resided nearer to her. 'He had a bird to catch' as a parishioner later succinctly and aptly put it.[11] The proposed arrangement was attractive to Patrick. The incumbency of Thornton would give him the considerably increased income of £140 a year, an important consideration with two daughters to support, and it also offered him the prospect of a deeper involvement in the much larger parish of Bradford. There was also a parsonage house available for the incumbent, which was an added inducement for a man with a young family.

Patrick readily agreed to the exchange and by the middle of March John Crosse, the vicar of Bradford, had nominated him to the perpetual curacy of Thornton. On 18 May 1815 Patrick took his final services at Hartshead, a funeral and two baptisms, and on the following day, accompanied by Maria and their two daughters, he made the thirteen-mile journey to their new home in Thornton.

'At Thornton ... happy with our wives and children' 1815–1820

> I can fancy, almost, that we are still at Thornton, good neighbours, and kind, and Sincere
> friends, and happy with our wives and children.
>
> *Patrick Brontë to the Rev'd Robinson Pool, 18 March 1858*[1]

Thornton was a small township situated about four miles from Bradford. Its chapelry, dedicated to St James, had been created out of the parish of Bradford to serve the inhabitants not only of Thornton but also of four other villages in the surrounding area: Clayton, Denholme, Allerton and Wilsden. Thornton itself was the site of an ancient settlement mentioned in the Domesday Book. It consisted of a few dwellings and several inns, grouped about Market Street, which formed part of the old highway from Bradford to Halifax. The majority of the inhabitants lived in farms and tied cottages in the surrounding hills. At the time of Patrick's arrival the population of the area was growing rapidly. In 1811 there were 5,500 souls in the chapelry; by 1821 this number had grown to just over 9,000.

The chapelry of Thornton had financial obligations to its mother parish and on 13 March, while he was still at Hartshead, Patrick signed a document agreeing to pay to the vicar of Bradford the dues which were customary:

> ten pence [4p] for every Funeral, if an Infant, and for every Adult twenty pence [8p], and
> sixpence [2½p] for every Christening. Which shall be done or performed at the Chapel of
> Thornton.[2]

For the first time in his clerical ministry Patrick now had the use of an official residence for himself and his family to live in. Thornton Parsonage stood in Market Street, one of a row of late Georgian stone buildings separated from the road by a narrow strip of garden surrounded by railings. Four steps led up to the front door, on either side of which were the two main rooms, each with a double window overlooking the street.

The kitchen was at the rear and upstairs were two bedrooms and a small dressing room. There was a large yard and some barns at the back of the building. A terrier (a document outlining the benefits, profits and endowments of a benefice) of 1817 noted that:

> This Chapel is endowed with a parsonage, situated in the village of Thornton, consisting of six rooms, three on the ground floor, and three bedchambers, having a stand for a Cow and Horse at one end, and a Cottage at the other – All built of stone and lime, purchased partly by contribution, and partly by the Governors of Queen Anne's Bounty &c – There is a road round the West End into a garden at the back of the House – which is enclosed by a stone wall, the greater part of the eastern side of which is built at the expense of the owner of the adjoining field, and the remainder by the Minister.[3]

Despite the advantage of having no rent to pay, Patrick found the parsonage at Thornton to be 'very ill-constructed' and 'inconvenient', and it required a considerable sum each year for repairs.[4]

The Old Bell chapel, as the church in Thornton was known, was in a dilapidated state of repair when Patrick arrived in 1815. It had been constructed in 1612 and was a functional building with no pretensions to architectural beauty. The interior was gloomy, dark and damp, with two galleries blocking out almost all the light from the small square windows. The aisles were paved with gravestones which were slippery when damp. The south wall was crumbling and the roof was in a dangerous condition. Patrick knew that considerable renovation would soon be required to get the building into an acceptable state.

His clerical duties at Thornton were not particularly onerous. Burials, which averaged about fifty-five a year, were the same as at Hartshead and the number of baptisms (at forty-three a year) were about half. The main reason for this was that Thornton was a major centre of nonconformity. Churchgoers in the chapelry were in a minority compared with the large number of Dissenters who attended the services held at nearby Kipping chapel. The minister at the time of Patrick's arrival in Thornton was the Revd John Calvert. His successor, appointed in 1816, was the Revd Robinson Pool, with whom Patrick enjoyed very good relations.

An imaginative description of the scene in Thornton on a Sunday morning at this time is given by Ivy Holgate, in an article in Brontë Society *Transactions* for 1959:

> The ringing of the bell … was a lengthy business, for few among the poorer households could boast of possessing a clock. As the bell tolled, sending its echoes down the long valley, the worshippers left their homes; some on foot, others on horseback. And, an essential detail in the scene, the dogs; dogs in packs; lone dogs; favourites, well-used to church-going; weaving about the hooves of the trotting horses. … They filed into the chapel as the bell tolled. The inhabitants of the respective townships had certain pews allotted to them. … All looked forward to the music and the lusty singing of hymns. … At this time instrumentalists accompanied the singing.[5]

In the conduct of the services Patrick was assisted by the parish clerk, John Drake, whose family had held that office in Thornton for many generations. In order to make a sufficient living he had to combine the post of clerk with those of sexton and caretaker. Some idea of the nature of the Sunday services taken by Mr Brontë was given in 1898 by the Bradford antiquarian, William Scruton:

> The service of the Church of England in the early years of the century was conducted in a very different fashion to what it is now-a-days. Instead of the procession of priest and choir to which we are now accustomed, the former was quietly ushered into the reading-desk by the verger, who bore his wand of office. ... The pulpit was of course the time-honoured "three-decker". Underneath the reading-desk was located the Parish Clerk ... who gave out the hymns, and at the end of each prayer solemnly intoned a loud "Amen!"
>
> The *Venite* and *Psalms* were read by the minister and clerk in alternate verses, the *Gloria Patri* being sung by the choir after each psalm. The *Te Deum* and other canticles were sung by the choir, usually to double chants of the most florid type. The metrical hymns consisted of the Psalms in metre by Tate & Brady, Sternhold & Hopkins, Bickersteth, or some such versifiers, and a selection of hymns. ... The hymns were usually sung to tunes of a sober sort, varied occasionally by others of a more ambitious kind. ... After morning prayer, a hymn was sung, and then came the Litany, usually a duet for parson and clerk. After the singing of a second hymn came the Ante-Communion Office in which the *Kyrie Eleison* was sung by the choir. This proceeded as far as the Nicene Creed, when a third metrical hymn was sung, during which the minister was solemnly conducted by the verger into the vestry, where he was robed in the black Geneva gown with white bands, then in vogue, and ushered back again by the same official to the pulpit, where the sermon was delivered – usually a performance of half-an-hour's duration. The whole service generally occupied over two hours.[6]

Patrick frequently took the opportunity to go to Church functions in the Bradford area. He regularly attended the annual meetings of the Bradford Auxiliary of the Bible Society. It is probable that he attended the consecration of the new Christ Church, Bradford, on 12 October 1815, performed by the Archbishop of York. His old friend William Morgan was nominated by Mr Crosse as the new church's first minister. In January 1816 Patrick, in common with ministers throughout the country, held special services of thanksgiving in the Old Bell chapel to celebrate the restoration of peace in Europe.

An interesting view of Patrick's activities in Thornton is given by the diary entries of a parishioner who lived at nearby Kipping House. Elizabeth Firth was eighteen years old at the time of Patrick's arrival in the parish and she rapidly became a close friend of the family. Her mother had died a year earlier in an accident to her gig and Elizabeth was keeping house for her father, who was a doctor. The family were well respected in the area and had a wide circle of friends. Frances Walker of Lascelles Hall, on whom

Thomas Atkinson, Patrick's predecessor, was bestowing his affection, was Elizabeth's cousin. Elizabeth kept a diary in which she made brief entries on family and local events.[7] She was away from Thornton staying with her cousin at Lascelles Hall on 19 May 1815, the day that the Brontë family arrived in the village, and her diary entry for that day laconically records: 'Mr Brontë came to reside at Thornton.' She returned home on 6 June and lost no time in calling on the Brontë family the next day. The two families rapidly became firm friends, as her diary records:

June 1815

9th.   We met Mr Brontë's family at Mr Kay[e]'s.

11th.   See St Matthew C. xiii. Vs. 3–9. The Parable of the Sower. The first time I heard Mr Brontë preach.

4th.   Drank tea at Mrs Brontës.

15th.   I called at Mr Brontës.

20th.   We had the Outhwaites, Brontës, and Miss M. Ibbotson to dinner.

26th.   We walked with Mr Brontès to the top of Allerton.

Maria Brontë's sister Elizabeth was staying with the family at that time. Miss Branwell had probably travelled from Penzance to assist the family in their move. She remained at Thornton for over a year and did not return home until the end of July 1816. She readily joined in the social activities at Thornton and with her sister was a frequent visitor to the Firths at Kipping House.

On 26 August 1815 Elizabeth Brontë, Patrick and Maria's second daughter, who had been born nearly seven months earlier, was baptised in the Old Bell chapel by John Fennell, the former Methodist headmaster of Woodhouse Grove School, who had just been ordained to the priesthood of the Church of England. The growing friendship with the Firth family is shown by the fact that both Elizabeth and her father were asked to be godparents. Two weeks later there was an additional local excitement with Mr Firth's remarriage, to Miss Ann Graeme of Exley, near Halifax. The ceremony was held in Bradford church and was taken by William Morgan.

Eight months later, on 21 April 1816, a third daughter was born to Patrick and Maria. She was named Charlotte, after her mother's youngest sister. Charlotte's birth was the cause of much celebration and Elizabeth Firth presented her with a little cap which she had made. The baby was baptised in Thornton by William Morgan on 29 June. This time, Elizabeth Firth's cousin, Frances Walker, was asked to be a godmother and Thomas Atkinson (by now engaged to Frances) was a godfather. Two weeks later, on 12 July, all the Brontë family were invited to Kipping House for a celebration dinner.

At the end of July Elizabeth Branwell, who had been assisting her sister Maria in looking after her young family for over a year, decided it was time that she went back to Penzance. Elizabeth Firth recorded the event in her diary:

July 1816

25th.   Mrs Brontë and Miss Branwell drank tea here for the last time.

28th.   I took leave of Miss Branwell. She kissed me and was much affected. She left Thornton
         that evening.

With the departure of Miss Branwell it was clear that some help was needed in the
parsonage for Maria, who now had to care for three children under the age of three. In
order to find a housemaid for the parsonage, Patrick applied to the Bradford School of
Industry, a charity school set up to train the daughters of poor parents. The thirteen-
year-old Nancy Garrs, one of twelve children of Richard Garrs of Westgate in Bradford,
was selected. This proved to be a very wise choice. Nancy became devoted to the Brontë
children and remained a loyal friend of the family long after she had left their service.

On 17 June 1816 the Rev'd John Crosse died. He had been the vicar of Bradford for
thirty-two years and, despite being blind, he had exercised an outstanding ministry. He
had promoted missionary activity both at home and abroad and had given his full support
to the Sunday school movement. He had also initiated the building of Christ Church to
serve as a daughter church in Bradford and had taken great care to appoint to positions in
his parish men who shared his evangelical beliefs. Patrick knew that John Crosse's death
would usher in a period of change and he was probably disappointed at the choice of
Henry Heap as Mr Crosse's successor. Mr Heap, who came from Todmorden in the Calder
Valley, was unable to match his predecessor's illustrious ministry. His time at Bradford
was also marked by a failure to maintain good relations, either with the Dissenters in the
parish or between the parish church of Bradford and its daughter churches.

Throughout his life Patrick showed a strong interest in education and in Thornton
he worked hard to develop the work of the Sunday school, which had been established
about five years earlier. Despite all his efforts, however, the existence of four Dissenting
Sunday schools in the chapelry made progress difficult. His answer to a questionnaire
from the National Society (the body responsible for Anglican church schools) reveals
the difficult position in which he was placed:

> There are five Sunday Schools, one in my chapel, containing forty nine boys, and fifty one
> girls: One belonging to the |Independent| Dissenters held in their meeting house, … in
> the village of Thornton, containing seventy boys and fifty girls: one of the same class of
> Dissenters in a neighbouring Hamlet – containing one hundred and thirty boys and one
> hundred and seventy girls: one of the Baptist Dissenters – consisting of one hundred boys
> and one hundred and fifty girls: and one of the Methodistical sect consisting of forty boys
> and fifty girls.[8]

With only 100 students in the church Sunday school, Patrick was in a considerable
minority, compared with the 760 children who attended the Dissenting schools in

the area. Nevertheless, he worked hard to achieve success. He introduced the new method of instruction recommended by the National Society and also persuaded Elizabeth Firth and two other local ladies to assist in the teaching. The inventory in the records of the Old Bell chapel reveals that among the limited resources available for use in the Sunday school, there were only twenty-one Bibles, twenty Testaments and five spelling books.

On 26 June 1817 Patrick and Maria were able to rejoice in the birth of their first son. He was given the name of Patrick, after his father, but he was always known in the family by his second name, Branwell, his mother's maiden name. Elizabeth Firth's diary account of this important event reveals that at this stage there was some confusion over which of the baby's names should come first:

June 26[th.] Went to see Mrs Brontë. . Branwell Patrick was born early in the morning.

On the following day she invited the three Brontë girls, Maria, Elizabeth and Charlotte, to tea at Kipping House. Branwell was baptised at the Old Bell chapel on 23 July by John Fennell, now the curate of Christ Church, Bradford. Elizabeth Firth's father and stepmother were asked to act as godparents.

Much of Patrick's time was spent attending the meetings of various evangelical organisations in Bradford. On 6 November, accompanied by Elizabeth Firth, he went to a missionary tea at the house of a leading Bradford churchman. On the next day they heard an address by the popular evangelical preacher Legh Richmond[9] at a meeting of the Church Missionary Society. A few days later, on 12 November, Patrick was invited to a dinner at Kipping House, where the other guests were the Rev'd Samuel Redhead (a fellow founder of the Bradford Auxiliary of the Bible Society) and the Rev'd James Franks of Sowerby Bridge and his wife. Their son, James, who was destined to marry Elizabeth Firth in September 1824, was enjoying a distinguished career at St John's College, Cambridge. On 23 December 1817 Thomas Atkinson achieved his desire of marrying Frances Walker. In the absence of a parsonage at Hartshead they set up home in Mirfield.

On 30 July 1818 a fourth daughter was born to Patrick and Maria. Emily Jane was christened on 20 August by William Morgan in the Old Bell chapel. In view of the extra work that would now be required in the parsonage for the care of five children, all under five years old, some changes were made in the Brontë household. Nancy Garrs, who had previously had the sole care of the children, was promoted to be cook and assistant housekeeper, and her place as nursemaid was taken by her younger sister, Sarah, who had also been trained at the Bradford School of Industry.

In the late autumn of 1818 Patrick devoted himself to the renovation of the Old Bell chapel. The main task was to restore the fabric of the building. The chapel was completely re-roofed and a cupola erected to house the bell. The south wall was pulled down and rebuilt. Patrick also took the decision to close the gallery at the east end of the chapel, which was in a dilapidated state. This gallery had previously accommodated the singers and instrumentalists who accompanied the services in the absence of an organ. Patrick rehoused them in a pew situated immediately in front of the pulpit. It may have been in compensation for what was probably an unpopular action – some new music books were purchased at the same time.

The Thornton parish records contain details of the musical instruments and books which were used in the church. These give some idea of the nature of the music which accompanied the services:

An account of the musical instruments and books belonging to this chapel and which it is the business of the minister and church-wardens always to take care of and preserve for the use of the said chapel:–

    1 Violincello and Bow,
    1 Tenor Violin and Bow,
    2 Treble Violins and Bows,
    I Holroyd's Psalmody,
    1 Stansfield's Psalmody,
    I Knapps Church melody,
    I Folio Orators of Joshua,
    2 Volumes of Anthems by Croft,
    A Copy of Purcell's Te Deum,
    Some Volumes of Manuscript Music,
    1 Steel fork for Pitching Tunes,
    1 Book of Hymns.

A note shows that great care was taken of the chapel service books:

Matthew Bairstow hath the Bible. Timothy Riley the Testament and Joseph Foster the Prayer Book belonging to the wardens Pew.[10]

An entry in Elizabeth Firth's diary shows that she was involved in the repair of some of the chapel books.

The interior of the chapel was also refurbished. On 10 November Elizabeth Firth's diary records that, 'We went to look at the angel in Thornton Chapel.' This was probably a reference to a painting on an interior wall executed by Thomas Driver. He was a carpenter by trade and also had some skill as an artist. The parish records give details of two payments made to him:

1818. Thomas Driver for painting different things in the chapel.   £6-0-0
      Thomas Driver joiner bill for work done at chapel   £4-8-4 [£4.42][11]

The Old Bell chapel was re-opened for services on 6 December 1819 and a board was erected at the entrance to commemorate the work which had been done:

> This chapel was repaired and beautified A.D. 1818. The Rev. P. Bronte, B.A. Minister, Joseph Robertshaw, Joseph Foster, John Hill, John Lockwood and Tim Riley, churchwardens.[12]

A royal coat of arms was painted below this inscription surmounted by the letters 'G.R'. At the foot of the board in small lettering the legend 'Painted by Thomas Rembrandt Driver' was inserted. The Old Bell chapel is now abandoned as a picturesque ruin, having been replaced in 1870 by a new building on higher ground on the other side of the road.

William Scruton's account of Patrick's ministry in Thornton describes an unusual incident.[13] In March 1819 Patrick took a large party of young people, said to number about sixty, on the four-mile journey to Bradford, to be confirmed in the parish church. As they arrived in Bradford and were walking down Kirkgate the weather deteriorated and it began to snow. Patrick became concerned for the welfare of the party on the return journey and he hurried into the Talbot Hotel and ordered hot dinners to be prepared for them. At the conclusion of the service he led the young people through the storm into the hotel, where they were provided with this refreshment before returning home. There clearly is some truth in this unusual story for the church wardens' accounts for 27 December 1819 reveal the payment of 9/10 (49p) under the entry:

> Children at Bradford when Bishop was in confirmation.[14]

The payment of 9/10 seems very cheap for sixty dinners. It may be that only hot drinks were provided or that the party numbered less than sixty. It is clear, however, that some act of kindness on Patrick's part at the time of the confirmation service was remembered in the parish for many years afterwards.

'Providence has called me to labour ... at Haworth'
1819–1820

I do humbly trust that it is my unvarying practice to preach Christ faithfully, as the only Way, the Truth, and the Life. ... I do think that Providence has called me to labour in His vineyard at Haworth.

Patrick Brontë to Stephen Taylor, 8 July 1819

At the end of May 1819, after four happy and busy years at Thornton, Patrick received a letter from the vicar of Bradford, the Rev'd Henry Heap, offering to nominate him to the perpetual curacy of Haworth, which lay within his parish. The incumbency of Haworth had recently become vacant by the death of James Charnock, who had held the perpetual curacy there since 1791 and had been suffering from a long illness. The vicar's offer took Patrick by surprise but, after careful consideration, he decided to accept the nomination as 'a gift and a call of Providence'.[1] Despite the happiness of his life and ministry at Thornton, he had been finding it increasingly difficult to support his growing family on its very small stipend. He was also influenced by the exciting challenge of moving to a parish made famous by the evangelical ministry of the Revd William Grimshaw some sixty years earlier.

Patrick's nomination to Haworth was supported by Michael Stocks, a well-respected magistrate in the Halifax area, who wrote to one of the Haworth Church Trustees, recommending him for the post:

May I beg leave to recommend the Revnd P. Brontë as a proper person to succeed my late Reverend Friend Mr. Charnock as perpetual curate of Haworth and I trust that you will feel no objection to him on account of his possessing the confidence of the vicar of Bradford, as I am confident you will find in him every qualification necessary to the spiritual Pastor of your Parish.[2]

Patrick soon learned, however, that his move to Haworth was not going to be a straightforward affair. The complication arose from a long-running dispute between the vicar of Bradford and a body of local trustees, both of whom claimed the right to nominate the perpetual curate of Haworth.

The church at Haworth had been built in the Middle Ages as a chapel of ease for the remoter districts of the parish of Bradford. It was served by a perpetual curate subject to the vicar of Bradford, who claimed the right to appoint his nominee to that position. Since Elizabethan times, however, this appointment had effectively been in the hands of the Haworth Church Lands Trustees, who were responsible for paying the curate's salary. When the reformed Church of England had been restored at the beginning of the reign of Elizabeth I, the inhabitants of Haworth had raised the sum of £36 for the establishment of a local trust. According to a deed of 18 December 1559:

> Andrew Heaton and Christopher Holmes are chosen and appointed Trustees in Trust by the inhabitants of the said Chappelrye to purchase lands and take and receive the rents due and profits annually arising therefrom and the same apply and pay over to the minister for the time being who doeth the usual duties of Divine Service in the said Chappel of Haworth being first lawfully licensed and admitted thereunto.

There was, however, an important proviso in the deed, that, if the Trustees 'be debarred in their choice or in the nomination of a minister when any vacancy shall happen', they had the right to withhold the income from the minister and distribute the money 'amongst the poor of the said Chapelry, of Haworth, or to any other good and charitable use, for the benefit of all the Inhabitants of the said Chapelry.' A minister who was negligent in the performance of his duties might similarly be deprived of his income from the church lands.[3]

The terms of this indenture of 1559 created the unusual and difficult situation whereby the vicar of Bradford could claim the right to appoint the perpetual curate of his daughter church at Haworth but the Haworth Church Lands Trustees had the power of thwarting that appointment by refusing to pay his stipend. This anomalous situation had given rise to previous disputes. In 1741, when the Vicar had declined to nominate William Grimshaw to Haworth, the trustees had secured his appointment by refusing to pay the salary of any other minister. There had also been a dispute over the nomination of James Charnock in 1791, when John Crosse was vicar of Bradford, but Mr Crosse had wisely made no attempt to proceed with the appointment until he had secured the full consent of the Trustees.

It soon became clear that the trustees were once again determined to exercise their rights over the appointment of their minister. When Mr Heap came to Haworth to take the services on Whit Sunday, they shut the doors in his face and told him:

They would have nothing to do with any person he might nominate, <u>without their Consent previously</u> obtained – They claim the ancient Privilege of <u>chusing their own Minister</u>.[4]

Heap's immediate reaction was to write to the Archbishop of York, formally nominating Patrick Brontë to the curacy of Haworth, which he stated 'doth of Right belong to my Nomination', and requesting him to grant a licence 'for serving the said Cure'.[5] Two weeks later the *Leeds Intelligencer* carried a report on the dispute:

> We hear that the Rev. P. Brontë, curate of Thornton, has been nominated by the vicar of Bradford, to the valuable perpetual curacy of Haworth, vacant by the death of the Rev. James Charnock; but that the inhabitants of the chapelry intend to resist the presentation, and have entered a caveat at York accordingly.[6]

At this juncture Patrick decided to seek the advice of Stephen Taylor, one of the Haworth Trustees with whom he was acquainted. Mr Taylor was a gentleman farmer who lived at the Manor House in Stanbury. His daughter Mercy was the wife of Benjamin Kaye of Allerton Hall, which lay within the chapelry of Thornton. Patrick enjoyed friendly relations with Mr Kaye, who was one of his leading parishioners, and he paid regular visits to Allerton Hall. Elizabeth Firth's diary records meeting Patrick and his family there. Patrick went over to Haworth and had a meeting with Mr Taylor and some of the other trustees in order to discover the full facts of the situation. They explained that, whilst they had nothing against him personally, they would vehemently oppose his appointment if it was made on the sole nomination of the vicar of Bradford.

Realising the strength of local opposition to the vicar's unilateral action, Patrick decided to take the matter no further and he informed Mr Heap that he intended to resign from the nomination. Henry Heap was not prepared to give in so easily, however. He informed Patrick that he could not withdraw with 'honour' or with 'propriety', and that an attempt to do so would incur the displeasure of the Archbishop. He was also given to understand that the Archbishop was willing for him to hold the incumbencies of both Thornton and Haworth until the matter was satisfactorily resolved. Patrick wrote to Stephen Taylor on 8 July to acquaint him with the situation:

> When the living of Haworth was offered to me by the Vicar of Bradford, I knew but little of the circumstances of the case, and consequently I accepted the nomination. This I was induced to do for two reasons, which I am persuaded no one can blame; first, because it seemed to hold forth some desirable advantages, and secondly, because as I never asked for it, it appeared to be a gift and a call of Providence. After I had seen you, however, and some of the other trustees, I doubted if it was my duty to have anything more to do with Haworth, and I therefore wrote several letters to some gentlemen who were nearly concerned, signifying my intention to proceed no further.

It seemed, however, to be the general opinion of my learned and pious friends, that I should not in honour, and with propriety recede, as I had gone so far: and that if I were to draw back … I should run the greatest hazard of seriously displeasing the Archbishop, who had received and approved my nomination. In consequence of this remonstrance, and a kind proposal of his Grace, to permit me to hold both Thornton and Haworth, till affairs should be settled to my satisfaction, I now feel it to be my duty, with the help of God, to go on till I see the conclusion.

He went on to give details of his background and to explain further why he now felt that he should persist with the nomination:

I have been educated at Cambridge, and taken my degree at that first of Universities; I have resided for many years in the neighbourhood, where I am well known – I am a good deal conversant with the affairs of mankind – and I do humbly trust that it is my unvarying practice to preach Christ faithfully, as the only Way, the Truth, and the Life. From considerations such as these, I do think that Providence had called me to labour in His vineyard at Haworth, where so many great and good men have gone before me.

He concluded by requesting that he should receive a fair hearing when he next came to preach at Haworth:

I therefore request your kindness, and your prayers, and that when I come to preach amongst you, you will use your endeavours to prevent people from leaving the church, and will exhort them to hear with candour and attention, in order that God's name may be glorified, and sinners saved.

It is not known whether Patrick took the services at Haworth on the following Sunday (11 July), or whether, if he did so, he received an unfavourable reception. At all events, on 14 July, he wrote again to Stephen Taylor telling him that he had decided to withdraw from the nomination:

I have just written to the Archbishop and the Vicar of Bradford to acquaint them with my resignation of my nomination to the living of Haworth – I thought it best to give you the earliest notice of this.

Patrick's speedy withdrawal seems to have surprised the trustees, who responded by inviting him to come to Haworth to preach a trial sermon, with the implication that they might then consider nominating him themselves. On 19 July Patrick wrote to Stephen Taylor giving his immediate response:

My conscience does not altogether approve to a circumstance of exposing myself to the temptation of preaching in order to please ... Through divine grace my aim has been, and I trust, always will be, to preach Christ and not myself and I have been more desirous of being made the instrument of benefit rather than of pleasure to my own congregation. Besides all this, I really am of the opinion that the best way by far is for the Trustees and some others of the people of Haworth, who are good judges of preaching to come and hear both me and others in our own Churches at a time when we do not expect them, and then they will see us as we usually are, and such as they would find us after many years' trial. It is an easy matter to compose a fine sermon or two for a particular occasion, but no easy thing always to give satisfaction. ... As I am but five or six miles off it will be no very difficult thing for such of the Trustees, and people of Haworth, as may be inclined to hear me in my own Church, to come over at a time when I do not expect them – and they may even learn my character, both as a preacher and a liver, from others.

He went on to define what many would believe to be the acid test of a faithful clergyman:

Believe me, the character and conduct of a man out of the pulpit is as much to be considered as his character and conduct in, and ... my wish is that if it should please the All-Wise Dispenser of events to call me to Haworth, rather to grow in the esteem and affection of my congregation, and neighbours, than greatly to please them at the first and then constantly to lose ground after the charms of novelty were over.

There is a note of subdued pride in the way in which Patrick rejected the idea of preaching a fine sermon especially to impress the inhabitants of Haworth. His suggestion that they should come unexpectedly to hear him at Thornton reveals a quiet confidence in the power and faithfulness of his ministry there. The trustees continued in their determination to assert their rights, and on 25 September they wrote to the Archbishop nominating the Rev'd William Fry to be the perpetual curate of Haworth, but it seems that nothing further came of this nomination.[7]

With the prospect of a move to Haworth now seeming remote, Patrick devoted himself to his pastoral ministry at Thornton. Due to industrial depression and a succession of bad harvests the summer of 1819 was a period of much discontent. In August Patrick, together with some of his evangelical friends, including the Revd Robinson Pool, the Dissenting minister at Thornton, addressed the annual meeting of the Bradford Bible Society, stressing the need for Christians to be active at this time of national crisis.

In the absence of an incumbent, the services at Haworth were being taken by various local clergy and on 8 October the Archbishop wrote to Patrick requiring him to take the services there on the following Sunday. Anxious not to cause offence to the trustees and to assure them that he was not seeking to gain the incumbency of Haworth by underhand means, Patrick wrote the next day to Stephen Taylor to explain the situation:

> His Grace the Archbishop of York sent me word yesterday that he wished me to take the duty at Haworth Church tomorrow. This, which was certainly very contrary to my inclination, I could not refuse – I therefore write to inform you of the circumstance, lest you should mistake my motive. My mind, and my inclination, are the same on the subject in question, as they were when I last saw you … I hope you will receive me in a friendly manner tomorrow, as I am obliged to go to you, in compliance with the wishes of the Archbishop.[8]

The nature of Patrick's reception at Haworth on 10 October is not known, but it may be assumed that it did not go too well from the fact that on 21 October his resignation was finally accepted by Mr Heap.

Mr Heap was unwilling to give way in the matter, however, and four days later he nominated the Revd Samuel Redhead, the minister of the New Horton chapel in Bradford parish, to the incumbency of Haworth. He again made his nomination without any reference to the trustees. On 30 October his action was reported in the *Leeds Mercury*, which stated that Mr Redhead had been licensed 'upon the nomination of the Rev. Henry Heap, Vicar of Bradford'.

In her *Life of Charlotte Brontë*, Mrs Gaskell wrote a vivid account of the scenes of disorder and chaos which ensued when Mr Redhead attempted to assume the incumbency. She told how, at his first service, on 31 October, during the reading of the second lesson the entire congregation walked out, stamping their clogs and making as much noise as possible, leaving Mr Redhead and the clerk to continue the service. On the second Sunday the disturbance was far worse. Again, during the second lesson:

> A man rode into the church upon an ass, with his face turned towards the tail, and as many old hats piled on his head as he could possibly carry. He began urging his beast around the aisles, and the screams and cries, and laughter of the congregation entirely drowned all sound of Mr. Redhead's voice.

On the third Sunday Mr Redhead arrived in Haworth accompanied by several gentlemen from Bradford. On this occasion the people brought forward a chimney sweep whom they had plied with drink:

> They placed him right before the reading desk, where his blackened face nodded a drunken, stupid assent to all that Mr. Redhead said. At last … he clambered up the pulpit stairs, and attempted to embrace Mr. Redhead. … Some of the more riotous pushed the soot-covered chimney-sweeper against Mr Redhead, as he tried to escape. They threw both him and his tormentor down on the ground in the churchyard where the soot-bag had been emptied,

> and though, at last, Mr. Redhead escaped into the 'Black Bull' ... the people raged without,
> threatening to stone him and his friends.

Eventually, with the help of the landlord of the Black Bull, Mr Redhead and his party managed to escape down the hill and rode away to Bradford.[9]

Mrs Gaskell's dramatic account was based on information given her by the Revd Dr William Scoresby, who had succeeded Mr Heap as vicar of Bradford in 1839, and by the landlord of the Black Bull who had assisted Mr Redhead in his escape. It should be remembered that her work was published over thirty years after the event and it seems that in the intervening years the story had grown in the telling. After the publication of *The Life of Charlotte Brontë* in the spring of 1857, Mrs Gaskell's version of events was challenged in the *Leeds Intelligencer* by Samuel Redhead's son-in-law, who quoted the relevant extracts from Mr Redhead's diary.[10] According to Mr Redhead's own account, he arrived at Haworth to take his first duty on 31 October, accompanied by Mr Rand, a leading Bradford churchman. After producing his licence he was admitted to the church, but the churchwardens refused to allow the bells to be rung. The congregation was small at first but slowly increased to about 500. The service proceeded normally enough until Mr Redhead entered the pulpit when, 'on a signal given by the churchwardens, trustees &c', the whole congregation stamped noisily out of church, shouting 'Come out, come out'. On leaving the church:

> Mr Rand and I were pursued and hooted and insulted by considerable numbers out of the
> village.

When Mr Redhead came to take duty on the following Sunday he brought with him Mr Crossley, a Bradford churchwarden. Once again, as he entered the pulpit, the congregation left their pews and began walking in and out of the church without any regard for the service which was taking place. The disorder continued into the afternoon:

> The afternoon service commenced in the midst of uproar and confusion, all decency seemed
> thrown aside, and laughing, talking, and noise frequently interrupted the prayers ... great numbers
> leaping over the tops of the pews, throwing to the pew doors with great violence, stamping with
> their feet, shouting and rushing out in the most outrageous and tumultuous manner.

Mr Redhead retired to the vestry and insisted that the churchwardens should remain with him while he conducted a burial in the churchyard. As he left Haworth he was pursued with 'hootings and pushing and shouting and insult.'

On the next day he went to York for an interview with the Archbishop and secured from him a threat that, if the disturbance at Haworth continued, the church would be closed and the matter referred to the Lord Chancellor. On the following Sunday Mr

Redhead returned to Haworth, for the third time, again accompanied by Mr Crossley. His diary reveals that any hopes that the Archbishop's intervention might ensure him a quieter reception were soon dashed:

> When we entered the village we were saluted with shoutings and insults, and pursued with the most indecent insolence. The same irreverent conduct was displayed all the way to the church. … Indecency and impiety marked their conduct during the prayers, and when I entered the pulpit all was uproar and confusion. I felt obliged to close the service without preaching. I gave directions to the churchwardens to shut up the church till they received instructions from the Archbishop, as I should lay the whole matter before him on the following day. I further told them that I should expect their protection through the town, with which they complied, and we went as we came, pursued more like wild beasts than human beings. Their shoutings continued, and we heard them for more than a mile and a half.

On the following day Mr Redhead wrote to the Archbishop and secured his agreement that he should resign from the incumbency.

A week later, the *Leeds Intelligencer* sternly criticised the people of Haworth for the disorders which had taken place:

> We regret to learn from a correspondent, that scenes, scarcely possible in an heathen village, have been witnessed on three successive Sundays, in the church of Haworth, merely in consequence of the minister officiating under the appointment of the Vicar of Bradford, and the licence of the Archbishop of York. The churchwardens are certainly liable to a prosecution for the wilful neglect of their duty and deserve to feel, that the house of God, and the hallowed ground of a church-yard, are not proper places in which to allow, by disturbance and howlings, the loudest and lowest marks of irreverence and insult.[11]

As the news of these proceedings filtered through to Thornton, Patrick must have been relieved that he had withdrawn from the nomination. In the absence of an incumbent, services still had to be performed at Haworth, however, and on Wednesday 17 November, just three days after Mr Redhead's last ignominious exit, Patrick was required to go there to take two funerals and a baptism, and a few days later he had to perform a marriage. Apart from these two occasions, however, he kept his distance from Haworth and devoted himself to his ministry at Thornton.

The new year of 1820 began auspiciously with the birth of Patrick and Maria's fifth daughter, Anne, on 17 January. The baby girl was given the name Anne after her maternal grandmother, Anne Branwell, and she was baptised on 25 March in the Old Bell chapel by William Morgan. The birth of his fifth daughter and the fact that he no longer had the prospect of moving to Haworth with its larger parsonage and increased income seems to have convinced Patrick that he must take steps to improve his financial situation. Life at Thornton was getting very difficult. The small parsonage, home to a family of six children, their parents and two servants, was very cramped and his limited stipend barely enabled him to provide support for them all. On 4 February 1820 he wrote to the Archbishop of York, enclosing a copy of a letter to the Governors of Queen Anne's Bounty which he had drafted a week before, in which he explained his financial problems as incumbent of Thornton:

> Thornton has generally been returned for one hundred and forty pounds a year; but in this have been included the Dues, which average about five pounds, and a voluntary contribution, frequently made under exceedingly unpleasant circumstances – amounting for the most part to seven or eight pounds. Nothing arises from pews, or from any other source. The Inhabitants, too, are so poor, in general, that presents, which in some Situations are very considerable, are here, not worth mentioning. So that all things duly weighed, and the proper deductions being made, the regular and certain Salary of this Living, is not more than one hundred and twenty pounds yearly. There is, it's true, besides this, a very ill constructed Parsonage House, which is, not only inconvenient, but requires, annually, no small sum to keep it in repair.

He described the Chapelry as 'very extensive, being about five miles long, and nearly four broad' with a population of 'at least nine thousand', and added: 'the place swarms with disaffected people, who omit no opportunity that offers, to bring our excellent Establishment into contempt.'

He concluded his letter with a heart-felt plea:

> If I were a single man, I might find what I have sufficient, but I have a wife, and six small children, with two maidservants, as well as myself to support, without I can obtain something more, in a just and honourable way, I greatly fear, that with the most rigorous economy, I shall be unable, any longer to uphold in appearance the due degree of Clerical respectability.

In his covering letter to the Archbishop he asked him to use his influence with the governors on his behalf to secure a grant for Thornton.

Four days later, much to his surprise, Patrick was again offered the nomination to Haworth, this time with the support of all the parties concerned. It seems that the receipt of his letter had prompted the Archbishop to take steps to resolve the impasse. Mr Heap had written to him suggesting that in his capacity as vicar of Bradford he should hold the living of Haworth himself, but in his reply the Archbishop had suggested that he should seek a meeting with the trustees to try to reach some compromise. A meeting between the two parties had been swiftly arranged and agreement had been reached. In a document drawn up on 8 February, Patrick Brontë was appointed to the perpetual curacy of Haworth in a joint nomination to the Archbishop of York by the vicar of Bradford and the Haworth Church Lands Trustees:

Whereas the parochial chapel of Haworth within the parish of Bradford and in your Grace's Diocese of York is now void by the resignation of the Reverend Samuel Redhead last Curate there: These are humbly to certify your Grace that We whose Names are hereunder written do hereby nominate the Reverend Patrick Bronte Bachelor of Arts to be Curate of the said parochial Chapel, humbly desiring your Grace's Licence to be granted to him for serving the said Cure. In witness whereof we have hereunto set our Hands and Seals this eighth – Day of February, in the Year of our Lord one thousand eight hundred and twenty –

The signatures at the foot of the document were headed by that of Henry Heap as vicar of Bradford, followed by those of five of the Haworth trustees: William Greenwood, John Beaver, James Greenwood, Stephen Taylor and Robert Heaton.[12]

The speed at which agreement was finally reached seems to show that, once their authority in this matter had been recognised, the Trustees were happy to join in nominating Patrick to the incumbency. Mr Heap wrote to the Archbishop on the following day describing the compromise that had been reached in terms as favourable to himself as he could:

I was honoured with your Grace's Letter. … The difficulties stated therein of my holding Haworth with Bradford appeared so many and great that I thought it better to wait upon the Trustees at Haworth in order, if possible, to settle the business. After many Altercations they have at last agreed to take Mr Brontë on my permitting them to join with me in a Nomination similar to what was done by Mr Kennett late Vicar of Bradford, when Mr Grimshaw was appointed to Haworth – I had offered to do this some time ago, but the Trustees positively refused then to have Mr Brontë – Your Grace will see by the nomination, which will be sent by this day's Post that the question of Right between the Vicar of Bradford & the Trustees remains untouched.

Although he was stubborn in church matters, Henry Heap was not an unkind man, and he added:

If your Grace could save Mr Brontë a journey to York, by permitting him to take the Oaths before me for his Licence, it would be considered a great favour & some expense would be saved by this means, which to Mr Brontè, with six small children, is certainly an object.[13]

Events now moved swiftly. Patrick's letters testimonial were drawn up on the day he received the nomination. They were signed by Henry Heap as vicar of Bradford, William Morgan, the perpetual curate of Christ Church, Bradford, and also, most magnanimously, by Samuel Redhead.[14]

Although Mr Heap had been compelled to give way over the matter of the nomination, he was determined that Patrick should be in no doubt over the primacy of the parish church of Bradford. Patrick was required to sign a document under which he promised to:

> pay or cause to be paid to the said Henry Heap & his Successors the Vicars of Bradford the half of all the dues for Marriages, Funerals, Baptisms or Churchings which shall be done or performed at the Chapel of Haworth aforesaid & which shall be paid on Easter Monday in every year – and … if required by the Vicar of Bradford, to preach a Sermon, In the Parish Church of Bradford, every Trinity Sunday in the afternoon, as a mark of Reverence to the Mother Church.[15]

Patrick for his part, as he contemplated the move to Haworth, was also anxious to safeguard his position and ensure that peace should be maintained. On the day after his appointment had been confirmed he wrote to the Archbishop requesting that the special nature of his nomination should be mentioned in his licence:

> I have sent my Testimonial and License to the Perpetual Curacy of Haworth – for the inspection of your Grace, and should they be approved, I beg leave to request that your Grace will mention in My License, that I am Licensed in consequence of the conjoint nomination of the Vicar and Trustees; for if the Vicar's name only, were to be inserted; on my reading myself in, it would in all probability give rise to very serious tumults in the Church, and might ultimately lead to the necessity of my resignation.[16]

His licence was granted by the Archbishop on 25 February.[17]

After all the legal formalities had been completed Patrick continued his ministry in Thornton for a further two months, although he probably travelled to Haworth to take some services. He may have wanted to ensure that there was absolutely no doubt about his acceptance by the people of Haworth before he moved his family there. Another reason for his delay may have been the spirit of unrest which swept the country following the death of George III on 29 January 1820. The king had reigned for sixty years and most people, including Patrick himself, had never known another monarch. The day of the King's funeral was kept as a day of national mourning, all shops were closed and special services were held. It was also a time of widespread poverty and there was much fear of unrest throughout the country. Elizabeth Firth's diary entry for Good Friday (31 March) reflected the general mood: 'We sat up expecting the Radicals.' Her feelings of fear were probably accentuated by Patrick himself. Her son later recorded how Patrick 'used to come in to Kipping & frighten my mother and her step mother with tales of the outrages past or probable.' In the event, these fears proved to be exaggerated and Elizabeth's diary records that those who called at Kipping: 'only asked for bread and that given, went off peaceably.'

At the beginning of April Patrick took the decision to make the move to Haworth. He must have been greatly excited at the prospect of starting a ministry in the parish made famous by William Grimshaw, who had been the incumbent of Haworth for twenty-one years (1742–1763). Mr Grimshaw had been the close friend of John and Charles Wesley, both of whom had preached in Haworth. It was said that on the occasion of Charles' visit a congregation of several thousand assembled in the churchyard. Mr Grimshaw had sought to maintain good relations with the growing Methodist movement and in 1758 he had built a chapel in West Lane for their use. As Patrick contemplated his move he must have had high expectations of a successful ministry which would fulfil the ambitious hopes which he had cherished since his ordination.

On 5 April Elizabeth Firth, knowing she would be away from home when the Brontë family left the village, called at the parsonage to say her farewells. On 10 April Patrick took his last funeral and some time between 10–20 April 1820 all the family possessions were packed in two flat wagons which had been sent over from Stanbury by Stephen Taylor. Patrick and Maria with their six young children and two maidservants then set off on the six-mile journey over the moors to Haworth.

PART TWO

Faithfulness and Sorrow, 1820–1846

'The greatest load of sorrows'
1820–1825

> I was at Haworth, a stranger in a strange land. It was under these circumstances, after every earthly prop was removed, that I was called on to bear the weight of the greatest load of sorrows that ever pressed upon me.
>
> *Patrick Brontë to the Revd John Buckworth, 27 November 1821*

In 1820 Haworth was a busy, industrial township with an expanding community. The Industrial Revolution had led to a considerable growth in population. Between 1811 and 1821 it had risen by 17% to 4,668 and this trend continued during the early years of Patrick's incumbency. In 1820 there were ten small textile mills sited alongside the River Worth and its tributaries, employing more than a third of the population. Others worked in their own homes, as hand-loom weavers or wool combers. There were many small farms in the area and some employment was provided in sandstone quarries in the surrounding hills. The community included a significant number of professional people and tradesmen. The town also had a strong musical tradition. The Haworth Philharmonic, founded in the 1780s, was one of the oldest music societies in the country and four concerts a year were regularly performed by the local Choral Society.

Despite some evidences of prosperity, however, there was a great deal of poverty in the township. Many of the inhabitants lived in small back-to-back cottages shared by several families. Some of the poorest lived in two-roomed cellar dwellings below street level, which were damp and poorly ventilated. The ill health of the inhabitants was made worse by the poor quality of the available water. In 1850, when the Babbage Report into the water supply and sanitary conditions in Haworth was issued, there were eleven pumps in the village and seven wells, of which only two were public. Much of the water was tainted by the outflow from privies, of which there were sixty-nine. Most of these were shared by several households. As a result of these conditions the mortality rates in Haworth rivalled those of the worst areas of London. Over 41% of children died before the age of six and the average age of death was twenty-five.[1]

The chapelry of Haworth covered a large area which included the settlements of Stanbury and Oxenhope. The church of St Michael and All Angels lay on an eminence at the top of Main Street, the steep hill running up from the valley of the Bridgehouse Beck. There had been a church on the site since the Middle Ages, but the building in Patrick's day dated back to the middle of the eighteenth century. Although there were six large arched windows on each side of the church, the west window was small and the galleries on the east, north and west walls made the church rather dark. The interior also had a rather cluttered appearance with high boxed pews filling the nave, the two aisles and the galleries above. A three-decker pulpit stood in the centre of the south aisle, with pews adjoining it on either side.

The parsonage was a rather elegant late Georgian house, built of the local millstone grit in 1779 for the Revd John Richardson, the incumbent from 1763 to 1791. A wide hall gave access to two large front rooms and at the back there was a small storeroom and the kitchen. Upstairs there were two larger bedrooms at the front, two smaller ones at the back and also a little room over the hall. There was a double-vaulted cellar beneath the house and a yard at the back, giving access on to the moors. In front of the house there was a lawn with flower beds at each side and the whole property was surrounded by a high stone wall. Although it was not a large building, Haworth Parsonage was a more suitable home for Patrick's young family than the house in Thornton, and the garden provided an area where the children might play in safety.[2]

Immediately on his arrival Patrick found himself busy with the performance of his ministerial duties, taking burials on 20, 21 and 22 April, four baptisms and two marriages on the 23rd and two more marriages on the 24th. Although the population was not significantly larger than that of Thornton, he found that his duties were considerably more onerous. He had to perform nearly double the number of funerals and marriages, and nearly seven times the number of baptisms. This latter increase may partly have been the result of his own ministerial zeal. Many of the entries in the registers were of older brothers and sisters of the baby being christened and it would appear that Patrick made a habit of persuading parents to have all their children baptised.

Patrick kept up his links with the Firth family in Thornton. On 6 June he stayed overnight at Kipping House so that he could attend the Archdeacon of Craven's visitation in Bradford parish church on the following day. Elizabeth Firth's diary shows that he stayed at Kipping House several times in the next few months while on his way to meetings in Bradford. On 8 September Elizabeth and her father came over to Haworth to have dinner in the parsonage. At the beginning of December, however, Mr Firth's health deteriorated and he became very ill. Patrick travelled over to see him on 13 December and he returned on the 21st, when Elizabeth reported that her father 'by God's blessing and Mr Brontë's conversation became more happy.' Mr Firth died on 27 December and Patrick took his funeral in the Old Bell chapel on 2 January.

The new year brought a great personal tragedy for Patrick and his young family. On 29 January, just nine months after the family's arrival in Haworth, his wife Maria collapsed with pains in her stomach and it became clear that she was very seriously ill. At a comparatively late stage in her life she had given birth to six children in as many years, and it is thought that she had cancer of the uterus. Patrick called in several doctors to examine her but none offered any hope of her recovery. Patrick engaged a local woman to take over his wife's care during the day, but he insisted on undertaking all the night nursing himself. After the arrival of Maria's sister Elizabeth from Penzance to supervise the nursing, Patrick was able to dismiss the nurse, who had proved to be unsatisfactory. The great pain which Maria suffered proved a serious test of her faith. In a long letter, written after her death to his former vicar, John Buckworth, Patrick described this unhappy time:[3]

> Death pursued her unrelentingly. Her constitution was enfeebled, and her frame wasted daily; and after above seven months of more agonizing pain than I ever saw anyone endure she fell asleep in Jesus. … During many years she had walked with God, but the great enemy, envying her life of holiness, often disturbed her mind in the last conflict. Still, in general she had peace and joy in believing, and died, if not triumphantly, at least calmly and with a holy yet humble confidence that Christ was her Saviour and heaven her eternal home.

Throughout this difficult time, although he had no curate to assist him Patrick, faithfully continued to carry out his parish duties. Out of sixty-three burials during Maria's illness he only missed taking one; he performed all but two of 192 baptisms and he solemnised all twenty-one marriages. But he felt very keenly the loneliness of his situation. As he told John Buckworth:

> For the first three months I was left nearly quite alone. … Had I been at D[ewsbury] I should not have wanted kind friends; had I been at H[artshead] I should have seen them and others occasionally; or had I been at T[hornton] a family there who were ever truly kind would have soothed my sorrows; but I was at H[aworth], a stranger in a strange land.

There was one occasion when he felt almost overwhelmed by his sorrows:

> One day, I remember it well; it was a gloomy day, a day of clouds and darkness, three of my little children were taken ill of a scarlet fever; and, the day after, the remaining three were in the same condition. Just at that time death seemed to have laid his hand on my dear wife in a manner which threatened her speedy dissolution. She was cold and silent and seemed hardly to notice what was passing around her. This awful season however was not of long duration. My little children had a favourable turn, and at length got well; and the force of my wife's disease somewhat abated. A few weeks afterwards her sister, Miss Branwell, arrived, and afforded great comfort to my mind.

Maria died on 15 September at the age of thirty-eight. Her funeral service, held on 22 September, was taken by Patrick's old friend and colleague William Morgan, who eight years earlier had officiated at their marriage. For two weeks following Maria's death Patrick gave himself up to his grief and performed no duties in the parish. He resumed his parochial work on 29 September, taking two baptisms and two burials on that day.

Throughout these difficult months Patrick had been sustained by his strong Christian faith. In his letter to Mr Buckworth, written two months later, he described his deep feelings of loss at Maria's death, and yet rejoiced that he did not sorrow 'as those without hope':

> Do you ask how I felt under all these circumstances? I would answer to this, that tender sorrow was my daily portion; that oppressive grief sometimes lay heavy on me and that there were seasons when an affectionate, agonizing something sickened my whole frame, and which is I think of such a nature as cannot be described, and must be felt in order to be understood. And when my dear wife was dead and buried and gone, and when I missed her at every corner, and when her memory was hourly revived by the innocent yet distressing prattle of my children, I do assure you, my dear sir, from what I felt, I was happy at the recollection that to sorrow, not as those without hope, was no sin; that our Lord himself had wept over his departed friend, and that he had promised us grace and strength sufficient for such a day.

Maria's long illness had brought him additional expenses and he was now considerably in debt. The family income was also reduced for on her death Maria's annuity of £50 came to an end and Patrick was left totally dependent on his salary of £170 a year. But help was at hand:

> Throughout all my troubles, [the Lord] stood by me and strengthened me and kindly remembered mercy in judgment; and when the scene of death was over, and I had incurred considerable debts, from causes which I could neither foresee nor prevent, he raised me up friends to whom I had never mentioned my straitened circumstances, who dispensed their bounty to me in a way truly wonderful, and evidently in answer to prayer. I received on one day, quite unexpectedly, from a few wealthy friends in B[radford] not less than one hundred and fifty pounds! I received also several pounds from my old and very kind friend at B[radford], fifty pounds as a donation from the Society in London; and what is perhaps not less wonderful than all, a few days ago, I got a letter containing a bank post bill of the value of fifty pounds which was sent to me by a benevolent individual, a wealthy lady, in the West Riding of Yorkshire. How true, how memorable the saying, 'Seek ye first the Kingdom of God and his righteousness, and all these things shall be added unto you.

Gradually he felt able to pick up the threads of his life again:

> The edge of sorrow, which is still <u>very</u> <u>keen</u> is somewhat blunted. The tide of grief, which once threatened to overwhelm me, has I trust been at its height, and the slowly receding waves often give me a breathing time though there are periods when they swell high and rush momentarily over me; yet I trust through the mercy of the Lord that time will produce its effects, and that I shall be enabled to pursue my ministerial labours with the necessary degree of alacrity and vigour.

Apart from his financial concerns Patrick was left with the pressing problem of how to care for his six young children. Maria's sister, Elizabeth Branwell, could not be expected to stay permanently to look after them. For the moment they were in the loyal and loving care of the two servants, Nancy and Sarah Garrs, but this situation could not continue for long. The obvious solution for someone in Patrick's circumstances was to provide a mother for his children by entering into a second marriage.

Overwhelmed by his great grief and by deep concern for the welfare of his young children, Patrick almost immediately took steps in this direction. On 8 December, when presumably he had business to transact in Bradford, he went over to Kipping House to stay with Elizabeth Firth. While there he seems to have come to the conclusion that the twenty-four-year-old Elizabeth could provide the answer to all his problems. He had known her throughout his ministry in Thornton. She had been very fond of his wife and of his children, and she was godmother to two of them. She was used to running a household, having had to do so for her widowed father before his remarriage, and, since her father's death, she was a wealthy woman. After his return home Patrick wrote to her, explaining his situation and asking her to marry him. Elizabeth received his letter on 12 December and was very upset by Patrick's proposal. The prospect of devoting the rest of her life to the support of a penniless clergyman and his six children was totally unacceptable to her. Unknown to Patrick she was being courted by a much more eligible clergyman, the Revd James Franks, the vicar of Huddersfield, whom she subsequently married in 1824. On 14 December she wrote to Patrick giving him a firm refusal and noting in her diary, 'I wrote my last letter to Mr Bronte'.[4] She had no further contact with the Brontë family for the next two years.

A year later Patrick seems to have made a second attempt to provide a mother for his children. One of his friends amongst the local clergy was the Revd Theodore Dury, the rector of Keighley. They shared a common interest in the local work of the Bible Society and Patrick had preached in Mr Dury's church. It seems that during the winter of 1822–1823 Patrick paid frequent visits to Keighley and that this gave rise to local gossip that he had proposed to Isabella Dury, the rector's sister. He might well have considered Miss Dury a suitable person to marry. She was a woman of independent means and was presumably an evangelical like her brother. Whatever the truth behind this rumour, Miss Dury wrote to her friend Miss Mariner, the daughter of a local manufacturer, on 14 February 1823:

> I heard before I left Keighley that my brother & I had quarrelled about poor Mr Bronte, I beg if you ever hear such a report you will contradict it as I can assure you it is perfectly unfounded, I think I never should be so very silly as to have the most distant idea of marrying anybody who had not some fortune, and six children into the bargain. It is too ridiculous to imagine any truth in it.[4]

It seems from the terms of this letter that Mr Dury, in an attempt to help Patrick, might have been a willing agent in this matter. Isabella's reaction, however, suggests that she would not have been a suitable stepmother for his young children.

As he reflected on the problem of bringing up his young family Patrick's mind now turned to Mary Burder, his former love at Wethersfield, to whom he had once been engaged. On 21 April 1823 he sought to renew contact by writing to her mother. He said that after leaving Wethersfield and receiving no answer to his letters he had concluded that his friends there were dead or had forgotten him and he continued:

> I married a very amiable and respectable Lady, who has been dead for nearly two years, so that I am now left a widower. I have at length removed to a Living, where I have been for upwards of three years. ... I should like to know whether Miss Davy be still alive, how you are yourself, how all your children are, whether they be married or single, and whether they be doing well. ... I shall probably go up into the South this summer, and may pass through your neighbourhood. I long to revisit the scene of my first ministerial labours, and to see some of my old friends.

After a delay of some months Mrs Burder eventually replied, and on 28 July Patrick wrote to Mary herself. Rather tactlessly he expressed his pleasure at learning that she was still unmarried:

> I experienced a very agreeable sensation in my heart ... on reflecting that you are <u>still</u> single, and am so selfish as to wish you to remain so. ... <u>You</u> were the <u>first</u> whose hand I solicited, and no doubt I was the <u>first</u> to whom <u>you promised to give that hand</u>.
> However much you may dislike me now, I am sure you once loved me with an unaffected innocent love, and I feel confident that ... you cannot doubt respecting my love for you.

He went on to give her news of himself and his family circumstances:

> It is now almost fifteen years since I last saw you. This is a long interval of time and may have affected many changes. It has made me look something older. ... Though I have had much bitter sorrow in consequence of the sickness and death of my dear Wife, yet I have ample cause to praise God for his numberless mercies. I have a small but sweet little family and I have what I consider a competency of the good things of this life. ... I want but one addition

to my comforts. . I want to see a dearly Beloved Friend, kind as I once saw her, and as much disposed to promote my happiness.

He added, rather oddly, that should she 'doubt the veracity' of any of his statements he referred her to his former vicar, John Buckworth, 'who is an excellent and respectable man, well known, both as an Author and an able Minister of the Gospel'. He concluded the letter by requesting her to reply as soon as was convenient and to tell him 'candidly' whether she or her mother would object to him visiting her at her home. He said that if she would consent to seeing him he would set off for the south as soon as he could get someone to cover his services at Haworth.

It is obvious from the tone of Patrick's letter that he felt a great sense of embarrassment in writing to Mary. He clearly had no assurance that Mary had any friendly feelings towards him or would be willing to receive him if he made the journey south. It seems clear that it was Patrick himself who had been responsible for breaking off their engagement. Whatever doubts he had felt about Mary's feelings for him were confirmed three weeks later when he received her bitter reply. Writing on 18 August she gave clear vent to her feelings:

Reverend Sir, As you must reasonably suppose a letter from you ... naturally produced sensations of surprise and agitation. You have thought proper after a lapse of fifteen years ... again to address me. ... The subject you have introduced so long ago buried in silence ... cannot I should think produce in your mind anything like satisfactory reflection. ... With my present feelings I cannot forbear in justice to myself making some observations which may possibly appear severe, of their justice I am convinced. This review Sir excites in my bosom increased gratitude and thankfulness to that wise ... Providence which then watched over me for good and withheld me from forming in very early life an indissoluble engagement with one whom I cannot think was altogether clear of duplicity. A union with you under then existing circumstances must have embittered my future days. ... Happily for me I have not been the ascribed cause of hindering your promotion, of preventing any brilliant alliance, nor have those great and affluent friends that you used to write and speak of withheld their patronage on my account, young, inexperienced, unsuspecting, and ignorant as I then was of what I had a right to look forward to.

She then roundly rejected his request for a meeting:

Your confidence I have never betrayed; whether those ardent professions of devoted lasting attachment were sincere is now to me a matter of little consequence. ... With these my present views of past occurrences is it possible think you that I or my dear Parent could give you a cordial welcome to the Park as an old friend? Indeed I must give a decided negative to the desired visit. I know of no ties of friendship ever existing between us which the last eleven or twelve years has not severed or at least placed an insuperable bar to any revival.

Mary went on to tell him that it was by her own choice that she was still single and that, despite an attack of typhus fever which had brought her to the verge of death, she was very happy with her state of life:

> My present condition upon which you are pleased to remark has hitherto been the state of my choice and to me a state of much happiness and comfort. ... Blessed with the kindest and most indulgent of friends in a beloved Parent, Sister and Brother, with a handsome competency which affords me the capability of gratifying the best feelings of my heart, teased with no domestic cares and anxieties and without anyone to control or oppose me I have felt no willingness to risk in a change so many enjoyments in possession.

But she ended her letter on a softer note:

> I can truly sympathise with you and the poor little innocents in your bereavement. The Lord can supply all your and their need. It gives me pleasure always to hear the work of the Lord prospering. May he enable you to be as faithful, as zealous, and as successful a labourer to His vineyard as was one of your predecessors the good old Mr Grimshaw. ... Cherishing no feelings of resentment or animosity, I remain, Revd Sir, sincerely your Well Wisher, Mary D. Burder.[5]

Mary had made her feelings plain and for most people that would have been the end of the matter. Patrick, however, was not a man to give up easily and he also wanted to justify himself against some of her attacks. On 1 January 1824 he wrote to her again:

> Dear Madam,
>
> In the first place I wish you the compliments of the season. My earnest wish and ardent prayer is that you may soon recover from the effect of your late severe illness. ... Yet, my dear Madam, I must candidly tell you that many things in that letter surprised and grieved me. ... You added many keen sarcasms, which I think might well have been spared, especially as you knew the pale countenance of death was still before my eyes and that I stood far more in need of consolation than of reproach. I confessed to you that I had done some things which I was sorry for, which originated chiefly in the very difficult circumstances that surrounded me, and which were produced chiefly by yourself. ... I do not remember the things you allude to, but as far as I can collect from your letter I must have said something or other highly unbecoming and improper. Whatever it was, as a Christian Minister and a gentleman, I feel myself called upon to acknowledge my great sorrow for it.
>
> You ... distinctly promised (they were nearly the last words I heard you utter) when I last saw you in Wethersfield, that if I called again you would see me as a friend. I, moreover, loved you, and notwithstanding your harsh and in some respects cruel treatment of me, I must confess I love you still. You may think and write as you please, but I have not the least doubt that if you had been mine you would have been happier than you now are or

can be as one in single life. You would have had a second self – one nearer to you than Father or Mother, sisters or brothers; one who would have been eternally kind, and whose great aim would have been to have promoted your happiness. … Our rank in life would have been in every way genteel, and we should together have had quite enough of the things of this life.

He made one last plea for a meeting:

Once more let me ask you whether Mrs Burder and you would object to my calling on you at the Park some time during next spring or in the summer? If you cannot see me as a friend, surely you can see me without feelings of revenge or hatred and speak to me civilly. … Surely you cannot object to this. It can do no one living any harm, and might I conceive, be productive of some good.

There is no record of Mary replying to this request and Patrick never raised the matter again.

By October 1823 Patrick's friendly relations with Elizabeth Firth had been restored and that month he called on her at Kipping House. He stayed two nights in Thornton and seems to have shared with her the dilemma he faced over the education of his children. Elizabeth Branwell had been with him for two years and now wanted to return home to Penzance. The two servants, Nancy Garrs (now aged twenty) and her younger sister, Sarah, were devoted to the children, but they were not sufficiently well educated to be responsible for their upbringing. Although Patrick himself could undertake the education of his son Branwell, it was essential that his five daughters should also receive a good education so that they could make their own way in life. Patrick was well aware that, should anything happen to him, his family would be homeless and without any means of support. Elizabeth recommended that he should try her old school at Crofton Hall, near Wakefield, a boarding school for young ladies, where she and her friend Fanny Outhwaite had been very happy. Shortly after Patrick's visit to Thornton, the two eldest children, Maria, aged nine, and Elizabeth, aged eight, were sent to this school. They were only there for a short time. Athough Elizabeth may have given him some financial assistance, the school fees of £28 a year presented Patrick with a heavy burden which he could not sustain for long.

In December 1823, however, a seemingly heaven-sent opportunity presented itself in the form of an advertisement in the *Leeds Intelligencer* under the heading 'School for Clergymen's Daughters'. It announced that a property had been purchased at Cowan Bridge in the parish of Tunstall, near Kirkby Lonsdale, to provide premises for a boarding school for the daughters of clergymen. The school would accommodate sixty pupils and the fees would be only £14 a year. It was particularly aimed to be of benefit to 'the necessitous Clergy; and especially to those who are the most exemplary in their Life and Doctrine'.[6] The opening of this school must have seemed to Patrick the ideal solution to his problems. It was supported by a prestigious list of patrons, including Charles Simeon and William Wilberforce. Patrick was probably acquainted with the school's founder, the Rev'd William Carus Wilson, a well-known evangelical clergyman who regularly preached at Bible Society and Sunday school services in the Bradford area. The school may also have been recommended to Patrick by his friend, Theodore Dury, who in its early years was a trustee.

The Clergy Daughters' School opened in January 1824, but it was not until 21 July that Patrick took his two eldest daughters, Maria, aged ten, and Elizabeth, aged nine, to Cowan Bridge. They would probably have gone earlier if both children had not been affected by whooping cough and measles in the spring. Patrick accompanied the two girls on the coach from Keighley and stayed overnight at the school. Patrick's choice of education for his two daughters shows that he was a shrewd judge of their abilities. He arranged for Maria, who, as he later told Mrs Gaskell, 'had a powerfully intellectual mind', to be given the education suitable for a future governess. She was to be instructed in 'the accomplishments' and he paid an extra £3 for lessons in French and drawing. That he was correct in his assessment is shown by the statement made years later by a former teacher at the school who referred to Maria as 'a girl of fine imagination and extraordinary talents'. Elizabeth, on the other hand, whom Patrick described as having 'good solid sense' was to be given a basic education. It was probably his intention that she should receive training as a housekeeper.[7]

Although our picture of the school is inevitably coloured by later events, life there in its early days may not have been unpleasant. There were only sixteen other pupils and two of them would have been known to the Brontë sisters. Margaret Plummer, aged fourteen, was the daughter of the Revd Thomas Plummer, the headmaster of the Free Grammar School at Keighley, who occasionally did duty for Patrick at Haworth. She had been a pupil since 21 February. Harriet Jenkins, aged ten, who had joined the school on 4 March, was the daughter of the Revd David Jenkins, Patrick's successor as curate at Dewsbury, who had often performed duties for him at Hartshead. Their presence shows that other local clergy shared Patrick's trust that the school would provide a good education for their children.

On their arrival the girls' names were entered in the register and their accomplishments were assessed. Of Maria it was recorded:

Reads tolerably – Writes pretty well. Ciphers [arithmetic] a little – Works [sewing] very badly. Knows a little of Grammar, very little of Geography & History. Has made some progress in reading French but knows nothing of the language grammatically.

Elizabeth's report read:

Reads little. Writes pretty well. Ciphers none – Works very badly – Knows nothing of Grammar, Geography, History or Accomplishments.

Although these entries might seem to reflect limited ability, the same comments were made of most of the other pupils in the school.[8]

During his brief visit Patrick shared meals with his daughters and had an opportunity to see how the school was operating. The girls were required to wear a distinctive uniform, discipline was strict and conditions were austere, but this was not unusual in schools of the time. Although the food was later a major cause of complaint Patrick did not seem to notice anything untoward while he was there. Three weeks later, on 10 August, he returned to Cowan Bridge, bringing the eight-year-old Charlotte, and once again he stayed the night at the school. Charlotte's abilities were also assessed:

Reads tolerably – Writes indifferently – Ciphers a little and works neatly. Knows nothing of Grammar, Geography, History or Accomplishments.

The register shows that she was to receive the education suitable to train her as a governess and under 'General Remarks' there is the perceptive comment:

Altogether clever of [sic] her age but knows nothing systematically.

With the education of his elder daughters now apparently settled, Patrick was able to devote his full attention to the affairs of his parish. On 31 August 1824 the Archbishop of York, Dr Edward Harcourt, came to Haworth to consecrate a new area of ground as an extension to the churchyard. His visit was in response to a letter which Patrick, jointly with the churchwardens, had written to him in April 1820, a few days before he actually moved to Haworth, requesting his permission to use this area for burials prior to its consecration.[9] After he had performed the ceremony, the Archbishop and the accompanying clergy retired to the Parsonage to partake of what the *Leeds Mercury* termed 'good English fare'.[10]

Two days later, on Thursday 2 September, a violent storm struck the Haworth moors, causing a landslip and flooding on nearby Crow Hill. Patrick visited the scene on the next day to view the damage and ten days later described what had occurred in a sermon which he preached in Haworth church:

The heavens over the moors were blackening fast. I heard muttering of distant thunder, and saw the frequent flashing of the lightning. Though, ten minutes before, there was scarcely a breath of air stirring; the gale freshened rapidly, and carried along with it clouds of dust and stubble; and, by this time, some large drops of rain, clearly announced an approaching heavy shower. ... The house was perfectly still. Under these circumstances, I heard a deep, distant explosion, something resembling, yet something differing from thunder, and I perceived a gentle tremour [sic] in the chamber in which

I was standing, and in the glass of the window just before me, which at the time made an extraordinary impression on my mind; and which, I have no manner of doubt now, was an effect of an Earthquake at the place of eruption. This was a solemn visitation of Providence.[11]

Although a team of experts sent out by the *Leeds Mercury* considered that the phenomenon was caused by a water spout, Patrick persisted in his opinion that it was an earthquake and wrote letters to both the *Leeds Intelligencer* and *Leeds Mercury* asserting this view.[12] He devoted much of his sermon to explaining how earthquakes were caused and urged his hearers to take it as a merciful warning from God and amend their way of life. He later rewrote this sermon in verse and offered his poem as a prize for the higher classes in the Sunday school.

In his sermon Patrick explained that he had a particular reason for taking an interest in this event. Branwell (aged seven), Emily (six) and Anne (four) were recovering from sickness at the time and, as the day had seemed fine, Patrick had sent them out for a walk on the moors in the care of Nancy and Sarah Garrs:

I had sent my little children, who were indisposed, accompanied by the servants, to take an airing on the common, and as they stayed rather longer than I expected, I went to an upper chamber to look out for their return. ... My little family had escaped to a place of shelter, but I did not know it. I consequently watched every movement of the coming tempest with a painful degree of interest.

Patrick made no mention of the fact that he had gone out into the full force of the storm to look for his children. Many years later Sarah Garrs' family described how the children had been out on the moor when the weather broke:

And they were frightened, and hid themselves under Sarah's cloak, and Mr Bronte went in search of them and found them in a Porch ... terrified, and so was he until he found them.[13]

They had in fact been in considerable danger, as had some other children who were out at that time. The *Leeds Mercury* reported that a torrent of mud, peat and water, seven feet high, had plunged down the valley from Crow Hill in the direction of Ponden. Fortunately, someone gave an alarm, 'and thereby saved the lives of some children, who would otherwise have been swept away'.[14]

Patrick now decided that it was time to send Emily (aged six) to join her sisters at Cowan Bridge. On 10 November he wrote to Mr Marriner, the head of a worsted-spinning firm in Keighley, who ran a savings bank:

> I take this opportunity to give you notice that in the course of a fortnight it is my intention
> to draw about twenty pounds out of your savings bank. I am going to send another of my
> little girls to school, which at the first will cost me some little – but in the end I shall not loose
> [sic] – as I now keep two servants but am only to keep one elderly woman now, who, when
> my other little girl is at school – will be able to wait I think on my remaining children and
> myself.

As his letter indicates, Patrick now planned to institute some changes in the running
of his household. With only Anne (aged four) and Branwell (seven) at home, he no
longer needed the two Garrs sisters to look after his children, and so he engaged Tabitha
Aykroyd, a fifty-three-year-old woman from Haworth, to serve at the parsonage as
housekeeper. This was a shrewd choice. Tabitha Aykroyd, 'Tabby' to the children,
developed a fierce loyalty to the family and was to remain in their service for the rest of
her life.

Patrick was careful not to leave the Garrs sisters without provision. Nancy was
engaged and wished to leave her position in order to get married. Years later she told
how, when Patrick heard of her engagement, he came into the kitchen:

> And said in his pleasant way 'Why, Nancy, is it true that you are going to marry a Pat? 'Yes,
> sir,' I replied, 'it is, and if he only proves one-tenth as kind a husband as you have been, I shall
> think myself very happy in having made a Pat my choice.'[15]

Patrick now sought to assist Sarah in finding employment. On his recommendation
she secured a situation travelling with a wealthy widow and her daughter. When her
mother objected to this plan she became apprenticed to a dressmaker in Bradford. In
1829 she married William Newsome and later emigrated with him to America.

On 25 November Patrick took Emily to Cowan Bridge. In order to be able to
accompany his daughter, Patrick arranged for the Revd Bernard Greenwood, the
headmaster of Oxenhope Grammar School, to take a baptism and a funeral on that day.
Emily, as the youngest child to enter the school, seems to have had favourable treatment.
The superintendent, Miss Evans, later referred to her as 'quite the pet nursling of the
school'. She was spared any criticism of her lack of abilities and her entry in the register
was brief:

> Reads very prettily & Works a little.

The onset of winter made life more difficult for the pupils at the school. On Sundays
they were required to walk two miles across the fields to attend the morning service
at Tunstall church (where Carus Wilson was the vicar). Since it was too far to return
to the school for a mid-day meal the girls used to eat a packed lunch in the church

and attend the afternoon service before walking back to Cowan Bridge. This routine meant that they were often sitting in the cold church for several hours in wet clothes. In December Maria began to show signs of consumption, but it seems that her father was not told of her illness until the middle of February, when her condition was seen to be serious. On hearing the news Patrick immediately travelled over to the school and took her home with him. She lingered on for eleven weeks, nursed by Patrick himself and by Aunt Branwell (as Elizabeth Branwell was known). Maria died on 6 May 1825, aged eleven years. The funeral service was taken by William Morgan, who eleven years earlier had performed her baptism, and she was buried next to her mother in the vault under Haworth church. When Patrick wrote to notify the school of her death he reported that, 'She exhibited during her illness many symptoms of a heart under divine influence.'[16]

It now became clear that Elizabeth was also suffering from consumption. Her condition was not helped by an outbreak of low fever (a type of typhus), which spread through the school and may have masked her symptoms. A doctor was called who recommended that the girls should be sent away from the cause of the infection. Carus Wilson arranged that all of them who were well enough should be taken to his holiday home at Silverdale, on the Lancashire coast near Morecambe, where they could enjoy the sea air. Elizabeth was too ill to profit from this move and on 31 May, the day the other children were taken to Silverdale, she was sent home in the care of a servant. Patrick's feelings at this time can only be imagined. Fearing for the health of his other two children, he set out the next day for Silverdale and brought both Charlotte and Emily home. Elizabeth died two weeks later, on 15 June.

Although the school register records that Charlotte and Emily left the school on 1 June 1825, on the day that Patrick brought them home, he himself gave a different account to Mrs Gaskell in 1855 when recalling this sad train of events:

> In about a year after they entered, Maria and Elizabeth became consumptive, I went for them and brought them home, they soon died within six weeks of each other – I left Emily and Charlotte, at the school – where they remain'd a year, and then came home.[17]

Patrick's statement implies that sometime after Elizabeth's death Charlotte and Emily returned to the school and were only taken away after Charlotte had been there a year (this would have been some time in mid-August 1825). It has usually been assumed that Patrick's memory was muddled when he wrote this (he was seventy-eight years old at the time and these events had occurred thirty years earlier). In her *Life of Charlotte Brontë*, however, Mrs Gaskell, who seems to have been using a different, possibly official school source, wrote:

> Both Charlotte and Emily returned to school after the Midsummer holidays in this fatal year. But before the next winter, it was thought desirable to advise their removal from school,

as it was evident that the damp situation of the house at Cowan's Bridge did not suit their health.[18]

In view of the conflicting evidence it is difficult to be sure of the exact sequence of events. If Charlotte and Emily did return to the school it is clear they only stayed for a few weeks.[19]

Any assessment of conditions at the school is inevitably coloured by Charlotte's bitter portrayal of it as 'Lowood' in *Jane Eyre*. It is unfortunate that the Brontë sisters were at the school in its early days, when funds were scarce and there was much mismanagement. It has to be noted that at the time Patrick did not seem to regard the school as responsible for his daughters' deaths. It must also be remembered that he had stayed there on two occasions and had shared his children's meals. Elizabeth Firth had also visited the Brontë girls at the school in September 1824 whilst on her honeymoon and had seen nothing untoward. It seems that the tragedy probably evolved through a combination of circumstances. The school had an undoubtedly harsh regime, but this could be paralleled at other schools of the time, including Woodhouse Grove. One of the chief causes of complaint was the food, which in the early days was inadequate for growing girls and often so badly cooked as to be inedible. It was produced by a cook who was both dirty and careless, although matters improved after she had been replaced. The school also lay in an unhealthy situation, being too near the river and consequently subject to damp. This was particularly injurious to the two elder Brontë children, who were already showing signs of consumption when typhus fever swept through the school in the spring of 1825.

The Rev'd Carus Wilson who founded the school was known to Patrick as a fellow evangelical and they had probably met at local Bible Society and Sunday school meetings. Unlike Patrick, however, Mr Wilson, was a committed Calvinist, who in his writings laid stress on the sinfulness of human nature and the certainty of punishment, rather than on the mercy of God. In 1815 Charles Simeon had warned him that he was 'unduly Calvinist' and apparently the Bishop of Chester had refused to ordain him for that reason. Charlotte's portrayal of him as the odious Mr Brocklehurst was probably highly exaggerated, but it does seems to have contained some truth. The daily routine of the school was dominated by religious observances, which prompted one fellow pupil of the Brontë children later to write:

> I trust I have ever been a firm advocate for making religion the groundwork of all education but the long hours devoted to sermons, lectures scripture lessons &c &c were so unreasonably long at Cowan Bridge, that I feel they were better calculated to hinder not promote the salvation of immortal souls.[20]

Some aspects of his beliefs may be deduced from *The Friendly Visitor* and *The Children's Friend*, the periodicals which he started in 1824, the year of the school's opening. These contain stories of children dying young and of death-bed repentances. They stress the natural sinfulness of children and the pressing need for them to repent before it should be too late. His theology may be discerned from a story which was included in a collection which he published in 1836:

> Do look at that bad child. … Oh! how cross she looks. And oh! What a sad tale I have to tell you of her. She was in such a rage, that all at once God struck her dead. She fell down on the floor, and died. No time to pray. No time to call on God to save her poor soul. She left this world in the midst of her sin. And oh! Where do you think she is now? I do not like to think of it. But we know that bad girls go to hell when they die. … My child, take care of such sins.[21]

And in a letter to his daughter, who was bedridden with a spinal disorder, he made no effort to spare her from the bleakness of his theology:

> You are early learning, my child to carry the cross. I would have spared you the cross if I could; but in so doing how I should have marred your real welfare.

Mr Wilson was undoubtedly motivated by charitable concerns when founding the school at Cowan Bridge and some of its defects may have been caused by the lack of funding in the early stages. His genuine concern for the poor is revealed in two letters he wrote in 1822 to Stephen Garnett, the administrator of poor relief at Kirby Lonsdale (where Wilson's father owned an estate). In these letters he took up the case of Mary Dixon, a poor lady who, with encouragement from Poor Law officials, had moved to Preston. She had two little children to support and, after her husband was put into in jail for poaching, her pension was withheld. After visiting her Wilson wrote angrily to Mr Garnett stating that hers was 'one of the most deplorable cases of distress' he had ever seen:

> She is lying in a wretched hovel. … Her two children appeared weak and poorly, and are wholly dependent on the neighbours for everything.

When Garnett failed to reply to his letter Wilson wrote again, stating that even if her pension had been restored it would not have been adequate for her needs:

> Where the husband was in prison, the wife and two children could not be expected to live on 3/- [15p] a week.

He concluded his letter with the threat to those responsible for the treatment of Mary Dixon:

Happy will it be if an awful account has not to be rendered hereafter in the case of Mary Dixon.

Later in his life Mr Wilson devoted considerable attention to the welfare of soldiers. In 1857, after the Indian Mutiny, he collected money in order to provide for the families of soldiers who were stationed in India, and he also established a Soldiers' Institute in Portsmouth. In St John's church, Newport, Isle of Wight, a large memorial was erected in his memory by the non-commissioned officers and private soldiers of the British Army 'as a token of their love and gratitude'.[22]

Carus Wilson was clearly a man of forceful personality imbued with a genuine sense of charity. There can be no doubting of his religious fervour, which greatly impressed many of his contemporaries. His narrow theological beliefs, however, rendered him unsuitable for running a school and for being responsible for the welfare of the young. It was most unfortunate for the Brontë children that, at an impressionable stage in their lives, they encountered such a man, whose views were so contrary to those of their father. Charlotte was later to wreak a terrible revenge in her portrayal of the odious Mr Brocklehurst in *Jane Eyre*. As she gleefully told her publisher's reader, Mr W. S. Williams:

"Jane Eyre" has got down into Yorkshire; a copy has even penetrated into this neighbourhood: I saw an elderly clergyman reading it the other day, and had the satisfaction of hearing him exclaim "Why – they have got – School, and Mr – here, I declare! And Miss – (naming the originals of Lowood, Mr Brocklehurst and Miss Temple). He had known them all: I wondered whether he would recognise the portraits, and was gratified to find that he did and that moreover he pronounced them faithful and just – he said too that Mr – (Brocklehurst) "deserved the chastisement he had got."[23]

'Always ... at my post'
1824–1841

You have rightly informed your readers, that I have always been at my post, as a practical supporter of Church and State.

Patrick Brontë to the Editor of the Leeds Intelligencer, *29 January 1829*

The education of his daughters at Cowan Bridge had been the cause of great sorrow for Patrick. It had also been a serious drain on his limited finances and he decided that he must make some effort to improve his position. On 25 August 1825 he wrote to Richard Burn, the Secretary to the Governors of Queen Anne's Bounty, to ask for their assistance. He particularly wanted to draw their attention to the peculiar situation at Haworth underlying the payment of his stipend. As he explained:

The perpetual Curacy of Haworth is nominally worth, about one hundred and eighty pounds a year; Besides the Surplice Dues amounting annually, to about fourteen pounds. In addition ... there is a house in which the Incumbents have been permitted to live rent free. ... This House, the adjoining garden, and the Lands from which the one hundred and eighty pounds, yearly, arise, are vested in Trustees, whose power, according to the respective Deeds, is almost unlimited.

If the trustees should disapprove of the incumbent or find him negligent in any way, they had the power to withhold his stipend and might let or even sell the house. He referred to their possession of this power as 'a studied attempt to keep the Incumbent in perfect thraldom' and concluded that:

the Minister can claim nothing with certainty, but the fourteen pounds a year, arising from the Surplice dues, inasmuch, as under one plea or another, however circumspectly he may walk, he may be deprived of his Salary.

He pointed out that the effective result of these terms was that 'this perpetual Curacy has no certain endowment, at all'. The situation was aggravated by the fact that:

in various instances … bills for repairs, and other things, have been brought … to me, by the Trustees – to a very large amount, rendering the salary inadequate to support my family, even with the most rigorous economy.

He explained that, although 'he had no quarrel with the Trustees' and was 'on good terms with the Inhabitants', the worst feature in the situation was the fact that:

a part of the Trustees, who are much the wealthiest, and who have a preponderating influence, are Dissenters, and have to support the Interest of a Baptist Chapel of their own, lately erected within about one hundred yards of the Church.

He concluded by stating that this was a situation, 'in which no Church, or Minister of our Excellent Establishment ought to be placed'. Twelve days later he received an unhelpful reply:

The Governors of Queen Anne's Bounty cannot in any manner interfere with respect to this Curacy as it has never been certified by your Diocesan, as a Living under £150 pr. Ann – & therefore is not in the Governors' List of augmble [augmentable] – Livings.[1]

Patrick was not a man to give up easily. On 1 December he sent another letter to Richard Burn in which he said he thought there must have been some misunderstanding on the part of the Governors:

For, otherwise, they surely, never would have judged it expedient, to leave this church almost entirely dependent, and without any certain Endowment at all, with the single exception of about fourteen, or sixteen pounds a year of Surplice dues.

He added that he had been encouraged to make his application by many neighbouring clergymen and particularly by the patron of his parish, the Rev'd Henry Heap, the vicar of Bradford. He sent this letter to Mr Heap who, a few days later, sent it on to the Governors with a strong recommendation of his own:

I think, from some years experience in the matters connected with this large Parish, that a stronger case for the Bounty of the Governors, has not appeared before them.

But it was all to no avail. Four days later Mr Heap received the Governors' reply, couched in typical civil servants' terms:

The Governors of Q.A.B. cannot augment this Living or otherwise deal with it until the Diocesan shall by a Supplemental Return under his hand & Seal certify the value of the

Living – I gave Mr. Brontë similar information on 6 Sept last expecting he would apply to the Archbishop of York or to his Grace's Secretary – It will be a great kindness to Mr Brontë if you will take the trouble to aid him by your advice conformably to these Instructions.[2]

Despite all his efforts Patrick never received any assistance from the Governors during his incumbency of Haworth.

Throughout his ministry Patrick laid great stress on the importance of reading and preaching from the Bible. In 1812 while still at Hartshead he had addressed the Bradford Auxiliary of the Bible Society and in 1823 he formed an Auxiliary in Haworth. On 19 September 1825 the second anniversary was celebrated by a service in the church. Patrick, as president, took the chair and delivered what the *Bradford and Wakefield Chronicle* described as a 'very animated speech'.[3] The church was packed and the twelve speakers included Henry Heap, William Morgan and the Baptist minister, Moses Saunders. The branch was celebrating an active and highly successful year during which they had raised £350 and distributed eighty copies of the Bible. Two weeks later the two branch secretaries, Thomas Andrew, the Haworth surgeon, and James Greenwood, a leading manufacturer, joined Patrick in writing a letter of protest to the Bible Society against their decision to distribute copies of the Bible which contained the books of the Apocrypha.[4] Along with many evangelical clergy Patrick did not consider the books of the Apocrypha to have the same inspired status as the rest of the Bible. In the following year it must have been with mixed emotions that Patrick found himself sharing a platform with the Revd Carus Wilson, when they both addressed the Keighley Auxiliary on 21 October 1826.

During the winters of 1825–1826 and 1826–1827 poverty was widespread in the West Riding of Yorkshire. Continuing poor trade and the collapse of a number of banks had led to a great increase in unemployment. In May 1827 a survey showed that out of 6,691 factory workers in Keighley, 4,524 were totally unemployed and the remainder were only working a three-day week. Patrick, as the chairman of the parish vestry meeting, was heavily involved in overseeing the raising and distribution of the poor rate and he was tireless in his efforts to relieve the distress of those out of work.

Since his early days in Ireland education had always been a cause close to Patrick's heart and in his previous ministries he had taken a leading part in the work of the Sunday school. Haworth was a poor area and, since there were many Dissenters in the population, the Anglicans found themselves in a minority.[5] In 1831 Patrick managed to persuade the Church Trustees to release a small plot of land in Church Street for the building of a Sunday school. Such a provision was all the more necessary because two years earlier the Methodists had opened a Sunday school of their own which was attracting large numbers of scholars.

On 8 August Patrick wrote to Mr Wigram, the Secretary of the National Society, thanking the Society for a grant of £80 towards the opening of a Sunday school and enclosing the consent form which the trustees had signed:

We, the undersigned, being Trustees, for the Church Lands, of Haworth, in the Diocese of His Grace, the Lord Archbishop of York, consent to give, at a Yearly rent of about five shillings, to be paid to the Incumbent – a sufficient plot of Ground, for building a Church, National Sunday School, forty five feet long, and thirty feet wide.

And, in typically forthright terms, he added in a footnote:

It would be deemed a great act of kindness, if you would give a few general directions, with respect to the manner, in which the Deeds are to be drawn up – and ... would also, peremptorily demand that a considerable share of power, in the management of the School, should be forever vested in the Incumbent, as one of the Trustees.

His aim in adding this postscript was to protect the incumbent from any arbitrary action on the part of the trustees at some time in the future.

The Sunday-school building in Church Street was opened in the summer of 1832. A plaque on the wall bears an inscription which was surely composed by Patrick himself:

This National Sunday School is under the management of trustees of whom the Incumbent for the time being is one. It was erected AD 1832 by Voluntary Subscription and by a grant from the National Society in London. Train up a child in the way he should go and when he is old he will not depart from it. Prov. xxii.6.

To raise money for the running of the school, Patrick initiated the custom of an annual Sunday-school sermon, always to be preached by a visiting clergyman. He also purchased a copy of *Hymns for the Use of the National Sunday Schools* to be used on these occasions, in which he wrote:

To be kept for the purpose of Selecting Hymns, for the Annual Sunday School Sermons – at Haworth – Those selected must be marked, in order to prevent any from being used a second time – as repetition must be avoided.[6]

Patrick had a deep love of music. He regularly took his family to concerts of the Haworth Philharmonic Society and in the autumn of 1833 he set about raising funds for the installation of an organ in the church to replace the orchestra which was accompanying the services. On 17 September he wrote to an unknown correspondent:

I have spoken to several people concerning the organ. All seem desirous of having one if the money can be procured. Miss Branwell says she will subscribe five pounds, and some others have promised to give liberally. Mr Sunderland, the Keighley organist, says he will give his

services gratis on the day of the opening of the organ, and, in general, the real friends of the
church are desirous of having one. A player can also be readily procured.

An organ committee was soon formed. Thomas Andrew, the Haworth surgeon, served
as its secretary and Patrick's son Branwell was one of its members. Special sermons
were preached on behalf of the fund and the money required was raised by public
subscription. The organ was opened on 23 March 1834 when sermons were preached
by the vicar of Bradford and by Charles Musgrave, the Archdeacon of Craven. In the
evening there was a performance of Handel's *Messiah*, organised and presided over by
Abraham Sunderland, the organist of Keighley Church.

Patrick was always anxious to be intellectually stimulated and in 1833 he joined the
Keighley Mechanics' Institute, which had been founded in 1825 by four local tradesmen
as 'a society for mutual instruction, and to establish a library for that purpose'. Patrick
paid 5/- (25p) as an admission fee and was given the membership number 213. His
contribution of 2d (1p) a week entitled him to use the reading room, the library and the
scientific apparatus, and to attend lectures and classes. In 1832 a popular series of lectures
on 'Ancient British Poetry' was given by William Dearden, the former schoolmaster
of Keighley and long-time friend of the Brontë family. In March 1835 Patrick was
appointed to a lecture sub-committee, along with his friend, Theodore Dury, the rector.
By the winter of 1835 lectures were being given on a wide range of subjects, including
a few by Patrick himself. Committee minutes in December 1840 record that his offer
to speak on 'The Influence of Circumstances' had been accepted by the committee.
Although Patrick does not seem to have played a very important part in the Institute's
affairs, his name remained on its membership books until 1846.

Throughout his ministry Patrick had tried to keep on friendly terms with
Dissenters, but when their campaign against the payment of church rates gathered
momentum, relations in Haworth, as in the rest of the country, seriously deteriorated.[7] One indication of this was the decline of the Haworth Auxiliary of the Bible
Society. Previously this had enjoyed the support of all the churches in the township
but in September 1833 Patrick had to cancel a meeting because he could not summon
enough local interest. On 3 September he wrote to Charles Dudley, the Secretary of
the Bible Society:

> I am very sorry to be under the necessity of informing you, that notwithstanding all the
> exertions I have made to raise a respectable Bible Society meeting on the 27th: of the present
> month, I have not been able to succeed. This is owing to a variety of local circumstances,
> which I cannot enter into in detail – And I deemed it necessary to apprize you of my
> disappointment in order that by writing to Mr Philipps, on the subject you might save him
> the fatigue of a fruitless journey.

Three years later the situation in Haworth had not improved. This is made clear in a letter from the secretary of the Keighley Auxiliary, in which, after clarifying details for a meeting in the town, he added:

> With regard to Haworth I fear there will be some difficulty in convening <u>a general</u> meeting as there is an unpleasant difference among the officers & friends.[8]

The system by which the twelve Haworth Church Lands Trustees operated was a cumbersome one and early in 1834 Patrick achieved a rationalisation of the process. On 1 February a document was drawn up over his signature and signed by all the trustees creating a new arrangement under which there would be four acting trustees each year by rotation. This would facilitate the administration of routine business. The full body and their chairman would be called together 'on all occasions of importance' in order that documents relating to the sale of land and other such matters might be signed.[9] Patrick also agreed with the trustees that the sum of £10 should be deducted from his salary each year to pay for the upkeep of buildings on the church lands for which he was responsible. This would avoid disputes over the excessive sums which had sometimes been charged him in the past.

In August 1834 Patrick tried to secure the appointment as a magistrate of Joseph Greenwood, the chairman of the trustees, a Tory and a loyal member of the church. On 11 August he wrote to the Earl of Harewood, the Lord-Lieutenant of the county, urging the appointment of a magistrate for the Haworth district and saying that he knew of a suitable person for this position. The earl replied that, since he had only recently recommended two magistrates for Keighley, he did not think this was necessary. When the Tory party came back into office in November, Patrick tried again, this time using the services of the vicar of Bradford, Henry Heap. He argued that a magistrate was needed in the Haworth area in order to enforce 'many late Legislative Enactments – And especially those in reference to Factories, and Factory Children', and he named Joseph Greenwood as the man most suitable for the office.

The Factory Act of 1833 had stipulated that no children under nine should work in factories and that those between nine and thirteen should not be employed for more than nine hours a day. Patrick was a friend and a supporter of the Revd George Bull, the vicar of Bierley, who had championed the cause of factory children and had campaigned tirelessly for the passing of the 1833 Act. On 11 September 1834 Patrick entertained Mr Bull at the parsonage and gave him the opportunity of speaking in the Sunday school to defend himself against the accusations of his detractors. These included the Baptist minister, John Winterbotham, who dubbed Mr Bull 'the pugnacious parson' and referred to him as 'a Tory Demagogue, under the MASK of pleading for the poor factory children'.[10]

Referring to Patrick as 'the <u>excellent</u> Incumbent of Haworth' Mr Heap forwarded his letter to the Lord-Lieutenant. The Earl, however, again declined, informing Mr Heap that he 'did not think it necessary to add to the Magistracy in the neighbourhood of Bradford at present'.[11] In October 1835, alarmed by the growing unrest in Haworth and by the action of the Dissenters in preventing the raising of a church rate for the coming year, Patrick wrote again to the Earl, renewing his plea. Once again he received a polite but firm refusal. In December he decided to raise the matter again. He wrote to Mr Heap, expressing his fears in a forceful manner:

> The enemies of the Church, in this place, are in active co-operation, and are determined to apply to Government to have a Whig Magistrate Appointed for Haworth, <u>over the head of the Lord Lieutenant</u>!!! ... I wish, that the Lord Lieutenant, could be informed of this, as soon as possible.

Rather reluctantly Mr Heap forwarded Patrick's letter to the Earl:

> My Lord,
>
> It is with a great degree of reluctance that I have made up my mind to forward the enclosed Letter to your Lordship. – But what can I do in these exciting Times, but endeavour to call forth well digested plans for ... the continued Establishment of Church and State. ...
> The Reverend P: Brontë the Incumbent of the Parochial Chapelry of Haworth in this Parish is a very warm Conservative. – If Mr Greenwood could be soon admitted to ye Privilege of becoming a Magistrate for that truly important part of my Parish, I should be grateful to your Lordship – but be it remembered that I feel much delicacy in even resuming the subject – if I have taken too great a liberty in forwarding Mr: Brontë's letter, pray forgive me.[12]

This time Patrick's efforts were rewarded with success. After due enquiries had been made, Joseph Greenwood was sworn in as a Justice of the Peace on 28 June 1836.

Patrick's work in the parish made him well aware of the harm done to family life by excessive drinking and in November 1834 he initiated the founding of a Temperance Society in Haworth. An inaugural meeting was held in the National Sunday school room, and in a spirit of cooperation he invited the other ministers in Haworth to address the gathering. The rector of Keighley, Theodore Dury, and his curate also spoke. So many people turned up that the meeting had to be adjourned to the West Lane Methodist chapel. At the end of the proceedings many of those present signed the Temperance Pledge. Patrick was appointed the president of the society and the three secretaries were the two Baptist ministers, Moses Saunders and John Winterbotham, and Patrick's son, Branwell (aged seventeen). It is clear that Patrick himself was not a complete teetotaller. We know from various wine orders to the Thomas brothers (James and Richard), wine merchants at Haworth, that he submitted regular orders for port and sherry.[13] Branwell's later career showed that he gained little profit from this early espousal of teetotalism! Nevertheless, the activities of the society were not without fruit. When in 1850 Benjamin Herschel Babbage came to Haworth to examine the sanitary conditions there, he was able to report that the consumption of beer and spirits was considerably below the average for other places in the neighbourhood.

In 1835 there was a rare return of Halley's Comet, last seen seventy-seven years earlier in 1758. Patrick celebrated this memorable occasion with a poem published in the *Leeds Mercury* on 31 October. He started by rejoicing in the comet's rare appearance:

> Our blazing guest, long have you been,
> To us, and many more, unseen;
> Full seventy years have pass'd away,
> Since last we saw you, fresh and gay –

He reflected on the changes which had occurred in the intervening years since the comet was last seen:

> Vast changes in this world have been,
> Since by this world you last were seen:
> The child, who clapped his hands with joy,
> Has pass'd long since, that dusky bourne,
> From whence no travellers return;
> Or sinking now in feeble age,
> Surveys thee as a hoary sage.

Then, after considering the comet's nature and changes in its orbit, he concluded by stressing the divine control of the universe exemplified in its passage:

> Nor man nor angels by their force
> Can for one moment stop thy course:
> The Mighty God himself alone
> Can rein thy speed, and guide thee on.
> Then fare thee well, thou mighty star –
> Go – do thy errand, near and far.
> Ere thou dost here return again,
> Few things that now are shall remain.
> Tell distant worlds, on whom you shine,
> The hand that made thee is divine.

By 1835, Patrick who was now aged fifty-eight, was finding it increasingly difficult to cope with the weight of his duties in the parish. The population of Haworth had increased by one third since his appointment in 1820 and there were now nearly 6,000 people in his chapelry. The number of funerals which he was required to take had increased from around 100 in his early years to 135 in 1834. The number of baptisms too had risen. The total for 1835 was 301, an average of twenty-five a month and on 19 and 20 July he baptised twenty children on each day. Although he occasionally had help from a neighbouring minister, most of these duties were performed by Patrick himself. By 1835 it had become essential to seek help.

He had already made one unsuccessful attempt to secure assistance. In July 1833 he had signed the nomination papers for a young man, James Bardsley, to be ordained to the curacy of Haworth. These papers were not fully completed. Although the month of July was named, the exact date was not mentioned and the amount of stipend was also left blank.[14] On the day before Mr Bardsley's ordination, the Archbishop of York decided to divert him to the curacy of Keighley instead. Dr Harcourt may have taken this action because he was not satisfied that Patrick had the means to pay the stipend for a curate. Despite this sudden change of plan, however, James Bardsley remained a close friend of the Brontë family and regularly came to the parsonage with his wife on Saturday afternoons to drink tea. He went on to have a distinguished career in the Church. After serving as curate to Theodore Dury at Keighley and further curacies at Bierley and Burnley, in 1857 he was appointed the rector of St Anne's, Manchester. He was later made an honorary canon of Manchester Cathedral and his elder son John was the Bishop of Carlisle from 1892 to 1905.

In December 1835 Patrick was at last successful in obtaining his first curate, William Hodgson, a newly ordained young man. Mr Hodgson took his initial duty, a burial, on Christmas Day 1835, but did not sign himself as curate in the Haworth registers until mid-April 1836. This delay may have been caused by some continuing difficulty over the payment of his salary. It seems that at first this was met by a voluntary subscription, and it was not until the spring of 1836 that Patrick secured a grant of £50 from the Church Pastoral-Aid Society to assist him in paying for a curate. Helpful though this grant was, it was not by itself adequate to pay the full amount and a voluntary subscription to augment it continued to be necessary.

Hodgson took lodgings with Mrs Grace Ogden at Cook Gate House in Change Gate, not far from the church. Mrs Ogden was a lady of independent means who lived there with her daughter, Susanna, and her three-year-old granddaughter. After the arrival of his curate, Patrick continued to perform most of the baptisms, marriages and burials himself, leaving Hodgson to take the Sunday schools and occasionally to relieve him of some Sunday duties. Hodgson's son-in-law later recorded one occasion shortly after his arrival in Haworth when this latter duty caused him some embarrassment:

It had been arranged that Mr Hodgson should preach in the morning and Mr Brontë in the afternoon, but while Mr Hodgson was in the afternoon Sunday School Mr Brontë sent for him and told him that he felt unequal to the task of preaching and that Mr Hodgson must take his place. To this Mr Hodgson demurred, urging that he had no sermon ready. 'Oh', said Mr Brontë, 'you must preach extempore; the people like it better.' Poor Mr Hodgson with much sinking of heart had to do as he was bid, and the Haworth folk used to remind him of that first extempore sermon and say he had never preached a better one.[15]

Few details are known of William Hodgson's curacy, and although he would have called at the parsonage in the course of his duties, he does not seem to have been on close terms with the Brontë family. He is only once mentioned in their correspondence, and that was after he had left Haworth. Although he was a loyal supporter of Patrick's ministry and appears to have been a lively young man, he seems to have been rather tactless and over-zealous in his denunciation of Dissenters and in the defence of the Established Church. The little we know of his activities is mainly derived from the local papers. In December 1836, at a time when Patrick was trying to solve the church rates problem in a peaceable manner by raising a voluntary subscription, an anonymous letter in the *Leeds Mercury* (probably written by the Haworth Baptist minister, John Winterbotham) made a sharp attack on Hodgson:

> The only drawback ... arises from the wild zeal and boisterous denunciation of a certain young man, who has lately assumed the gown, and who discredits his holy vocation by repeated tirades and invective against those who do not attend the place where he is permitted to officiate. Having been suddenly raised from a very humble situation in life, his head seems too weak to bear the elevation. ... There is nothing more seemly in young men, and especially young ministers, than modesty. There is nothing more unbecoming the pulpit than a bold condemnatory spirit.[16]

Two weeks later Hodgson wrote to the paper admitting that he was of humble birth and saying that he thought the attack had been made on him because of, 'my preaching on certain doctrines, Ecclesiastical Establishment, Episcopacy, Infant Baptism, the use of a Litugy, and the purity of our Formularies.'[17]

On 1 March 1837 civil registration came into force, whereby Dissenters were given the legal right of performing their own baptisms, marriages and burials. Prior to this date all nonconformists were required to be married in the parish church and the only legal records of births and deaths were those contained in the parish registers. On 4 March Hodgson wrote to the *Leeds Intelligencer* announcing that on the previous Sunday he and Patrick had between them baptised seventy-two children and that a further sixty baptisms had been performed on the next two days. He provocatively declared that this showed that Dissenters really preferred the services of the Established Church. The nonconformists in Haworth did not immediately take advantage of this change in the law and it was not until the end of December that Moses Saunders performed the first Baptist wedding at Hall Green chapel. The service was delayed by the late arrival of Thomas Umpleby, the Keighley registrar, whose presence was a legal requirement. According to the *Halifax Guardian* Patrick himself attended the ceremony and is intriguingly described as appearing 'prim as a shrimp'.[18]

Despite the opposition which Hodgson aroused, however, it seems that he was popular with the church people of Haworth. When, in April 1837, he intimated that he would be leaving his curacy, Patrick, in an attempt to make him change his mind, drew up a requisition affirming appreciation of his services and assuring him that the financial support of a voluntary subscription would continue to be forthcoming:

> We the undersigned inhabitants of Haworth being fully satisfied with your faithful and diligent services, both in the desk, pulpit, Sunday School, and parish, earnestly desire (if you can see it to be the path of duty pointed out by Providence) that you would continue in your present situation for another year, at least, or as long as you conveniently can. And at the same time we wish to state it is our hope and belief that, notwithstanding trade is depressed, your subscription will be conducted in a spirit, similar to that which gave rise to it, last year.

Within a few hours Patrick secured 236 signatures to the document and he added a note saying that, given the opportunity, he thought that all the church people in the chapelry would have signed it. But it was all to no avail. William Hodgson had been offered the post of vicar of the newly built Christ Church in Colne, and after signing the registers for the last time on 11 May he left to take up his new post in Lancashire, where he remained until his death in 1874. Patrick was not able to find a replacement for nearly two years.

By the beginning of 1837 the effects of the Poor Law Amendment Act, introduced by the Whig government in 1834, were beginning to be felt in Yorkshire. Under the Act outdoor relief, which had been administered locally by the parish, was brought to an end. Those who through old age, infirmity or unemployment were unable to support themselves were required to reside in workhouses in which there was strict segregation of the sexes, whereby husbands were parted from their wives and parents from their children.[19] In March the three Tory Guardians of the Poor resigned from their positions to show their opposition to the Act. Feelings in Haworth ran very high. The Tories said that they would not put up any Tory candidates in the forthcoming elections for parish officers. The Dissenting and Whig constables had no hesitation in putting their names forward and an election meeting was called for noon on Easter Monday in the church vestry. This was calculated to raise trouble. There was always a church service on that day, at which the vicar of Bradford, to whom Haworth had to pay substantial church rates, was usually the preacher. Patrick worked hard to prevent a confrontation. He persuaded the constables that the meeting should be held after the completion of the church service and that it should be in the Sunday school. He also persuaded Henry Heap to absent himself on the plea of ill health.

Patrick took the chair himself and succeeded in preventing it from degenerating into an unseemly row. The proceedings lasted four hours and the *Leeds Intelligencer* praised Patrick for his 'able, patient, and impartial conduct' as chairman, which had been acknowledged at the meeting by a vote of thanks. The paper added its own tribute to him:

> Though he is far advanced in years, and has suffered much from ill health, [he] displayed his pristine energies and faithfulness. That his life and services in his place may be long continued, is the fervent prayer of every churchman, to which every dissenter, who has the cause of religion at heart, will not fail to add his hearty Amen.[20]

The death of William IV on 20 June 1837 necessitated a general election. Patrick's keen interest in politics meant that he closely followed the issues involved. On 17 July the Tory candidate, James Stuart Wortley, spoke at the hustings in Haworth, and, rather surprisingly in view of Haworth's Whig sympathies, he was given a quiet hearing. Two days later Lord Morpeth, the Whig candidate, came to Haworth. Patrick had been invited to tea by Mrs Taylor (the wife of his churchwarden George Taylor[21]) at Stanbury Manor on that afternoon and he wrote to her to defer the invitation:

> As Lord Morpeth is coming to Haworth, tomorrow evening at four O'Clock and Miss Branwell and my Children, wish to see and hear him – and it is likely that there will be a good deal of drunkness, and confusion on the roads, I must request that you will excuse us, for not accepting your kind invitation.[22]

Benjamin Binns, the son of the Haworth tailor, later gave the *Bradford Observer* his memories of the occasion:

> Elections at Haworth in those days were very violent affairs. … The Tories, or 'Blues', were very few in number, and dared hardly show their faces. On this occasion the platforms for the two parties were erected nearly opposite each other, the Liberals being located against a laithe which stood in the now open space in front of the Black Bull Inn. The vicar and his son Branwell were on the 'Blue' platform. … The Liberals were there in great numbers. … When Mr Brontë began to question Lord Morpeth a regular 'hullabulloo' was set up. Branwell, in his impetuous way, rushed to the front crying, 'If you won't let my father speak, you shan't speak'.[23]

But Patrick and Branwell's intervention was all to no avail. Lord Morpeth was elected as Member of Parliament for the West Riding and the Whig ministry of Lord Melbourne remained in office.

Throughout 1838 relations with Dissenters continued to deteriorate. Because of their opposition at vestry meetings it had not been possible to lay a church rate at Haworth since 1835 and Patrick had been compelled to resort to a voluntary subscription. He was clearly under great strain as he sought to perform his parish duties and this seems to have affected his health. In the autumn he consulted John Milligan, a young surgeon in Keighley, about the dyspepsia from which he was suffering. Milligan recommended that he should take a glass of wine or spirits with his main meal. Patrick realised that this practice might be open to misrepresentation. He was a founder member of the Haworth Temperance Society and, aware of the hostility between himself and local Dissenters over the payment of church rates, he thought he might be made the object of attack. On 9 October he wrote to Mr Milligan:

> I have frequently thought, that You might have Wondered, why I was so particular in requiring your signature – The truth is – I wished to have Medical Authority for what I might do – in order that I might be able to counteract – (under providence) the groundless, yet pernicious censures of the weak – wicked – and wily – who are often on the alert – to injure those who are wiser and better than themselves.

Patrick was now aged sixty-one and it was two years since he had last had a curate to assist him in ministering to his far-flung chapelry. In January 1839 he wrote to several friends asking for their advice and help in obtaining a curate. Among those he approached was the Revd James Franks, the vicar of Huddersfield, whose wife, Elizabeth (*née* Firth), Patrick's old friend from Thornton days, had died in 1837. This letter written on 10 January is important for Patrick's forthright rejection of any colleague holding Calvinist beliefs:

> I have lately written to several Clergymen, requesting that they would exert themselves to find for me a suitable Clerical Assistant. I have got a grant from the Pastoral Aid Society, in case I can procure a man congenial with their sentiments, and who would be active, as well as zealous. … Will you be so good … as to give me your advice and assistance On this Occasion? The Bishop[24], to whom I have applied has been very kind, and attentive to my case, and offers, if no better may be, to Ordain on my Nomination. I know not what your religious Opinions |may be,| on some particular points, but it is expedient that on this Occasion I should candidly tell you some of mine; lest inconvenience might arise, from a collision with my future Assistant in our preaching and exhortation. As far as I know myself, I think I may venture to say, I am no Bigot – Yet, I could not feel comfortable with a Coadjutor who would deem it his duty to preach the appaling [*sic*] doctrines of personal Election and Reprobation. As I should consider these, decidedly derogatory to the Attributes of God – so, also I should be fearful of evil consequences to the hearers, from the enforcement of final perseverance as an essential Article of belief. … I want, for this region, a plain rather than an Able preacher; a

zealous, but at the same time a judicious man – One, not fond of innovation, but desirous of proceeding <u>on the Good Old plan</u> – which, alas! Has <u>often</u> been <u>mar'd</u> but <u>never improved</u>.

This time Patrick was successful in his search and the Revd William Weightman took up his duties on 18 August 1839.

On 17 January 1839, the Revd Henry Heap, the vicar of Bradford for the past twenty-two years, died. This created a new situation in the problem over church rates. Because the chapelry of Haworth lay within the parish of Bradford, the people of Haworth were required to pay two sets of church rates, to their own church and to Bradford parish church. A significant proportion of the vicar of Bradford's income came from the rates paid by Haworth. Mr Heap's death raised the possibility of changing this anomalous and highly unpopular system. On 30 January, less than two weeks after the event, Patrick wrote to the Bishop of Ripon:

> The demise of the Late Vicar of Bradford, in conjunction with the nature of the patronage, as well as the Late Act of Parliament, authorizing the division of parishes where it may be proper for the Interest of the Establishment, and the very great extent of the Parish And its population, all combine, as far as I am able to discover, to render it highly desirable, that the Chapelry of Haworth, should be converted into a parish by itself, distinct, and independent.[25]

Patrick gave details of the size of the parish and the number of the inhabitants and then went on to inform the bishop of disputes which had taken place in the past over the payment of church rates to Bradford which had caused much ill-will, 'which even the lapse of time, has not yet, totally eradicated'. He also informed the bishop of the peculiar nature of the joint nomination to the incumbency of Haworth and of the powers of the trustees to withhold almost all the incumbent's salary if the vicar of Bradford tried to make a nomination without reference to them.

Patrick realised very well what the feelings of the people of Bradford would be on this matter, and he was careful to add a rider to his letter:

> One thing however, I would remark, I think, Your Lordship will be of opinion – that, as the future Vicar of Bradford, might possibly be biased, against, a separation – by some adverse counsellers, The important end, might be more easily effected – before such vicar is appointed.

He added that, if the bishop desired it, he was sure that all the inhabitants of the chapelry would readily sign a petition in favour of the separation from Bradford. Two days later a petition was sent to the bishop. On 26 March a church meeting was held at which several resolutions were passed, the first of which was:

That it is desirable and expedient, that there should be a final, and complete separation of
|Chapelry of| Haworth, from Bradford, and that Haworth, should be made an Independent
Parish, and its Incumbency be changed into an Independent Vicarage.[26]

As a result of these representations the bishop drew up a scheme to make Haworth a
parish in its own right.

These proposals were widely welcomed in Haworth, but Patrick's fears over the
attitude of the authorities at Bradford were fully justified. The patrons of the parish,
the Simeon Trustees (of whom the Revd Carus Wilson was a member) pointed out
that, if Haworth became a separate parish and no longer paid church rates, the vicar
of Bradford would lose a fifth of his income. It has to be said that the Simeon Trustees
were in a difficult position. If the people of Haworth achieved their aim of separating
from Bradford, many other chapelries in the parish would seek to do the same,
thereby creating a difficult situation at a time when they were seeking to appoint a
new vicar.

In October 1839 the Revd Dr William Scoresby was appointed vicar of Bradford.
Dr Scoresby was a more forceful man than his predecessor and he refused to accept
the situation. He swiftly ensured that the bishop's scheme for Haworth to be separated
from Bradford should be abandoned and within six months he had devised a scheme
of his own. He drew up a plan to reorganise his parish into smaller districts, based on
a population of about 3,000. He planned to build three new churches immediately
and six others later. He reserved to himself alone the right of marriage, and thus
ensured that his own income should remain adequate. At the same time, by this
scheme he would be reducing the income of the incumbents of the various chapelries
by restricting them to a smaller population. Patrick had one of the largest chapelries
with over 6,000 inhabitants and he now felt seriously threatened. Dr Scoresby's
arrangements caused a lot of bitter feeling and by January 1840 William Morgan, the
incumbent of Christ Church, Bradford, was so incensed that he was not willing to
reply to his vicar's letters.

Patrick was now enjoying the services of his new curate. William Weightman was
aged twenty-six and came from Appleby in Westmorland. He was a graduate of the
recently founded Durham University, where he had received a good grounding in
classics and theology. He came to Haworth on the recommendation of the Bishop of
Ripon, whom Patrick had approached for assistance over securing a curate. Haworth
was his first curacy and he was licensed there on the day after his ordination as
deacon.

The depression in trade throughout the winter of 1839/1840 had led to a fall in
wages and a great increase in unemployment. The weather had also been particularly
severe and the peat crop, the main source of fuel for the poor, had almost totally
failed. The great hardship felt by the people of Haworth led to much discontent.

Patrick and his curate, together with the Dissenting ministers in the chapelry, worked hard to relieve the sufferings of the poor. The sum of £260 was raised through subscription and by gifts. This money was used to purchase 1,800 yards of cotton shirting, 180 pairs of blankets, 30–40 loads of oatmeal and 60–70 loads of potatoes. Patrick was kept very busy ensuring that these goods were distributed to the most needy in the parish.

Patrick's friend Theodore Dury, who had served for twenty-six years as rector of Keighley, now decided to retire to a rural parish in Hertfordshire. He was succeeded by the Revd William Busfield. Mr Busfield had scarcely arrived in Keighley when he had to deal with a scandal involving the curate, John Collins. Mr Collins was well known to the Brontë family and had preached a memorable sermon in Haworth church in March attacking Dissenters.[27] Writing to her old school friend, Ellen Nussey, on 12 November, Charlotte gave details of his disgrace:

You remember Mr and Mrs C[ollins]? Mrs C– came here the other day, with a most melancholy tale of her wretched husband's drunken, extravagant, profligate habits. She asked Papa's advice; there was nothing she said but ruin before them. They owed debts which they could never pay. She expected Mr C–'s immediate dismissal from his curacy; she knew from bitter experience, that his vices were utterly hopeless. He treated her and her child savagely; with much more to the same effect. Papa advised her to leave him for ever, and go home, if she had a home to go to. She said that this was what she had long resolved to do; and she would leave him directly, as soon as Mr B[usfield] dismissed him.

It is interesting to note Patrick's instant grasp of the situation and his forthright and unconventional reaction to what he had heard. In the event, Mr Collins was not immediately dismissed by Mr Busfield, but he continued his dissolute career and subsequently abandoned his wife in Manchester. Six years later Charlotte was able to give Ellen news of a happy outcome for Mrs Collins:

Do you remember my telling you about that wretched and most criminal Mr Collins after running an infamous career of vice both in England and France – abandoning his wife to disease and total destitution in Manchester, with two children and without a farthing in a strange lodging house – ?

Yesterday evening Martha came up stairs to say – that a woman – 'rather lady-like' as she said wished to speak to me in the kitchen – I went down – there stood Mrs Collins pale and worn but still interesting looking and cleanly and neatly dressed as was her little girl who was with her – I kissed her heartily – I could almost have cryed to see her for I had pitied her with my whole soul – when I heard of her undeserved sufferings, agonies and physical degradation – she took tea with us and stayed about two hours and entered frankly into the narrative of her appalling distresses – her constitution has triumphed over the hideous disease – and her excellent sense – her activity and perseverance have enabled her to regain a decent position in society and to procure a respectable maintenance for herself and her children – She keeps a lodging house in a very eligible part of the suburbs of Manchester ... and is doing very well.[28]

'Intelligent companionship
and intense family affection'
1824–1841

They lived in the free expanse of hill moorland, its dells and glens and brooks ... in the charm
of that solitude & seclusion which sees things from a distance. ... It was not the seclusion
of a solitary person ... it was seclusion shared & enjoyed by intelligent companionship and
intense family affection.

Ellen Nussey, Reminiscences of Charlotte Brontë

The home life of the young Brontë children after the death of their mother has often
been depicted as a sad and gloomy affair. This impression is largely based on the account
of their childhood given by Mrs Gaskell, who referred to the children as being 'grave
and silent beyond their years'. It is unfortunate that in her *Life of Charlotte Brontë*,
published in 1857, Mrs Gaskell relied on the evidence of Martha Wright, a Haworth
woman who was then living in Burnley. She had been engaged by Patrick to assist in
the care of his wife during her last illness and had subsequently been dismissed when
he found her to be unsatisfactory.[1] Martha Wright clearly bore a resentment against
Patrick. After Charlotte's death she spread unfavourable rumours about him and gave a
distorted view of the children's family life.[2] When questioned about her experiences in
the parsonage, she told Mrs Gaskell:

You would not have known there was a child in the house, they were such still, noiseless,
good creatures. ... I used to think them spiritless, they were so different to any children I had
ever seen. In part, I set it down to a fancy Mr Brontë had of not letting them have flesh meat
to eat. ... He thought that children should be brought up simply and hardily: so that they
had nothing but potatoes for their dinner.[3]

It is natural that during the time of their mother's illness the children should have been
quiet and subdued when they were in the house. They undoubtedly felt great sadness at
the loss of their mother and two elder sisters at such an early stage in their lives. There

is evidence, however, to show that they generally lived normal, happy and boisterous lives. When Francis Leyland, a close friend of Branwell, wrote an account of the Brontë family, he recorded that on one occasion the children's imaginative playing became so noisy and exuberant that the family servant, Tabby Aykroyd, ran down the street to the house of her nephew, William Wood, and asked him to come up to the parsonage:

> 'William! Yah mun gooa up to Mr Brontë's, for aw'm sure yon childer's all gooin mad, and aw darn't stop 'ith hause ony longer wi' 'em; an' aw'll stay here woll yah come back!' When the nephew reached the parsonage, 'the childer set up a great crack of laughin',' at the wonderful joke they had perpetrated on faithful Tabby.[4]

There was also an episode remembered by Sally Garrs, who as the children's nurse was a regular companion in their activities, which shows that they played the usual imaginative games of childhood. She had been roped in to play a part in one of their plays:

> As an escaping Prince, with a counterpane for a robe, I stepped from a window on the limb of a cherry tree, which broke and let me down. There was great consternation among the children, as it was Mr Brontë's favourite tree, under which he often sat. I carried off the branch and blackened the place with soot, but the next day, Mr Brontë detained them a moment and began with the youngest, asking each pleasantly, 'Who spoiled my tree?' The answer was, 'Not I,' until it came to my turn.[5]

In a different version of this story, given by the biographer, Mrs Chadwick, the culprit was Emily, who was playing the part of Prince Charles escaping after the Battle of Worcester. There seems no reason to doubt that the Brontë children enjoyed a happy childhood, content with their own company and enlivened by a fertile imagination.

There is also clear evidence that the children regularly had meat in their diet. Emily and Anne jointly wrote a diary paper every few years and on 24 November 1834 they recorded, 'We are going to have for Dinner Boiled Beef Turnips, potato's [sic] and applepudding.'[6] Moreover, in a letter written to Emily from Brussels in October 1843, Charlotte wishes she was at home in the kitchen under Emily's watchful eye ensuring that she 'save the best pieces of the leg of mutton for Tiger (the Parsonage cat) and Keeper (Emily's dog).'[7]

It is regrettable that Mrs Gaskell gave credence to the gossip of this disgruntled nurse and did not rely on the statements of Nancy and Sarah Garrs, the servants employed at the parsonage until the winter of 1824. Years later, Nancy Garrs, who had been the family cook, used to point out to visitors who came to her house the meat spit from the parsonage which had been left to her after Patrick's death, and she emphatically stated that the children had been given meat to eat every day of their lives. It was this statement that he had restricted his children to a vegetable diet that Patrick most resented in Mrs Gaskell's life of Charlotte, and that he referred to as 'the principal mistake in the memoir'.[8]

A detailed picture of the children's home life after their mother's death was given many years later by their nursemaid, Sarah Garrs.[9] Sarah recorded how after the children had been washed and dressed, the day began with the whole family, including the servants, assembling in Patrick's study for prayers. The children then accompanied him across the hall for a 'plain but abundant' breakfast of porridge and milk, bread and butter. Apart from the baby Anne, they then returned to the study for a morning session of lessons with their father. Once that was over, they were committed to Sarah's care until dinner-time, when they dined with their father. They were given plain roast or boiled meat and various desserts, including bread and rice puddings and custards. In the afternoons, while Patrick was out visiting in the parish, the children went for walks on the moors, unless the weather was too bad. Sarah recalled that these walks were the highlight of their day:

> Their afternoon walks, as they sallied forth, each neatly and comfortably clad, were a joy. Their fun knew no bounds. It was never expressed wildly. Bright and often dry, but deep, it occasioned many a merry burst of laughter. They enjoyed a game of romps, and played with zest.

On their return home they had their tea in the kitchen. When Patrick came back he took tea in his study and then gathered the children about him, 'for recitation and talk, giving them oral lessons in history, biography or travel.' While their mother was still alive and able to listen to them, the children said their nightly prayers at her bedside, kissed her goodnight and then went to their own 'warm clean beds'. On Sunday evenings, the whole family gathered in Patrick's study for Bible study and catechism. The servants were again included and, as Sarah noted, they were always treated as superiors in the presence of the children.

This picture of a stable and happy home life is corroborated by the account given in Emily and Anne's 1834 diary paper. Although this document exposes the sixteen-year-old Emily's appalling spelling and punctuation, it provides a rare and intimate insight into the details of the children's daily life:

> November the 24 1834   Emily Jane Bronte   Anne Bronte
> I fed Rainbow, Diamond, Snowflake Jasper pheasent … this morning Branwell went down to Mr Drivers. And brought news that Sir Robert peel was going to be invited to stand for Leeds Anne and I have been peeling Apples for Charlotte to make an apple pudding … Charlotte said she made puddings perfectly and she was of a quick but limited Intellect Taby said just now come Anne pillopatate (ie pill a potato[)] Aunt has come into the kitchen just now and said where are your feet Anne Anne answered on the floor Aunt papa opened the parlour Door and gave Branwell a Letter saying here Branwell read this and show it to your Aunt and Charlotte … Sally mosley is washing in the back Kitchin

It is past Twelve o'clock Anne and I have not tidied ourselves, done our bed work or our
lessons and we want to go out to play We are going to have for Dinner Boiled Beef Turnips,
potato's and applepudding the Kitchin is in a very untidy state Anne and I have not Done
our music exercise which consists of b majer Taby said on my putting a pen in her face Ya
pitter pottering there instead of pilling a potate I answered O Dear, O Dear, O Dear I will
derictly with that I get up, take a Knife and begin pilling the potatos[10]

It is also clear that Patrick, far from being the remote father depicted by Mrs Gaskell,
took an active part in his children's upbringing. William Dearden, a schoolmaster from
Keighley and a friend of both Patrick and Branwell, later recorded:

Branwell told me, when accidentally alluding to this mournful period in the history of his
family, that his father watched over his little flock with truly paternal solicitude and affection
– that he was their constant guardian and instructor – and that he took a lively interest in all
their innocent amusements.

Mr Dearden also stated that Patrick often took the children with him on his walks:

His children were the frequent companions of his walks. I have seen him, more than once,
conversing kindly and affably with them in the studio of a clever artist who resided in
Keighley; and many others, both in that town and in Haworth, can bear testimony to the
fact of his having often been seen accompanied by his young family in his visits to friends,
and in his rambles among the hills.[11]

Patrick himself told Mrs Gaskell that he was occasionally asked to intervene in the
children's disputes:

When mere children, as soon as they could read and write, Charlotte and her brother and
sisters, used to invent and act little plays of their own, in which the Duke of Wellington
my Daughter Charlotte's Hero, was sure to come off the conquering hero – when a dispute
[wou]ld not infrequently [ari]se amongst them regarding [th]e comparative merits of him,
Beaunaparte [sic], Hannibal, and Caesar – When the argument got warm, and rose to its
height, as their mother was then dead, I had sometimes to come in as arbitrator, and settle
the dispute, according to the best of my judgement.[12]

He also recorded an occasion when he questioned his children under cover of a mask:

When my Children were very young, when as far as I can re[me]mber the oldest was about
ten years of age, and the youngest about four – thinking that they knew more, than I had
yet discover'd, in order to make them speak with less timidity, I deem'd that if they were put

under a sort of cover, I might gain my end – and happening to have a mask in the house, I told them all to stand, and speak boldly from under |cover of| the mask. I began with the young-est [Anne] – I asked what a child like her most wanted – She answered, age and experience – I asked the next [Emily] what I had best do with her brother Branwell, who was sometimes, a naughty boy, She answered, reason with him, and when he won't listen to reason whip him – I asked Branwell, what was the best way of knowing the difference between the intellects, of men and women – He answer'd, by considering the difference between them as to their bodies – I then asked Charlotte, what was the best Book in the world, She answered the Bible – And what was the next best, She answer'd, the Book of Nature – I then asked the next [Elizabeth], what was the best mode of education for a woman, she answered, that which would make her rule her house well – Lastly, I asked the Oldest [Maria], what was the best [mode] of spending time, She answer'd by laying it out in preparation for a happy eternity – I may not have given you precisely their words, but I have nearly done so, as they made a deep and lasting impression on my memory – the substance however, was what I have stated.[13]

The children were provided with the normal amusements of childhood. They had various toys to play with, including a wooden lion and a set of ninepins. The girls had wax-headed dolls with hats and frocks, a doll's wickerwork cradle, and a children's tea service, while Branwell had a set of Indians and two sets of Turkish musicians. Moreover it was their father who was responsible for a momentous occasion in their lives when on 5 June 1826, he returned from a visit to Leeds with a parcel for Branwell. Charlotte later described the occasion:

Papa bought Branwell some soldiers at Leeds when papa came home it was night and we were in Bed so next morning Branwell came to our Door with a Box of soldiers Emily and I jumped out of Bed and I snat[c]hed up one and exclaimed this is the Duke of Wellington it shall be mine!! … when I said this … Emily likewise took one and said it should be hers when Anne came down she took one also. Mine was the prettiest of the whole and perfect in every part Emilys was a Grave Looking ferllow we called him Gravey Anne's was a queer little thing very much like herself. he was called waiting Boy Branwell chose Bonaparte.[14]

This present from their father immediately sparked off the children's vivid imagination. They invented a history for their soldiers and went on to write a whole saga of their adventures. This was the origin of their juvenile writings, those little books, written in minuscule script on sugar-paper or other scraps and bound together to form little books. Charlotte and Branwell described the exploits of these soldiers in their Glass Town saga, while Emily and Anne later created the imaginary kingdom of Gondal. In 1829 Charlotte explained how their plays had developed. Her account is also important for giving us a vivid insight into intimate details of the children's daily life and of their relationship with the old family servant Tabby Aykroyd:

The play of the Islanders was formed in December 1827 in the following manner. One night about the time when the cold sleet and ... |drear| fogs of November are succeeded by the snow storms & high peircing nightwinds of confirmed ... winter we were all sitting around ... the warm blazing kitchen fire having just concluded a quarel with Taby concerning the propriety |of| lighting a candle from which she came of victorious no candles having been produced a long pause suceeded which was at last broken by B saying in a lazy manner I don't know what to do This was reechoed by E & A

T   wha ya may go t'bed

B   Id rather do anything [than] that

&C   Your so glum tonight T suppose we had each an Island.

B   if we had I would choose the Island of Man

C   & I would choose the Isle of Wight

E   the Isle of Arran for me

A   & mine should be Guernsey

C   the Duke of Wellington should be my chief man

B   Her[r]ies should be mine.

E   Walter |Scott| should be mine

A   I should have Benti[n]ck

Here our conversation was interrupted by |the| to us dismal sound of the clock striking 7 & we were summoned to bed. The next day we added several others to our list of names till we had got almost all the chief men in the Kingdom.[15]

Patrick was clearly aware of his children's literary activities. He must have seen them busily writing and, as he told Mrs Gaskell in 1855, as they grew older, 'their compositions and plots were more matur'd'.[16] Although he made no attempt to restrict their activity, he seems to have felt that their writing should be conducted in a less secretive manner. At Christmas 1833 he gave Charlotte a manuscript notebook and wrote on the top of the first page:

1833   All that is written in this book must be in a good, plain and legible hand.   PB

Charlotte seems at first to have made an effort to comply with his instructions, but by the end of 1835 she had only inserted five poems in the book.

After their return home from Cowan Bridge, Patrick himself took responsibility for his children's education. It seems from the textbooks known to have been in the parsonage that he used the standard educational works of the day: Thomas Salmon's *New Geographical and Historical Grammar*, the one-volume edition of Oliver Goldsmith's *History of England* (which is heavily annotated by Patrick), Rollin's *History* and an edition of J. Goldsmith's *A Grammar of General Geography* (heavily annotated by the children). The family also had other books: John Bunyan's *Pilgrim's Progress*, John

Milton's *Paradise Lost* and Walter Scott's *The Lay of the Last Minstrel*, which Patrick had purchased while he was at Cambridge. They also had copies of Aesop's *Fables* and the *Arabian Nights' Entertainment* and in 1828 Aunt Branwell gave them Walter Scott's *Tales of a Grandfather*.

It is clear that Patrick encouraged his children to take an active interest in the political questions of the day and was willing to discuss these issues openly with them. The family had access to several newspapers and journals and in 1829 the thirteen-year-old Charlotte gave a vivid description of the excitement they all felt when the news of the passing of the Roman Catholic Relief Bill was received at the Parsonage:

> O those 3 months from the time of the Kings speech to the end! Nobody could think speak or write on anything but the catholic question and the Duke of Wellington or Mr Peel I remember the day when the Intelligence extraordinary came with Mr Peels speech in it containing the terms on which the catholics were to be let in with what eagerness papa tore off the cover & how we all gathered round him & with what breathless anxiety we listend as one by one they were disclosed & explained & argued upon so ably & so well & then when it was all out how aunt said she thought it was excellent & that the catholics [could] do no harm with such good security. I remember also the doubts as to wether it would pass into the house of Lord[s] & the prophecys that it would not & when the paper came which was to decide the question the anxiety was almost dreadful with which we listened to the whole affair the opening of the doors the hush the Royal Dukes in theire robes & the Great Duke in green sash & waistcoat the rising of all the peeresses when he rose the reading of his speech papa saying that his words were like precious gold & lastly the majority one to 4 in favour of the bill.[17]

Patrick also encouraged his children to think independently for themselves. In 1831 he gave his support to the Whigs' Reform Bill, which proposed the abolition of rotten boroughs and the extension of the franchise. When the bill was thrown out by the House of Lords in May 1832, Charlotte, although she knew her father's views on the subject, wrote to Branwell expressing her joy at the Bill's defeat:

> Lately I had begun to think that I had lost all the interest which I used formerly to take in politics but the extreme pleasure I felt at the news of the Reform-bill's being thrown out |by| the House of Lords and of the expulsion or resignation of Earl Grey, &c. &c. convinced me that I have not as yet lost all my penchant for politics.[18]

Patrick exerted influence over his children in other ways. He ensured that each of them owned a copy of the Bible and a Prayer Book. In 1827 he gave the nine-year-old Emily a Bible which was inscribed on the flyleaf, 'To Emily Jane Brontë, by her affectionate Father, Feb 13th, 1827'. On the same day Anne was given a Prayer Book by her godmother, Fanny Outhwaite. She had already been given a Bible four years earlier in October 1823 by her other godmother, Elizabeth Firth. Charlotte owned a New Testament given to her by William and Jane Morgan. The children were strongly influenced by this biblical background and their writings revealed an extensive knowledge of scripture.

The Brontë children were also influenced by their father's classical training. Patrick was proud of the classical education he had received at Cambridge and he still possessed the prizes which he had won: Richard Bentley's 1728 edition of the works of Horace and Samuel Clarke's 1729 edition of Homer's *Iliad*. In his juvenile writings Branwell frequently displayed the knowledge of Latin and Greek which he had acquired from his father. In 1839 Patrick decided to undertake a wider course of classical reading with Branwell. He wrote his plans down on the flyleaf of his concordance to the Bible:

> In June 1839 – I agreed with Branwell, that, under Providence, we should thoroughly read together, the following classics, in the following order only –
>> 1st the first 6 Books of the Aeneid – and the four Gospels – in Greek.
>> & 2ndly the first 3 … or 6 Books of Homer's Iliad –
>> And some of the first Odes of Horace, and the Art of Poetry – besides – translating
> some English into Latin – The progress of the reading is to be regularly set down in this and the following pages. B.

Branwell clearly had ability and in 1840 his translation of the first book of Horace's *Odes* won the praise of Hartley Coleridge. Charlotte and Emily also showed knowledge of the classical world. Although Charlotte never quoted from Greek and only rarely from Latin, her work contains many classical allusions. Fragments remain of Emily's translations of some portions of Virgil's *Aeneid* and of her notes on the tragedies of Euripides and Aeschylus.[19] Anne, too, while working as a governess at Thorp Green, purchased a Latin textbook, presumably for use with her pupil, Edmund Robinson.

In addition to the skills which he imparted to his children himself, Patrick also made arrangements for them to receive expert tuition in other areas. Some time around 1829 the children began to have art lessons from John Bradley of Keighley, a well-known local artist. William Dearden recalled meeting Patrick, accompanied by Charlotte and Branwell, on several occasions in Mr Bradley's studio in Keighley, 'where they hung in close-gazing inspection and silent admiration over some fresh production of the artist's genius.'[20]

Patrick also wanted to foster the musical talents of his children and he arranged for them to have lessons from Abraham Sunderland, the Keighley church organist. Sometime in late 1833 or early 1834 he bought a piano for the parsonage so that the children could play at home. Both Emily and Anne had musical talent. Emily became an accomplished pianist and Anne developed an attractive singing voice. Patrick also

paid for Branwell to have lessons on the flute from Mr Sunderland. Patrick had a deep
love of music and, according to Benjamin Binns, the son of the Haworth tailor, he
regularly took his family with him to attend the concerts of the Haworth Philharmonic
Society, which were held in a large room at the Black Bull.

There was one interest which Patrick shared with Emily, who of all his children was
probably the closest to him. In 1843, while Charlotte was away in Brussels and Anne and
Branwell were with the Robinson family at Thorpe Green, Emily was the sole member
of the family in the parsonage with her father. Patrick admired her strong character and
her vivid imagination and seems to have regarded her as a kindred spirit. It has been
said that he saw in her the son which Branwell had failed to be. He had a great interest
in firearms and it was during this time that he decided to teach Emily to shoot with a
pistol. John Greenwood, the Haworth stationer, recorded in his diary how father and
daughter used to go into the garden to shoot at a mark:

> Mr Brontë formerly took very great pleasure in shooting – not in the way generally
> understood by the term, but shooting at a mark, merely for recreation. He had such
> unbounded confidence in his daughter Emily, knowing, as he did her unparalleled intrepidity
> and firmness, that he resolved to learn her to shoot too. They used to practice with pistols.
> Let her be ever so busy in her domestic duties, whether in the kitchen baking bread at which
> she had such a dainty hand, or at her ironing, or at her studies, raped [rapt] in a world of
> her own creating – it mattered not; if he called upon her to take a lesson, she would put all
> down. His tender and affectionate 'Now, my dear girl, let me see how well you can shoot
> today,' was irresistible to her filial nature and her most winning and musical voice would be
> heard to ring through the house in response, 'Yes, papa' and away she would run with such a
> hearty good will taking the board from him, and tripping like a fairy down [to] the bottom
> of the garden, putting it in its proper position, then returning to her dear revered parent, take
> the pistol, which he had previously primed and loaded for her. 'Now my girl' he would say,
> 'take time, be steady'. 'Yes papa' she would say taking the weapon with as firm a hand, and as
> steady an eye as any veteran of the camp, and fire. Then she would run to fetch the board for
> him to see how she had succeeded. And she did get so proficient, that she was rarely far from
> the mark. His 'how cleverly you have done, my dear girl', was all she cared for. She knew she
> had gratified him, and she would return to him the pistol, saying 'load again papa', and away
> she would go to the kitchen, roll another shel[f-]ful of teacakes, then wiping her hands, she
> would return again to the garden, and call out 'I'm ready again, papa', and so they would go
> on until he thought she had had enough practice for that day. 'Oh!' He would exclaim, 'she is
> a brave and noble girl. She is my right-hand, nay the very apple of my eye!'[21]

Although it is improbable that either Patrick or Emily spoke in the terms attributed to
them, John Greenwood had plenty of opportunities to observe Patrick and his daughter
engaged in this activity. At the time Patrick was suffering from cataracts and feared

that he would go totally blind. He must have taken comfort from Emily's prowess, which provided the assurance that, should an emergency arise, there would be someone capable of defending the parsonage.

The most vivid account of the family and their daily life is that given by Charlotte's school friend, Ellen Nussey, who came to the parsonage for the first time in July 1833. She stayed two weeks and recalled the details of her visit when writing her *Reminiscences* many years later.[22] She first described her arrival at the parsonage:

> When we reached the top of the village there was apparently no outlet, but we were directed to drive into an entry which just admitted the gig; we wound round in this entry and then saw the church close at hand, and we entered on the short lane which led to the parsonage gate-way. Here Charlotte was waiting, having caught the sound of the approaching gig. When greetings and introductions were over, Miss Branwell (the aunt of the Brontës) took possession of their guest and treated her with the care and solicitude due to a weary traveller. Mr Brontë, also, was stirred out of his usual retirement by his own kind consideration, for not only the guest but the man-servant and the horse were to be made comfortable. He made enquiries about the man, of his length of service, etc., with the kind purpose of making a few moments of conversation agreeable to him.

Ellen then gave her impressions of the family:

> Mr Brontë struck me as looking very venerable. … His manner and mode of speech always had the tone of high-bred courtesy. He was considered somewhat of an invalid, and always lived in the most abstemious and simple manner. His white cravat was not then so remarkable as it grew to be afterwards. … We always had to wind for him the white sewing-silk which he used. Charlotte said it was her father's one extravagance. …
> Mr Brontë's tastes led him to delight in the perusal of battle-scenes, and in following the artifice of … war, had he entered on military service instead of ecclesiastical he would probably have had a very distinguished career. The self-denials and privations of camp life would have agreed entirely with his nature, for he was remarkably independent of the luxuries and comforts of life. The only dread he had was <u>fire</u>, and this dread was so intense it caused him to prohibit all but silk or woollen dresses for his daughters.

She described Aunt Branwell as:

> A very small, antiquated little lady. She wore caps large enough for half a dozen of the present fashion, and a front of light auburn curls over her forehead. She always dressed in silk. She had a horror of the climate so far north, and of the stone floors in the parsonage. She amused us by clicking about in pattens whenever she had to go into the kitchen or look after household operations.

She talked a great deal of her younger days; the gaieties of her dear native town, Penzance, in Cornwall. ... The social life of her younger days she used to recall with regret; she gave one the idea that she had been a belle among her own home acquaintances. She took snuff out of a very pretty gold snuff-box, which she sometimes presented to you with a little laugh, as if she enjoyed the slight shock and astonishment visible in your countenance.

Ellen also gave valuable portraits of Emily (aged seventeen) and Anne (aged fifteen):

Emily Brontë had by this time acquired a lithesome, graceful figure. She was the tallest person in the house, except her father. Her hair, which was naturally as beautiful as Charlotte's, was in the same unbecoming tight curl and frizz, and there was the same want of complexion. She had very beautiful eyes – kind, kindling, liquid eyes; but she did not often look at you: she was too reserved. ... She talked very little. She and Anne were like twins – inseparable companions, and in the very closest sympathy. ...
Anne – dear, gentle Anne – was quite different in appearance from the others. She was her aunt's favourite. Her hair was a very pretty, light brown, and fell on her neck in graceful curls. She had lovely violet-blue eyes, fine pencilled eyebrows, and clear, almost transparent complexion. She still pursued her studies, and especially her sewing, under the surveillance of her aunt.

She said little of Branwell, except that he:

studied regularly with his father, and used to paint in oils, which was regarded as study for what might eventually be his profession.

She also gave her impression of the old servant, Tabitha Aykroyd:

'Tabby', the faithful, trustworthy old servant, was very quaint in appearance – very active, and in these days, the general servant and factotum. We were all 'childer' and 'bairns,' in her estimation. She still kept to her duty of walking out with the 'childer', if they went any distance from home, unless Branwell was sent by his father as a protector.

Ellen's account described the parsonage as it appeared in the early 1830s:

The interior of the now far-famed parsonage lacked drapery of all kinds. Mr Brontë's horror of fire forbade curtains to the windows; they never had these accessories to comfort and appearance till long after Charlotte was the only inmate of the family sitting-room. ... There was not much carpet anywhere except in the sitting-room, and on the study floor. The hall floor and stairs were done with sand-stone, always beautifully clean, as everything was about the house; the walls were not papered, but stained in a pretty dove-coloured tint; hair-seated chairs and mahogany tables, book-shelves in the study, but not many of these elsewhere. Scant and bare indeed, many will say, yet it was not a scantiness that made itself felt. Mind and thought, I had almost said elegance, but certainly refinement, diffused themselves over all, and made nothing really wanting.

She also gave an interesting glimpse into the daily life of the Brontë family:

Every morning was heard the firing of a pistol from Mr Brontë's room window, – it was the discharging of the loading which was made every night. In summer Miss Branwell spent part of the afternoon in reading aloud to Mr Brontë. In the winter evenings she must have enjoyed this; for she and Mr Brontë had often to finish their discussions on what she had read when we all met for tea. She would be very lively and intelligent, and tilt arguments against Mr Brontë without fear.

At meal times Patrick would sometimes regale the family with a fund of strange and weird stories:

Mr Brontë at times would relate strange stories, which had been told to him by some of the oldest inhabitants of the parish, of the extraordinary lives and doings of people who had resided in far-off, out-of-the-way, places, but in contiguity with Haworth, – stories which made one shiver and shrink from hearing; but they were full of grim humor and interest to Mr Brontë and his children.

Ellen also described the walks she took on the surrounding moors with Charlotte, Branwell, Emily and Anne:

In fine and suitable weather delightful rambles were made over the moors, and down into the glens and ravines that here and there broke the monotony of the moorland. … Emily, Anne, and Branwell used to ford the streams, and sometimes placed stepping-stones for the other two; there was always a lingering delight in these spots – every moss, every flower, every tint and form, were noted and enjoyed. Emily, especially had a gleesome delight in these nooks of beauty, her reserve for the time vanished. One long ramble made in these early days was far away over the moors to a spot familiar to Emily and Anne, which they called 'The Meeting of the Waters'. It was a small oasis of emerald green turf, broken here and there by small clear springs; a few large stones served as resting-places; seated here, we were hidden from all the world, nothing appearing in view but miles and miles of heather, a glorious blue sky, and brightening sun. A fresh breeze wafted on us its exhilarating influence; we laughed and made mirth of each other, and settled we would call ourselves the quartette.

In the evening before he retired to bed Patrick held family prayers:

> Mr Brontë's health caused him to retire early. He assembled his household for family worship at eight o'clock; at nine he locked and barred the front door, always giving as he passed the sitting-room door a kindly admonition to the 'children' not to be late; half-way up the stairs he stayed his steps to wind up the clock.

The Brontë family had a deep love of animals, although this was not greatly to Aunt Branwell's liking:

> During Miss Branwell's reign at the parsonage, the love of animals had to be kept in due subjection. There was then but one dog, which was admitted to the parlour at stated times. Emily and Anne always gave him a portion of their breakfast, which was, by their own choice, the old north country diet of oatmeal porridge. Later on, there were three household pets – the tawny, strong-limbed 'Keeper', Emily's favourite: he was so completely under her control, she could quite easily make him spring and roar like a lion. 'Flossy', – long, silky-haired, black and white 'Flossy', was Anne's favourite; and black 'Tom', the tabby, was everyone's favourite. It received such gentle treatment it seemed to have lost cat's nature, and subsided into luxurious amiability and contentment.

Ellen concluded her account with a sensitive appreciation of the values which the whole family held dear:

> <u>They lived</u> in the free expanse of hill moorland, its purple heather, its dells and glens and brooks, The broad sky view, the whistling winds, the snowy expanse, The starry heavens, and in the charm of that solitude & seclusion which sees things from a distance without the disturbing atmosphere which lesser minds are apt to create. It was not the seclusion of a solitary person which becomes in time awfully oppressive – it was seclusion shared & enjoyed by intelligent companionship and intense family affection.

In June 1830 for the first time in his life the fifty-three-year-old Patrick became seriously ill. He developed inflammation of the lungs and for three weeks he was too ill to get out of bed. During this period his clerical duties were taken by the Revd Thomas Plummer, the headmaster of Keighley Grammar School. On 22 June, when his illness was at its height and his life seemed to be threatened, a strange visitor called at the parsonage door. Charlotte was sufficiently alarmed by this event to record it in detail that same evening:

> The following strange occurence happened on the 22 of June 1830. At that time papa was very ill, confined to his bed and so weak that he could not rise without assistance. Tabby and I were alone in the kitchen, about half past 9 ante-meridian. Suddenly we heard a knock at the door. Tabby rose and opened it. An old man appeared standing without, who accosted her thus:

Old Man: Does the parson live here?

Tabby: Yes.

Old Man: I wish to see him.

Tabby: He is poorly in bed.

Old Man: Indeed. I have a message for him.

Tabby: Who from?

Old Man: From the LORD.

Tabby: Who?

Old Man: The LORD. He desires me to say that the bridegroom is coming and that he must prepare to meet him; that the cords are about to be loosed and the golden bowl broken; the pitcher broken at the fountain and the wheel stopped at the cistern. Here he concluded his discourse and abruptly went away. As Tabby closed the door I asked if she knew him. Her reply was that she had never seen him before nor anyone like him. Though I am fully persuaded that he was some fanatical enthusiast, well-meaning, perhaps, but utterly ignorant of true piety, yet I could not forbear weeping at his words, spoken so unexpectedly at that particular period.[23]

News of Patrick's serious illness had spread through the parish and it later transpired that the caller was an eccentric gentleman farmer who later died in a lunatic asylum.

It is not surprising that the incident had such a powerful effect on Charlotte. Patrick's illness was a very worrying time for the children. They knew that if he were to die they would lose their home and be left without any support. The eldest, Charlotte, was aged only fourteen and their aunt was not in a financial position to give them help. In the event, Patrick recovered, but remained for some time physically very weak. He also became depressed and found it a struggle to return to his clerical duties. A year later he described his illness to his old friend Mrs Franks (formerly Elizabeth Firth):

I have for nearly a year past, been in but a very delicate state of health. I had an inflammation in my lungs, last summer – and was in immediate, and Great danger, for several weeks – For the six months, last past, I have been weak in body, and my spirits have often been low – I was for about a month unable to take Church Duty. I now perform it – though, with considerable difficulty. I am certainly a little better, Yet I fear I shall never fully recover – I sometimes think that I shall fall into a decline. But, I am in the Lord's hands.[24]

Patrick now decided that he must take urgent steps to provide a secure future for his family. While he could assume that Branwell would eventually be able to provide for himself, he knew that for his daughters to make their way in the world and to find posts as teachers or governesses, they would have to have some educational qualifications. In January 1831 he decided that his eldest daughter, Charlotte, should be given a formal education.

The school which he chose was Roe Head on the outskirts of Mirfield, near Dewsbury. It was run by a Miss Margaret Wooler, with the help of her sisters, Catherine, Susan, Marianne and Eliza. Patrick probably had several reasons for choosing it. It was situated only half a mile from his old church at Hartshead and he would probably have walked past the building on many occasions. He knew that it lay in a healthy and open position and, from his previous ministry in the area, he was acquainted with some of the parents of pupils there. The fact that these wealthy men had chosen the school for their children probably gave him additional reassurance. He also had friends nearby who would be available to keep an eye on Charlotte's welfare. Her godparents, the Revd Thomas Atkinson (Patrick's successor as incumbent of Hartshead) and his wife Frances lived less than a mile from the school, and Elizabeth Firth, his old Thornton friend (now married to the Revd James Franks, the vicar of Huddersfield), was not much further away. Frances Atkinson and Elizabeth Franks were both acquainted with Miss Wooler and her sisters. Elizabeth's diary records that they had both taken tea with them in May 1829. Frances' niece Amelia was also a pupil there and it may have been Frances who recommended the school to Patrick.

Charlotte arrived at Roe Head on 17 January 1831. She soon settled in to school life and made rapid progress. By the end of her first half-year she had risen to the top of her class and won three prizes and also the silver medal for achievement. At the end of her second term she won the school prize for French and during the rest of her time at the school she always remained top of her class. She was popular with her fellow pupils and her friendships with Ellen Nussey and Mary Taylor were to last for the rest of her life. Charlotte was well aware of the financial sacrifices that her father was making for her education and she devoted herself to her studies with the utmost application. As Ellen Nussey said of her:

> She always seemed to feel that a deep responsibility rested upon her; that she was an object of expense to those at home, and that she must use every moment to attain the purpose for which she was sent to school, i.e., to fit herself for governess life.[25]

Her father's liberal and unorthodox attitude to her education is clearly seen in Mary Taylor's later comment to Mrs Gaskell:

> We thought her very ignorant, for she had never learnt grammar at all, and very little geography. She would confound us by knowing things which were out of our range altogether.[26]

Ellen Nussey later recalled that Charlotte had a deep knowledge of the Bible and took great delight in some of its 'sublimest passages, especially those in Isaiah.' She also recorded that Charlotte was confirmed while she was at the school.

In June 1832, after Charlotte had spent eighteen months at Roe Head, Patrick took the decision that she should return home. She was now sixteen and, by conscientiously applying herself to her studies, she had acquired the skills which would later be essential to her as a governess. She could also take over from Patrick the education of her two sisters.

Three years later, in the summer of 1835, significant changes occurred in the Brontë family circle. At the beginning of July Charlotte (now aged nineteen) accepted an offer from Miss Wooler to return to Roe Head as a teacher, and to bring the seventeen-year-old Emily with her as a pupil. This would enable her to gain invaluable teaching experience, while Emily would have the advantage of some formal education. Patrick, anxious to safeguard the welfare of both girls, wrote to Elizabeth Franks to ask for her assistance:

> My dear Madam,
> As two of my dear children, are soon to be placed near you, I take the liberty of writing to you a few lines, in order to request both you and Mr. Franks, to be so kind, as to interpose with your advice and counsel, to them in any case of necessity – and if expedient to write to Miss Branwell, or me, if our interference should be requisite.

One of his concerns may have been that Charlotte, while she was away from the close supervision of her father and her aunt, might attract the attentions of some unsuitable admirer:

> They, both have good abilities, and as far as I can judge their principles, are good also, but they are both very young, and unacquainted with the ways of this delusive and insnaring world, and though, they will be placed under the superintendance of Miss Wooler, who will I doubt not, do what she can for their good, yet, I am well aware, that neither they, nor any other, can ever, in this land of probation, lie beyond the reach of temptation.

He also outlined his plans for the other members of the family:

> It is my design, to send my son … to the Royal Academy for Artists, in London – and my dear little Anne, I intend to keep at home, for another year, under her aunt's tuition, and my own.[27]

In the event, things did not quite turn out as Patrick had planned. Charlotte and Emily travelled to Roe Head on 29 July, but after only three months Emily's health broke down and she had to return home. As Charlotte later wrote:

> Liberty was the breath of Emily's nostrils; without it, she perished. The change from her own home to school, and from her own very noiseless, very secluded, but unrestricted and inartificial mode of life, to one of disciplined routine (though under the kindest auspices), was what she failed in enduring. … Every morning when she woke, the vision of home and the moors rushed

on her, and darkened and saddened the day that lay before her. Nobody knew what ailed her but me – I knew only too well. In this struggle her health was quickly broken: her white face, her attenuated form, and failing strength threatened rapid decline. I felt in my heart she would die if she did not go home, and with this conviction obtained her recall.[28]

Towards the end of October Emily's place at the school was taken by her sister Anne, now aged fifteen. It was Anne's first time away from home. She, too, was home-sick but, well aware how important it was for her to obtain a good education, she resolutely stuck it out and remained at the school until December 1837.

It seems that the ambitious plans made for Branwell also came to nothing. It is not clear why this happened, but it is certain that he never presented his papers to the Royal Academy, and it is probable that he never visited London at all. Years later an acquaintance of his described how, after closely studying maps of London, Branwell would convince the 'commercial gents' who came to the Black Bull that he was 'an old Londoner', and then he would astonish them 'by saying that he was never in London in his life'.[29]

At Christmas 1836 an incident occurred which showed that the Brontë children had inherited much of the spirited temperament of their father. A few days after Charlotte and Anne returned to Haworth for the Christmas holidays, the sixty-five-year-old Tabby Aykroyd, their servant for the past twelve years, suffered a serious accident after falling on the ice while on an evening errand in the village. Charlotte wrote to Ellen Nussey to tell her what had happened:

> She was gone out into the village on some errand, when as she was descending the steep street her foot slipped on the ice, and she fell – it was dark and no one saw her mis-chance, till after a time her groans attracted the attention of a passer-by. She was lifted up and carried into a druggist's near and after examination it was discovered, that she had completely shattered, and dislocated one leg. Unfortunately the fracture could not be set until six o'clock the next morning as no Surgeon could be had before that time, and she now lies at our house, in a very doubtful and dangerous state.[30]

The nursing of Tabby caused serious disruption to the normal life of the parsonage and Aunt Branwell thought that she should be moved elsewhere. The Brontë girls, however, who regarded Tabby as one of the family, insisted on looking after her themselves. The druggist, Elizabeth Hardaker, who was also the village nurse, later told Mrs Gaskell that the girls 'struck eating' until they had forced their aunt to agree that they should nurse her in their own home. Tabby recovered well, although she was left with a pronounced limp.

In December 1837 Anne was taken seriously ill at Roe Head. Her condition was exacerbated by the fact that she also went through a crisis in her religious beliefs which led her to consult the Revd James la Trobe, the Moravian minister at Well House in Mirfield. He visited her several times at Roe Head during her illness and soon won her confidence. Some years later he described the physical condition in which he had found her:

> She was suffering from a severe attack of gastric fever which brought her very low, and her voice was only a whisper; her life hung on a slender thread.

He also explained the religious problems with which she was wrestling:

> I found her well acquainted with the main truths of the bible respecting our salvation, but seeing them more through the law than the gospel, more as a requirement from God than His gift in His Son, but her heart opened to the sweet views of salvation, pardon, and peace in the blood of Christ, and she accepted His welcome to the weary and heavy laden sinner, conscious more of her not loving the Lord her God than of acts on enmity to Him, and, had she died then, I should have counted her His redeemed and ransomed child.[31]

Thanks to the ministrations of this wise and kindly man, Anne's mind was quickly set at rest. She was brought home and soon recovered from the worst effects of her physical illness. Her continuing delicate state of health, however, meant that she did not return to Roe Head, and at the beginning of 1838 Charlotte set out alone to resume her teaching duties.

Since his plan for Branwell to train to be an artist at the Royal Academy in London had come to nothing, early in 1838 Patrick made another attempt to settle the question of his son's future career. On 22 February he wrote to John Driver, the son of one of his churchwardens, who was a grocer with premises in West Lane, and asked him whether he might be able to assist in procuring Branwell an opening 'as Clerk in some Respectable Bank'. Patrick knew Branwell's inclinations and weaknesses well and the doubtful influence which some of his friends had on him, and he told Mr Driver:

> I have made no attempt – either in Halifax, Bradford, or Leeds, since, I think it would be to his advantage to go farther from home. And to see a little more of the World. London, Liverpool, or Manchester, would Answer better on many accounts. And would open a wider field, for talent, and suitable connexions.[32]

Nothing came of this approach, however, and in July Branwell, now aged twenty-one, was sent to Bradford to set up as a professional portrait-painter under the patronage of Patrick's old friend and former colleague, William Morgan, who had been the incumbent of Christ Church, Bradford, since 1815. Branwell took up lodgings with a

Mr and Mrs Kirby in a house in Darley Street, very near to Mr Morgan's church. He had been having painting lessons from the Leeds artist William Robinson since 1835 and was a competent, though not a very good, painter. He was now well placed through Mr Morgan's contacts in Bradford to make a modest success of his new career.

In September 1838 Emily felt that she also should make an attempt to earn her living and she took up a teaching post at Law Hill, a girls' school at Southowram on the outskirts of Halifax. It was run by a Miss Elizabeth Patchett, a forty-two-year-old spinster and sister of a Halifax banker. The school had about forty pupils between the ages of eleven and fifteen, nearly half of whom were boarders. There were only two other teachers and Emily's work-load, as Charlotte told Ellen Nussey, seems to have been very hard:

> My Sister Emily is gone into a Situation as teacher in a large school of nearly forty pupils near Halifax. I have had one letter from her since her departure – it gives an appalling account of her duties – Hard labour from six in the morning until near eleven at night. With only one half hour of exercise between – this is slavery I fear she will never stand it.[33]

It soon became clear that Patrick's plans for the future of his family were not meeting with much success. Anne had remained at home since her return from Roe Head in December 1837. When Charlotte came home for Christmas 1838 she told her family that she had given her notice to Miss Wooler and would not be returning to the school. Some time in the early spring of 1839 it also became apparent that Branwell's attempt to establish himself as a portrait-painter in Bradford was not going to be successful and he returned to Haworth. By the middle of April, Emily, too, was back at the parsonage, having ended her employment at Law Hill. It must have been worrying for Patrick that all four of his children were now back at home, and that three of them had failed in their attempts to gain secure employment.

It was Anne who at this juncture decided that she must make an effort not to be a burden on the family finances. On 8 April she left home to take up the post of governess to the Ingham family at Blake Hall, near Mirfield. She showed her resolute courage by insisting on making the journey unaccompanied. As Charlotte told Ellen:

> Poor child! She left us last Monday – no one went with her – it was her own wish that she might be allowed to go alone – as she thought she could manage better and summon more courage if thrown entirely upon her own resources.[34]

Anne later immortalised her frustrating experiences with the Ingham family in her novel *Agnes Grey*. Although it was obviously a great effort to leave the family circle and go out on her own, if her novel in any way indicates her own feelings, Anne was eager to make her own contribution in the world:

How delightful it would be to be a governess! To go out into the world; to enter upon a new life; to act for myself; to exercise my unused faculties; to try my unknown powers; to earn my own maintenance, and something to comfort and help my father, mother, and sister, besides exonerating them from the provision of my food and clothing; to show papa what his little Agnes could do; to convince mama and Mary that I was not quite the helpless, thoughtless being they supposed.[35]

The others in the family had always protected Anne as the youngest child, but she was eventually to prove the only one of Patrick's children with sufficient determination successfully to make her own way in the world. Within a month of her departure, Charlotte took up a temporary position as governess to the Sidgwick family at Stonegappe, at Lothersdale. She found the role of governess a humiliating one and was glad when her temporary employment came to an end in the middle of July.

At the end of November 1839 there was another break in the life of the parsonage. Tabby's leg, which had been so badly broken three years before, had become so ulcerated that she was now too lame to perform her duties. A year or two previously she had used her savings to buy a little house and she now took up residence there with her sister. With Tabby's departure the main household duties now fell on Charlotte and Emily, though for running errands they also employed the services of the eleven-year-old Martha Brown, eldest daughter of John Brown, the Haworth sexton. Charlotte told Ellen how they were managing:

I manage the ironing and keep the rooms clean – Emily does the baking and attends to the Kitchen – We are such odd animals that we prefer this mode of contrivance to having a new face among us. Besides we do not despair of Tabby's return and she shall not be supplanted by a stranger in her absence.[36]

Tabby did return in 1842, when Charlotte and Emily went to Brussels, and, although her help was of limited value, Patrick continued to employ her until her death in 1855. Martha Brown remained in the employment of the Brontë family until Patrick's own death in 1861.

At Christmas 1839 Anne returned to Haworth after being dismissed by the Ingham family. She had failed to make any impression on their badly behaved children and Mrs Ingham held her responsible for their lack of improvement. The Brontë family was now reunited once again. All the children had had some experience of employment but none of them had succeeded in gaining a secure position. It was now Branwell's turn to make a second attempt to forge a career for himself. On 21 December 1839 he saw an advertisement in the *Leeds Intelligencer* which seemed to offer him the opportunity for which he was looking:

Patrick Brontë – a portrait painted by a local artist during his early years in Haworth

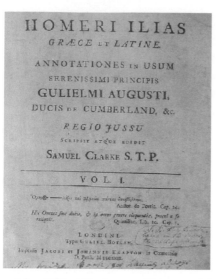

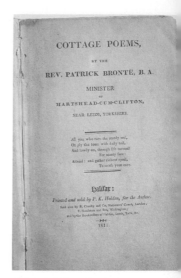

2. *(above left)* Patrick's prize copy of Homer awarded to him at St John's College, Cambridge

3. *(above right)* Title page of *Cottage Poems*, 1811

4. *(above left)* Maria Branwell

5. *(above right)* Elizabeth Branwell

All Saints' Church and Vicarage, Dewsbury (by kind permission of the vicar and PCC)

St Peter's Church, Hartshead

8. *(above left)* The Old Bell Chapel, Thornton

9. *(above right)* The Parsonage, Thornton

10. Haworth Church and Parsonage, *c.* 1860

2. Haworth Old Church and churchyard, c. 1861

2. Haworth Old Church interior, pre-1879

13. *(top left)* The three-decker pulpit in Haworth Old Church

14. *(top right)* Entrance hall and stairs

15. *(above)* Haworth Parsonage, after 1859

6. *(top)* The dining room

7. *(above)* Patrick's study

8. *(right)* The long case clock on the stairs

19. *(above left)* Charlotte Brontë. A portrait by J. H. Thompson

20. *(above right)* Ellen Nussey – a drawing by Charlotte

21. Anne Brontë – a miniature painting by Charlotte

22. Emily's dog, Keeper – a watercolour by Emily

23. Emily and Anne's 'diary paper' of 26 June 1837

24. Some of the little books made by the Brontë children

25. Haworth Sunday School and John Brown's house

6. *(above left)* William Morgan

7. *(above right)* Dr William Cartman (by kind permission of Mr W. R. Mitchell)

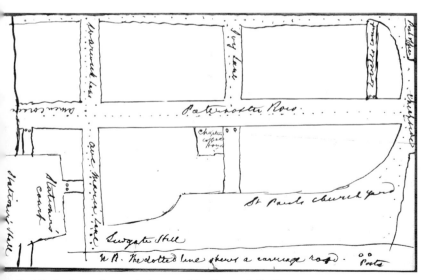

8. Patrick's sketch map showing the location of the Chapter Coffee House

29. *(above left)* Patrick's notes on his visit to Brussels in his French phrase book

30. *(above right)* Two pages of French phrases in Patrick's notebook

31. Hymn sheet for a service in Haworth Church, Sunday 19 July 1840

32. William Weightman (Charlotte's portrait drawing)

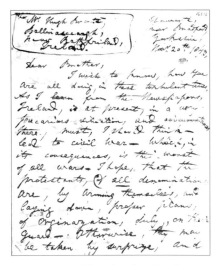

3. *(above left)* A letter from Patrick to Eliza Brown, 10 June 1859, in which he informs her of her baby daughter's death and seeks to comfort her

4. *(above right)* A letter from Patrick to his brother, Hugh, 20 November 1843, in which he urges the Protestants of Ireland to be on their guard, but not to act illegally

5. *(above left)* A letter from Patrick to Mrs Franks, 6 July 1835, in which he asks her to keep an eye on Charlotte and Emily, who were going to Roe Head School

6. *(above right)* Patrick's annotated copy of Graham's *Domestic Medicine*

37. *(above left)* Arthur Bell Nicholls

38. *(above right)* Martha Brown

39. *(above left)* Branwell Brontë – a self portrait, *c.* 1840

40. *(above right)* Branwell's *Parody of Death*

1. *(above left)* Mrs Elizabeth Gaskell – a portrait by Samuel Laurence (courtesy of Mrs Trevor Dabbs)

2. *(above right)* Mrs Gaskell's sketch of Haworth Church and Parsonage

3. *(above left)* George Smith

4. *(above right)* Two pages from Patrick's account book

45. Patrick in old age

TUITION. – WANTED, IN A SMALL Town in the Neighbourhood of the Lakes, A
PRIVATE TUTOR, competent to instruct Two boys, Ten & Eleven Years old, in a general
course of Education, including the Classics, with the strictest attention to Grammar.

For some months now, Patrick's supervision of his studies had been preparing Branwell
for just such an appointment as this and his application for the post was successful. His
new employer was Robert Postlethwaite, whom Branwell described to his friend, John
Brown (the Haworth sexton), as, 'a retired County magistrate, a large landowner and of
a right hearty and generous disposition'.[37] He lived at Broughton House in Broughton-
in-Furness, a small market town on the banks of the River Duddon. Branwell left to
take up his position there on 31 December.

Patrick was now enjoying the services of his new curate, William Weightman, who
had performed his first duties in Haworth on 19 August 1839. His youth and attractive
personality immediately made him a popular figure in Haworth. He rapidly became a
favourite with the Brontë family and was a regular visitor to the parsonage, where he
joined in many of their activities. The girls greatly appreciated his company and gave
him the nickname of 'Celia Amelia'.

In February 1840, at a time when Ellen Nussey was staying at the parsonage, Mr
Weightman was invited to give a lecture entitled 'The Advantages of Classical Studies'
to the Keighley Mechanics' Institute. He wanted the four girls to hear his lecture and he
arranged for a married clergyman in Keighley to invite them to tea beforehand, while
he himself offered to escort them on their journey. Patrick and Aunt Branwell agreed
to this arrangement. All went well except that, on their late return to the parsonage
around midnight, Aunt Branwell had not provided enough coffee for the two clergy
escorts as well as the four girls. As Ellen later recalled:

Poor Miss Branwell lost her temper, Charlotte was troubled, and Mr Weightman, who
enjoyed teasing the old lady, was very thirsty. The great spirits of the walking party had a
trying suppression, but twinkling fun sustained some of them.[38]

On hearing that none of the girls had ever had a Valentine before, Mr Weightman
sent one to each of them, having walked to Bradford to put them in the post in order
to escape detection. The Brontë girls all enjoyed his company and it has often been
said that Anne developed a special affection for him, but this may also have been true
of Charlotte. Her letters at this time are full of references to him and it was she who
decided to paint his portrait. According to Ellen, 'the sittings became alarming for
length of time required'.

In May 1840 Anne left Haworth to take up a post as governess to the five children
of the Rev'd Edmund Robinson, a wealthy clergyman who lived at Thorp Green, near
York. Branwell, meanwhile, was still engaged in his tutorship at Broughton and seems

to have used his spare time to do a lot of walking. In April he sent some of his poems and five translations from Book I of Horace's *Odes* to Thomas De Quincey, who was now living at Dove Cottage in Grasmere. De Quincey, who was ill at the time, seems to have made no reply. Branwell also sent two of his Horace translations and a long poem to Hartley Coleridge, who was living at Nab Cottage by Rydal Water. To his surprise and delight he received a reply from Coleridge inviting him to visit Nab Cottage. Branwell spent 1 May with Coleridge, who encouraged him to finish his translation of the first book of Horace's *Odes*. Two months later, however, at midsummer 1840, after six months in his post as tutor, he was dismissed by Mr Postlethwaite. The reasons for this are not clear. It may be that the encouragement given him by Coleridge led him to concentrate on his poetry to such an extent that he neglected his tutorial duties. A few days after his return to Haworth he sent Coleridge a revised version of his translation of the First Book of Horace *Odes*. His work showed considerable merit but, unfortunately, although Coleridge drafted a letter praising Branwell's translations, this letter was never sent.[39]

On 14 July William Weightman travelled to Ripon for his ordination as a priest and then went home to Appleby for a short holiday. Charlotte, who was coming to realise that the attentions he paid to the family circle at the parsonage were also being offered to other young ladies of his acquaintance, seems to have altered her previously favourable opinion of him. She expressed her feelings in a letter written to Ellen at the end of June:

> I am afraid he is very fickle – not to you in particular but to half a dozen other ladies – he has just cut his inamorata at Swansea and sent her back all her letters – his present object of devotion is Caroline Dury [the daughter of the Vicar of Keighley] to whom he has just despatched a most passionate copy of verses.[40]

William Weightman returned to Haworth and resumed his duties in the middle of September. Writing to Ellen Nussey at the end of the month, Charlotte told her that she had recently overheard a conversation between him and Patrick which had led her to revise her opinion of the fickleness of his character:

> Last Saturday night he had been sitting an hour in the parlour with Papa; and as he went away, I heard Papa say to him – "what is the matter with you? You seem in very low spirits to-night." "Oh, I don't know. I've been to see a poor young girl, who, I'm afraid, is dying." "Indeed, what is her name?" "Susan Bland, the daughter of John Bland, the superintendent." Now Susan Bland is my oldest and best scholar in the Sunday-school; and when I heard that, I thought I would go as soon as I could to see her. I did go, on Monday afternoon, and found her very weak, and seemingly far on her way to that bourne whence no traveller returns. After sitting with her some time, I happened to ask her mother if she thought a

little port wine would do her good. She replied that the doctor had recommended it, and that when Mr. W[eightman] was last there, he had sent them a bottle of wine and a jar of preserves. She added, that he was always good-natured to poor folks, and seemed to have a deal of feeling and kind-heartedness about him. This proves he is not all selfishness and vanity.[41]

The church registers show that Mr Weightman worked hard to relieve Patrick (now aged sixty-three) of most of the daily burdens of the parish. He performed almost all the baptisms and burials, leaving just the marriages for Patrick to take. He was also an assiduous visitor.

At the beginning of August 1840 a cousin of Mrs Maria Brontë, John Branwell Williams, together with his wife and daughter, Eliza, spent a day at the parsonage. They had come north to stay for a month at Cross-Stone, near Todmorden, with John Fennell, Mrs Brontë's uncle. Although any contact with her mother's family was a rare event, Charlotte was not impressed by them:

> They reckon to be very grand folks indeed – and talk largely – I thought assumingly I cannot say I much admired them – To my eyes there seemed to be an attempt to play the great Mogul down in Yorkshire – Mr Williams was much less assuming than the womenites – he seemed a frank, sagacious kind of man – very tall and vigorous with a keen active look – the moment he saw me he exclaimed that I was the very image of my Aunt Charlotte. Mrs. Williams sets up for being a woman of great talents, tact and accomplishment – I thought there was much more noise than work. My cousin Eliza is a young lady intended by nature to be a bouncing good-looking girl. Art has trained her to be a languishing affected piece of goods.[42]

Throughout this period Charlotte seems to have been content to remain in Haworth, making few attempts to obtain another position as a governess. It was Branwell who found a new job, working on the railway. On 31 August he was confirmed in his appointment as 'assistant clerk-in-charge' at Sowerby Bridge station, near Halifax, on a newly completed section of the unfinished Leeds to Manchester line. His salary was £75, rising by £10 each year to a maximum of £105. Patrick and Aunt Branwell showed their confidence in him and in his chances of promotion by standing surety for him for the huge sum of £210 (a figure representing more than Patrick's annual income). Branwell took up his post in time for the grand opening of the line on 5 October 1840. Spurred on perhaps by Branwell's success, Charlotte at last secured herself a job as governess in the family of John White at Upperwood House in Rawdon. This was very close to Woodhouse Grove School, where Patrick had first met and courted her mother, Maria. She took up her position on 2 March 1841.

'I went to Brussells'
1841–1846

I went to Brussells, Lille, Dunkirk, & Calais, in Feby 1842.

Patrick Brontë's French notebook, 1842

The winter of 1841/1842 brought further hardship and suffering to the poor of Haworth. Once again, in conjunction with the Dissenting ministers, Patrick and his curate were fully involved in attempts to relieve the distress. A general subscription was set up among the gentlemen and tradesmen of the chapelry and a considerable sum was raised, which, together with a grant of £200 from the London Committee for the Relief of the Distressed Manufacturers, was put to good use to provide practical help.

Early in the new year of 1842 Patrick decided to break his habit of seclusion and embark on an adventurous journey, accompanying two of his daughters to the Continent. Since the summer of 1841 a plan had been mooted in the family for the girls to found a school of their own. On 19 July Charlotte had told Ellen:

> There is a project hatching in this house – which both Emily and I anxiously wished to discuss with you – … Papa and Aunt talk by fits & starts of our – id est – Emily Anne and myself commencing a School! I have often you know said how much I wished such a thing – but I never could conceive where the capital was to come from for making such a speculation – I was well aware indeed that Aunt <u>had</u> money – but I always considered that she was the last person who would offer a loan for the purpose in question – A loan however she <u>has</u> offered or rather intimates that she perhaps <u>will</u> offer in case pupils can be secured, an eligible situation obtained &c. &c.

Charlotte herself was undoubtedly the driving force behind this idea. On 29 September she wrote to her aunt from Upperwood House suggesting that the best preparation for founding a school would be for her and Emily to spend some time in a school on the Continent:

My friends recommend me, if I desire to secure permanent success, to delay commencing the school for six months longer, and by all means to contrive, by hook or by crook, to spend the intervening time in some school on the continent. They say schools in England are so numerous, competition so great, that without some such step towards attaining superiority we shall probably have a very hard struggle, and may fail in the end.

She argued that the best place to go would be Belgium:

The cost of the journey there, at the dearest rate of travelling, would be £5, living is there little more than half as dear as it is in England, and the facilities for education are equal or superior to any other place in Europe. In half a year, I could acquire a thorough familiarity in French. I could improve greatly in Italian, and even get a dash of German.

She concluded by reminding her aunt of the ambition which her father had shown when setting out from Ireland to further his career:

Papa will perhaps think it a wild and ambitious scheme; but who ever rose in the world without ambition? When he left Ireland to go to Cambridge University, he was as ambitious as I am now. I want us all to go on. I know we have talents, and I want them to be turned to account.

Aunt Branwell was persuaded by Charlotte's arguments and agreed to give £50 to fund the scheme. Charlotte gave up her post as governess with the White family and arrived home on Christmas Eve. The family now had to choose a suitable school in Belgium. Charlotte's school-friend Mary Taylor was in Brussels on a Continental tour with her brother John and younger sister Martha. The two girls were attending school at the Château de Koekelberg, but it was clear that this establishment would be too expensive. Patrick wrote to the Church of England chaplain in Brussels, the Revd Evan Jenkins (the brother of David Jenkins, Patrick's former clerical colleague at Dewsbury) for advice. After consultation with his wife he recommended the Pensionnat Heger, run by Madame Heger with the assistance of her husband, Constantin.

Despite his heavy commitments in Haworth, with the continuing dispute over the payment of church rates and his time-consuming efforts to relieve the distress of the poor, Patrick was determined to accompany his daughters to Brussels himself. Before setting out he purchased a notebook in which he jotted down some French phrases which might be useful during his time away. On the first page he made a note about the use of the book:

The following conversational terms, suited to a Traveller, in France, or any part of the Continent of Europe – are taken from Surenne's New French Manual – for 1840 – And …

will be sufficient, for – me – And must be fully mastered; and ready semper –... These are first the French – 2 – the ... right pronunciation – and lastly the English.

There followed a list of nouns and phrases set out on this principle:

> A droit = a droa – to the right
> Quand partirez vous? = Quand partire voo? When do you sail?
> Demain = de mang – tomorrow[1]

The party left Haworth on 8 February 1842, accompanied by Mary Taylor and her brother Joe. They travelled to London by train from Leeds, a journey of eleven hours. On arriving at Euston Station Patrick took them to stay at the Chapter Coffee House in Paternoster Row, near St Paul's Cathedral, where he himself had stayed at the time of his ordination as deacon thirty-five years earlier. The next three days they spent sight-seeing under Charlotte's enthusiastic guidance. While in London they had to purchase their passports. In his notebook, Patrick was pleased to record a bargain:

> My passport, procured at the Belgian Consuls Office in London cost 5s= Though at the French Consuls it would have amounted to ten.

Early on the morning of Saturday 12 February they went down to London Bridge Wharf and boarded the Ostend packet, which sailed twice weekly with mails and passengers for the Continent. The voyage took nearly fourteen hours and they arrived late in the evening. They stayed in Ostend until Monday morning and then took the diligence (public stagecoach) for the seventy-mile journey to Brussels. They arrived there in the evening and took rooms for the night at the Hotel d'Hollande. In the morning Mr Jenkins and his wife came to the hotel to escort them to the school.

The Pensionnat Heger was in the Rue d'Isabelle, in the ancient quarter of the city, close to the central park. The building itself was forty years old and there was an attractive garden lined with ancient fruit trees. The two schoolrooms were large and airy and above them ran the dormitory containing about twenty beds. Monsieur and Madame Heger, with their three small daughters, lived on the school premises. Madame Heger, who was thirty-eight years old, was the *directrice* of the school. Her husband, an eminent teacher at the nearby Athenée Royal School for boys, gave literature lessons to the girls of the *pensionnat*. The cost for six months' schooling was to be about 1,055 francs, equivalent to £42. This was within the budget of £50 which Aunt Branwell had said she was prepared to contribute. According to Mrs Gaskell's *Life*, Charlotte had written to the Hegers asking the amount of any extra charges. The Hegers were struck by the 'simple earnest tone' of her letter and discussed what arrangement to make:

These are the daughters of an English pastor, of moderate means, anxious to learn with an ulterior motive of instructing others, and to whom the risk of additional expense is of great consequence. Let us name a specific sum, within which all expenses shall be included.[2]

Charlotte and Emily were given permission not to attend the daily mass and they were also assigned a curtained-off recess at the end of the dormitory to provide them with a little privacy.

The school lay in one of the healthiest parts of the city and Madame Heger seemed actively concerned with the welfare of her pupils. Once he had inspected the school Patrick must have felt that his daughters were being placed in safe hands. Mr and Mrs Jenkins promised that they would keep a close eye on the girls and gave them an open invitation to spend Sundays and half holidays at their house in the Chaussée d'Ixelles. Patrick remained in Brussels for another week, staying with Mr and Mrs Jenkins and seeing the sights of the city. During this time he achieved what had probably been a lifetime's ambition, a visit to the site of the Battle of Waterloo. Years later, Benjamin Binns recalled Patrick 'describing in vivid and vigorous language the field of Waterloo which he had visited from Brussels'.[3] Patrick then made the journey home via Calais and London. When he was back in Haworth, he recorded a few comments on his experiences abroad:

I went to Brussels, Lille, Dunkirk, & Calais, in Feby 1842 =And found the expenses of travelling, under All circumstance, generally, to be neither below, nor above one fifth less there than in England. ... I was only between 2 and 3 weeks away – And the whole expences of my journey, amounted to about £23-10-0 [£23.50] not more.

The notebook concludes with a telling comment:

A traveller, may and must, always have a good bedroom to himself alone.

Soon after Patrick's return to England a sad event occurred in the township with the death on 30 April 1842 of Thomas Andrew, the surgeon there for the past twenty-four years. He had been a close friend of Patrick, who took the funeral himself. So many people wanted to pay their respects to him that his corpse had to be taken out of his house and displayed in the street. Thomas Andrew is commemorated in Haworth church by a marble statue sculpted by Branwell's friend J. B. Leyland. Branwell himself was commissioned to compose the inscription, which, after detailing his career, concluded:

This Tablet was erected by those who knew his worth, and who feel that, while in his death the neighbourhood has lost an honourable & upright man, the poor have lost an able adviser in their calamities, & a generous friend in their need.

There had been significant developments in Branwell's life, too. In April 1841 he had been promoted from his position at Sowerby Bridge to become the clerk-in-charge at Luddenden Foot, the next station up the line, on a much higher salary of £130 a year. In March 1842, however, he was dismissed from his position with the Leeds & Manchester Railway. A company audit of the ledgers at Luddenfoot revealed a discrepancy in the accounts, with the sum of £11-1-7 (£11-08) unaccounted for. There was no suggestion that Branwell was suspected of theft or fraud, for in that case he would almost certainly have been prosecuted. The Leeds & Manchester Railway had a reputation for taking a very hard line with its staff. Branwell was responsible, however, for the accuracy of the accounts, and was clearly guilty of negligence. According to his friends he occasionally had the habit of wandering off from the station, leaving one of his subordinates in charge. The missing amount was deducted from his quarter's salary and he was summarily dismissed.

In August 1842 Haworth and the surrounding area was disrupted by an outbreak of political unrest. Under the influence of Chartist activists, thousands of factory-workers marched on the mills and forced them to stop production. Riots broke out in Bradford, Bingley, Keighley, Skipton, Todmorden, Halifax and Huddersfield, and on 14 August the local newspapers estimated that 10,000 Chartists had gathered on Lees Moor, near Haworth. The authorities were quick to react. By 19 August some order had been restored and most of the mills at Keighley were working again. There were further alarms, however, when disgruntled mill-workers sabotaged machinery by removing the plugs from the boilers which powered the looms, and special constables were sworn in at Haworth.

The sixty-five-year-old Patrick does not seem to have been much involved in these proceedings. Although he sympathised with the sufferings of the poor and tried to render them assistance, he always disapproved of violence and the taking of illegal action. On 22 September, in a reference to the Conservative administration of Sir Robert Peel which in September 1841 had replaced the Whig government under Lord Melbourne, he expressed his feelings to John White, Charlotte's former employer:

> In regard to Politics, it must now appear to all rational and unprejudiced men, that had the poor, unprincipled, temporizing Whigs, remain'd much longer in power, we should have been utterly ruined, as a nation. ... May the Most high, enable the Conservatives to do their duty, and protect them from all the evil designs of their enemies!

In the midst of all this turmoil Patrick suffered a sad loss in the death of his curate, William Weightman, on 6 September at the age of twenty-eight. He had been an assiduous visitor of the sick in the parish and had fallen ill of cholera. In his funeral sermon Patrick related how he had visited him during his last illness:

I generally visited him twice a day, joined with him in prayer, heard his request for the prayers of this congregation, listened to him while he expressed his entire dependence on the merits of the Saviour, heard of his pious admonitions to his attendants, and saw him in tranquillity close his eyes on this bustling, vain, selfish world; so that I may truly say, his end was peace, and his hope glory.

Patrick took his funeral on 10 September in Haworth church, and he preached a funeral sermon in his memory at the afternoon service on Sunday 2 October. On this occasion, knowing that some parishioners had asked him to publish what he was going to say, Patrick departed from his usual custom of preaching extempore and prepared a written sermon which was later printed for wider distribution in the parish.[4]

Patrick, who had been very fond of his young curate and seems to have regarded him almost as a son, was deeply moved by his grief. He took as his text I Corinthians 15: vv. 56–58:

The sting of death is sin, and the strength of sin is the law. But thanks be to God, which giveth us the victory, through our Lord Jesus Christ. Therefore my beloved brethren, be ye steadfast, unmoveable, always abounding in the work of the Lord, for as much as ye know that your labour is not in vain in the Lord.

He opened his address with these words:

For more than twenty years, during which time I have ministered amongst you, this will be the first sermon I shall have read to this congregation, and it may be the last.

He then went on to praise William Weightman's character and ministry:

In his preaching and his practising, he was, as every clergyman ought to be, neither distant nor austere, timid not obtrusive, nor bigoted, exclusive, nor dogmatical. He was affable, but not familiar; open, but not too confiding. He thought it better, and more scriptural, to make the love of God, rather than the fear of hell, the ruling motive for obedience. ... Though he preached the necessity of sincere repentance, and heart-felt sorrow for sin, he believed that the convert, in his freedom from its thraldom, should rejoice evermore in the glorious liberty of the gospel. ... In the Sunday School, especially, he was useful in more than ordinary degree. He had the rare art of communicating information with diligence and strictness, without austerity, so as to render instruction, even to the youngest and most giddy, a pleasure, and not a task.

After outlining his career before coming to Haworth, he continued with a heartfelt tribute:

For about three years our Reverend Friend in his sacred office has laboured amongst us, faithfully preaching the doctrines expressed and implied in our text. … As it ought to be with every Incumbent, and his clerical coadjutor, we were always like father and son – according to our respective situations – giving and taking mutual advice, from the best motives, and in the most friendly spirit; looking on each other, not as rivals, but as fellow labourers in the same glorious cause, and under the superintendence of our common Lord and Master. …

As he was himself a friend to many, and an enemy to none, so by a kind of reaction, he had, I think I might say, no enemies and many friends. He was a conscientious Churchman, and true Protestant – but tolerant to all his differing brethren; where he could not cordially unite, he determined that separation should be no ground of hostility. …

He concluded that it was right to mourn his death, but not without Christian hope:

Our friend is gone the way of all flesh, and the people and places which knew him once, shall know him no more. But let us not grieve, as those without hope. … Our privilege as Christians is to look forward to a joyous resurrection, in the hope of being for ever re-united above, with those who have been taken from us by death, and whom we have loved here below.

The sermon was printed privately in Halifax and priced at 6d (2½p), with any profits going to the Sunday school.

Branwell, who had had a close relationship with Weightman and had regularly visited him throughout his illness, was greatly upset. At this time of their grief Patrick and Branwell were deprived of the support of Charlotte and Emily, who were studying in Brussels, and of Anne, away at her post at Thorp Green. A few weeks later they had to bear another grievous loss. Aunt Branwell was taken ill and, after enduring great pain from an internal obstruction, she died on 29 October 1842. Branwell was particularly affected by her death. In a letter to his friend Francis Grundy, written a few days before her death, he wrote:

I have had a long attendance at the deathbed of the Rev. Mr. Weightman, one of my dearest friends, and now I am attending at the deathbed of my aunt, who has been for twenty years as my mother.[5]

He wrote again a few days later expressing his grief at her death:

I have now lost the [guide] and director of all the happy days connected with my childhood.[6]

The news of Aunt Branwell's serious illness was conveyed to Charlotte and Emily in Brussels. They had already decided to return home when a second letter brought news of her death.

Aunt Branwell's funeral was held on 3 November and was taken by the Revd James Bradley, the curate of Oakworth. In accordance with her expressed wish, her remains were deposited in the church, 'as near as convenient to the remains of my dear sister'. Anne arrived home from Thorp Green in time for the funeral and she was given permission by the Robinson family to remain a few weeks at home. Her assistance at the parsonage was in fact essential, since with the death of Aunt Branwell, and in the absence of Charlotte and Emily, the whole responsibility for running the household would otherwise have fallen on the twelve-year-old Martha Brown. Charlotte and Emily arrived back in Haworth on 8 November.

They brought with them a letter from Monsieur Heger, praising Patrick for the qualities he had instilled in his daughters and commenting on their progress at the school:

> Sir,
>
> ... I have not the honour of knowing you personally, and yet I feel for you yourself a sentiment of sincere veneration, for in judging the father of a family by his children there is no risk of being mistaken; and in this respect the education and opinions we have found in your daughters could only give us a very high idea of your worth and your character. No doubt you will be pleased to hear that your children have made very notable progress in all the branches of instruction, and that this progress is entirely due to their love of work and their perseverance; in dealing with such pupils we have had but little to do; their progress is your handiwork much more than ours; we have not had to teach them the value of time and instruction, they had learnt all that in their father's house, and we for our part have had the minor merit of guiding their efforts and providing suitable material to foster the admirable activity that your daughters have derived from your example and your lessons.

Coming from such a wise and experienced schoolmaster this was a remarkable tribute to the way in which Patrick had brought up his daughters. Monsieur Heger added that while at the school the girls had developed in other ways. Emily was now losing some of her shyness. She had received piano lessons from the best teacher in Belgium and was now teaching the instrument herself. Charlotte was gaining the 'assurance and aplomb so essential in teaching' and was beginning to give lessons in French. He said that within a year he would have been able to offer one of the girls a position at the school. He made an indirect appeal for them to return to the school:

> This is not, please believe me sir, this is not a question of our personal advantage, but a question of affection; you must pardon me if we speak to you of your children and concern

ourselves with their future as if they formed part of our family; their personal qualities, their good will, their extreme zeal are the only reasons leading us to venture in this way.[7]

In her will Aunt Branwell had left the three Brontë girls, together with their cousin, Eliza Kingston in Penzance, an equal share in her estate, which amounted to just under £300 each. Over the Christmas holidays much thought was given to the future of the family. Emily was now needed to take on the role of housekeeper at home, something she was only too willing to do. Charlotte, on the other hand, had already decided to return to Brussels. Anne, who was greatly appreciated by the Robinson family, was going to return to Thorp Green and Branwell was going to accompany her as tutor to the young Edmund Robinson.

Charlotte was determined to return to Brussels as soon as she could. It is a sign of Patrick's confidence in her resourcefulness that she managed to persuade him to agree to her making the long journey without anyone to accompany her. On 27 January 1843 she left home and travelled to Leeds to take the nine o'clock train to London. She arrived at Euston after a thirteen-hour journey and immediately took a cab to London Bridge Wharf, where she managed to persuade someone on the packet-boat to let her on board. The boat sailed early next morning and she arrived in Ostend at nine in the evening. After staying the night there she caught a train to Brussels and arrived at the Pensionnat Heger the next day, Sunday 29 January 1843, at seven in the evening. She was now to work as a teacher at the school with a salary of £16 a year, out of which she had to pay for her German lessons.

For the six months following William Weightman's death, Patrick had no curate to assist him. It was not until the beginning of March 1843 that he was joined by the Rev'd James William Smith, a graduate of Trinity College, Dublin. Although he was zealous in the performance of his duties, Patrick found him to be a fiery and intemperate man and never developed a close relationship with him. Charlotte's portrait of Mr Malone in *Shirley* is said to be based on him.

Shortly after Mr Smith's arrival Patrick was required to travel to York to give evidence in a case held at York Assizes on 20 March 1843. This concerned an alleged forged deed relating to the will of John Beaver, a Haworth Church Lands Trustee. Patrick had been a witness to the original will. In the event it seems that, prior to the trial, some deal was done between the parties, as a result of which the prosecution presented no evidence and the defendants were acquitted. Patrick was concerned over the effect the case had on two of his parishioners, William Thomas, a wine and spirit merchant at Haworth, and Enoch Thomas, the landlord of the King's Arms, and he tried to assist them in their difficulties.[8] He also took the opportunity when he was in York to visit Anne and Branwell at Thorp Green.

During the course of 1843 Patrick became very worried over the disturbed situation in Ireland. Irish agitation for the repeal of the Act of Union of Great Britain and Ireland had reached a climax under the leadership of Daniel O'Connell, and on 27 May 1843 Patrick wrote to the *Leeds Intelligencer* to express his concern. Six months later he wrote to his younger brother Hugh, who was living at Ballynaskeagh, near Rathfriland. He urged the Protestants in Ireland to be doubly on their guard but not to take any illegal action:

> I wish to know how you are all doing in these turbulent times. As I learn from the Newspapers, Ireland, is at present in a very precarious situation, and circumstances there, must, I should think – lead to civil War – which in its consequences, is the worst of all wars – I hope, that the Protestants of all denominations, Are, by Arming themselves, and laying down, proper plans of orginazation [*sic*] duly, on their Guard – Otherwise, they may be taken by surprise, And murdered by their insidious, And Malignant enemies. … Yet, whilst I say these things, I would admonish You, And All my Brothers, and Friends, not to be rash, and neither to break the Laws of God or Man.[9]

During much of 1843 Patrick was busy in a campaign to open a National Society day school in Haworth. He was assisted in his efforts by the vicar of Bradford, who paid a visit to Haworth to give him advice. In another way, however, Dr Scoresby's intervention was not so welcome. For the past six years the Free Grammar School near Oxenhope had been run by a Mr Ramsbottom, a local Wesleyan Methodist preacher. This was, in fact, contrary to the terms of the seventeenth-century foundation of the school, which required the master to be a graduate of Oxford or Cambridge, thus effectively excluding all Dissenters from the post. On 4 January 1844 Dr Scoresby wrote to Patrick pointing out this irregularity. He accused Patrick and the trustees of being culpably negligent and he urged Patrick to call a meeting in order to dismiss Mr Ramsbottom and appoint 'a proper master' in his place. The trustees had no alternative but to give Mr Ramsbottom notice to leave at midsummer. In July 1844 he was replaced as master by the Rev'd Joseph Brett Grant, who was to prove useful to Patrick by occasionally assisting him in his clerical duties.

The manner of Mr Robinson's dismissal infuriated the Dissenters. They took their revenge by accusing Patrick of saying in a recent sermon that he would no longer bury anyone not baptised in the Church of England. Patrick responded by writing to the *Bradford Observer* on 15 February 1844, pointing out that they had distorted what he had said. His refusal to bury those who had not been baptised was aimed not at Dissenters but at his own parishioners who had registered their children's births with the civil registrar but had made no attempt to have them baptised in church. He stated categorically that he would continue to bury nonconformists:

> As I would wish the dissenters to live long and to live well, it would be my desire that our burial ground of not narrow limits, would amply suffice for them all for many years to come.

At the beginning of January 1844 Charlotte returned from Brussels in a state of great depression following her estrangement from Madame Heger over her growing attachment to Monsieur Heger. Although her long-term plan in going to the Pensionnat Heger had been to found a school of their own in some suitable location, she now felt that the state of her father's health prevented her from leaving Haworth. As she told Ellen on 23 January 1844:

> Every one asks me what I am going to do now that I am returned home and every one seems to expect that I should immediately commence a school – In truth Ellen it is what I should wish to do – I desire it of all things – I have sufficient money for the undertaking – and I hope now sufficient qualifications to give me a fair chance of success – yet I cannot yet permit myself to enter upon life – to touch the object which seems now within my reach and which I have been so long striving to attain – you will ask me why – It is on Papa's account – he is now as you know getting old – and it grieves me to tell you that he is losing his sight – I have felt for some months that I ought not to be away from him – and I feel now that it would be too selfish to leave him (at least so long as Branwell and Anne are absent) in order to pursue selfish interests of my own – with the help of God – I will try to deny myself in this matter and to wait.

Some provision had to be made for the family's future, however, and during the summer of 1844 it was decided that an attempt would be made to start a school at the parsonage, which would obviate the necessity for the girls to leave home. As Charlotte told Ellen:

> I have seriously entered into the enterprise of keeping a school – or rather taking a limited number of pupils at home – that is I have begun to seek in good earnest for pupils.[10]

She wrote round to some of her former contacts in an attempt to secure pupils. The White family of Upperwood replied that they would happily have sent their daughter to Haworth but had unfortunately just committed her to a school in Batley. Mrs Busfield, the wife of the rector of Keighley, wrote saying that she thought they would find it difficult to attract pupils. Although the fees proposed were moderate and the small number of pupils would enable individual attention to be given, the 'retired situation' of Haworth would probably outweigh all other benefits. Charlotte sent copies of the prospectus to Ellen for her to distribute around Dewsbury. Despite all efforts, however, no applications were received, and in October the scheme was abandoned.

At the end of June 1844 Ellen Nussey paid another visit to the parsonage. It seems that during her stay the curate, James Smith, paid considerable attention to her, causing Patrick to make an uncharacteristic intervention in the affairs of his family. In a letter to Ellen written at the end of July, shortly after her return home, Charlotte told her that most unusually Patrick had been very worried over this matter:

Papa has two or three times expressed a fear that since Mr Smith paid you so much attention he will perhaps have made an impression on your mind which will interfere with your comfort – I tell him I think not as I believe you to be mistress of yourself in those matters. Still he keeps saying that I am to write to you and dissuade you from thinking of him – I never saw papa make himself so uneasy about a thing of the kind before – he is usually very sarcastic on such subjects.

The reason for Patrick's fears may be deduced from another passage in Charlotte's letter:

Mr Smith has not once mentioned your name since you left – except once when papa said you were a nice girl – he said – "yes – she – is a nice girl – rather quiet – I suppose she has no money" – and that is all – I think the words speak volumes – they do not prejudice one in favour of Mr Smith – I can well believe what papa has often affirmed – and continues to affirm – i.e. that Mr Smith is a very fickle man – that if he marries he will soon get tired of his wife – and consider her a burden – also that money will be a principal consideration with him in marrying.[11]

James Smith left Haworth in October to become the curate of Keighley. Patrick's assessment of his character was shown to be soundly based when, four years later, he absconded to Canada, leaving many debts behind him, including money given him for charitable purposes which he had appropriated to his own use. In view of this, it may be significant that after his departure from Haworth Patrick had to write to the National Society in March 1845 reporting that the accounts of the school which had been kept by Mr Smith could not be found.

For some time Patrick's eyesight had been gradually failing and it now seemed that he might go completely blind. As Charlotte told Ellen on 13 June 1845:

I feel reluctant indeed to leave papa for a single day – his sight diminishes weekly and can it be wondered at – that as he sees the most precious of his faculties leaving him, his spirits sometimes sink? It is so hard to feel that his few and scanty pleasures must all soon go – he now has the greatest difficulty in either reading or writing – and then he dreads the state of dependence to which blindness will inevitably reduce him – He fears he will be nothing in his parish – I try to cheer him, sometimes I succeed termporarily – but no consolation can restore his sight or atone for the want of it. Still he is never peevish – never impatient only anxious and dejected.

Patrick also had an additional problem. The lotion that he had been taking for his eyes seems to have been alcohol-based and had given rise to rumours that he had taken to drink. As the president of the Haworth Temperance Society, Patrick was very sensitive to this charge. In a letter to Joseph Greenwood on 4 October 1843, he had threatened to prosecute those responsible for the rumours:

> They keep propagating false reports – I mean to single out one or two of these slanderers, and to prosecute them, as the Law directs. I have lately been using a lotion for my eyes, which are very weak – and they have ascribed the smell of that to a smell of a more objectionable character.

This situation clearly caused him great embarrassment. When, five years earlier, in October 1838, the Keighley surgeon John Milligan had recommended him to take a glass of wine or spirits before his main meal to counteract dyspepsia, Patrick had been most particular to obtain his signature to the prescription to prevent such rumours.

In May 1845 the arrival of the new curate, the Rev'd Arthur Bell Nicholls, once again provided Patrick with assistance in the performance of his clerical duties. Arthur Nicholls was a twenty-six-year-old Irishman who, like Patrick, came from an impoverished family background. His father was a poor farmer near Belfast, but from the age of seven he had been brought up by his maternal uncle, Dr Alan Bell, the headmaster of the Royal School at Banagher. Dr Bell had supported his nephew through his education at the school and then at Trinity College, Dublin, which Nicholls had entered as a fee-paying pensioner in July 1836. He had taken his B.A. degree in February 1844 and had been ordained deacon at Ripon Cathedral on 18 May 1845. He took up his post at Haworth on the following Sunday, 25 May.

Within a few months of his arrival Arthur Nicholls had taken over almost all of Patrick's parochial duties, including the oversight of the National School. The knowledge of his support must have been a great relief to Patrick, whose failing eyesight had made it increasingly difficult for him to carry out his role as incumbent.

Towards the end of April 1845 Patrick convened a meeting to discuss raising a subscription to replace the existing three bells at Haworth by a peal of six, which would enable the Haworth bellringers to take part in change-ringing competitions. The first bell at Haworth had been placed in the tower in 1664 and the other two in 1742 and 1747, during the incumbency of William Grimshaw. This proposal was enthusiastically received and, by the beginning of June, £230 had been raised. The new bells were in place by the end of October and in the following March their installation was celebrated by a change-ringing competition and a dinner at the Black Bull. An inscription in the belfry tower records that:

> This peal of bells was hung by William Wood, Joseph Redman being the architect, and was opened and prizes given, March 10th, 1846.

The tenor bell is inscribed:

> C. and G. Mears London. These bells were raised by subscription. Rev. Patrick Brontë, A.B., Incumbent, Mr George Feather, Mr James Lambert, Churchwardens.

In June there were dramatic changes in the life of the Brontë family. When Anne and Branwell came home from Thorp Green for their summer holidays, Anne announced that she had given up her post as governess to the girls of the Robinson family. She did not explain her reasons for doing this, but they soon became apparent. Branwell was only at home for a week, before returning to resume his duties, with the intention of taking the rest of his holdays while the Robinson family were away at Scarborough. He returned to Haworth early in July. On 17 July Mr Robinson wrote to him from Scarborough dismissing him from his post as tutor to his son. Charlotte, who had been away for three weeks staying with Ellen Nussey at her brother's vicarage at Hathersage in Derbyshire, wrote to Ellen on 31 July, explaining the situation which she had found on her return home:

> It was ten o'clock at night when I got home – I found Branwell ill – he is so very often owing to his own fault – I was not therefore shocked at first – but when Anne informed me of the immediate cause of his present illness I was greatly shocked, he had last Thursday received a note from Mr Robinson sternly dismissing him ... intimating that he had discovered his proceedings which he characterised as bad beyond expression and charging him on pain of exposure to break off instantly and for ever all communication with every member of his family.

The truth of what had happened is hard to ascertain with certainty, but it seems most probable that Branwell had had an affair with Mrs Robinson and that this situation had been brought about with her active encouragement. In 1857 the passages in Mrs Gaskell's *Life of Charlotte Brontë*, which stated that this had been the reason for Branwell's dismissal, had to be withdrawn under threat of legal action for libel. Patrick himself remained firmly convinced that Mrs Robinson had been responsible for the affair. In his first letter of appreciation to Mrs Gaskell after the publication of Charlotte's life he praised her for 'the picture of my brilliant and unhappy Son, and his diabolical Seducer', which he described as a 'Masterpiece'.[12] As is the nature of such things, however, evidence which would stand up in court was hard to gather. George Smith, the publisher of Mrs Gaskell's work, later recalled a conference which was held between the author's and publisher's solicitors:

> It was determined to employ detectives in order to ascertain what evidence was available to justify the alleged libel. Much gossip, it was found, existed; but it was gossip of the kind which

is apt to dissolve into mere vapour when tested in a court of law. The following Memorandum
will show the sort of information which the Rev. Patrick Brontë, Branwell's father, regarded
as 'evidence' in this case. I am not much of a lawyer but I think I can conceive the opinion a
lawyer would have of such 'evidence' – Branwell constantly received letters from Mrs – but
Mr Brontë himself never saw them; could not say whether they were signed with her name;
he 'understood' that the letters showed guilt; often remonstrated with Branwell, but he would
keep up the correspondence. After his death (Branwell's) 'the children' made the letters into a
bundle and burnt them. A servant who went by the name of 'Cherry' was privy, he believed,
to a good deal. A gardener – whose name he did not know – had definite proofs of guilt and
had informed, as he understood, Mrs –'s husband. A surgeon who attended the family, he
had been told, was cognizant of the intimacy. His conversations with his son, who frequently
spoke freely with him, left no doubt as to the nature of the intimacy, etc., etc. All this, of
course, was mere unverifiable gossip, quite insufficient to justify a public accusation.[13]

Whatever the truth of the matter, the effect on Branwell was devastating. He was dis-
traught and suffered a complete breakdown. In her letter to Ellen of 31 July reporting
the matter, Charlotte wrote:

We have had sad work with Branwell since – he thought of nothing but stunning, or
drowning his distress of mind – no one in the house could have rest – and at last we have
been obliged to send him from home for a week with some one to look after him.

Patrick had decided that, to give Branwell some relief, he should be sent away for a
short holiday in the care of his friend John Brown. They set out for Liverpool on 29
July and from there went into Wales for a week. During a trip down the Welsh coast
Branwell did some sketches at Penmaenmawr and also wrote some poetry. Although he
seems to have recovered some of his spirits during his time away, two months later he
gave a miserable report on his condition to his friend Francis Grundy:

I have lain during nine long weeks utterly shattered in body and broken down in mind. …
I dreaded the wreck of my mind and body, which God knows during a short life have been
severely tried. Eleven continuous nights of sleepless horror reduced me almost to blindness,
and being taken to Wales to recover, the sweet scenery, the sea, the sound of music caused me
fits of unspeakable distress.[14]

One distraction for Patrick at this time was the promotion of a new railway line to run
from Hebden Bridge to Oxenhope and on via Haworth and Oakworth to Keighley.
This link to the main railway system would greatly increase Haworth's prosperity
and Patrick joined the principal inhabitants as a promoter of the plan. Applications
for shares were advertised in the *Leeds Intelligencer* on 11 October 1845. Branwell was

stirred into activity by the prospect of employment which this scheme seemed to present. Sometime in October he applied for the post of secretary to the new Railway, but with his past record it is hardly surprising that his application was not successful. Unfortunately the new line had been proposed at a time when many railway schemes were coming to grief and the plan was soon abandoned. It was not for another twenty-two years that Haworth secured its railway link.

In the early summer of 1846 the first publication of the Brontë sisters appeared in print. Charlotte later recounted how a chance find had brought this about:

> We had very early cherished the dream of becoming authors. … One day in the autumn of 1845, I accidentally lighted on a MS. Volume of verse in my sister Emily's handwriting. Of course, I was not surprised, knowing that she could and did write verse. I looked it over, and something more than surprise seized me, – a deep conviction that these were not common effusions, nor at all like the poetry women generally write. I thought them condensed and terse, vigorous and genuine. To my ear, they had also a peculiar music – wild, melancholy, and elevating.[15]

It was only with great difficulty, however, that Charlotte was able to overcome Emily's furious rage at this unwarranted trespass on her privacy. Encouraged by Charlotte's discovery, Anne produced some of her verses, which in Charlotte's opinion 'had a sweet sincere pathos of their own'. Eventually the decision was taken to publish a collection of poems by all three sisters. After much enquiry, Charlotte managed to secure the agreement of the small publishing house, Aylott & Jones, of No. 8 Paternoster Row, London, to publish the poems at the sisters' own expense. On 3 March 1846 Charlotte sent a banker's draft for £31 10-0 (£31.50) to enable printing to begin. Emily had insisted that the poems should be published under a pseudonym. As Charlotte later explained:

> Averse to personal publicity, we veiled our own names under those of Currer, Ellis, and Acton Bell; the ambiguous choice being dictated by a sort of conscientious scruple at assuming Christian names positively masculine, while we did not like to declare ourselves women. … We had a vague impression that authoresses are liable to be looked on with prejudice.[16]

The first copies of the *Poems* reached the parsonage on 7 May 1846. The volume ran to 165 pages of text and and was priced at four shillings (20p). Sadly, it attracted little attention in the critical journals and only two copies were bought by the public. The purchaser of one of these was a Mr Frederick Enoch of Warwick, who wrote through the publishers to ask for their autographs.

During the winter of 1845/1846 the three sisters had each been writing a novel. They spent over a year seeking to have them published and it was not until the summer of 1847 that Emily's *Wuthering Heights* and Anne's *Agnes Grey* were accepted by the unscrupulous Thomas Newby. Charlotte's novel *The Professor* was either rejected by Newby or not published by him because Charlotte refused to accept his terms. Eventually, after several rejections, she was encouraged by a percipient reader at Smith Elder & Co. to submit an alternative manuscript and the publication of *Jane Eyre* in October 1847 brought her instant fame and success. Although Patrick had noticed that his daughters always seemed to be engaged in some literary activity, he was unaware of their publications until Charlotte informed him of her success with *Jane Eyre* early in 1848.[17]

Patrick's eyesight was continuing to deteriorate. In February 1846, while Charlotte was staying with Ellen Nussey, she took the opportunity of consulting William Carr, an experienced surgeon who had married a cousin of Ellen's, over whether anything could be done for her father's eyes. He advised that an operation might be successful in restoring Patrick's eyesight, but that it should be deferred until the cataracts that were causing the problem had hardened enough to be removed. Charlotte returned home on 2 March and on the next day reported to Ellen:

> Papa was much cheered by my report of Mr Carr's opinion … but I could perceive he caught
> gladly at the idea of deferring the operation a few months longer.

By the summer of 1846 Patrick was almost totally blind and his faithful curate, Arthur Nicholls, continued to carry out the great majority of his pastoral duties. Although he was now unable to read or write for himself, Patrick continued to preach sermons on Sundays, but he had to be guided to the pulpit. His disabled situation made him increasingly depressed. In a letter written to her former teacher, Margaret Wooler, in November 1846,Charlotte looked back to this time:

> when Papa's vision was wholly obscured – when he could do nothing for himself and sat all
> day-long in darkness and inertion.

Patrick found it very frustrating not to be able to play a full part in the running of the parish. Although on Whit Monday he gave the annual sermon to the teachers and children of the Sunday school, he was not able to join the processional walk through the village. Two weeks later he could not attend the ceremonial laying of the foundation stone for a National School at Oxenhope, particularly frustrating since education was a cause so dear to his heart. He was also not in a position to play his full part in alleviating the continuing distress in the township caused by the poor state of trade and the decline in wages.

One event that he was able to attend was the performance on 20 July of an oratorio in Haworth church. The soloists for this performance were Thomas Parker, a well-known Haworth tenor, and Mrs Sunderland from Halifax. Unfortunately, the concert was boycotted by all the high-church Puseyite clergy in the district on the grounds that Thomas Parker was a Baptist. Nonetheless, the performance was a great success. The

Leeds Intelligencer for 25 July reported that the church was 'crowded to suffocation'. It also noted that Patrick, 'the venerable incumbent ... who is now totally blind' was sitting in a prominent position in the west gallery with his clerical friends Thomas Crowther, who was staying at the parsonage, having preached the annual Sunday-school sermons on the previous day, and Thomas Charnock, the son of the previous incumbent of Haworth. They were also joined by Joseph Greenwood, the chairman of the Haworth trustees. On the next day Patrick was also able to go to the half-yearly public examination of the scholars in the National School at Haworth, which he had worked so hard to establish,[18] and he must have taken great pleasure in the good progress of the school.

By July 1846 five months had elapsed since Charlotte had consulted the surgeon William Carr about Patrick's eyes, and it was decided that it was now time to make arrangements for an operation to remove his cataracts. Charlotte and Emily went to Manchester to find a suitable surgeon and were recommended to consult Mr William James Wilson. He was a highly skilled oculist, and an honorary surgeon at the Machester Royal Infirmary, with a private practice at his consulting rooms at 72 Mosley Street. He had helped to found the Manchester Institution for curing the Diseases of the Eye in 1814. Mr Wilson told Charlotte that he could not say whether an operation was possible until he had examined Patrick's eyes. As Charlotte told Ellen on 9 August 1846:

> In a fortnight I hope to go with papa to Manchester to have his eyes couched – Emily and I made a pilgrimage there a week ago to search out an operator and we found one in the person of a Mr Wilson – He could not tell from description whether the eyes were ready for an operation – Papa must therefore necessarily take a journey to Manchester to consult him – if he judges the cataract ripe – we shall remain – if on the contrary he thinks it not yet sufficiently hardened we shall have to return – and papa must remain in darkness a little while longer.

On Wednesday 19 August Charlotte and Patrick made the journey to Manchester. Two days later Charlotte wrote to Ellen:

> Papa and I came here on Wednesday, we saw Mr Wilson the Oculist the same day; he pronounced papa's eyes quite ready for an operation and has fixed next Monday for the performance of it – Think of us on that day dear Nell.

Charlotte and Patrick stayed the first night in a hotel, but the next day they moved into lodgings recommended by Mr Wilson at 83 Mount Pleasant, Boundary Street, off Oxford Road, where they remained for the next month. Charlotte was anxious about the housekeeping. As she told Ellen:

> We got into our lodgings yesterday – I think we shall be comfortable, at least our rooms are very good, but there is no Mistress of the house (she is very ill and gone out into the

country) and I am somewhat puzzled in managing about provisions – we board ourselves
– I find myself excessively ignorant – I cannot tell what the deuce to order in the way of
meat – etc.

I wish you or your sister Anne could give me some hints about how to manage – For
ourselves I could contrive – papa's diet is so very simple – but there will be a nurse coming
in a day or two – and I am afraid of not having things good enough for her – Papa requires
nothing you know but plain beef & mutton, tea and bread and butter but a nurse will
probably expect to live much better – give me some hints if you can.[19]

The operation was performed by Mr Wilson and two other surgeons on Monday
24 August 1846 in Mr Wilson's consulting rooms. It was carried out without any
anaesthetic and the surgeons were impressed by the sixty-nine-year-old Patrick's
great fortitude. Charlotte reported to Ellen on the next day:

The operation is over – it took place yesterday – Mr Wilson performed it, two other
surgeons assisted – Mr Wilson says he considered it quite successful but papa cannot
yet see anything – The affair lasted precisely a quarter of an hour – it was not the simple
operation of couching Mr Carr described but the more complicated one of extracting
the cataract. ...
Papa displayed extraordinary patience and firmness – the surgeons seemed surprised.
I was in the room all the time, as it was his wish that I should be there – of course I
neither spoke nor moved till the thing was done – and then I felt that the less I said
either to papa or the surgeons, the better – papa is now confined to his bed in a dark
room and is not to be stirred for four days – he is to speak and to be spoken to as little
as possible.

Patrick himself took a great interest in the proceedings and later made notes under the
heading 'Cataract' in the margin of his copy of Graham's *Modern Domestic Medicine*:

In Augt 1846 – Mr Wilson, Surgeon, 72 Mosley St. Manchester, operated for cataract on
one of my eyes – the left one. He informed me ... that, generally, they do not operate on
both eyes – for fear of inflammation, which would destroy the sight. Belladonna a virulent
poison, prepared from the deadly nightshade, was first applied, twice, in order to expand the
pupil – this occasioned very acute pains for only about five seconds – The feeling, under the
operation – which lasted fifiteen minutes, was of a burning nature – but not intolerable – as
I have read is generally the case, in surgical operations. My lens was extracted so that cataract
can never return in that eye.

He also described the great care that was taken to avoid inflammation:

> I was confined on my back a month in a <u>dark</u> <u>room</u>, with bandages over my eyes for the greater part
> of the time and had a careful nurse, to attend me both night and day – I was bled with 8 leeches, at
> one time, and 6, in another, (these caused little pain) in order to prevent inflammation.[20]

Although Mr Wilson considered that the operation had been entirely successful, Patrick's progress was slow. When his bandages were removed five days after the operation, Charlotte reported to Ellen that he could see dimly, although 'Mr Wilson seemed perfectly satisfied and said all was right'. Two weeks later on 13 September she wrote:

> Papa thinks his own progress rather slow but the Doctor affirms he is getting on extremely well
> – he complains of extreme weakness and soreness in the eye but I suppose that is to be expected for
> some time to come – he is still kept in the dark – but he now sits up the greatest part of the day.

Writing to Ellen again on 22 September she said that Patrick continued to do well and that the nurse was being dispensed with that day.

On 29 September Charlotte was able to bring Patrick back to Haworth. After returning home his sight continued to improve and he was delighted with the result. By the middle of November he was sufficiently recovered for Mr Nicholls to take a well-earned holiday. During his three-week absence in Ireland Patrick was able to take all three Sunday services and most of the baptisms and funerals which occurred. In the following January he noted that:

> Through Divine Mercy, and the skill of the Surgeon, as well as my dear Charlotte's attention,
> and the assiduity of the nurse – after a year of blindness – I was so far restored in sight, as to
> be able to read, and write, and find my way, without a guide.

He also stated that Mr Wilson had only charged him £10 instead of his normal fee of £20 or £30 and that all his other expenses in Manchester amounted to nearly £50.

It was not only the recovery of his eyesight which made the stay in Manchester significant. During the five weeks that they spent there Charlotte had received yet another rejection slip for her novel, *The Professor*. Although suffering from raging toothache which kept her awake at night, she was spurred into action and she spent most of those dreary days writing the first draft of a new novel, *Jane Eyre*.

In December that year the weather at Haworth, which had been unusually mild, became bitter. All the Brontë family caught severe colds. Anne's developed into bad attacks of asthma and Patrick's into influenza. It was also a time of great hardship amongst the people of Haworth. There had been depression of trade and low wages all year and yet the price of bread and potatoes was unusually high. In August the powerloom workers and wool-combers had come out in strike, but demand was so low that the manufacturers were able to hold out for over three months. It was probably

with reference to this, the most serious strike during Patrick's time in Haworth, that
Mrs Gaskell stated in her *Life of Charlotte Brontë* that Patrick gave his support to the
workers:

> Mr Brontë thought that they had been unjustly and unfairly treated, and he assisted them
> by all the means in his power to 'keep the wolf from their doors,' and avoid the incubus of
> debt. Several of the more influential inhabitants of Haworth and the neighbourhood were
> mill-owners; they remonstrated pretty sharply with him, but he believed his conduct was
> right, and persevered in it.[21]

It is clear that his determination to do what seemed right was as strong as it had ever
been.

PART THREE

A Varied Ministry

'Employment ... full of real, indescribable pleasure'

When released from his clerical avocations, the Author was occupied in writing the Cottage Poems; from morning till noon, and from noon till night, his employment was full of real, indescribable pleasure such as he could wish to taste as long as life lasts.

Patrick Brontë in the Advertisement to Cottage Poems, *1811*

Patrick Brontë was the first member of his family to appear in print. As a young curate he had seen his vicars publish their writings in an effort to extend the range of their evangelistic ministry. While he was in Wellington the sermon preached to celebrate the naval victory at Trafalgar by his vicar John Eyrton had been published by a local bookseller. John Buckworth had regularly published collections of his sermons in Dewsbury and on Patrick's departure to Hartshead he had presented him with his latest volume.

It was in 1810 while he was a curate at Dewsbury that Patrick's first piece of writing was published. This was a poem entitled *Winter Evening Thoughts*. It seems to have been inspired by a Day of National Humiliation for the war against France which was held on 28 February 1810. The poem was published anonymously, but Patrick sent a copy to his friend John Nunn with the inscription:

To my dear Friend Nunn, with my unfeigned love, and Christian regards. P Brontè.
By P. Brontè. B.A.[1]

It had the subtitle 'A Miscellaneous Poem' and covered a variety of issues, including a description of the sufferings of the poor, the tale of an innocent girl seduced in her youth and reduced to prostitution, and an account of a ship lost at sea in a winter storm. The poem included patriotic references to the war against France and its overriding message was that sin was the root of all the problems affecting the country and its people.

After moving to Hartshead Patrick embarked on a more ambitious project. In 1811 he published a collection of twelve poems under the title *Cottage Poems*.[2] In the advertisement which preceded the work he wrote:

Cottage Poems … is chiefly designed for the lower classes of society. … For the convenience of the unlearned and poor, the Author has not written much, and has endeavoured not to burthen his subjects with matter, and much as he well could, has aimed at simplicity, plainness, and perspicuity, both in manner and style.

He also expressed the philosophy underlying his writing:

The Author has had recourse, for assistance, only to that Book of Books, the Bible, in which the wisest may learn that they know nothing, and fools may be made wise; and in which the divine, the philosopher, and the poet, may find a richer magazine, than in the best productions of Greece and Rome. … Some, in reading this work may be ready to say, that it is too religious, others, that it is not religious enough. In answer to both these characters, the Author would just observe, that he has written not only for the good of the pious, but for the good of those who are not so. … It is generally difficult, and sometimes impossible, in the same thing to please both. The great Apostle, says, "I am made all things to all men, that I might by all means save some:" and may not the Author, acting from the same good motive, endeavour to walk in the same steps?

Bearing in mind the later literary achievements of his family, it is revealing to note the great pleasure which Patrick took in his writing:

When released from his clerical avocations, he was occupied in writing the Cottage Poems; from morning till noon, and from noon till night, his employment was full of real, indescribable pleasure, such as he could wish to taste as long as life lasts.

The collection begins with a poem dedicated to the Rev'd John Buckworth, 'whilst journeying for the recovery of his health'. Although the tone is tendentious and the imagery is highly affected, there is no doubting the great affection with which Patrick regarded his former vicar. Another poem is addressed to the Rev'd John Gilpin, the rector of Wrockwardine, in which Patrick praises 'his improved edition of the Pilgrim's Progress'. This would seem to demonstrate Patrick's continuing loyalty to his former friend rather than his literary judgment, for in the words of the local antiquarian J. Horsfall Turner, Mr Gilpin's work 'met with the failure it deserved'.

In 'Verses sent to a Lady on her Birth-day' Patrick adopted a sombre tone and, rather than celebrating the joy of the day, he seems keen to remind her of the inevitability of her death:

But, hark, fair maid! Whate'er they say,
You're but a breathing mass of clay,
    Fast ripening for the grave.
    …

Attend with care, to what I sing;
Know, time is ever on the wing,
  None, can its flight detain;
Then like a pilgrim, passing by,
Take home this hint, as time does fly,
  "All earthly things are vain."

Five poems extol the virtues of the humble poor. 'The Cottage Maid' describes a girl who lives with her mother in a little cottage:

Aloft, on the brow of a mountain,
And, hard by a clear running fountain,
  In neat little cot,
  Content with her lot,
Retired, there lives a sweet maiden.

Her father is dead, and her brother –
And now she alone with her mother,
  Will spin on her wheel,
  And sew, knit and reel,
And cheerfully work for their living.

She is a model of restrained and simple living. She visits the sick, regularly studies the Bible, always wears plain dress and will have no truck with plays, dances and shows. When she meets a poor old woman carrying a baby who begs for aid she gave her 'her apron of blue, though handsome and new' and led them to her cottage to give them hospitality:

All peace, my dear maiden be thine
Your manner and looks are divine,
  On earth you shall rest,
  In heaven be blest,
And shine like an angel, for ever.

The 'Epistle to the Labouring Poor' is addressed to 'All you who turn the sturdy soil'. It adopts a similar theme, that the poor should be satisfied with their simple life and not be envious of the rich:

What, though you dwell in lowly cot,
And share, through life, a humble lot?
Some thousands, wealth and fame have got
     Yet know no rest:
They build, pull down, and scheme, and plot,
     And die unblest.

For those who give God his due place, a glorious future is in store:

But, all, who worship God aright,
In Christ, his Son and image bright;
With minds illumed by Gospel Light,
     Shall find the way,
That leads to bliss: and take their flight
     To heavenly day.

There, rich, and poor, and high, and low,
Nor sin, nor pain, nor sorrow know:
There, Christ with one eternal glow,
     Gives, life, and light,
There, streams of pleasure, ever flow,
     And pure delight.

The welcoming message of the gospel is clearly expressed:

Behold my hands, my feet, my side,
All crimsoned with the bloody tide!
For you, I wept, and bled, and died,
     And rose again:
And throned, at my Father's side,
     Now plead, amain!

Repent, and enter mercy's door,
And though you dwell in cots obscure,
All guilty, ragged, hungry, poor,
     I give in love,
A crown of gold, and pardon sure,
     To each above.

Although the poem is naïve in tone, there is no doubting the sincerity of the writer or his urgency in expressing the gospel message. The expressions may occasionally be trite and the picture of rustic simplicity depicted gives no hint of the poverty and misery soon to erupt in the violence of the Luddite riots. The gospel message conveyed, however, gives us a clearer impression of Patrick's evangelical fervour as a young clergyman than is to be found anywhere in his later writings.

The 'Epistle to a young Clergyman' illustrates the high ideals which Patrick had of his calling. It takes the form of advice to someone recently ordained:

> A graduate you've just been made,
> And lately passed the Mitred Head;
> I trust, by the Blest Spirit, led,
> > And Shepherd's care;
>
> …
>
> Divide the word of truth aright,
> Shew Jesus in a saving light,
> Proclaim to all, they're dead outright,
> > Till Grace restore them:

The young clergyman is also reminded that his conduct is as important as his preaching:

> Remember still to fear the Lord,
> To live, as well as preach, his word …
> Example only, can afford
> > To precept, power.

He should also be concerned about his appearance and ensure that he 'dress not slovenly nor gay'.

In 1813 Patrick published a second collection under the title *The Rural Minstrel*.[3] This contained eleven poems and is of a much higher standard than *Cottage Poems*. Two poems related to his own circumstances. The first was addressed to his wife Maria on her thirtieth birthday. It was written nine months after their marriage and reveals the depth of his love for her.[4] The second, entitled 'Kirkstall Abbey,' portrays the scene beside the ruins of the mediaeval Cistercian Abbey, on the banks of the River Aire near Leeds, when seen at night in the beautiful light of the moon:

> When Luna's lovely rays,
> Fall trembling on the night,

> And round the smiling landscape, throw,
> And on the ruined walls below,
>> Their mild uncertain light.

Patrick's affection for the place is clear to see:

> Who would be solemn, and not sad,
> Who would be cheerful, and not glad,
> Who would have all his heart's desire,
> And yet, feel all his soul on fire,
> To gain the realms of his eternal rest,
> Who would be happy, yet not truly blest,
> Who in the world, would yet forget his worldly care,
>> With hope fast anchored in the sands above,
>> And heart attuned by sacred love,
> Let him by moonlight pale, to this sweet scene repair.

His emotional fervour is easy to understand when one remembers that he and Maria had been there on several occasions in the previous year with family gatherings from Woodhouse Grove, and that it is thought that this was the spot where he had proposed to her.

A vigorous poem reflects on the onset of winter and on the plight of birds and also of the wandering traveller:

> See! How the winter's howling storms,
> Burst forth, in all their awful forms,
>> And hollow frightful sound!
> The frost is keen, the wind is high,
> The snow falls drifting from the sky,
>> Fast whitening all around.
>> ...

> In hops the redbreast, half afraid –
> Ah! Lend the little stranger aid,
>> Throw gently o'er the floor,
> With silent twitch, a fallen crumb;
> And lest grimalkin, prowling come, –
>> Close fast the dreaded door.
>> ...

May he, who clothes the lilies fair,
And feeds the wandering birds of air, –
    Relieve their great distress !
Haste ye, who lie on beds of down,
With bounteous hand, their table crown,
    And make their sorrow less.

    ...

I think upon the storming wave,
Which, thundering, opes a watery grave,
    For the faint, shivering crew:
And ye that wander in the air,
Through drifting snows, ye know not where,
    I grieving, think on you.

The collection is brought to a fitting conclusion by 'The Harper of Erin.' In a lively and effective poem Patrick imagines an aged harpist perched on a rock high above Lake Killarney, singing not of the glories of Ireland and the beauty of the lake below, but in praise of God for the wonders of his redemption:

An ancient harper, skilled in rustic lore;
When summer hailed the mild departing spring;
High on a rock, on sweet Killarney's shore,
With flying fingers, touched the tuneful string.
    A wildly sentimental grace,
Each feature marked, of his expressive face;
And whilst his fingers swept the mellow chords along,
In sweet accord, with his seraphic lyre,
His soul spoke through his eyes, its wild poetic fire;
    And thus he raised his song.
I shall not sing of Erin, beauteous isle,
Nor of her courteous sons, for valour famed,
Nor of Killarney, queen of lakes, –
Adorned with nature's sweetest smile,
And every grace that can be named, –
    To view whose charms,
    Insensibility herself awakes
Whilst soft sensation, her dull bosom warms,
I would, with soaring mind, to higher note aspire;
    Beyond the pole,

My glowing soul,
Would catch a spark, of pure seraphic fire,
Where flows a Fount of life, through the divine abode, –
I'd sing the praise of my Redeeming God.

O, for a seraph's tongue!
And harp immortal strung,
And sweetly tuned, by Gabriel's hand,
For highest themes divine!
O, for a choral seraph-band,
To join their aid to mine!
But, even then, our notes would feeble prove;
And in their greatest flight,
Could never reach the height
Of his due praise;
The Ancient of eternal days
And God of love.

He died! He died! The King of glory died!
To rescue from his heavenly Father's ire,
A guilty world, just sinking in eternal fire.
I see! I see the fatal wood,
Stained with his pure atoning blood!
Whilst looks benign,
Beam from his face divine,
On the relentless band, by whom that face was marred,
Repent ye murderous crew,
There's mercy e'en for you.

In 1815, soon after arriving in Thornton, Patrick submitted a short story to *The Pastoral Visitor*, a magazine run by his friend William Morgan. It was written in the first person and recounted the conversion of a sinner. It was printed in three instalments of the magazine from July to October. Later that year, Patrick published another short story, this time accompanied by four poems. It was entitled 'The Cottage in the Wood or the Art of becoming Rich and Happy.'[5] This tells the story of Mary, a poor young cottager, who was taught to read the Bible at Sunday school and then brought about the conversion of her parents through reading the scriptures to them at night. She received a small income from teaching in the Sunday school and went occasionally to a day school where she learned to write and acquired a competent knowledge of English grammar. When a wealthy drunken man, William Bower, asked her to be his mistress she indignantly refused. After her parents had died Mary worked as a servant for an old lady who on her death bequeathed her £4,000. William Bower, who had fallen into poverty through riotous living, was converted after a narrow escape from death when his two companions were shot by robbers. After becoming an assistant teacher in a large day school, he gave his services free to poor children in the Sunday school. Here he met Mary when she came to distribute prizes and they were married. The couple subsequently lived a long and happy life together rejoicing in their shared Christian faith. Patrick's story enjoyed considerable local success and received a highly favourable review from William Morgan in *The Pastoral Visitor*:

> This is a very amusing and instructive tale, written in a pure and plain style. Parents will learn in this little Book the Advantages of Sunday Schools, while their children will have an example well worthy of their closest imitation. Young women may here especially obtain a knowledge that the path of virtue leads to happiness. We would therefore most cordially recommend this Book to all sorts of Readers.

It was about this time that Patrick's wife Maria also wrote an article on conversion and education, under the title, 'The Advantages of Poverty, in Religious Concerns'. Although it is somewhat naïve in sentiment, this essay reveals the sincerity and piety of its author. The article does not seem to have been published, but it is important as the only extant piece of writing by Maria, apart from her letters to Patrick before they were married.[6]

In April 1818 *Blackwood's Magazine* announced the publication of Patrick's most ambitious and longest literary work, a short novel entitled *The Maid of Killarney, or Albion and Flora, a modern tale, in which are interwoven some cursory remarks on religion and politics.*[7] The story was divided into eleven chapters and covered sixty-eight pages. It was published by Baldwin, Cradock & Joy of Paternoster Row, London. Although the book appeared anonymously, many years later, Patrick acknowledged his authorship when, in April 1860, he signed a copy for a clerical friend. It tells the story of the wanderings in Ireland of a young Englishman named Albion.

Albion, accompanied by a friend, visits an Irish cabin where an old woman lies dying. He is greatly struck by seventeen-year-old Flora Loughlean, who has been tending the poor old lady. After attending the Irish wake which follows her death, Albion makes friends with Flora's father, Captain Loughlean, and is invited to their house, Loughlean Hall, for dinner. Here he meets Flora's uncle, Dr Laurence O'Leary, a lively and opinionated man. There is much discussion at the dinner table on many religious and political topics dear to Patrick's heart, including conversion, Roman Catholic Emancipation and the reform of the criminal justice system. Albion is impressed by the simple Christian faith of Flora and her father and is invited to stay at Loughlean Hall. During the night, Flora displays great bravery when there is an attack by bandits.

Albion then has to return to England to deal with the affairs of his late father. Among his father's effects he finds a letter addressed to him in which his father urges him to become a Christian. Albion is greatly moved by this and, after consultation with the local vicar, he is converted. Two months later he returns to Ireland, where Flora accepts his proposal of marriage.

Captain Loughlean gives them his blessing and his final remarks surely reflect the realistic and practical advice which Patrick was in the habit of giving to marriage couples in the weddings which he conducted:

> Now, my children, in two months hence, through Divine permission, you shall be married; and I hope your lot will be as good as can be expected, in this uncertain and sinful world. But do not look forward to an uninterrupted flow of happiness. This is not the portion of mortals on this side eternity. Make up your minds for some difficulties, that when they come, you may rather meet them as the common lot, than struggle under them with impatience. When the young fancy is warm, it sees nothing but a gay prospect before it. But sage experience removes the delusion, and teaches more moderate expectations. Let me advise you both, then, whether in prosperous or adverse circumstances, to be fully resigned to the Divine will, constantly preserving a tranquil equanimity. Let each look upon the other as the best earthly friend. And be not blind to faults on either side, but cover them with a mantle of charity. Either never let your minds be ruffled at all, or be not angry at the same instant, let not the sun go down on your wrath. Differ but seldom in your opinions; but if at any time you cannot agree, the law of God and nature requires, that the husband shall bear the rule. And above all things, my children, remember that you have immortal souls; encourage each other in the great work of laying up treasure for them in heaven.

The Maid of Killarney was Patrick's last attempt to write a connected story. In the following years, however, he did write several pamphlets, sermons and letters to the press. His writings are uneven and clearly not of great literary merit. At their best, however, they do convey considerable emotion, and they also provide explicit statements of the Christian faith to which he devoted his life. The most important aspect of his literary activity is that his children grew up knowing their father to be a published writer and could see the results of his work on the shelves of the parsonage. Who can say what influence that had in shaping the young minds of Charlotte, Emily and Anne?

'An advocate for temperate reform'

It appears, that some, whose opinions, I highly value, greatly misunderstand my motives, in being an advocate for temperate reform, both in church and state.

Patrick Brontë to Mrs Franks, 28 April 1831

Patrick always considered it to be part of his role as a clergyman to make a public contribution to discussions of the major issues of the day. In this way he sought to exert an influence well beyond the borders of his parish. His letters to the local newspapers, and especially to the Tory *Leeds Intelligencer* and the Whig *Leeds Mercury*, constitute an important element of this wider ministry. Despite a tendency to verbosity on occasions, he usually had the knack of penetrating to the heart of the subject under discussion. His letters covered a wide variety of issues and were cogently expressed. Several were related to the religious controversies of his day; others dealt with general concerns.

Throughout his clerical career Patrick was a firm believer in the necessity for the continuing establishment of the Church of England, which during his ministry at Haworth seemed to its supporters to be under constant threat. The attack came mainly from two directions: from Roman Catholics pressing for the removal of their civil disabilities and from Dissenters objecting to the privileged position of the established Church, and especially the legal requirement that they should pay rates for the upkeep of their local parish church.

By 1829 the demand for the removal of many of the restraints on Roman Catholics was rapidly gaining momentum. From the time of the Reformation their civil liberties had been severely restricted and, although their position had been somewhat alleviated towards the end of the eighteenth century, they were still subject to many disabilities. They had the right to vote if they were qualified to do so, but they could not stand for Parliament or hold important civil, judicial or administrative offices under the Crown. Having been brought up in Ireland, where the Roman Catholic Church was in a majority, Patrick Brontë had always been a fervent critic of its beliefs and practices. In January 1829, however, he wrote two letters to the *Leeds Intelligencer* showing that, although he had not lost his dislike of Roman Catholicism itself, he had come to feel that some concessions were due. The repeal of the Test and Corporation Acts in 1828 had formally given to nonconformists their civil rights (although in practice they had enjoyed these some time earlier) and Patrick now considered that Roman Catholics should be treated in a similar way, provided that the Protestant establishment was adequately secured.

In his first letter, which appeared on 15 January, Patrick urged a rational and unprejudiced consideration of the question:

> Sir,
>
> You must have perceived, as well as myself, that the writers on both sides of the Catholic question, have, in many instances, been powerfully swayed by prejudice, party spirit, selfishness, or personal resentment, and have diverged into opposite and dangerous extremes. … There are those who would have us to believe, that no danger would result from admitting Roman Catholics into power, without any securities whatsoever; and there are those, who maintain, that under the wisest and best securities, the most terrible consequences would follow. … After duly weighing these things the question evidently is, whether it is best to endeavour to maintain, at all hazards, the Protestant ground which we now occupy, or under certain securities to raise the Roman Catholic part of our community to our own level in political power and consequence: taking it at the same time for granted, that the Act of Settlement shall for ever continue in force, and that the Sovereign must, of consequence, necessarily be a Protestant.

Patrick's support for limited Catholic emancipation in a Tory newspaper was so unusual that the editor attached a footnote, defending him from the charge of having subversive intentions or of being a Radical:

> This much is due, from us to Mr Brontë to declare – that, whatever his speculative opinions, he has, to our knowledge, been always at his post, as a practical supporter of Church and State.

Patrick returned to the question of securities two weeks later. His second letter reveals a clear sense of realism and a willingness to reach some compromise:

> You have rightly informed your readers, that I have always been at my post, as a practical supporter of Church and State. … No one can be more thoroughly convinced than I am, of the necessity of maintaining the Protestant ascendancy. … Yet, after all, it is absolutely necessary to take various other considerations into our account, if it be our object to see what had best be done, under all the circumstances of the case. What we might *wish* to have done, and what is *really practicable*, may be very different things, and I fear, most of us will find them so, in the

instance before us. ... The question of *securities*, is what chiefly ought to occupy Protestants of all denominations, at the present [cr]itical juncture. We can have no just reasons for excluding Roman Catholics from power, if it would be safe to admit them. The Act of Settlement precludes, and must for ever preclude them from the Throne; nor could it ever be right to admit a Roman Catholic to the office of Lord-Lieutenant in Ireland, or Lord Chancellor in England, as those who fill these places of trust and power, immediately represent his Majesty, and are in intimate connexion with our Protestant Establishment. But could no securities be devised that would render it safe to admit a number of Roman Catholics into Parliament, and other responsible situations? ... Let every member of society, who has the welfare of his country at heart, weigh these things well in an unprejudiced mind. ... It may be, that they will find themselves reduced to the necessity of choosing one out of two evils. In such a case, they will not hesitate in preferring the less of these. And would not this be, cautiously to open the door of British privileges to Roman Catholics, under adequate securities?[1]

Patrick's liberal stance on this matter brought him into conflict with some of his evangelical colleagues. His friend and former fellow curate at Wellington, William Morgan, wrote to the same issue of the paper roundly criticising the arguments which Patrick had made in his first letter. Three months later, however, on 13 April 1829, the Government led by the Duke of Wellington, with Robert Peel as Home Secretary, secured the passing of the Roman Catholic Relief Bill, giving Roman Catholics the right to sit in Parliament, and making them eligible for all military, civil and corporate offices except those of Regent, Lord Chancellor of England and Lord-Lieutenant of Ireland. The news was received with great excitement at the parsonage, where Patrick had clearly imbued his family with a consuming interest in the debate.[2]

Some of Patrick's concerns were not purely ecclesiastical. State provision for the poor had been the duty of the parish since the time of Elizabeth I and took the form of outdoor relief given to those in need, enabling them to remain in their homes. The necessary funds were raised from the poor rate which was a charge on every parish. By the early nineteenth century, this system had become very costly and in 1834 the Poor Law Amendment Act was passed. This sought to reform the system under which local relief was administered by the parish and to reduce the amount of money which had to be paid. Under the terms of the Act unions of several parishes were created, supervised by elected boards of guardians. Outdoor relief in the parish was abolished and all who needed assistance, through old age, infirmity or unemployment, were obliged to reside in union workhouses. Conditions in these workhouses were made deliberately harsh in an effort to deter the poor from 'going on the parish'. Families were split up, with separate provision being made for men, women and children, and the able-bodied were required to work for their keep, usually by hard labour.

In common with many other clergymen in the country, Patrick strongly opposed the provisions of this Act. Although some of his colleagues were influenced by the fear of losing the local influence they had enjoyed under the previous system, most of them, like Patrick, were appalled by the harsh conditions introduced by the new regime. By 1837 the provisions of the Act were beginning to take effect in Yorkshire. In February that year Patrick called a meeting of the inhabitants of Haworth in the Sunday school with the aim of drawing up a petition to Parliament for the repeal of the Act. So many people turned up for the meeting that it had to be adjourned outside into the open air. Patrick chaired the meeting and, along with several other speakers, addressed the crowds. He reminded them that they had not met for any party political purposes, but 'to plead the cause of the poor', and he urged the people of Lancashire and Yorkshire to oppose the Act. The petition was carried unanimously and was sent to one of the Yorkshire M.P.s and also to the Archbishop of Canterbury. The meeting attracted considerable publicity and *The Times* carried a full report of the speeches and of the resolutions which had been made.[3]

Two months later, on 22 April 1837, Patrick wrote to the *Leeds Intelligencer* on the subject. His letter appeared under an uncompromising heading:

Liberty or Bondage

To the Labourers, Mechanics, and Paupers or Slaves of England

My dear friends ... I would take the liberty of addressing you a few words of advice, in this most important crisis of our affairs. All who know me, are fully aware, that I am a conscientious Conservative, but at the same time, a genuine reformer, and that I regard not men but measures. ... A law has lately been passed called the Poor Law Amendment Bill – a greater misnomer I never read or heard. It is a monster of iniquity, a horrid and cruel deformity. I know that a committee is sitting to *amend* the bill – but let me tell you, my dear friends, that it *cannot be amended; it must be repealed altogether.*

After recounting an anecdote of a shopkeeper who forced any customer requiring change to take it out of one of the large bags of spurious coins which he kept on his counter, he continued:

The whole poor law amendment bill is an assemblage of base metals, therefore resolutely reject it as such, and be not deceived. ... We are told in the five books of Moses that *the poor shall never cease from the land,* and are exhorted to *open our hands wide to relieve them.* ... But a set of unfeeling, antiscriptural men, have lately arisen ... who ... teach doctrines in direct opposition to the *law* and to the *gospel.*

He then urged his readers to oppose the Act by any legal means possible:

What, then, my friends are we to do under these circumstances? Why, verily, I see no plan better for us than that adopted by the Apostles, namely *to obey God, rather than man.* We will *not* therefore submit to go to their *bastilles. We will not live* on their water gruel, and on their two ounces of cheese, and their fourteen ounces of bread per day. We will not suffer ourselves to be chained by their three *tyrannical commissioners*; *and we will never endure* the idea, of men, rolling in affluence and luxury, prescribing to us the most extreme line which can keep body and soul together. We have religion, reason, justice and humanity, on our side, and by these we are determined to stand or fall. ... Then let me request you to do *your duty* – petition, remonstrate, and resist powerfully but *legally*, and God, the father and friend of the poor, will crown all your efforts with success.

I remain your sincere Friend,

P. Bronte.

Patrick was also firmly opposed to the widespread use of capital punishment, which as late as 1830 was the stated penalty for 220 offences. In his tale *The Maid of Killarney*, published in 1818 while he was still at Thornton, Patrick put into the mouth of one of his characters (Dr O'Leary) a strong condemnation of the present situation:

> Consider, moreover, the inadequacy of punishment. A man will be hanged for stealing a fat sheep, though he be hungry; – he will incur no greater punishment for murdering twenty men! In the name of common sense, what is the necessary tendency of this? Most undoubtedly, the man who robs, will find it his interest to murder also, for by so doing, he will be more likely to prevent discovery, and will, at all events, incur no greater punishment. It has always been a sorrowful reflection to me, when I have heard of robbers being hanged on the evidence of the person robbed, that in all probability they came to their melancholy end, through that little remains of conscience, and tenderness of heart, which they still possessed, and which prevented them, even at their own peril, from imbruing their hands in their fellow creatures' blood.[4]

He repeated these arguments eleven years later in a letter published in the *Leeds Mercury* on 10 January 1829, in which he offered support for the paper's campaign for a liberalisation of the criminal code and argued that the indiscriminate use of capital punishment was itself an inducement for a greater crime:

> If a man steals a sheep, or breaks into a dwelling house burglariously, and is detected and prosecuted, he will be hanged. If, at the same time, he murders the owners, he will only be hanged. Now, it often happens, that the owners are the very persons who bring him to trial and punishment; unless, therefore, he has some conscience or feeling of humanity left, he will take away their life, in order the more effectually to secure his own.

He returned to this theme in the same paper on 14 November that year:

> A long series of crimes, scarcely resembling each other in magnitude, are all visited by death! – This appalling state of things often prevents the humane from prosecuting,

propels transgressors to the commission of murder, as affording them a greater chance of secrecy and escape, and hardens the feelings of the multitude. … Where man's blood has been malignantly shed, an unrepealed law of God requires that the blood of man should be shed in return, but, nearly in all other cases whatsoever, fine, imprisonment, and hard labour, duly moderated as to durance and degree, would … answer the ends of justice infinitely better. People of all descriptions would under such circumstances be more ready to prosecute; transgressors would be more sparing of the lives of others, in order more effectually to secure their own; and by a judicious regulation of our gaols, many criminals, such as are now taken off by a violent death in the midst of their sins, would have time given them for repentance and amendment, and through divine mercy, ultimately become useful members of society.

Patrick's words have a curiously modern ring to them and would surely meet with the approval of many present day advocates of penal reform.

In 1830 he promoted a petition to both Houses of Parliament seeking a revision and mitigation of the criminal code. As he told readers of the *Leeds Intelligencer* on 6 May:

All the dissenting and Methodist ministers in the parish gave their consent and assistance with a cheerful alacrity that did credit alike to their piety, good sense, and humanity: and out of a population of more than four thousand, not one objected to – but all approved of, those measures of mercy and justice which we had in contemplation.

He also noted that:

The Quakers, with their characteristic humanity and wisdom, have exerted and are now exerting themselves, infinitely to their credit, in order to induce our legislators to amend and mitigate our criminal code. And it is much to be lamented that all other denominations do not act in a similar manner.

Patrick's efforts and those of others urging the reform of the criminal code were not in vain. By 1837 the number of capital offences had been reduced to fifteen and in 1861 capital punishment was only retained for the crimes of murder, treason, piracy with violence and setting fire to Her Majesty's vessels, dockyards and arsenals.

Patrick also wrote on the subject of duelling. In a duel fought at Camden Town on 1 July 1843 Colonel David Fawcett was killed by Lieutenant Alexander Munro. This incident attracted considerable attention and details of the duel appeared in the *Leeds Intelligencer* of 2 September. In the same issue of the paper a letter from Patrick appeared, condemning the practice. It was written in his usual forthright and uncompromising style:

In a duel, two worthless fellows place themselves in opposition to each other, owing to some worthless cause – and all this they do with loaded pistols, which in a moment may send one or both of them to eternity – and perhaps, as has often been the case, leave a mourning widow, and fatherless children, in the greatest depths of distress. Horrid practice – and most horrid result. And yet the most religious, civilized, and powerful nation in the world, connives at this!

Patrick proposed a simple and effective solution to the problem:

What then is the simple and efficient remedy? Why, simply to pass a law that would make it transportation for life to give, or accept a challenge. This, like the decree of Frederick the Great, that all duellists should fight under a gallows, and that the survivor, or survivors should be immediately hanged, would put an end to the delusive and damning sin for ever. Nothing less than this will answer the end. And it would be the best kind of punishment, since the weak, wicked, and reckless class of duellists are not at all fitted for immediately appearing before the bar of God, and not worth a rope at the public expense. Till we shall have got entirely rid of this bloody and abominable practice of duelling, we shall not have freed ourselves from a state of barbarism.

Throughout his life Patrick took a deep interest in the subject of health and his copy of *Modern Domestic Medicine* by Dr Thomas Graham, published in 1826, is extensively annotated, recording his own medical experiences and those of his family. In January 1841 he wrote to the *Leeds Intelligencer* supporting the medicinal use of brandy and salt:

It appears to me that every genuine Minister of the Gospel should … venture occasionally to recommend to his poor hearers especially, some proper medicinal measures for the body as well as for the soul; and of all the safe and salutary medicines I know of, after much reading and observation, I am fully of opinion that Brandy and Salt, used according to Mr Lee's directions, deserves the preference. It can seldom or never do harm, and will generally do much good.

And, as a precaution, he added:

Should any timid, over-scrupulous person imagine that this might lead to habits of intemperance, let him consider that such a melancholy result could never take place except where there was a previous bias, and that even where such a bias existed, the nauseous taste of the mixture I speak of would be far more likely to give a disrelish than an inclination for intoxicating liquors.[5]

His opinion on the efficacy of brandy and salt was shared by other clergy. Mr Andrews, the vicar of Ketteringham in Norfolk, is recorded to have given it to a woman patient and Benjamin Philpot, the incumbent of Little Cressingham and Bodney in Suffolk, regularly made use of it, commenting:

> Brandy and salt was much given in those days and I used it a great deal.

Patrick also took an informed interest in new developments in medicine. In June 1847 he wrote to the *Leeds Mercury* criticising those who opposed the newly emerging practice of using sulphuric ether to deaden pain in operations:

> Notwithstanding the vapour of ether has been administered with great success by some of the ablest surgeons in this or any other age or country – notwithstanding, as the necessary result of this, human suffering has been greatly diminished – notwithstanding as great a proportion of patients after the operation, have lived and done as well as if the old torturing plan had been acted upon, and notwithstanding every friend to humanity ought to cry "all hail" to such a messenger of good tidings … not a few begin to raise objections, to start theories, and use arguments far-fetched and sophistical, and to deduce imaginary consequences of a doleful nature. What a maze of difficulties they would plunge us into by the changes they tell us which take place, all changes of a fearful nature of course; in the heart, the lungs, the brain, and the blood. … Resting and arguing from these data, many surgeons, in towns and villages, go on as usual, screwing out teeth, amputating limbs, and using the scalpel as freely as they do the carving knife. The patients, who through ignorance or indifference allow them to do so, cannot fairly claim much of our sympathy. Having read both sides of the question, and judging from the opinion of some of the most learned, able and humane of the faculty, it appears to me to be evident, that as it regards the inhalation of the vapour of ether, a great, a useful, and important discovery has been made, and one that ought to be patronized by every friend to humanity.[6]

In addition to writing to the papers Patrick also made his views known in other ways. Through the tireless efforts of William Wilberforce and his associates, the slave trade had been abolished by Parliament in February 1807, but the practice of slavery still continued to operate in the British dominions. In April 1830, in common with many other evangelical clergymen all over the country, Patrick organised petitions to be sent to both Houses of Parliament urging that slavery itself should be abolished. Their efforts were crowned with success three years later when, in 1833, an act was passed freeing all slaves from 1 August 1834, subject to an interim apprenticeship of not more than six years.

In 1831 Patrick risked alienating many of his Tory friends by expressing his support for the attempts by the Whigs in Parliament to introduce a Reform Bill, which would disenfranchise the rotten boroughs, give the vote to some of the new towns which had grown up since the Industrial Revolution and halve the property qualifications for registering as a voter. Unlike most of his evangelical colleagues and despite the opposition of his hero, the Duke of Wellington, Patrick was convinced that a limited amount of reform was necessary.

His support for the Whig government's first Reform Bill of March 1831 caused some of his old friends openly to express their criticism. On 28 April he wrote to Elizabeth Franks[7] to explain his position:

It appears, that some, whose opinions, I highly value, greatly misunderstand my motives, in being an advocate for temperate reform, both in church and state. I am, in all respects, now, what I was, when I lived in Thornton – in regard to all political considerations. A warmer, or truer friend to church, and state, does not breathe the vital air. But, after many years, mature deliberation, I am fully convinced, that, unless, the real friends of our Excellent Institutions, come forward, and advocate the cause of Temperate reform – The inveterate enemies – will avail themselves of the opportunity, which this circumstance would give them, and will work on the popular feeling – already but too much excited – so as to cause, in all probability, general insurrectionary movements, and bring about a revolution – We see, what has lately been done in France – We know, that the Duke of Wellington's declaration, against reform, was the principal cause, of the removal, of him, & the other Ministers from power – And there is now, another instance before our eyes, of the impolicy of this perverseness. The Anti-reformers, have imprudently thrown the Ministers into a Minority, and consequently Parliament is dissolved by the King in person, and in all probability another Parliament will soon be returned, which may be less particular than the other, and perhaps go too far in the way of reformation – Both, then, because I think moderate, or temperate reform, is wanted – and that this would satisfy all wise & reasonable people, and weaken the hands of our real enemies, & preserve the church and state from ruin – I am an advocate for the Bill, which has just been thrown out of Parliament.

He went on to defend the independent line which he was taking:

It is with me merely an affair of conscience and judgment, and sooner than violate the dictates of either of these, I would run the hazards of poverty, imprisonment, and death. My friends – or some of them, at least – may differ from me, as to the line of conduct which ought to be followed – but our motives, and our good wishes, towards, Church, and State, are the same.

Patrick's liberal attitude towards such matters clearly caused tension between him and some of his Tory friends. A few years later he seems to have received a patronising letter from Dr John Outhwaite, whose sister Frances had been a close friend of the Brontë family during their time at Thornton. She had been at school with Elizabeth Franks and was one of Anne Brontë's godmothers. Whatever Dr Outhwaite had said in his letter it clearly rankled with Patrick. In reply he wrote a dignified, forceful and succinct rejoinder, in which he revealed his independence of mind and his refusal to be browbeaten by his friends:

> Sir,
>
> I thank You for Your Laconic Letter – I will try to abide by your – prescription for in good sooth, I have much need of patience, especially, when under affliction, such as may arise from Old Age and Old Friends. – But that God to whom you refer, will judge You and [me], on the day of Doom, when we shall be more on a Level than we now are – You have in times past done me |and mine| good for which I shall ever be thankful, whatever <your conduct now is> you now do, or may do, in time to come –[8]

The Brontë family seem to have taken a keen and informed interest in the political manoeuvring in London in late 1834 and throughout 1835. In Emily and Anne's Diary Paper of 24 November 1834 they recorded that:

> This morning Branwell went down to Mr Drivers and brought news that Sir Robert peel was going to be invited to stand for Leeds.[9]

During that month the King dismissed the Whig ministry led by Melbourne and imposed a Tory minority government under Sir Robert Peel. In the ensuing election Peel failed to command a majority in the Commons but, despite suffering several defeats, remained in office with a programme of reform until finally resigning on 8 April 1835. Feelings had been running high in the country and, at the beginning of April 1835, Haworth, along with many other towns in the West Riding of Yorkshire, sent an address to Sir Robert Peel, supporting his minority government. Patrick was the first to sign this document, which he may well have drafted, as it bears all the hallmarks of his style.

> SIR – With glowing and unfeigned delight we hail all your measures of Reform, and witness the glorious struggle which you and your colleagues, in conjunction with our gracious Sovereign, are making at the present eventful crisis, in order to stem the factious torrent which assails you, and which threatens to overwhelm the best institutions of our country: in the name and on behalf of the numerous Friends to Church and State in our chapelry, we entreat you *not* to resign your high office, but to *persevere* even to the *dissolution* of Parliament, if necessary, being fully convinced, as we are, that by such an event you would find a great accession of true and loyal hearts to support you from every quarter of the United Kingdom.

When this address was printed in the *Leeds Intelligencer* of 11 April 1835 it caused a great furore in Haworth. Of the 124 registered voters there, ninety-six were supporters of the two Whig candidates in the forthcoming election. This meant that there were only twenty-eight voters, led by the vicar and the churchwardens, who supported Sir Robert Peel and wished him to continue in office, and yet this address had been presented to Peel in the name of all the voters in Haworth. A Whig supporter, John Foster, wrote to the *Leeds Mercury* on 18 April roundly denouncing the document as not representing the views of the Haworth voters.

Shortly after the election Patrick wrote a pamphlet entitled 'The Signs of the Times,' which bore the subtitle 'A Familiar Treatise on some Political Indications in the Year 1835'.[10] This document set out his political beliefs in a measured and restrained style. The majority of the contents were aimed at defending the established Church. Patrick argued that the state had a moral duty to lay down a system of religious instruction for its people. Although the Church of England was best suited to be the Church supported by the state, there should be full liberty of conscience and all religions should be tolerated. He conceded that the Church of England was not perfect, but argued that what was required was reform not destruction. Church rates, in their present form, should be abolished and tithes should be fairly commuted. The Church of England should be financed on a fairer system which did not impose on Dissenters.

He ended his argument by objecting to the party violence which had been prevalent during the election. In a heart-felt personal statement he expressed his belief that truth would prevail:

> If there be one privilege greater than another, in all our charter of liberty, it is that which consists in full permission to write and speak our sentiments with propriety and decorum. Take but this privilege away, under any name or pretence, and you sap and undermine the foundation, and ruin the very fabric of our freedom. No cause is good that will not admit of discussion; and no number of men can long benefit any undertaking by force and violence, especially in England. If men will not hear, it is because they dare not: and vociferation, and missiles, and brute force, are but poor substitutes for argument and liberality and justice. I would therefore say to all who are friendly to our Church and State, whatever others may do, take care that you act uprightly, and with courage, wisdom, and vigour. Where the laws are broken, let the laws be enforced: and be mild and just, but firm and persevering. Try to convince rather by reasoning than by violence: always taking the Scriptures for your rule of faith and practice; common sense and common decency will guide you, – your good conduct will go far towards recommending your good cause; – God will approve, – man will be convinced, – and the wicked will be intimidated and abashed, and you will finally prevail.

This statement would seem to be not a bad yardstick by which to judge Patrick Brontë's political philosophy and his own personal integrity. It would seem to encapsulate the civilised values which are vital to any nation state.

'I never was friendly to Church Rates'

I never was friendly to Church Rates in their present form. I always earnestly desired, and often advocated the commutation of Tithes and Church Rates, in order to prevent that disagreeable collision, that must otherwise take place between the clergyman and his differing brethren.

Patrick Brontë to the Editors of the Leeds Mercury, *5 November 1836*

The repeal of the Test and Corporation Acts in 1828, and the passing of the Roman Catholic Relief Act in 1829, had given Dissenters and Roman Catholics the right to enjoy full civil liberties and to hold public office in the state. Encouraged by this success, Dissenters now directed their opposition against the compulsory payment of church rates by all parishioners, regardless of their religious affiliation. Church rates were levied to pay for the necessary expenses of the church; its lighting and heating, the provision of communion wine and robes for the minister and his clerk, the salary of the parish clerk and the sexton, and the payment of the bellringers and singers. They also paid for the maintenance and repair of the church building and the surrounding churchyard. The legal background to the payment of church rates was slightly ambiguous. The payment of a rate proposed by the churchwardens and approved at a vestry meeting could be enforced by law. If the meeting refused to levy a rate, the only sanctions that could be applied were ecclesiastical, which obviously would have no effect on those who did not attend the parish church.

Until the start of the nineteenth century there had been little opposition to these payments, which were regarded as a legitimate charge on the parish. By the 1830s, however, this tax had come to be greatly resented by Dissenters, who argued that they should not be required to pay money for the upkeep of a parish church which they did not attend. They also pointed out that they had their own place of worship to maintain, and that they did so out of their own voluntary contributions. Their resolute campaign aroused feelings of great concern in the minds of many churchmen, who feared that the establishment of the Church of England was under serious threat.

This dissension was a very serious matter at Haworth, which was a poor parish and contained a large number of Dissenters. Members of the Church of England were in a minority in the township, only comprising about a quarter of the worshippers,[1] and the situation was not helped by the fact that several of the Church Lands Trustees were themselves Dissenters. When Patrick had arrived in Haworth his evangelical background had led him to establish good relations with both the Methodists and the Baptists. From the appointment of the Rev'd John Winterbotham as minister of West Lane Baptist chapel in 1831, however, there was a marked deterioration in Patrick's relations with Dissenters. Mr Winterbotham's hard line over co-operation with the Church of England was supported by the Revd Moses Saunders, the minister of Hall Green Baptist chapel at Haworth.

Patrick decided to meet this growing challenge from Dissenters head-on. At the beginning of 1834 he wrote to the *Leeds Intelligencer* and the *Leeds Mercury*, defending the establishment of the Church of England and attacking the proposals of the Dissenters to remove bishops from the House of Lords, to abolish tithes and other church dues and to open the universities of Oxford and Cambridge to non-Anglicans. In an effort to concentrate on the issues involved and to avoid upsetting the large number of Dissenters in Haworth, he signed his letter of 18 January 1834 to the *Intelligencer* merely by his initials. But his attempt to avoid local controversy was in vain. The following week's issue of the *Mercury* carried a furious rebuttal by the Revd John Winterbotham, who also wrote to the paper again at the beginning of February.[2]

As the arguments continued they became more bitter in tone. Patrick could not resist a sarcastic rejoinder to Mr Winterbotham's demand that the universities be opened to all:

> Amongst many things he would obtain, he wants the three universities to be widely opened. Now I would seriously ask him, what good this opening would do to him? He seems not to be aware that, however the universities might be opened, it would be requisite, that before anyone entered them, he should have at least a competent knowledge of Greek and Latin. When he went therefore to procure admission, the inexorable examiner would put Homer and Horace into his hands, and just then and there, alas! would for ever terminate the university peregrination of the Revd John Winterbotham.

Mr Winterbotham responded to this attack by stating that the recent repairs and redecoration of Haworth church had been paid for out of the church rates to which Dissenters as well as Anglicans had been required to contribute.

In 1835 matters in Haworth came to a climax. At the annual vestry meeting to fix the parish rate held on 22 September, the Dissenters vehemently opposed the imposition of a church rate. They were led by James Greenwood, the owner of Bridgehouse Mills, Haworth. He was a Baptist and, as a result of a family dispute, he had a serious grudge against his brother, Joseph Greenwood, the chairman of the Haworth trustees and a loyal churchman.[3] James Greenwood pointed out to the meeting that the churchwardens still had a surplus of £10 from the previous year and he secured the passing of a motion that the laying of a church rate should be deferred until the following year. The churchwardens' case was not helped by the disclosure that the items under sundry expenses included 'a bottle of wine here and another there, when the churchwardens had their meetings'. As a result of the passing of this motion no payments of a church rate could legally be required. Patrick was seriously alarmed by the outcome of the meeting. He had never encountered such a situation before and he became convinced that the establishment of the Church of England was directly under threat. He was also left in a very difficult situation. The £10 which the wardens had in reserve was totally inadequate to meet the expenses of the church.

Patrick was anxious, however, not to get involved in a dispute with his parishioners, and in September 1836 he permitted a meeting to be held in the church which had been advertised as:

> an opportunity of stating in vestry assembled whether they did really consider it right for one sect to tax all others to support its own religion.[4]

Patrick did not take the chair himself and he also appears not to have played any part in the discussion. Despite a strong defence by George Taylor, one of the churchwardens, it was again decided, by an almost unanimous vote, to defer the laying of a rate to September of the following year. In order to avoid any confrontation Patrick forbade his churchwardens to make any attempt to raise a rate.

On 5 November he wrote to the *Leeds Mercury*, giving a clear statement of his views on the subject:

> I never was friendly to Church Rates in their present form. I always earnestly desired, and often advocated the commutation of Tithes and Church Rates, in order to prevent that disagreeable collision, that must otherwise take place between the clergyman and his differing brethren. But why a reasonable commutation of Church Rates, as long as the church and church yard are to be considered a kind of public property, should be considered a *grievance*, is, I must confess, to me an entire mystery. Vestry meetings, are often held for the convenience of all denominations. The Dissenters have even church pews, which they let. Notices of a public nature are given out in the church, a clock is often kept in the church tower, and bells rung for the convenience of the *whole* parish. The Dissenters have burial places, both in the church and church yard; and these must be guarded by walls, that must be kept in repairs, by regular contributions.
>
> On what ground then of reason or of justice can those who derive benefit from an estate be exempted from the necessity of keeping it in repairs. ... Dissenters may support their

religion, and ought exclusively to do so, because none but themselves, have anything to do with it. It is however far different with respect to churches and church yards, with which, in general, all the parishioners are immediately concerned, and from which they derive more or less of benefit, and must continue to do so till there is something equivalent to a revolution. ... But times, some people say, are changed. ... I believe that ... *persons* only are changed. I am moreover of the opinion, that the laws of true religion and morality are unchanged and unchangeable. ... We may turn our political or religious code as we turn our coat, but "Jesus Christ is the same, yesterday, to-day, and for ever."

Despite his moderate stance, however, the *Leeds Mercury* carried an editorial in the same issue of the paper, critically examining Patrick's arguments and concluding:

We wish no other than that the Church Rates question should be settled in the very principle indicated by Mr Brontë, namely that the Dissenters should just pay towards the expenses of the church "as far as they have anything to do with it," but no further. Let the estimate be made liberally; we will not begrudge a single farthing of the allowance. But when Dissenters are taxed for the expenses of maintaining divine service in the church and of maintaining the edifice itself which they never enter but once or twice a year, we say that the reverend gentleman's argument plainly and fully exonerates them; for as to these things, they have "nothing to do with them."

Sensing that the argument was now going against him, Patrick gave up the attempt to lay a church rate and in December he opened a voluntary subscription to raise the money necessary to cover church expenses. His moderate stance was in marked contrast with that adopted by the Revd William Busfield, the rector of Keighley. When the annual church meeting refused to fix a rate, Mr Busfield is said to have ordered the church clock to be stopped so that Dissenters should be deprived of its services.

The moderation which Patrick displayed in public is all the more notable for the bitterness which he felt in private over the concession he had been forced to make. He believed that the established position of the Church of England was an important bulwark of the state and he strongly resented any attempt to erode it. In a letter to the Secretary of the National Society on 4 August, 1843, written at a time when he was negotiating with that body over the opening of the National School at Haworth, he revealed the strength of his feelings over the predicament in which he had been placed:

We have not been able to lay on a legal Church rate for these three years. We have consequently been compell'd to succumb to the degrading Anti church Mode of a voluntary contribution. For Some time, Our Church Clock was at a stand, and our bellringers, engaged only in ringing their peals elsewhere, on account of their having no remuneration. We can hardly get our surplices kept decently clean, for want of money – and our Sexton and Clerk, are deprived of one third their wonted and proper emoluments.

It is ironical to notice that in Haworth, as in Keighley, the church clock had been stopped, but this was through lack of money for its repair rather than a desire to deprive Dissenters of its benefit.

On 27 February 1837, accompanied by his curate William Hodgson and by his son Branwell, Patrick went to a meeting which had been arranged at Hall Green Baptist chapel with the aim of drawing up a petition to Parliament for the total abolition of church rates. The hostile *Bradford Observer* (which was campaigning for the abolition of church rates) reported that Patrick and his two companions had come:

with the intention of disturbing the harmony of the meeting, but finding themselves unsupported they prudently contented themselves with holding up their hands against the resolution.[5]

Their action caused great amusement because they were the only ones in the meeting to vote against the motion. According to the *Bradford Observer*, Patrick's reaction to the decision to send an anti-church rate to Parliament in the name of the people of Haworth was one of great anger:

The church parson and his curate have been in a dreadful state of excitement ever since. On last Sabbath morning one of them commenced a fierce attack upon all Dissenters; and in the afternoon both of those meek-spirited clergymen let loose a whole volley of vulgar abuse, in a double lecture in the church, to the great consternation of the congregation.[6]

Relations with Dissenters continued to deteriorate and in April 1838 the annual attempt to raise a rate in Haworth failed yet again.

The situation in Haworth was further complicated by the fact that, as a daughter church of Bradford, the parishioners were required to pay an additional rate to the church there. In the summer of 1838 several people in Haworth, including James Greenwood, were prosecuted for failure to pay that portion which went to Bradford, where a legal rate had been successfully raised. This tense situation clearly put Patrick under great strain. On 17 January 1839, the death occurred of the Revd Henry Heap, who had been vicar of Bradford for the past twenty-two years. In October the Revd Dr William Scoresby was appointed as his successor. His first vestry meeting was attended by many Dissenters. They were led by the Haworth Baptist minister, John Winterbotham, and they were successful in voting down the motion for a Bradford church rate.

The dispute continued unabated and on 26 March 1840 there was a meeting in the school-room at which Patrick took the chair, supported by his curate, Mr Weightman, and Mr Collins, the curate of Keighley. Charlotte told Ellen that it was 'most stormy' and that Patrick had great difficulty in controlling the Irish Mr Collins, but managed to keep him quiet, 'partly by persuasion, and partly by compulsion'. The meeting refused to fix a church rate, but agreement was reached that, since the churchwardens had already incurred expenses of £21, collections in church might be used to pay off their debts. Charlotte also described the two sermons on Dissent and its consequences, which had been preached on the previous Sunday, by Mr Weightman, and Mr Collins:

> All the Dissenters were invited to come and hear and they actually shut up their chapels and came in a body; of course the church was crowded. Miss Celia Amelia [Weightman][7] delivered a noble, eloquent high-Church, Apostolical succession discourse – in which he banged the dissenters most fearlessly and unflinchingly – I had thought they had got enough for one while, but it was nothing to the dose that was thrust down their throats in the evening – a keener, cleverer, bolder and more heart-stirring harangue I never heard than that which Mr Collins delivered from Haworth Pulpit last Sunday Evening – he did not rant, he did not cant he did not whine, he did not snivel, he just got up and spoke with the boldness of a man who is impressed with the truth of what he is saying who has no fear of his enemies and no dread of consequences – his sermon lasted an hour yet I was sorry when it was done.[8]

The winter of 1840/1841 was a difficult time in Haworth, with considerable unemployment and great poverty. On 1 January the vicar of Bradford called a meeting of all the clergymen in his daughter parishes. Fearing further confrontation, Patrick brought with him a petition signed by 160 of his parishioners acknowledging the vicar's right to the dues from Haworth but asking for his forbearance:

> In consequence of the hard times & want of sufficient employment, we pray the Vicar to take our case into his kind consideration & if he pleases to remit, for this year what is due from us, we conscientiously declaring that we are at present unable to pay the same.[9]

The Dissenters also made the current distress of the poor a reason to redouble their efforts to oppose the granting of a church rate in Bradford.

The legal issue over the payment of church rates by all those living in the parish had been further complicated by a recent decision in the law courts which had received considerable national publicity. At Braintree in Essex one of the churchwardens had claimed that there was a legal precedent for a minority of parishioners to make a legal rate even if the majority rejected it. The case was brought before the Queen's Bench Division and on 1 May 1840 Lord Denman had made a ruling that no churchwarden had the power to make a rate without the consent of the parish. Although this ruling had been upheld in the Exchequer Court on 8 February 1841, when giving his judgement the Lord Chief Justice, Lord Tindal, had suggested that, if the churchwardens had made the rate at the vestry meeting which had rejected it, instead of separately from the meeting, it was possible that it would have been valid.[10]

Lord Tindal's suggestion had the effect of leaving the matter undecided. On 13 March 1841 Patrick wrote to the *Leeds Intelligencer*. He began by commenting on the recent legal decision in the Braintree case:

> Church-rates have long been the a subject of dispute, and in reference to them, there have been legal proceedings which have occupied a good deal of public interest. ... The somewhat equivocal decision of a Court superior to that of Lord Denman's had given an advantage to Churchmen, inasmuch as it holds out a *hope* that if *another protracted* course of litigation should take place ... the issue of the case, would, in all probability, be *otherwise*.

He went on to say that few clergymen and churchwardens would wish to enter upon 'a contest of this nature', and he argued that the law should be changed so that no ambiguity remained. He then attacked the Dissenters for their hidden agenda of wanting to destroy the Establishment of the Church of England and urged that the dispute about church rates:

> should be *set at rest* by well defined laws, which in their execution, would admit of but little or no grounds for litigation. Any law that brings or that would bring, the clergyman and his differing parishioners into annual collision, would be detrimental and wrong; and any law which would have a contrary effect, would be so far right.

Two months later, on 13 May 1841, Patrick returned to the subject again, this time in a letter to the *Bradford Observer*, in which he made it clear that he opposed the present method of raising Church Rates:

> I do not, and never did like, the present mode of laying on Church-rates. It gives rise to annual irritation, and raises those bad passions which had better be left dormant. ... Some commutation such as that proposed by Lord Althorp, would, in my humble opinion, be a good plan, the very best, I should imagine, that could be suggested.

He then came out in open opposition to the system whereby daughter churches were required to pay a rate for the upkeep of the mother church, as Haworth had to do for Bradford. This was a brave thing to do, since it brought him into direct collision with his vicar, Dr Scoresby:

> It appears to me, that when a new church is built in a large parish, and has ... a district assigned to it, there should be absolute independency there – so that, in no one instance, the parishioners should be answerable for any rate, but that which should be requisite for

the repairs of their own church. As for the laying on of two or three rates annually on any one district, to keep in repairs churches, it has nothing to do with; this is unreasonable and preposterous, and if there be laws which require it, they should, for the general good, be altered and amended, as soon as possible.

He went on to point out that church rates had been paid from time immemorial and that there had been very little opposition to them until 'about eight or ten years last past'. He attacked those who said they could not pay them because to do so would violate 'the dictates of conscience':

Our forefathers paid the Church rates without ever dreaming that they violated the dictates of conscience by so doing. But lately a new light I fear, has broken in upon us; our consciences have all at once become morbidly sensitive, and some of us have gone, and are quite ready to go to prison, and to suffer martyrdom, rather than pay eightpence of a Church rate! ... I myself am a warm advocate for liberty of conscience, but, at the same time, I am strongly opposed to an abuse of the term, and cannot help thinking that it has often been abused by the opponents of Church-rates. ... These conscientious men say, that because they do not approve of the Church Establishment they will give nothing to support it.

He declared his support for the principle that all parishioners, regardless of their personal religious allegiance, should be required to make payments in support of their parish church. He referred to the example of Christ, who performed a miracle 'rather than leave Caesar without his dues' and to the divine injunctions given in scripture: 'Obey magistrates'; 'Owe no man anything – pay to all their dues'; 'tribute to whom tribute is due'. He concluded by giving an account of a conversation he had recently had on this subject with one of his own parishioners:

Not long since, I met with a man who objected to the payment of Church-rates, under the plea that to do so would violate the dictates of his conscience. Well knowing his circumstances, I said to him, 'James, do you pay your rents without any such religious scruple?' 'Yes,' said he, 'I do, and why not?' 'Do you know,' I observed, 'that part of these rents go towards keeping beer shops, and part, I fear, towards upholding a gambling house?' 'Yes,' he observed, with rather a downcast countenance, conjecturing, as I suppose, what I was after. 'Well,' I remarked, 'how can you conscientiously do this; do you really think, that even, according to your way of thinking, Church-rates would go to so bad a purpose?' He only observed – 'I have been wrong, but I trust that, by Divine grace, I shall be right for the future, and that no one shall ever mislead me any more by false arguments.' He went home and I heard no more of his opposition to Church-rates. Had it not been for this providential interference, he might, for ought I know, have been numbered with Mr Thurogood, and Mr Baines, and others, amongst the Church-rate martyrs of the day.

The 'Mr Thurogood and Mr Baines' mentioned by Patrick in his conclusion were well-known examples of Dissenters who had refused to pay their church rates because of the dictates of their conscience. John Thorogood (Patrick had not spelt his name correctly) was a Quaker who in September 1838 had been summoned to appear before the Consistory Court of the Diocese of London for not paying his church rate of 5s 6d (27½p). He said that he had refused to pay because he did not believe it was right to pay a compulsory rate for religion. When he failed to appear before the court he was committed to Chelmsford jail for contempt. Since he refused to purge his contempt he remained in prison. Great embarrassment nationally was felt about this case and in July 1840 a special act of Parliament was passed, enabling a judge to release a prisoner for contempt if he had been in custody for six months and his debt and costs were paid.[11]

William Baines was a prosperous shopkeeper in Leicester who in November 1840 had also ignored a summons to appear before the ecclesiastical court over non-payment of the rate and had been committed to jail for contempt of court. Baines was a popular figure in Leicester and he was elected a town councillor while he was still in prison. He was eventually released in June 1841 under the same act which had secured Thorogood's release. The churchwarden at Braintree, a solicitor named Mr Augustus Veley, who had brought the original case which had led to the Lord Chief Justice's intervention, continued with his legal action for another thirteen years, until the House of Lords ruled against him on 12 August 1853. By that time, his case had been heard in four different courts by twenty-six different judges.[12]

A few days after Patrick's letter appeared, the Baptist minister, John Winterbotham, went to a church rates meeting in Bradford, at which he denounced the vicar and churchwardens for:

> the awful fact that they oppress and rob the poor of Haworth to furnish the Lord's Table at Bradford.[13]

Dr Scoresby's response was to obtain a legal requisition from the ecclesiastical court demanding the payment of £76-12-10 (£76.64) in church rates due to Bradford, and threatening imprisonment for failure to pay. This placed an impossible burden on the people of Haworth, many of whom were dependent on charity relief. In July Patrick called a church rate meeting, making it clear from the start that its purpose was not to lay a rate but merely 'to consider a demand' from the churchwardens of Bradford. He then called on the sexton and constable of the chapelry formally to propose the rate, and immediately invited John Winterbotham to speak. Mr Winterbotham's motion, that no church rate for the parish of Bradford should be granted, was carried. Patrick then thanked all those present and, according to the *Halifax Guardian*, 'the meeting separated with good temper and cordiality'.[14]

In January 1842 the Bradford churchwardens again presented their demands for a rate of £76-12-10. This time, Patrick felt so strongly that he roundly denounced them for their action at this time of great hardship. The *Bradford Observer* for 13 January 1842 gave a full report of the vestry meeting which Patrick chaired. At the outset he declared that:

> The rate now demanded, had not, according to his opinion, the sanction of either law or custom, having been laid in quite an unusual way, contrary to the vote and voice of a great majority of the rate payers. ... He entreated the body of the ratepayers then before him to consider the dilemma in which the chapelwardens of Haworth were placed, by having such a heavy demand pressed upon them at this time when even the poor's rate could only with the greatest difficulty be obtained and hoped that all parties, both Whigs, Radicals, Tories, Dissenters, Methodists, and Churchmen would unite heartily to save them from the jeopardy and peril to which they are exposed by the strange and unprecedented proceedings of the Bradford churchwardens. The Rev. gentleman then told the people that his mind was quite made up never more to attempt a compulsory Church Rate either for Bradford or Haworth so long as the law stood as it does.

Direct confrontation with Bradford was avoided by a vote to adjourn the discussion to a future date. A proposal of the Dissenters that any legal costs incurred by the churchwardens of Haworth in opposing the Bradford demands should be met by the vestry was agreed.

Three weeks later, in a letter to the *Bradford Observer* of 3 February 1842, Patrick returned to the subject and set out his views for the last time in public:

> What I chiefly find fault with is the present mode of collecting church rates, and the undefined state of the law respecting them. I have ever considered the circumstance of annually collision in this matter a serious evil. ... Were I to be asked how the evil was to be remedied, I should answer, by Lord Althorp's proposed measures, till you can find a better.

In April 1834 the Whig Chancellor of the Exchequer, Lord Althorp, had proposed that church rates should be abolished and that the repair of churches should be made a charge on the Treasury, but no further action had been taken due to the fall of the Whig government a few months later. Patrick went on to give a clear statement of his own position:

> With respect to the legality of churchwardens being able, in conjunction with the minority, to tax the parishioners, that remains to be tried, and till it is tried, or the parliament make a new and defined law on the subject of church rates, I am not disposed to proceed, except by a majority, or if that cannot be got, by voluntary contribution.

He then attacked the actions of the Bradford churchwardens:

> Against the Bradford churchwardens, as gentlemen and Christians, I would say nothing. They appear, however, to me to have acted precipitately, and with respect to the inhabitants of Haworth, strictly, if not severely. What we wished here was, that they would first try the cause for the township of Bradford. If they succeed there, no opposition, or but little at any rate, would then be made elsewhere; and if they failed, they would then deem it prudent handsomely to retire.

Patrick concluded by attacking the system under which the people of Haworth had to pay dues to Bradford as well as to their own church:

> The mainspring of all this may be … traced to the anomalous circumstance of having a parish within a parish. … Let any candid observer look only at our case. First, we are called upon to pay a disproportionally large share of church rates to Bradford, and then, before we have had time to breathe, to raise a rate to keep our own venerable and ancient church from crumbling to pieces!! Can any true Christian look with complacency on this state of things? I think not.

In May the churchwardens of Bradford applied to the court of the Queen's Bench for a writ against the Haworth churchwardens for refusing to pay the church rate. After long deliberation the judges decided that they could not issue a writ and the case was dropped. Two months later John Winterbotham, who had orchestrated much of the opposition to raising a rate, retired from his ministry in Haworth to take up a post at a Baptist chapel in Upper Canada. The ship in which he sailed bore the appropriate name of *Nemesis*, for, as he reported to the *Bradford Observer* in October, it ran aground off New York.[15] It was not until 1868, seven years after Patrick's death, that the system of compulsory church rates was abolished.

'My aim has been ... to preach Christ'

Through divine grace my aim has been, and I trust, always will be, to preach Christ and not myself and I have been more desirous of being made the instrument of benefit rather than pleasure to my own congregation.

Patrick Brontë to Stephen Taylor, 21 July 1819

Patrick always considered preaching to be the most important of his clerical duties and he continued to perform this function virtually to the end of his life. He persisted in doing this even in 1846, when cataracts had made him virtually blind and he had to be led to the pulpit. In old age, despite suffering from persistent bronchial attacks, he regularly preached once each Sunday, usually at the afternoon service, and as late as December 1858 at the age of eighty-one he was able to claim to his brother Hugh:

I am yet able to preach once or twice on the Sundays, and to do some duty besides.

It was a feature of his preaching on almost all occasions to speak extempore.[1] This habit went back to his earliest days as a clergyman. When in 1806 he paid a return visit to Ireland shortly after his ordination as deacon and was invited to preach in Drumballyroney Church, according to his sister Alice:

He preached a gran' sermon, and never had anything in his han' the whole time.[2]

In his sermons Patrick seems to have concentrated on expounding the scriptures in terms which were accessible to the humblest of his listeners. Ellen Nussey later wrote an account of her first visit to Haworth in 1833 and her impressions of worshipping in Haworth church:

The people assembled, but it was apparently to <u>listen</u>. Any part beyond that was quite out of their reckoning. All through the prayers, a stolid look of apathy was fixed on the generality of their faces. There they sat, or leaned, in their pews; some few, perhaps, were resting, after a long walk over the moors. The children, many of them in clogs (or sabots), pattered in from the school after service had commenced, and pattered out again before the sermon. The sexton, with a long staff, continually walked round in the aisles, 'knobbing' sleepers when he dare, shaking his head at and threatening unruly children; but when the sermon began there was a change. Attitudes took the listening forms, eyes were turned on the preacher. It was curious, now, to note the expression. A rustic, untaught intelligence, gleamed in their faces; in some, a daring, doubting, questioning look, as if they would like to offer some defiant objection. Mr Brontë always addressed his hearers in extempore style. Very often he selected a parable from one of the Gospels, which he explained in the simplest manner – sometimes going over his own words and explaining them also, so as to be perfectly intelligible to the lowest comprehension.[3]

Ellen Nussey's account is supported by a later description of Patrick's preaching given by Abraham Holroyd of Bradford, who came to Haworth on a Sunday in the summer of 1853:

Mr Brontë came in from the vestry. Having given out his text, he delivered an extempore sermon, devoid of all oratorical display, and remarkable for studied simplicity. He spoke to his hearers of the hollowness of all earthly pleasures, the uncertainty and brevity of human life, and advised everyone to seek religion, and therein, he assured them, they would find 'that peace of God which passeth all understanding'.[4]

This impression is also borne out by the account of James Hoppin, a professor from Yale, who came to Haworth sometime around 1858. After being invited to call on Patrick at the parsonage, he heard him preach at the afternoon service:

In the afternoon I heard Mr Brontë preach from Job iii 17: 'There the wicked cease from troubling; and there the weary be at rest.' It was the simple extemporaneous talk of an aged pastor to his people, spoken without effort, in short, easy sentences, – and was drawn, it appeared to me, *right out of that old graveyard*, among whose stones his feet had walked, and his imagination had lived so long. In parts it was pathetic, especially where he alluded to the loss of children. He branched off upon the sorrows, convulsions, and troubles then in the world, and he seemed to long for wings like a dove to fly away from this changeful scene, and be at rest.[5]

Throughout his clerical career Patrick was well aware of the need to minister to the pastoral and practical needs of his parishioners. During the winter of 1825/1826 poverty was widespread in the West Riding of Yorkshire. Although his powers of action were limited, Patrick did what he could to assist in individual cases. In April 1826 he had the duty of appointing a new parish clerk after the death of the previous holder of the post, Stephen Paslow. Two candidates applied for the position, Joseph Redman and Joseph Whitehead, and Patrick decided to provide practical assistance to both of them. On 12 April he wrote to Mrs Taylor (the wife of Stephen Taylor, a churchwarden and one of the Haworth trustees) reporting on the action he had taken:

> Dear Madam,
>
> Thinking that Mr. Taylor might be from home, I write a few lines, to you, which I will thank you to show him, when he comes – After mature deliberation, I have acted according to my best Judgment and conscience – in reference to the Clerkship. The affair is now finally settled – The following is the copy of the agreement between the parties – I think I see Mr Taylor smile whilst he reads it – …
>
> "Owing to the hardness of the times, and very nearly the equality of merit, in Joseph Redman, And Joseph Whitehead, as Candidates, for the Clerkship of Haworth, I appoint them both till further notice from me, to officiate in the Parish aforesaid, as Clerks in alternate months as follows – Joseph Whitehead, shall officiate in the months of January – March – May – July – September – and November – And Joseph Redman – in the months of February – April – June – August- October – And December – And, each, shall receive, all the Clerks Dues, for himself, during the months, in Which he officiates – and each – when the other, is unable to take the Duty, shall act for him, and receive all the dues for the time being – and the Amount of the Collection, made at Easter, shall be equally divided between them both.[6]

By the following winter continuing poor trade and the collapse of a number of banks had led to a great increase in unemployment. In May 1827 a survey showed that out of 6,691 factory workers in Keighley, 4,524 were totally unemployed and the remainder were only working a three-day week. Patrick, as the chairman of the parish vestry meeting, was heavily involved in overseeing the raising and distribution of the poor rate and he was tireless in his efforts to relieve the distress of those out of work. His determination to relieve the distress of the poor of Haworth, even at the risk of alienating the local mill-owners, was noted by Mrs Gaskell in her *Life of Charlotte Brontë*.[7]

Patrick had always had a fear of fire and in his early days in Haworth he did not allow the use of curtains in the parsonage. In March 1844, in a letter which reflected his many years of pastoral experience and his deep concern for his younger and more vulnerable parishioners, he wrote to the *Leeds Mercury*, warning against the danger of fire caused by the nature of some children's clothing:

> You know … that all garments of linen and cotton, are peculiarly inflammable, and that clothes of woollen, or silk, are much less so, and cannot be ignited at all, without the most careless and wanton neglect. Hence it is evident that if women and children were, in general, or always, to have their garments of silk or wool, there would be little or no danger of their

losing their lives by accidental ignition. … I have been at Haworth for more than twenty years, and during that long interval of time, as far as I can remember, I have performed the funeral service over ninety or a hundred children, who were burnt to death in consequence of their clothes having taken fire, and on inquiry in every case I have found that the poor sufferers had been clothed in either cotton or linen. Believing this to be an important lesson, and by giving it to the world, in all its simplicity, I shall be amply gratified that I should be the means of saving only one life in this our state of probation.[8]

Mindful of how he had been assisted in fulfilling his own ambitions, Patrick was always anxious to help young people to develop themselves and make something of their lives. Benjamin Binns later recorded an occasion when, as a boy, he was sent to do some work at the parsonage. While he was in the study he became fascinated by the pictures on the wall. Patrick, noticing his interest, took him round the room explaining the various subjects which were depicted. These included several black-and-white engravings of dramatic biblical scenes by John Martin.[9] Patrick also showed a sympathetic understanding of human nature when in May 1844 he wrote to the secretary of the National Society in support of a young Haworth man who had applied to train as a teacher:

The young man James Feather, has started for London, with his Documents, duly signed – knowing him, as I well do, I think, he would be an acquisition to the Society. I am only afraid, that as he will very probably be abashed, the Examiner may not discover his intrinsic worth, whilst many of far less merit, might shew off, to greater advantage.[10]

In the summer of 1831, however, his attempt to help a local man met with failure. He had been asked by Mr Metcalfe, a Keighley schoolmaster, to recommend his brother Anthony as a candidate for ordination. Although Anthony Metcalfe was an educated man, he was not a university graduate. Nevertheless, Patrick wrote to the Archbishop of York supporting his application to be ordained. The archbishop replied, however, that he was unwilling to vary his rule of not ordaining any non-graduate who was over thirty years of age.[11]

The writing of references and testimonials was a frequent requirement of a clergyman and Patrick was conscientious in performing this task. Several examples survive from the last years of his life. On 22 June 1850 he wrote to the secretary of the Society for the Propagation of the Gospel in support of an application by the Rev'd W. R. Thomas to work as a teacher overseas:

Revd Sir,
    In reply to your letter of enquiry respecting the Revd. W.R. Thomas's qualifications, for the situation of an emigrant teacher, I would briefly but faithfully remark, that I have known him

for many years, And that from what I know of him, and what you want, I do not think that you could easily get another, who would suit your purpose better – or so well – He is steady, judicious, pious, and consequently moral, & would I am sure, be most ardently devoted to his avocation, he is active and persevering, and a warm climate would far better suit him than a cold one. ... He has, as far as I know, been hitherto, under independent circumstances, and cannot, I imagine, be under any pecuniary embarrassment, nor do I think, that he is a character, that would, ever likely to be so.

In July 1859 he wrote in support of Richard Greenwood, the eldest son of John Greenwood, the Haworth stationer who wished to practise as a dentist:

Richard Greenwood, the bearer hereof, is a young man, the son of respectable parents, and is a native of my chaperly [sic]; He is moral, and steady, and well qualified, for performing his duty, in the line of life he has chosen.[12]

In September that year, in conjunction with Arthur Nicholls and several leading local inhabitants, he signed a testimonial for Greenwood Dyson, a young man who wished to join the Keighley police force.[13] In a similar, undated, testimonial he recommended Joseph Holmes for employment as a 'Porter or Policeman on a Railway'.[14] Despite the weakness of old age and recurrent bouts of ill health Patrick continued this task almost to the end of his life. The last surviving document which he wrote, at the age of eighty-three on 20 October 1860, just eight months before his death, is a testimonial in support of the application of a local man, Squire Thornton, to be a Railway Porter.

The individual pastoral needs of his parishioners might take a variety of forms. On 1 August 1843 he wrote to William Thomas, a wine and spirit merchant at Haworth. William, like Patrick, had been required to give evidence in a case at York Assizes in the previous March, concerning a forged deed relating to a will.[15] He had been one of the executors of this will and was now contemplating taking the matter to court. Patrick wrote to dissuade him:

I would say to you, as an old neighbour and friend, settle, if you can your affairs with a certain personage, as soon as you possibly may do, without law. It would be far better to do this, at the loss of two or three hundred pounds, than to spend as many thousands, with the lawyers, and be nothing better. ... Send for this weak man, who has got into the snares of those who are cunning and designing, ... And endeavour to persuade him, to come to Scriptural and just terms.

Seven months later Patrick made a similar effort to support another man who had been affected by the York case. Enoch Thomas was the landlord of the King's Arms and one of the churchwardens at Haworth. He had been a witness to a second deed relating disowning the forged one, and he was now suffering from acute depression from his involvement in the affair. On 29 February 1844 Patrick wrote to George Taylor of Stanbury, also a churchwarden, with a novel suggestion for assisting Mr Thomas:

> I doubt not, you have heard of Mr. Enoch Thomas's, very severe and great affliction, one of the greatest that can fall to our human nature – In consequence of this, I requested him to come up here, this morning, and when he came, I gave him the most consolatory advice, within my power – But what can console a man, under his circumstances? – I am aware, that you have kindly sent for him, and given him good advice, but I wish you, to have a tea party, soon, and to invite him among, the number of the guests; His mind, which is, in a very disordered state should be diverted, as much as possible, from his present way of thinking – He is a good, well-meaning, and honest man; and, in many respects, unfit, for his present arduous, situation – yet still, his friends, ought to do for him, all that lies, within their power.

In July 1858 Patrick wrote to Dr McLaw of Ben Rhydding seeking to arrange a consultation for one of his parishioners who was a tailor:

> Greenwood Wood, of this parish, who has formerly been under your care, and been greatly benefited by it, is earnestly desirous of your advice and aid, and wishes to know, whether you have a vacancy for him – He is labouring under the sad effects of indigestion and is very reduced, and feeble – His employment, as a Tailor, being ill suited, to his condition.[16]

Occasionally it was his duty to convey bad news. When William Cannan died at Haworth on 18 October 1842 it fell to Patrick to inform his wife, Elizabeth. She was the daughter of James Greenwood, one of the Haworth trustees and the sister of Joseph Greenwood, the chairman. She had married William in 1818, but it seems that she was now separated from him and living at Clitheroe in Lancashire. Patrick's letter is significant for the sensitive and delicate way in which he broke the sad news:

> Happening to be at Mr Greenwood's of Spring Head … he has desired me to write to you on a solemn Occasion. Mr Cannan, surgeon, in this place has been rather unwell, for some weeks past, but for three or four days lately, he became very ill – and this morning at two O'Clock he died – His funeral, and its consequent expenses are now to be thought of – And therefore, as you stood in such close connexion with him, it was judged proper to acquaint you with the circumstance as soon as possible. I saw him a little before his death, and had some spiritual conversation with him, and After that went to prayer – in which he join'd with great earnestness – I trust you will be supported and comforted by the Lord.

Patrick's concern to promote the welfare of young people is clearly seen in the letter he wrote on 2 November 1855 to Eliza Brown, the younger sister of Martha Brown, the parsonage servant. Eliza was the third daughter of John Brown, the Haworth sexton. She had worked briefly at the parsonage in the previous June while Martha was unwell and away in Leeds and during that time she had been a witness to Patrick's will. After the death of her father in August, she had taken up a post in service to a family who lived near Edenbridge. In November, at Martha's request, Patrick wrote to Eliza, giving her the latest news of her family:

> Your mother and sisters are as well as could be reasonably expected under their trying circumstances. Martha's health is much better than formerly, and they are all very glad to hear from you, and wondered that you were so long in writing. They all think much about you, and feel truly desirous that you should do well, in regard to this world and that which is to come.

He went on to encourage her to be faithful in her new post:

> I am pleased to know, that you give a good account of those in whose service you are. I hope that they will continue to do their duty to you, and I am sure that you will do your duty to them, as an honest, and able, and faithful servant.

Eliza now had a boyfriend, James, and Patrick praised her for the way she and James were conducting their friendship:

> You both have acted very properly. You have done all things openly and wisely – which is ever the best way. As the times are hard, and likely to be so, during the winter you should be in no haste about marriage. You should not marry till you have a fair prospect of being able to live without debt and poverty. You are now very well off. You are not far from home. You are with decent people – and you can see, or hear from your relations frequently. ... All your relations will be glad to see you when you come home, and they all send their affectionate regards.

This friendly and encouraging letter must have brought considerable comfort to a lonely girl away from home so soon after her father's death. It bears the mark of a kindly, caring and experienced pastor.

Four years later, on 10 June 1859, Patrick wrote to Eliza again. It seems that she was now an unmarried mother and had left her little baby girl with her family in Haworth while she was living and working near Bingley:

> Eliza,
> This is a sorrowful world, and I write to you on a sorrowful subject. You have already been informed that little Jane was in the Scarlet fever; after some time, it was hoped she was recovering, and that the danger was past, However, She rather suddenly got worse, and worse, till at last she seem'd to sleep away, till she closed her eyes, on time, and open'd them

in eternity, I doubt not in an Eternity of glory and bliss. Thus she has made an exchange infinitely for the better.

It should be noted how gently and sensitively Patrick breaks the news of the little girl's death. He went on to give her some apposite advice for the future:

> This will, as it ought to do, give You trouble for a time, but on reflection, after a while, under all the circumstances of the case, You will perceive that for her, for You, And many others, it is a merciful dispensation. And that the best use You can make of it, is for yourself, to live the remainder of your days, a holy life, to be wise and good, avoiding temptation to evil, ... so that you may be prepared for death, come where, how, and when it will.

Then, as a kindly reassurance, he added:

> Every thing has been done for little Jane, that could be done. She has been duly attended to by Mr Ingham, Betty Lambert And your kind Mother and Tabitha; Martha also has Sometimes seen her – so that there is nothing to regret, left behing [*sic*] – You will of course come home, as soon as you conveniently can –

This letter reveals Patrick's skill in responding to the needs of a sad and troubled individual. It should also be noted that his account book shows that for the last few months of his life Eliza was again employed at the parsonage. And at Patrick's funeral, Eliza, along with her sister Martha, was described as a 'chief mourner'. It can surely be said of Patrick, as he himself had said of his curate, William Weightman:

> He thought it better, and more scriptural, to make the love of God, rather than the fear of hell, the ruling motive for obedience.[17]

16

'Our School has commenced'

Our School has commenced, under more favourable circumstances, than I, with my most sanguine notions, ever anticipated.

Patrick Brontë to the Rev'd W. J. Kennedy, 9 January 1844

From his childhood Patrick had been imbued with a passion for education. Despite being born in humble circumstances, his natural abilities and the complete dedication to his studies which he showed in early life had enabled him to gain a place at St John's College, Cambridge, and to be ordained into the Church of England. Throughout his clerical ministry, education continued to be a major interest. During his curacy at Dewsbury he took a leading role in the running of the Sunday school, giving religious instruction and also teaching the basic skills of reading and writing. At Thornton, despite competition from four large nonconformist schools, he laid great stress on the importance of the Sunday school. He introduced the new method of instruction recommended by the National Society and he persuaded his friend, Elizabeth Firth, and two other local ladies to assist in the teaching.

At Haworth progress was slow, but in 1831 he managed to persuade the trustees to release a small plot of land in Church Street for the building of a Sunday school. As late as 1843, however, there was no Church of England day school in Haworth. The National Society had been founded in 1811 and by 1833 7,000 schools had been either built or assisted by the society. The provision of a National school in Haworth would appear to be much delayed. There were, however, reasons for this. The people of Haworth were in general very poor, and a large proportion of the inhabitants were Dissenters, who were keen to organise their own schools.[1] Also, the adoption of a voluntary church rate in 1835 meant that money which might otherwise have been devoted to the cause of education had to be spent on parish maintenance.

In July 1843 Patrick added his name as a founder member of the Bradford Church Institution, which was set up to promote the building of Church of England schools in the area. On 22 July he wrote to the *Leeds Intelligencer* bitterly criticising the Dissenters for their part in causing the failure of a parliamentary bill aimed at providing manufacturing districts with a centralised education system. This had proposed that children should be educated in state schools, under the influence of the established Church. According to this scheme the schoolmaster would be required to be a member of the Church of England and the school was to be managed by seven trustees, amongst whom must be the clergyman and the two churchwardens. Dissenters had opposed the bill, fearing that it gave too much influence to the ministers of the Church of England.

A few weeks later Patrick received a circular from the secretary to the National Society, the Rev'd John Sinclair, urging the foundation of Church day schools in every parish. Patrick immediately sprang into action. On 4 August he wrote to Mr Sinclair, explaining the situation in Haworth:

> Revd. And Dear Sir,
>
>   I have just received Your circular, which is too important, to be pass'd over in Silence. I wish I could do Something more substantially beneficial, than merely writing, on the subject. … As a Minister of the gospel, I have resided in Yorkshire, above thirty years, and … from my reading, personal observation, and experience, I do not hesitate to say, that the populace in general, are either ignorant or wicked, and in most cases, where they have a little learning, it is either of a schismatical, vainly philosophical, or treacherously political nature. We have not been able to lay on a legal Church rate for these three years. We have consequently been compell'd to succumb to the degrading Anti Church Mode of a voluntary contribution. … One thing … I would mention. After a great deal of time and labour, we got erected a Church National Sunday School – And could any Good Institution in the United Kingdom, procure us a proper Master, with a Suitable Salary, to carry on a School, throughout the week it would be of especial benefit, to the Chapelry at large, and might, And under God, I doubt not, would extend its benefits much farther.

This letter marked the beginning of a remarkable correspondence between Patrick and the National Society, whose archives contain twenty-six letters written by Patrick between August 1843 and April 1845.[2] This correspondence reveals the unflagging energy of a sixty-six-year-old incumbent, determined to overcome all obstacles to the foundation of a day school in Haworth and to raise the funds necessary for its continued maintenance.

In response to Patrick's letter, Mr Sinclair sent him an application form for a grant from the society. On 12 August Patrick replied saying that he had sent the necessary documents to the bishop for his signature. He now felt confident that everything was in order for the foundation of a day school and in October he jauntily told an unidentified correspondent:

I have lately had communication with the Bishop, who has been very, and unusually kind, respecting getting a curate for Oxenhope. I am also in the way of procuring a daily teacher for the National Church Sunday School. The salaries in both cases will be paid by the London Institutes – So that if the Lord should spare my life a few years longer, our Church affairs will be put into a better condition than they were ever before.

On 9 October he wrote to Mr Sinclair thanking the National Society for the promise of a grant and saying that he had informed the bishop of his successful application. On 16 November he wrote again to arrange further practical details:

We hope it will not be long, ere our National Schoolmaster arrives – The Room, is sufficiently fitted up, to make a begin[in]g – but I thought it best, not to go far in this way – but to leave the Master who will best understand his own plans, to buy the greater part of the books, and furniture – when he comes – soon after he is appointed, it might be well – if he would write a few lines, before his arrival – informing what kind of Lodgings he would like, and what sum he would be disposed to pay for them – in order that, we may look out, and have them ready.

The receipt of this letter seems to have caused some confusion at the National Society over what had been promised to Haworth. During the intervening weeks since Patrick had last contacted the society, Mr Sinclair had been appointed an archdeacon and had been replaced as secretary by the Revd W. J. Kennedy. Mr Kennedy now wrote to Patrick querying the promise of a grant for Haworth. In great concern Patrick replied on 27 November:

Revd. & Dear Sir,
   I take the liberty of sending You a correct copy of Mr. Sinclair's letter – it is as follows
      "Octr 6th. 1843. –
   "Revd & Dear Sir,
   I have the pleasure to inform You, that the Committee agree to vote a grant of £50- towards the Salary of an efficient Master for one Year, the case to be reconsidered at the close of that period. They will allow £10- for a supply of Books and School materials. The Committee will not be able to send a Master before November. ...
                     Sign'd
                     J. Sinclair

After requesting the society to send a master of their own choosing and 'to be so kind as to pay all expenses', he continued:

We are so hard press'd at present, by Voluntary Subscriptions (as we can get no churchrates) that we cannot possibly do any thing more in a pecuniary way – The Dissenters are numerous, inveterate, and active – Whilst we are deliberating, And going through a long form of routine, they are coming at once to their work, And will with their Schoolmasters, get a long way before us. – This has greatly distress'd me, but I cannot help myself.

It is clear that there was still some confusion over the amount of salary which would have to be paid to a master and a week later Patrick contacted the society again. He was so upset over the misunderstanding that he wrongly addressed the Secretary as 'W.J.Kennedy Esqr.' He referred once more to the plans of the Dissenters to open their own schools and continued:

All this greatly distresses me – but what can I do? Having had a Churchrate refused, for Several Years, I am thrown upon voluntary subscriptions – … My Salary does not exceed, £160- Yearly, and I have a family to maintain – Had I any money to spare, I would freely give it. … £50- has been liberally granted by Your Honourable Committee, for the Maintenance of a Master, and £10- for proper furniture for the School – for all this I am duly thankful – Yet I must plead for more – for the requisite salary. It appears that we cannot have a Master from Westminster, under £60- or [£]65 a year – Will you, therefore be so kind, as to lay this letter before Your Honourable Committee, and to let me know, their decisions, as soon as You conveniently can? The people here, are very impatient, and trouble My Clerical Coadjutor and me with many enquiries – owing to their having heard that a Master has been appointed for the adjoining rich parish of Keighley – at a salary of £60- Whilst, we, who are very poor – have been obliged to remain, without a National teacher.[3]

Four days later he wrote again to apologise for not addressing Mr Kennedy as a clergyman in his previous letter. He made skilful use of his error to press home his request:

I am glad to find that you are a Clergyman, Since, on this account, You will be better enabled from personal experience, to judge of a Clergyman's difficulties, in these precarious and perplexing times. I have the original Document by me, in which Archdeacon Sinclair, stated that Your Honourable Committee, voted for us, £50, for one Year, towards a master, and £10- in order to procure, suitable furniture or apparatus – For want of knowing better, I expected, and so did the people a Schoolmaster from London, or Westminster, properly qualified – Some time in the last month, as seem'd to be implied in Archdeacon Sinclair's letter – But, Your last, has greatly embarrasd, and distress'd me – It would appear, that we can entertain but little hope of Succeeding in our very important undertaking, unless, we can raise £10- or £15- in addition – Owing to the people being generally poor, And being oppressed with Voluntary Subscriptions – Since we can lay on no churchrate – it really seems to me, that as well might You require us to raise £1500- as £15- Had I, any money to spare, I would, myself, subscribe liberally, but My humble means, are already exhausted – Yet, notwithstanding all these things, that Chapelry is a very important portion of the United Kingdom – Containing 6301 – inhabitants. ... Surely then, there can be only a few applications, stronger or more just than mine – I beg that You will leave these considerations, before Your Honourable Committee, with Your own recommendation, and let me know their decision, at your early convenient opportunity. If we fail in this Affair, much harm will be done. ... I tremble to consider the consequences, of Your Honourable Committee, leaving us, in this our time of need.

The strength of Patrick's feelings is clearly revealed in this heartfelt letter. Most unusually, instead of signing himself 'P. Brontë' as he almost invariably did in all his other correspondence, he signed the letter with his full Christian name. He also added a postscript:

Be so kind as to excuse mistakes, as I am now advanced in Years, and my sight has become dim.[4]

This powerful and moving letter obviously made an impression on the officials of the society. Among the annotations on the last page of the letter one hand has written, 'For how small a Sum can you send a Master?', and below in another hand is written: 'Mr Rand – 7 months in training – age 23 – will accept a salary of £50-.' Four days later Patrick made one last attempt to press home his case:

Since I last wrote to You, I have been amongst the Inhabitants, respecting A Master, And they Are All willing to do what they can. –
I therefore beg that a Master may be sent to us, as soon as possible.[5]

Three days later, on 15 December, after hearing that his application had been successful and that the society would be sending a master, Patrick wrote again to thank the committee. He promised that they would pay 'moderate travelling expenses' and continued:

I do believe, that if absolutely necessary, we could raise, £60- or £65, Annually, that is with the grant of £50- The Children might be made to pay one penny, or two pence a week, and Something might be done by Subscription. Having made these remarks, I beg leave to commit, entirely to You, the Choice of the Master – And have only, in addition to request, that You will be so kind as to let us have him as soon as possible.

On 18 December Patrick sent £2 to cover the travelling expenses of the master, and in a sudden rush of enthusiasm he added:

We hope to be able to raise the Master's wages, to 70£ - or £80 a year.

On 27 December he wrote again making some shrewd financial comments:

> They are very willing, here, to pay two pence a week for each child – and thinking
> that they will value more, and attend to better, what they have something to pay for,
> in this trading District – I have consented to this plan – But I have heard, that your
> Honourable Committee expect, that in such cases, the money thus got should go to
> them, and not to the Master – Now, if they will permit me, to give my humble opinion,
> it is this, the Master, I should think ought to have, a well pointed stimulus, for his
> greatest exertions.

The committee's decision on this matter is not known. On 28 December an announcement appeared in the *Bradford Observer*:

> Haworth – Education – On the 2nd of January next we are to have a day school opened
> in the National School Room, to be conducted by Mr Rand, from the National Society's
> Central School, London. The posted advertisements inform us that the system will comprise
> a complete English education. ... The requisites for the school such as books, slates, pencils
> &c. are to be provided gratis; but the charge will be twopence a week for each child irrespec-
> tive of age or proficiency. The Wesleyan Methodists are upon the alert to open a school in the
> Wesleyan school-room.

At the beginning of January 1844 the long-awaited master, Ebenezer Rand, arrived, and the day school opened as promised on 2 January. Mr Rand was twenty-three years old and had trained at the National Society's school at Westminster. The school was an immediate success and within a month there were 170 pupils. Patrick was delighted and on 9 January he wrote to Mr Kennedy again:

> The Master You have chosen for us, does exceedingly well, and I would not, if it were left to
> me, exchange him, for any other. Our School has commenced, under more favourable circum-
> stances, than I, with my most sanguine notions, ever anticipated. We have, now, between one
> and two hundred children, and the Church people seem to be highly pleased with the whole
> concern. The little creatures also find that the way to wisdom, is the road to pleasure, and go on
> in their work for the acquisition of knowledge, with alacrity and delight. This, is, I conceive, as
> it ought to be, for, "wisdom's ways are ways of pleasantness, and all her paths are peace".

He again referred to the activities of 'the Methodists and Dissenters' and, then, eager to build on what had been achieved, he made a further request:

> I have, already told you, that our population, according to the last census, amounts to 6301
> – and that this is a Manufacturing District, abounding with Methodists, and Dissenters, either

open, or conceal'd, and Active |inveterate| enemies, of our truly Apostolical Establishment – They have done, are doing, and will, no doubt, do, all they can, against us – They are appointing mistresses in their Schools – which is a strong inducement, And unless we meet them, in this way, we shall suffer loss – Now, I very much want a Mistress, here, for the Girls. But, how She might be supported is the question. On talking with our Master, I find, that he thinks "it is not good for man to be alone" – and that he would have no objection, to have a fit conjugal partner in his labours, his joys, and sorrows |such a person I believe, he has in view – I must say, that I encouraged the idea.

Ten days later he gave a glowing report of the school's progress and repeated his request for a grant towards the expense of appointing a schoolmistress:

Our Scholars, now, nearly amount to two hundred, and our Master, appears, well to understand, and perform his Office – He wishes, however, to marry – and I wish him to do so – too – admitting he could get a wife of good education, who was well qualified to act as Mistress – He says, that he has one such in view – and might have her soon, if Your Honourable Society would make her only a small grant. These things, I have already taken the liberty of stating to You – and I only mention them again, lest You should have forgotten what I have said – A suitable Mistress, would greatly strengthen our hands.[6]

On 5 February Patrick wrote to the society to thank them for the £10 towards the cost of books and furniture which they had sent and added the sad comment:

As You have said nothing respecting the grant of a small Salary for a National School Mistress, I am afraid that my important suit, has been rejected.

The success of the National School at Haworth encouraged Patrick to consider opening a school at Oxenhope, which lay within the chapelry of Haworth. On 26 February he submitted to the National Society the necessary application form and two months later was told that the society would make a grant of £20 for this purpose. He wrote thanking Mr Kennedy for this grant but asked that it might lie over until he had been able to raise sufficient funds to rent a room and pay the salary of a master. Despite the fact that Patrick's request for support for a schoolmistress had met with no response from the society, Mr Rand had now married and soon after her arrival in Haworth his wife Sarah began to assist in the teaching. On 15 April Patrick wrote to Mr Kennedy asking that Mr Rand's quarter's salary should be paid, adding shrewdly:

He has brought with him a wife, and all married men know, by experience, that an acquis[i]tion of this kind, necessarily occasions some expense.

On 3 May he acknowledged receipt of this payment and once again raised the question of a grant for a schoolmistress:

> Our Master has got a wife, who attends regularly, and teaches, and as far as I am able to discover, both understands, and does her duty according to the National Plan – Yet, I believe that she has not been trained in the Normal School – I have thought, that should it not be contrary to your rules, £20 – a year could hardly be laid out better than in recompensing her for her labours. Should Your Honourable Committee object to making, such a Grant, I cannot Yet see what must be done – Since it would be unreasonable to expect her to labour, without any adequate remuneration.

It seems, however, that once again Patrick's appeal for assistance in this matter fell on deaf ears. The school continued to make good progress, however, and on 29 July the *Leeds Intelligencer* carried a report on an examination of the children in which they praised the work of Mr and Mrs Rand:

> The children were examined in the Scriptures, history, Geography, English Grammar, Arithmetic &c., and the answering gave great satisfaction. The school has been open only for six months, yet within so short a time, owing to the excellency of the system, and the diligence of the master and mistress, the children have made considerable progress in learning, and in good manners. The school numbers 160 children.

Patrick now directed his efforts to ensuring a secure future for the Haworth school. National Society grants were only intended to be short-term, usually for one year, after which parishes were expected to support themselves. Although the school at Haworth was doing well, the financial situation remained precarious. On 2 August 1844 (seven months after its foundation) Patrick was forced to write to the society requesting a grant for a second year:

> I am under the Necessity of applying for another Grant in aid of our Excellent National School. I had thought that the liberal Grant of £50 – for one year, would have been sufficient. And so it would have been, had all things gone on, as I expected they would have done. But, soon after our School Opened, the Methodists, set up a School of their own, within a hundred yards of ours, and used all their influence, to thwart and hinder us, in every Way they could. This laid us under the necessity, of making low charges for the Children, and providing them, in every possible accommodation. Our Master, married, and we encouraged his Partner, to enter upon the instruction of the Girls, in which department she has been exceedingly useful – so much so, that, I do not see how we could have got on, rightly, without Her – Circumstances demand that the Master and Mistress, should have a decent competency, which could not be, on

less than £80 – or £90 – a year: and besides this, money must be expended for books, slates, – and coals, in the winter, and for cleaning, and Keeping in Order, the Room, and the various Articles in it – We have its true, from 150- to, 160, scholars, and are as to numbers, in a flourishing condition, but are afraid of charging high, lest the children, Should be taken away, to where they might have to pay less. The good effects, already visible, in regard to the National School, are Most encouraging. And I scarcely know of any circumstance that would distress me more, than a failure, in this Matter, or a retrograde movement. I do hope, that after what I have said, shall have been duly considered, by the proper Authorities, they will lend a little pecuniary aid for another Year.

At the end of September he sent a completed grant application form to the society. Three weeks later, after not having received a reply, he wrote again pointing out the stark position in which he found himself:

The time is now drawing near, when I must either, retain our Master, or give him notice to leave.[7]

When Mr Kennedy wrote to suggest ways in which money might be raised in Haworth, Patrick was quick to respond:

I hasten to answer by return of post, Your kind and considerate letter. We had the will here, to do all we could by way of Subscriptions, and Collections, but owing to circumstances over which we had no control, we could never find the way – We, are however willing to do all within the compass of our power, during the course of the ensuing Year. I will undertake to make a collection in the Church, and follow up as far as shall be reasonably practicable, any plan, which may be laid down, by the Society – Nevertheless, in candour, I must state, that No great Sum, can be anticipated, by the greatest exertions, which I can make – And this is owing to our being under the necessity of making a <u>Voluntary</u> or I should rather say, on my part, an involuntary subscription, & collections, in lieu of a Churchrate – in order to keep the church in decent repair, and to pay the Church Officers, their small salary … should the Committee seriously consider, all the peculiarities, and the urgency, and importance of our case, as I feel assured they will do – I hope they will afford us a little pecuniary aid, for one other Year.
After which, we have reason to think, that we shall be able to support ourselves.[8]

His plea was successful and two weeks later he was able to thank the society for the £20 grant which he had received. He promised to be careful over its use and to comply with the instructions which he had been given.[9]

Despite the society's help, however, the financial position of the school remained in doubt and on 31 January 1845 Patrick was compelled to write a letter to the principal inhabitants of Haworth seeking further assistance. He informed them that, although Mr and Mrs Rand had performed their duties exceedingly well, 'want of money' was likely to lead to the closure of the school:

> Only £20 is granted by the Society and the Scholars which attend or are likely to attend for a time at least do not afford a competent Salary. There has also been sickness and this has occasioned extra expenses.

He made a plea for 'a little liberality at the present Crisis'. His request seems to have met with a satisfactory response and the school was able to continue.

On 31 March Patrick contacted Mr Kennedy again to ask for the first £10 of the school grant. He said this was needed because:

> Our Master, having had an increase in His Family, since I last wrote, is in need of a little pecuniary aid.

Patrick was referring to the birth of Ebenezer Bacon Rand, who was baptised at Haworth on 16 April. He later went to Gonville & Caius College, Cambridge, and became a clergyman, being ordained priest in 1872. In the spring of 1845 Mr and Mrs Rand decided to leave Haworth and move to the National School at Dukinfield, near Stalybridge in Cheshire. Despite having established a warm friendship with the Brontë family, the main factors in their decision to move were probably the constant doubt about the future of the school combined with the continuing opposition from the many Dissenters in Haworth. Mr Rand's place as schoolmaster was taken by Joseph Purnell, and May Wright became the new schoolmistress.

In his letter of 31 March Patrick also requested help over an unfortunate problem which he had encountered over the school accounts:

> We are in a difficulty about one thing, My Curate who managed the National School concerns, has gone to another Curacy, and we have lost the accounts He kept, respecting the money expended for Books slates and pencils, and other things pertaining to the institution – I believe however, that the duplicate of these was sent to You – And if it should be of no use to You, and should be still in Your possession, if You would be so Kind as to let me have it, at least for a time, it would satisfy the Managers.

The curate referred to was James Smith, who had left Haworth in the previous October to be the curate of Keighley. In view of the fact that in 1848 he absconded to Canada, leaving numerous debts behind him, including money given him for charitable purposes, it is probably significant that after his departure from Haworth the school accounts could not be found.

Although the National School at Haworth continued to have financial problems, by the spring of 1845 Patrick felt that his main aim had been established. On 4 April 1845 he wrote to Mr Kennedy what proved to be his last surviving letter to the National Society. It is once again signed with his full Christian name and seems deliberately couched in valedictory terms:

Revd. & Dear Sir,

I acknowledge the receipt of £10- and beg leave to thank the National Society, for their kindness and consideration – I feel also, greatly obliged to You, for your ready Compliance, and politeness, under circumstances, sometimes of a trying Nature – but I may be excused for the trouble which I have given when I state, truly, that I am in one of the Most difficult though important positions, in the United Kingdom – Though, not personally, assaulted, Yet the Church, which lies near my heart, is assaild from all points of the compass, by Schism, Radicalism, and Scepticism – Yet notwithstanding these adverse circumstances, we are doing well – And if we can keep up, our National School – we shall, under Providence, still do better – ... As I see but very dimly, kindly excuse all inaccuracies, as to spelling, and composition –

I remain, Revd. & Dear Sir,

Your Obedient,

And obliged Servant,

Patrick Brontë

Patrick had fought a good fight on behalf of the children of Haworth and he could now rest from his labours. All subsequent correspondence with the society was undertaken by Patrick's new curate, Arthur Bell Nicholls, who took up his post on 25 May.

'There is now a great want of pure water'

There has already been long, and tedious delay – there has been a deal of sickness amongst us, and there is now a great want of pure water, which ills might have been prevented, or palliated, had the remedial measures we hope for, been duly applied.

Patrick Brontë to the Secretary of the General Board of Health, 10 July 1851

Between 1811 and 1821 the population of Haworth increased by over 17% to 4,668, and during the next twenty years it rose again by over a third. Although this growth led to the prosperity of some individuals, there was a great deal of poverty in the township, most of whose inhabitants lived in small back-to-back cottages shared between several families. The situation was made worse by the lack of pure water. There were only two public wells in the village and much of the supply was tainted by the outflow from privies. As a result of these conditions the mortality rate in Haworth equalled that of some of the worst districts in the country.

In 1844, with the backing of the local Health Committee, Patrick began a campaign to seek improvements in the water supply and sanitation arrangements of the village. In July that year he chaired a meeting to discuss what might be done to alleviate the growing problem over the shortage of water in the township. It was agreed to set up a committee to investigate the feasibility of drawing on a spring at West End. For Patrick this meeting marked the beginning of a campaign which would last fourteen years and would barely be completed in his lifetime.

During the next five years little progress was made and in August 1849 it was decided to take the matter further. Patrick headed a petition which was also signed by his curate, Arthur Nicholls, and by Mr Hall and Mr Wheelhouse, the two surgeons in the township. After many of the inhabitants had also signed, it was sent to the General Board of Health in London, requesting assistance in procuring an improvement to the water supply at Haworth. The petition stated that, although there were two good springs in the village, this water was only of benefit to the wealthy who owned the land in which they were situated. It pointed out that it would only need the provision of a few pipes to make this supply available to the many poor in the township. There was always water pouring down from the hills and all they wished for was 'to procure the salutary beverage in question'.[1] In reply the board stated that it could take no action in this matter unless one-tenth of the ratepayers signed a petition. A second petition containing the requisite number of signatures was duly sent on 9 October. The board responded by promising that they would give the matter 'early' consideration and that an inspector would be sent.

On 23 January 1850, since no inspector had visited Haworth, John Hudson, the chairman of the Haworth Health Committee, wrote to ask 'why he has not come'. No reply to this letter was received from the board and on 5 February Patrick wrote to the secretary seeking an explanation for the Board's inactivity:

> Having long since petitioned for an authorized Agent, to come and look into our situation, with regard to a sufficient supply of pure water, we are much disappointed, at not having seen any such Agent, nor having got any satisfactory answer to our petition: we would, therefore request, that you would be so kind as to inform us, what we are to expect, or do; and we are the more anxious on this head, as spring and summer are drawing nigh, when the want of pure water, would be extremely detrimental and the privilege of it, a great blessing –
> We consequently beg an answer, at your earliest opportunity.
>
> P. Brontë, A.B.
> Incumbent

Patrick's letter met with the desired response and an inspector, Benjamin Herschel Babbage, was sent to conduct an enquiry. Later that year he published a comprehensive and damning report. This revealed that the average age of death in Haworth was twenty-five, and that over 41% of children died before reaching the age of six, a mortality rate equalling those of the worst districts in London. There were no sewers in the township, and the surface water and outflow of privies and midden-steads ran along open channels and gutters down the streets. There was not a single water-closet and only sixty-nine privies. Only two-dozen households (including the parsonage) had their own privy. There were at least two instances where twenty-four households were sharing a single privy. The churchyard was over-full and burials often took place where there was very little earth and just a flat stone over the coffin. To supply water to the township there were eleven pumps (only nine of which were operational) and seven wells (one belonging to the parsonage), only two of which were for public use. 150 inhabitants were dependent on the supply from Head Well, which in summer ran so slowly that the poor had to start queuing at 2 or 3 o'clock in the morning to get their water for the Monday wash. The report recommended the installation of sewers, a piped water supply from a reservoir, at least one water closet for every three houses, the setting up of a public slaughterhouse and the immediate closure of the churchyard. Payment for these improvements should be financed by a rate levied on each house over thirty years.[2]

After the publication of Mr Babbage's report nothing further was heard from the board and on 12 February 1851 Patrick wrote again to the secretary:

> Having made application, long since, to the General Board of Health, respecting their assisting us, in making improvements here, by securing a supply of pure water, which is much wanted. – We are greatly surprised and grieved that nothing has yet been done towards the furtherance of this desirable end – We hope, however, that the board will take our case into their early consideration, and promote our object as soon as practicable. Mr Babbage, who has visited this place, can give them, the requisite information.

After a further exchange of letters (those from Haworth being written by Joseph Redman, the parish clerk who also served the local Health Committee) it became clear that the cause of the delay was not just the dilatoriness of the board but also the opposition of several of the wealthy inhabitants to some of the recommendations. In March Patrick called a public meeting to discuss the details of what was proposed. As a result of the objections raised on this occasion, he wrote to the board on 1 April, requesting the removal from the scheme of several outlying farms. He pointed out that the expense of supplying them with piped water would be too high and that such provision was not necessary because they already had an adequate supply from springs on the moors. He also requested that the churchyard should not be closed until a new burial ground had been found to replace it.

Several of the wealthiest landowners in Haworth (many of them members of Patrick's own congregation) now caused further delay by independently writing to the board to seek exemption from the new water rate which would have to be imposed to pay for the new supply. They argued that they should not be required to pay, since they already possessed adequate wells and springs. These objectors included the Merrall brothers, William Thomas, Richard Thomas of the White Lion Inn, Tobias Lambert of Hall Green and Joseph Hartley of Sowdens.[3] After he became aware of these objections, Patrick wrote to the Board again on 10 July:

> Our sanitary Committee held a meeting last night, and requested me to write to the General Board of Health, in order to petition them to proceed with our case as soon as practicable –
>
> There has already been long, and tedious delay – there has been a deal of sickness amongst us, and there is now a great want of pure water, which ills might have been prevented, or palliated, had the remedial measures we hope for, been duly applied. A few interested individuals, might try to throw difficulties in the way, but by the large majority, consisting chiefly of the working people, there is an anxious desire that the work should on the earliest opportunity be done.

In view of the board's previous dilatoriness, he added a postscript:

> Please to send me an early answer.

Two months later, since no further action had been taken, Patrick wrote again to express his anger and frustration:

> After, tedious delay, they, have, as far as we know done almost nothing – We might have thought, that this arose from a press of more urgent business, had it not been, that we have learned from good authority, that their salutary rules have been adopted, and enforced, in various other places, where there was less necessity for them, and from whence application was made, at a date long after ours – What we have to request, therefore, is that you will be so kind as to inform us, as soon as you conveniently can – whether, our case has been entirely given up – and if not, at what time we may expect a decisive, and final arrangement.[4]

In answer to this letter the board replied that an 'order in Council for the purpose is now in progress'. They then wrote, however, to say that boundary alterations would probably cause a delay.

On 10 December 1851 a petition signed by leading inhabitants and property owners in the township was sent to the General Board alleging malpractice in the elections to the local Board of Health which had recommended the improvements to the water supply.[5] The board responded by sending another inspector, William Ranger, to Haworth. Patrick was recovering from a minor stroke which he had suffered earlier in the month and he was unable to attend the meeting which Mr Ranger held in the village on 30 July 1852. As a result of this meeting the inspector came down on the side of those making complaints about the elections and recommended in his report that the property qualification should be raised from £5 to £10. Patrick angrily protested that this change would disenfranchise all but ten houses in the township, and five of these were inns. The clerk, Joseph Redman, later admitted that Patrick's claim was an exaggeration and that there were forty-three houses rated at £10 or above.

Despite this continued opposition on the part of the landowners, however, some progress was achieved. In June 1854 the Haworth Board of Health constructed a main sewer in the lower part of the main street, 172 yards in length, and charged the nearby owners with the expense. When they objected to this action, the clerk explained that these pipes had been put in to prevent buckets of filth being thrown down the street, and he insisted that they should make the necessary payment. In May 1856 the Haworth Health Committee started work on Church Hills Reservoir in the fields above the Parsonage. They borrowed £800 and levied a water-rate to pay for it. The work was completed in 1858 and the installation of pipes by the end of the year made a constant supply of fresh water available for every cottage in Haworth. It had taken fourteen years to achieve this objective and the eighty-one-year-old Patrick could be well satisfied with the successful outcome of his long campaign.

PART FOUR

Grief and Determination, 1847–1861

'My Son! My Son!'

1847–1849

Much and long as he had suffered on his account – he cried out for his loss like David for that of Absalom – My Son! My Son! And refused at first to be comforted.'

Charlotte Brontë to William Smith Williams, 6 October 1848

The restoration of Patrick's sight after his cataract operation in 1846 gave him a new lease of life. In March 1847 he resumed his former habit of writing to the local newspapers on a variety of issues. His recovery of spirits is also seen in a light-hearted poem which he wrote at this time. His curate Arthur Nicholls had been fighting a long battle with the washerwomen of Haworth over their habit of spreading their laundry over the tombstones in the churchyard. In November 1847 he succeeded in banning this custom and Patrick celebrated his victory with a frivolous poem which he entitled 'Church Reform.' He began with a reference to his achievement two years earlier of installing a new peal of bells:

The Parson, an old man, but hotter than cold,
Of late in reforming, has grown very bold,
And in his fierce zeal, as report loudly tells,
Through legal resort, has reformed the bells –

He went on to refer to Nicholls's recent success:

His curate who follows – with all due regard –
Though Foil'd by the Church, has reform'd the Churchyard –

He concluded by predicting the awful fate which awaited his curate:

The females all routed have fled with their clothes
To stackyards, and backyards, and where no one knows,

And loudly have sworn by the suds which they swim in,
They'll wring off his head, for his warring with women.
Whilst their husbands combine & roar out in their fury,
They'll Lynch him at once, without trial by Jury.
But saddest of all, the fair maidens declare,
Of marriage or love, he must ever despair.[1]

The last line would seem to be highly ironic in view of Arthur Nicholls's later marriage to his daughter Charlotte.

At the end of October 1847 Patrick was greatly saddened to hear of the death by suicide of a long-standing clerical friend, Thomas Brooksbank Charnock, the son of the former incumbent of Haworth, James Charnock. Thomas Charnock was a man of independent means and, after taking his degree at Oxford, he had returned to live in the Haworth area. Having no parish responsibilities of his own, he had frequently assisted Patrick by taking services for him at Haworth. Mr Charnock could have been refused a church burial because of his suicide but Patrick insisted on taking the funeral himself, although at this time Arthur Nicholls was performing virtually all the parish duties.

The winter of 1847/1848 was harsh with a prevailing east wind, and Patrick, along with the rest of his family, suffered from bad colds and influenza. He had, however, another worry on his mind. Branwell had now resumed his old habit of heavy drinking and his physical condition had seriously deteriorated. In early January 1848 Branwell wrote to his friend, the sculptor Joseph Leyland, attempting to explain two fainting fits which he had recently suffered in Halifax:

I was not intoxicated when I saw you last, Dear Sir, but I was so much broken down and embittered in heart that it did not need much extra stimulus to make me experience the fainting fit I had, after you left, at the Talbot, and another more severe at Mr Crowthers – the Commercial Inn near the Northgate.[2]

It is now thought that these fainting fits were brought on by his excessive drinking and were a symptom of *delirium tremens*.

Another incident involving Branwell brought further cause for alarm. On one occasion when he was lying in his bedroom in a drunken stupor he accidentally set his bedclothes on fire. Anne, who was passing the room at the time, could not rouse him and, realising the seriousness of the situation, rushed to get Emily's assistance. Emily unceremoniously dragged Branwell out of bed and ran to the kitchen to get a can of water to douse the flames. Patrick had always been concerned over the danger of fire, and, realising that Branwell was now an irresponsible alcoholic, he insisted that his son should sleep in the same room as himself. This fatherly act of responsible kindness caused him untold harassment. As Charlotte told Ellen on 11 January:

We have not been very comfortable here at home lately – far from it indeed – Branwell has contrived by some means to get more money from the old quarter – and has led us a sad life with his absurd and often intolerable conduct – Papa is harassed day and night – we have little peace – he is always sick, has two or three times fallen down in fits – what will be the ultimate end God knows.

In her *Life of Charlotte Brontë* Mrs Gaskell described the desperate state of Branwell's condition:

For some time before his death he had attacks of delirium tremens of the most frightful character; he slept in his father's room, and he would sometimes declare that either he or his father should be dead before morning. The trembling sisters, sick with fright, would implore their father not to expose himself to this danger; but Mr Brontë is no timid man, and perhaps he felt that he could possibly influence his son to some self-restraint, more by showing trust in him than by showing fear. ... In the mornings young Brontë would saunter out, saying with a drunkard's incontinence of speech, 'The poor old man and I have had a terrible night of it; he does his best – the poor old man! But it's all over with me;' (whimpering) 'it's her fault, *her* fault.'[3]

The strain on Patrick must have been intolerable. After a night of prolonged disturbance from his son he had, at the age of seventy-one, to cope with the busy life of running a large parish. He was also well aware of the danger he was running. In his copy of Graham's *Modern Domestic Medicine*, the passage on 'Insanity or Mental Derangement' has been marked with an asterisk. And alongside he wrote:

There is also "delirium tremens", brought on, sometimes by intoxication – the patient thinks himself haunted by demons ... has frequent tremors on the limbs, if intox-n, be left off – this madness, will in general, gradually diminish.

As he read Graham's text Patrick could not fail to recognise his son's symptoms:

Unrestrained behaviour ... an irritability which urges on the patient in an extravagant pursuit of something real or imaginary, to the ruin of himself, or annoyance of his friends; and ultimately leads him, if opposed in his disordered wishes, to acts of extreme violence.

Charlotte, thinking that her father was in need of some comfort at this time of great stress, decided to inform him of her literary success with *Jane Eyre*, which had been published on 19 October 1847. In a letter to Catherine Winkworth dated 25 August 1850 Mrs Gaskell described the occasion as she had heard it from Charlotte herself:

Their father ... had never heard of Jane Eyre when 3 months after its publication she promised her sisters one day at dinner she would tell him before tea. So she marched into his study with a copy wrapped up & the reviews. She said (I think I can remember the exact words) – 'Papa I've been writing a book.' 'Have you my dear?' and he went on reading. 'But Papa I want you to look at it.' 'I can't be troubled to read MS.' 'But it is printed.' 'I hope you have not been involving yourself in any such silly expense.' 'I think I shall gain some money by it. May I read you some reviews.' So she read them; and then she asked him if he would read the book. He said she might leave it, and he would see. But he sent them an invitation to tea that night, and towards the end of tea he said, 'Children, Charlotte has been writing a book – and I think it is a better one than I expected.'

Despite Patrick's encouraging response it seems that he was not told on that occasion that Emily and Anne had also written novels. According to Mrs Gaskell Patrick later said that he had suspected all along that his daughters were engaged in some sort of writing activity:

He says now that he suspected it all along, but his suspicions could take no exact form, as all he was certain of was, that his children were perpetually writing – and not writing letters.[4]

Branwell, in addition to his deteriorating physical condition, also had the problem of fending off his creditors. In June the landlord of the Old Cock inn at Halifax had written to Patrick demanding settlement of Branwell's bills and threatening to obtain a court summons. Branwell sent his friend John Brown with 10 shillings [50p] and an offer to pay the rest as soon as he could. He expressed his despair in a letter to Joseph Leyland:

If he refuses my offer and presses me with law I am RUINED. I have had five months of such utter sleeplessness violent cough and frightful agony of mind that jail would destroy me for ever.[5]

He was now desperate to to feed his drug habit and Mrs Gaskell recorded how he would steal out of the house while all the family were at church and beg a lump of opium from the village druggist. His last surviving letter reveals the depths which he had reached. It was addressed to John Brown:

Sunday. Noon.

Dear John

I shall feel very much obliged to you if [you] can contrive to get me Five pence worth of Gin in a proper measure.

Should it be speedily got I could perhaps take it from you or Billy at the lane top, or what would be quite as well, sent out for, to you.

I anxiously ask the favour because I know the good it will do me.

Punctually at Half-past Nine in the morning you will be paid the 5d out of a shilling given
me then.

Yours,

P.B.B.[6]

The end was not long delayed. In the third week of September Branwell's old friend
from his railway days, the surveyor and engineer, Francis Grundy, came over to
Haworth to pay him a visit. After ordering dinner for two in a private room at the Black
Bull, he sent a message up to the parsonage. As he waited for Branwell, to his surprise,
he received a visitor. Patrick, greatly touched by Grundy's kindness towards his son, had
come down to see him and to warn him of the great change in Branwell's appearance.
Grundy later wrote his account of the meeting:

> Much of the Rector's old stiffness of manner was gone. He spoke of Branwell with more
> affection than I had ever heretofore heard him express, but he also spoke almost hopelessly.
> He said that when my message came, Branwell was in bed, and had been almost too weak for
> the last few days to leave it; nevertheless, he had insisted upon coming, and would be there
> immediately.

When Branwell at last arrived, Grundy was greatly shocked at his appearance:

> Presently the door opened, cautiously, and a head appeared. It was a mass of red, unkempt,
> uncut hair, wildly floating round a great, gaunt forehead; the cheeks yellow and hollow, the
> mouth fallen, the thin white lips not trembling but shaking, the sunken eyes, once small now
> glaring with the light of madness, – all told the sad tale but too surely.

Grundy concealed his surprise and greeted him in a lively manner and forced a glass
of hot brandy on him. Soon 'something like the Brontë of old returned', although
Branwell remained grave throughout the evening and said that he was:

> waiting anxiously for death – indeed longing for it, and happy, in these his sane moments, to
> think that it was so near.[7]

As they were parting he took a carving knife from his sleeve and confessed that he had
imagined Grundy's message to have been a call from Satan. He had determined to rush
into the room and stab the occupant, but the sound of Grundy's voice and his friendly
manner had 'brought him home to himself'.

Two days before his death Branwell was well enough to walk down the lane into the
village, but on his return he was overcome by faintness and shortness of breath and had

to be helped home by William Brown, John's brother. An observer of their progress was Tabitha Brown, William's thirteen-year-old niece. Years later she recalled the scene:

> There was a low step to mount and I can always remember seeing him catch hold to the door side – it seemed such hard work for him.[8]

The next day he was confined to bed. John Wheelhouse, the Haworth surgeon was called and he told the family that Branwell was close to death. Patrick was in an agony of sorrow and despair. He knelt at the bedside fervently seeking his son's spiritual welfare. It seems that in his final hours Branwell showed the repentance which Patrick was seeking and to the last prayer that Patrick offered at his bedside he was heard to add 'Amen'. He died soon after nine o'clock on the morning of Sunday 24 September. In a letter to Mr William Smith Williams (of Smith, Elder & Co., Charlotte's publishers) Charlotte described the final scene:

> The remembrance of this strange change now comforts my poor Father greatly. I myself, with painful, mournful joy, heard him praying softly in his dying moments, and to the last prayer which my father offered up at his bedside, he added "amen". How unusual that word appeared from his lips – of course you who did not know him, cannot conceive. Akin to this alteration was that in his feelings towards his relatives – all bitterness seemed gone.[9]

The cause of his death was certified by John Wheelhouse as 'Chronic bronchitis – Marasmus', though it seems that he may also have been suffering from consumption.

Despite Branwell's persistent waywardness, the death of his only son caused Patrick great distress. As Charlotte wrote to Mr Williams on 2 October:

> My poor Father naturally thought more of his <u>only</u> son than of his daughters, and much and long as he had suffered on his account – he cried out for his loss like David for that of Absolom – My Son! My Son! And refused at first to be comforted.

As time passed, however, Patrick came to display the fortitude which had sustained him throughout his long life and on 14 October Charlotte was able to tell Ellen's sister Ann:

> Papa, I am thankful to say, has borne the event pretty well – his distress was great at first, to lose an <u>only</u> son is no ordinary trial, but his physical strength has not hitherto failed him, and he has now in a great measure recovered his mental composure.

Branwell's funeral was held on Thursday 28 September. It was taken by Patrick's old friend William Morgan. After the service Branwell's body was interred in the family vault beside the remains of his mother, his aunt and his younger sisters. Many years later, in his account of his friendship with Branwell, Francis Grundy wrote what is probably his most appropriate epitaph:

> Patrick Branwell Brontë was no domestic demon – he was just a man moving in a mist, who lost his way. More sinned against, mayhap, than sinning, at least he proved the reality of his sorrows. They killed him.[10]

The harshness of the weather was unremitting throughout that autumn and all the Brontë family suffered from colds. Charlotte was taken ill with a headache and nausea on the day of Branwell's death and was confined to her bed for a week, but it was Emily's condition that was to give the greatest cause for concern. Charlotte's letters to Ellen Nussey and to William Smith Williams reveal her rapid decline. On 29 October, she wrote to Ellen revealing her deep anxiety about Emily:

> I feel much more uneasy about my sisters than myself just now. Emily's cold and cough are very obstinate; I fear she has pain in the chest – and I sometimes catch a shortness in her breathing when she has moved at all quickly – she looks very, very thin and pale. Her reserved nature occasions one great uneasiness of mind – it is useless to question her – you get no answers – it is still more useless to recommend remedies – they are never adopted. Nor can I shut my eyes to the fact of Anne's great delicacy of constitution. … Papa has not quite escaped, but he has so far stood it out better than any of us.

Three days later she wrote to Mr Williams explaining how difficult it was to give assistance to Emily, who was refusing to make any acknowledgement of her illness:

> My sister Emily has something like a slow inflammation of the lungs. … I would fain hope that Emily is a little better this evening, but it is difficult to ascertain this: she is a real stoic in illness, she neither seeks nor will accept sympathy; to put any question, to offer any aid is to annoy; she will not yield a step before pain or sickness till forced … you must look on, and see her do what she is unfit to do, and not dare to say a word.

Gradually it became clear that Emily was very ill indeed, and that there was little hope of her recovery. On 23 November Charlotte wrote again to Ellen to let her know the seriousness of the situation:

> I told you Emily was ill in my last letter – she has not rallied yet – she is _very_ ill: I believe if you were to see her your impression would be that there is no hope: a more hollow, wasted pallid aspect I have not beheld. The deep tight cough continues; the breathing after the least exertion is a rapid pant – and these symptoms are accompanied by pain in the chest and side. … In this state she resolutely refuses to see a doctor. … God only knows how all this is to terminate.

In this situation Patrick showed a stoic fortitude and tried to prepare Charlotte and Anne for what now seemed the inevitable end. As Charlotte reported to Mr Williams on 7 December:

> My Father is very despondent about her. Anne and I cherish hope as well as we can … but my father shakes his head and speaks of others of our family once similarly afflicted, for whom he likewise persisted in hoping against hope, and who are now removed where hope and fear fluctuate no more.

Although Emily refused to see a doctor and resolutely persisted in carrying out her usual daily tasks, she was in the final stages of consumption and the end was near. Charlotte admired her stoical fortitude:

> While full of ruth for others, on herself she had no pity; the spirit was inexorable to the flesh; from the trembling hand, the unnerved limbs, the faded eyes, the same service was exacted as they had rendered in health. To stand by and witness this, and not dare to remonstrate, was a pain no words can render.[11]

On Tuesday 19 December she arose as usual, dressed herself and slowly made her way downstairs. As Charlotte watched her attempting to pick up her sewing she wrote a brief note to Ellen:

> I should have written to you before if I had had one word of hope to say – but I have not – She grows daily weaker. … Moments so dark as these I have never known – I pray for God's support to us all. Hitherto he has granted it.

During the morning Emily's condition deteriorated and by noon she could only whisper in gasps. At last she gave way and said to Charlotte, 'If you will send for a doctor, I will see him now.' Dr Wheelhouse was rapidly summoned, but it was too late: Emily died at about two o'clock. Charlotte wrote to Mr Williams on the next day:

> Tuesday night and morning saw the last hours, the last agonies, proudly endured till the end. Yesterday Emily Jane Brontë died in the arms of those who loved her. …
> The last three months – ever since my brother's death seem to us like a long, terrible dream. We look for support to God.

Emily's funeral service was held on 22 December and was taken by Patrick's curate, Arthur Nicholls. When the small family procession left the parsonage, Patrick was accompanied by Keeper, Emily's faithful dog. The local paper described them as 'walking first side by side'.[12] They were followed by Charlotte and Anne, and then by the two faithful servants, Tabby Aykroyd and Martha Brown.

Both Patrick and Anne were also far from well and it was Charlotte who now became a source of strength for the household. On 23 December she wrote to Ellen to inform her of Emily's death:

> Emily suffers no more either from pain or weakness now. She never will suffer more in this world – she is gone after a hard, short conflict. She died on Tuesday, the very day I wrote to you. … Yesterday we put her poor, wasted mortal frame quietly under the Church pavement. We are very calm [a]t present, why should we be otherwise? – the anguish of seeing [he]r suffer is over.

And on Christmas Day she wrote to Mr Williams:

> My father and my Sister Anne are far from well – as for me, God has hitherto most graciously sustained me – so far I have felt adequate to bear my own burden and even to offer a little help to others – I am not ill – I can get through daily duties – and do something towards keeping hope and energy alive in our mourning household. My Father says to me almost hourly "Charlotte, you must bear up, I shall sink if you fail me." … The sight too of my Sister Anne's very still but deep sorrow wakens in me such fear for her that I dare not falter. Somebody must <u>cheer</u> the rest.

Anne's condition now began to give serious cause for alarm. Since early in December she had been complaining of a pain in her side and over Christmas she had another attack of influenza. Patrick decided that specialist medical help was required and he arranged for a leading doctor from Leeds, Thomas Teale, to come to Haworth to examine Anne. The consultation took place on 5 January. Ellen Nussey, who had been staying at the parsonage since the end of December, later wrote an account of the occasion:

> Anne was looking sweetly pretty and flushed, and in capital spirits for an invalid. While consultations were going on in Mr Brontë's study, Anne was very lively in conversation, walking round the room supported by me. Mr Brontë joined us after Mr Teale's departure and, seating himself on the couch, he drew Anne towards him and said, 'My *dear* little Anne.' That was all – but it was understood. … Charlotte afterwards told me that Mr Teale said – The disease of consumption had progressed too far for cure.[13]

Ellen's account provides a brief glimpse of Patrick's undemonstrative, yet deep, affection for his children, and especially for his youngest daughter.

Despite Anne's brave attitude towards her illness, it is clear that she was greatly affected by Mr Teale's diagnosis. Two days after his visit she began a poem which reflected her anguish at knowing she was shortly to die:

A dreadful darkness closes in
    On my bewildered mind;
O let me suffer and not sin,
    Be tortured yet resigned.

    …

Weary I am – O give me strength
    And leave me not to faint;
Say Thou wilt comfort me at length
    And pity my complaint.

    …

I hoped amid the brave and strong
    My portioned task might lie
To toil amid the labouring throng
    With purpose pure and high.

    But Thou hast fixed another part,
    And Thou hast fixed it well;
I said so with my breaking heart
    When first the anguish fell.

For Thou hast taken my delight
    And hope of life away,
And bid me watch the painful night
    And wait the weary day

    …

As the month unfolded, Anne's strong religious faith came to the fore and she began to accept the situation. On 28 January she added a further nine verses to her poem:

Shall I with joy thy blessings share
    And not endure their loss?
Or hope the martyr's crown to wear
    And cast away the cross?

    …

Weak and weary though I lie,
    Crushed with sorrow, worn with pain,

Still may I lift to Heaven mine eyes
    And strive and labour not in vain.

      …

Thus let me serve Thee from my heart
    Whatever be my written fate,
Whether thus early to depart
    Or yet awhile to wait.

If Thou shouldst bring me back to life
    More humbled should I be;
More wise, more strengthened for the strife,
    More apt to lean on Thee.

Should Death be standing at the gate
    Thus should I keep my vow;
But, Lord, whate'er my future fate
    So let me serve Thee now.[14]

Although he considered Anne's case to be hopeless in any long term, Mr Teale had thought that with care she might yet live a little longer. As Charlotte told her publisher, George Smith, on 22 January 1849:

Mr Teale said it was a case of tubercular consumption with congestion of the lungs – yet he intimated that the malady had not yet reached so advanced a stage as to cut off all hope; he held out a prospect that a truce and even an arrest of the disease might yet be procured; till such truce or arrest could be brought about, he forbade the excitement of travelling, enjoined strict care and prescribed the use of cod-liver oil and carbonate of iron.

Patrick had realistically come to realise the hopelessness of the situation. When George Smith suggested that Dr John Forbes, a distinguished physician and an expert on cases of consumption, should come from London at his expense to visit Anne, Patrick rejected the idea. As Charlotte told Mr Smith:

Did he think any really useful end could be answered by a visit from Dr Forbes he would – notwithstanding his habitual reluctance to place himself under obligations – unhesitatingly accept an offer so delicately made. He is however convinced that whatever aid human skill and the resources of science can yield my Sister is already furnished her in the person of her present medical attendant, in whom my father has reason to repose perfect confidence, and he conceives that to bring down a Physician from London would be to impose trouble in quarters where we have no claim, without securing any adequate result.[15]

She described Mr Teale's diagnosis and course of treatment and asked for Dr Forbe's comments. Dr Forbes swiftly replied saying that he knew Mr Teale well and thought highly of his skill. The remedies he was using were those he would have recommended himself. He also added a warning against entertaining sanguine hopes of a recovery.

Although there were occasional periods of improvement, Anne's condition continued to decline. Throughout this difficult period Patrick was sustained by his strong religious faith. This is clearly seen in his reply on 26 February 1849 to a letter from Mr Rand, the former schoolmaster at Haworth, who was now living in the Manchester area:

I have indeed had my ample share of trouble – But it has been the Lord's will – and it is my duty to resign – My Only Son has died, and soon after him, a beloved Daughter, died also – for these things we may weep, since Christ himself wept over his dead friend … Yet, whilst we grieve, it should not be without hope.

Towards the end of March, Ellen Nussey wrote to Charlotte inviting Anne to come to her home in Birstall, where she could be looked after by Ellen and her sisters. Anne felt that this would be too much of an imposition, but she did ask Charlotte to write to Ellen to ask whether in May she might be willing to accompany her to 'the sea-side or some inland watering-place'.

Writing to Ellen on 29 March, Charlotte said that both she and Patrick were opposed to the idea that Anne should go away:

She continues to vary – is sometimes worse and sometimes better, as the weather changes – but on the whole I fear she loses strength. Papa says her state is most precarious – she may be spared for some time – or a sudden alteration might remove her ere we were aware – were such an alteration to take place while She was 'far' from home and alone with you – it would be too terrible – the idea of it distresses me inexpressibly, and I tremble whenever she alludes to the project of a journey.

When Ellen, on Charlotte's instigation, replied to Anne saying that 'her friends' were reluctant for her to undertake the responsibility of accompanying an invalid, and adding that May was generally a bad month for weather, Anne decided that she would write to Ellen herself:

I do not think there would be any great responsibility in the matter: I know, and everybody knows that you would be as kind and helpful as anyone could possibly be; and I hope I

should not be very troublesome. It would be as a companion not as a nurse that I should wish
for your company.

She admitted that the earlier part of May could sometimes be cold, but said that there
was often warm weather in the latter part, and added:

I have a more serious reason ... for my impatience of delay: the doctors say that change of air
or removal to a better climate would hardly ever fail of success in consumptive cases if 'the
remedy were' taken in time, but the reason why there are so many disappointments is, that it
is generally deferred till it is too late. Now I would not commit this error.

She went on to describe her present condition:

[Though] I suffer much less from pain and fever than I did when you were with us, I am
decidedly weaker and very much thinner, my cough still troubles me a good deal, especially
in the night, and, what seems worse than all, I am subject to great shortness of breath going
up stairs or any slight exertion. Under these circumstances I think there is no time to be lost.

She faced the prospect of her death with calm courage:

I have no horror of death: if I thought it inevitable I think I could quietly resign myself to the
prospect. ... But I wish it would please God to spare me not only for Papa's and Charlotte's
sakes, but because I long to do some good in the world before I leave it. I have many schemes
in my head for future practise [sic] – humble and limited indeed – but still I should not like
them all to come to nothing and myself to have lived to so little purpose. But God's will be
done.[16]

Anne's resolute persistence won the day. When the matter was referred to Mr Teale he
said that he had no objections and he recommended Scarborough, which had been
Anne's first choice of destination. She had many happy memories of accompanying the
Robinson family on their holidays there. Patrick later copied Mr Teale's advice into his
copy of Graham's *Modern Domestic Medicine*:

Change of place & climate, could prove beneficial, only in the early stage of consumption
– that afterwards, the excitement caused by the change of scenes, and beds, and strange
company, did harm.

The matter was finally settled when Patrick declared that he had no objection to
Charlotte also accompanying Ellen, leaving him in the care of their two servants, Tabby
Aykroyd and Martha Brown. Charlotte wrote to Ellen on 16 May:

You ask how I have arranged about leaving papa – I could make no special arrangement – he wishes me to go with Anne – and would not hear of Mr Nicholls coming – or anything of that kind.

Ellen came over to Haworth on Wednesday 23 May and the party set off on the following day. As they said their goodbyes, Patrick, Tabitha and Martha realised that in all probability they would never see Anne alive again. Charlotte, Ellen and Anne travelled to Keighley, where they caught the 1.30 p.m. train to Leeds, and then travelled on by rail to York, where they stayed the night at the George Hotel in Coney Street. After a rest and a meal, Anne felt well enough to go out in a bathchair and they did a little shopping. Before leaving next morning Anne insisted that they visit York Minster, which had always impressed her. On arriving in Scarborough they took rooms at No. 2 The Cliff, where Anne had previously stayed with the Robinson family. On the next day, Saturday 26 May, they went down to the beach, where Anne drove herself in a donkey cart, having taken over the reins for fear the boy would drive the donkey too hard. On the Sunday Anne wanted to go to church, but Charlotte and Ellen dissuaded her. She spent much of the time sitting at the window, looking down on to the sea. That night there was a wonderful sunset over the harbour. Ellen Nussey later wrote:

The evening closed in with the most glorious sunset ever witnessed The castle on the Cliff stood in proud glory, gilded by the rays of the declining sun. The distant ships glittered like burnished gold; the little boats near the beach heaved on the ebbing tide … the view was so grand so fine so far beyond description the dear invalid was drawn in her easy chair to the window to enjoy the scene with her friends. Her face became illumed almost as much as the glorious scene she gazed upon.[17]

The next morning, Monday 28 May, Anne managed to come down stairs, but about mid-morning she spoke of feeling a change. A doctor was sent for and, after Anne had told him to speak frankly, he told her that death was near at hand. Seeing that Charlotte could barely restrain her grief, Anne said to her, 'Take Courage, Charlotte; take courage.' She was moved to a sofa and died at about 2 o'clock. Her cause of death was certified by Ellen as 'Consumption six months'. Charlotte took the decision that Anne should be buried in Scarborough. In a letter to Mr Williams on 4 June she explained the reason for her action:

I have buried her here at Scarbro' to save papa the anguish of the return and a third funeral.

The parish church of St Mary was closed for extensive repairs and the funeral service was held in the daughter church, Christ Church. The only other person present at the service was Miss Wooler, the former teacher of Anne, Charlotte and Ellen, who was now living in Scarborough. Anne was buried in the churchyard of St Mary's, on a headland overlooking a wide sweep of the bay which she had loved so much and where she had experienced such happiness.

Patrick, realising the strain which Charlotte must be suffering, wrote her a letter in which he 'ordered' her to remain at the seaside for a while. He also told her that he and the servants had known when they parted from Anne that they would see her no more. A few days after Anne's death Charlotte and Ellen moved to Filey, where they spent a week, before going on to Bridlington for a few days. They left for home on 20 June, after being away for nearly a month. Charlotte wrote to Ellen on 23 June with an account of her homecoming:

> I got home a little before eight o'clock. All was clean and bright waiting for me – Papa and the servants were well – and all received me with an affection which should have consoled. The dogs seemed in strange ecstasy. I am certain they regarded me as the harbinger of others – the dumb creatures thought that as I had returned – those who had been so long absent were not far behind. I left Papa soon and went into the dining room – I shut the door – I tried to be glad that I was come home – I have always been glad before – … but this time joy was not to be the sensation. I felt that the house was all silent – the rooms were all empty – I remembered where the three were laid – in what narrow dark dwellings – never were they to reappear on earth. So the sense of desolation and bitterness took possession of me. … I do not know how life will pass. … The great trial is when evening closes and night approaches – At that hour we used to assemble in the dining room – we used to talk – Now I sit by myself – necessarily I am silent.

'I can, yet ... take two Services on the Sundays'
1849–1852

> Now being in the 75th year of my age, I have lost something of the elasticity of youth ... I can, yet, and generally do, take two Services on the Sundays – but I am unable to run over these hills, as I once did.
>
> *Patrick Brontë to the Rev'd A.P. Irvine, 15 April 1851*

Although grievously saddened by the deaths of three of his children within a space of eight months, Patrick showed his usual fortitude as he picked up the threads of life again. With the assistance of Arthur Nicholls, who took most of the regular duties, he continued to involve himself in parish affairs and, aware of his wider responsibilities as incumbent of Haworth, he began his campaign for an improvement in the water supply and sanitary arrangements in the locality.[1] Life at the parsonage was quiet and governed by an orderly routine. Charlotte now devoted herself to finishing her second novel, *Shirley*, which had been two-thirds completed at the time of Branwell's death. When, in August, her publishers suggested to her that James Taylor, the managing clerk of Smith, Elder & Co., should collect the manuscript on his way back from a holiday in Scotland, she wrote to the firm's reader, Mr Williams, agreeing that he should come, but stipulating that it should be just for the day. She said that she would have invited him for longer:

> if the peculiar retirement of papa's habits were not such as to render it irksome to him to give much of his society to a stranger even in the house: without being in the least misanthropical or sour-natured – papa habitually prefers solitude to society, and Custom is a tyrant whose fetters it would now be impossible for him to break.[2]

After receiving this letter it is not surprising that the staff of Smith, Elder & Co. should have come to regard Patrick as a solitary, unfriendly and eccentric character. Charlotte's description of him is misleading. Throughout this period Patrick took a keen interest in visitors to the parsonage and treated them with great courtesy and friendliness. It was only a few days after Mr Taylor's brief visit that Patrick welcomed his old friend the Rev'd Thomas Crowther, the vicar of Cragg Vale, to stay at the parsonage while he preached two sermons in Haworth church on Sunday 16 September, to raise funds to meet the cost of installing gas lighting in the church.

Shirley was published on 26 October and its portrait of local figures soon caused a sensation in the district. One man who took his portrayal in good part was her father's curate, Arthur Nicholls, who is depicted as Mr Macarthey, the curate of Briarfield. On the whole he is given a favourable character in the novel, where he is described as 'decent, decorous, and conscientious' and is said to have made the Sunday and day schools flourish. But his faults were also unsparingly exposed:

> Being human, of course, he had his faults, these, however, were proper, steady-going, clerical faults; what many would call virtues: the circumstance of finding himself invited to tea with a Dissenter would unhinge him for a week; the spectacle of a Quaker wearing his hat in the church – the thought of an unbaptized fellow-creature being buried with Christian rites – these things could make strange havoc in Mr Macarthey's physical and mental economy; otherwise he was sane and rational, diligent and charitable.[3]

On 29 January 1850 Charlotte reported to Ellen Nussey Mr Nicholls' reaction when reading the book in the lodgings which he rented from John Brown, the sexton:

> Mr. Nicholls has finished reading "Shirley" he is delighted with it – John Brown's wife seriously thought he had gone wrong in the head as she heard him giving vent to roars of laughter as he sat alone – clapping his hands and stamping on the floor. He would read all the scenes about the curates aloud to papa – he triumphed in his own character.

Arthur Nicholls' good-humoured and exuberant enjoyment in his portrayal reveals him as a rather different character from his usual depiction as a stern and rigid individual.

In November Charlotte travelled to London, where she spent two weeks staying with her publisher, George Smith. She devoted her time to sightseeing and visits to art galleries and the theatre. On 4 December the Smiths gave a dinner party where she met her hero, William Makepeace Thackeray. On the next day she wrote to her father reporting on her experiences:

> I have seen a great many things since I left home about which I hope to talk to you at future tea-times at home. I have been to the theatre and seen Macready in Macbeth. I have seen the pictures in the National Gallery. I have seen a beautiful exhibition of Turner's paintings, and yesterday I saw Mr Thackeray. He dined here with some other gentlemen.

A few days later she paid a visit to Harriet Martineau, the writer and political economist.

At Christmas that year Patrick wrote a hymn, part of which was printed for use during the services in church. He composed it on 18 December, the eve of the anniversary of Emily's death, and it was published over his initials in the *Leeds Intelligencer*. Although it does not reflect much of the joy of the Christmas season, it reveals the strength of his Christian faith, despite all the personal tragedies which he had suffered:

Our Church it is pure and unstain'd,
    And founded on Christ as a Rock;
His truth it has ever maintained
    And cherished and shielded His Flock.

Though winds of iniquity blow,
    And enemies come like a flood,
This building they cannot o'erthrow,
    For it is the building of God.

Then haste at the sound of its bell,
    The Sabbath bell calls you away,
With God for a season to dwell,
    In his temple to praise and to pray.

To those who meet there in his name,
    His presence and blessings are sure,
And these will ever be the same
    When time shall no longer endure.[4]

Shortly after her return from London, Charlotte invited Ellen to come to the parsonage. Ellen arrived on 22 December and stayed for three weeks. Her presence gave Charlotte much-needed comfort. Patrick was clearly aware of the depression from which Charlotte was suffering. He had read *Shirley* and he probably recognised in Caroline's longing for her mother something of Charlotte's own sense of loss in the early death of her own mother. Some time in mid-February he placed in her hand some letters which he said she could read. Charlotte wrote to Ellen describing her father's action:

A few days since a little incident happened which curiously touched me. Papa put into my hands a little packet of letters and papers – telling me that they were Mamma's and that I might read them – I did read them in a frame of mind I cannot describe – the papers were yellow with time all having been written before I was born – it was strange to peruse now for the first time the records of a mind whence my own sprang – and most strange – and at once sad and sweet to find that mind of a truly fine, pure and elevated order. They were written to papa before they were married – there is a rectitude, a refinement, a constancy, a modesty, a sense – a gentleness about them indescribable. I wish She had lived and that I had known her.[5]

Charlotte's fame now attracted some unexpected visitors to the parsonage. One such was the Revd Andrew Cassels, the vicar of Batley. He appeared just after dinner one day and demanded to see Mr Brontë. Charlotte, who had not seen the visitor, asked Martha who it was and received the reply, 'Some mak' of a tradesman he's not a gentleman I'm sure'. Writing to Ellen Charlotte described the occasion:

Yesterday – just after dinner – I heard a loud bustling voice in the kitchen demanding to see Mr. Brontë – somebody was shown into the parlour – shortly after wine was rung for. … The personage stayed for about an hour – talking in a loud vulgar key all the time. At tea-time I asked papa who it was – "Why" said he "No other than the Revd Andrew Cassels Vicar of Batley. … Martha said he looked no more like a parson than she did.

Even Patrick, who treated all visitors with courtesy regardless of their appearance, admitted that he was 'rather shabby-looking' but added that 'he was wondrous cordial and friendly'.[6]

Any hopes that Charlotte might have had of preserving her local anonymity were finally dashed by a statement in the *Bradford Observer* on 28 February 1850, which read:

It is understood that the only daughter of the Rev P Brontë, incumbent of Haworth is the authoress of *Jane Eyre* and *Shirley*, two of the most popular novels of the day, which have appeared under the name of "Currer Bell".

Patrick took a great interest in Charlotte's literary fame and with his shrewd practical sense he urged her to be careful how she invested the money she received. After being paid £500 on handing over the manuscript of *Shirley*, Charlotte wrote to George Smith asking for advice over 'the wisest and safest manner of investing this £500' and added:

I should like to take great care of this money: it is Papa's great wish that I should realize a small independency.[7]

Another visitor to the parsonage was the physician and educationalist Sir James Kay-Shuttleworth, who came with his wife on 1 March 1850. Charlotte had previously turned down their invitation to visit them at their home, Gawthorpe Hall near Burnley.

At the conclusion of their visit to Haworth they renewed their invitation. Patrick had seen how Charlotte's visit to London had improved her spirits and, to her great dismay, he sided with the Kay-Shuttleworths in urging her to go. As she told Ellen:

> Papa took their side at once, would not hear of my refusing; I must go, – this left me without plea or defence. I consented to go for three days.[8]

In the event Charlotte enjoyed her visit and after her return she admitted:

> Now that the visit is over, I am, as usual, glad that I have been. … The brief absence from home – though in some respects trying and painful in itself – has I think given a better tone to my spirits – all through the month of Feby I had a crushing time of it – I could not escape from or rise above certain most mournful recollections – the last days – the sufferings – the remembered words – most sorrowful to me – of those who – Faith assures me – are now happy. At evening – and bedtime such thoughts would haunt me – bringing a weary heartache.[9]

It is often assumed that Patrick's desire for Charlotte to visit some of her distinguished well-wishers arose from a feeling of selfish pride and snobbery, but his encouragement for her to accept the invitations which she received may well have arisen from his awareness that such journeys away from Haworth did much to alleviate her sense of loss and depression.

On 1 April Patrick was one of three speakers at the second anniversary *soirée* of the Haworth Mechanics Institute. The *Leeds Mercury* of 6 April praised his speech, which it described as being:

> as usual, characterised by the sterling good sense which his great experience as an observer of human nature, and his general tact in delineating the workings of the mind so fully capacitate him for.

Later that month Charlotte received an invitation from the Kay-Shuttleworths to join them when they were in London. She was at first unwilling to go, but Patrick was again keen that she should accept. As she told Ellen:

> Papa is eager and restless for me to go – the idea of a refusal quite hurt him.[10]

In the event, Sir James became ill and was unable to make the journey.

At the end of May Charlotte received an invitation from George Smith and his mother to stay with them instead. She travelled to London on 30 May and a few days later she wrote to her father describing some of her experiences:

I have been to the Opera; to the Exhibition of the Royal Academy, where there were some fine paintings, especially a large one by Landseer of the Duke of Wellington on the field of Waterloo, and a grand, wonderful picture of Martin's from Campbell's poem of the 'Last Man'. ... The secretary of the Zoological Society also sent me an honorary ticket of admission to their gardens, which I wish you could see. There are animals from all parts of the world inclosed in great cages in the open air amongst trees and shrubs – lions, tigers, leopards, elephants, numberless monkies, camels ... There are also all sorts of living snakes and lizards in cages ... and a cobra di capello snake. I think this snake was the worst of all: it had the eyes and face of a fiend, and darted out its barbed tongue sharply and incessantly.[11]

During her visit she was taken to the Ladies' Gallery at the House of Commons and, much to her delight, she caught sight of the Duke of Wellington at a service in the Chapel Royal. She also met Thackeray again. While Charlotte was in London George Smith persuaded her to sit at his expense for a portrait by George Richmond.

After a stay of nearly a month Charlotte left London on 25 June and went to spend a few days with Ellen Nussey at her home, Brookroyd House, in Birstall near Dewsbury. A week later she broke into her visit to travel to Edinburgh to spend two days with George Smith and his sister Eliza, who had gone to Scotland to bring George's youngest brother home from school for the holidays. During these two days Charlotte was taken round all the places associated with Sir Walter Scott. She then travelled back with the Smiths as far as York and returned to Birstall to resume her holiday with Ellen.

While Charlotte was away from Haworth major repairs were undertaken at the parsonage and it was completely reroofed. This clearly caused great inconvenience for the household, as Charlotte made clear in a letter to Martha, written from London on 12 June:

It appears from a letter I received from Papa this morning that you are now all in the bustle of unroofing, and I look with much anxiety on a somewhat clouded sky, hoping and trusting that it will not rain till all is covered in. ... I am rather curious to know how you have managed about a sleeping-place for yourself and Tabby.

In a letter to Ellen Nussey written on 12 July Patrick asked her to inform Charlotte of the progress that had been made:

After a host of labour amidst, decayed laths and rafters, and broken lime plaster, and busy carpenters, Masons, and repairers of various descriptions, we have at length, got our house put into order – And that moreover, amidst all this bustle, both workmen, and servants, as well, as the more important Trustees – have acted in good will, fidelity, and harmony. I have often thought, that when it has been otherwise, it has been as much owing to the Employers, as the Employed – In general, people can be more easily, led than driven, and respect, has a far more prevailing influence than fear.

Benjamin Binns, the Haworth tailor, later recalled that when Patrick discovered that one of the men working on the parsonage was a Roman Catholic, instead of expressing any disapproval, he told him to keep up to his faith and he would be all right at the last.[12]

After her return to Birstall Charlotte became ill and was forced to take to her bed. She was suffering from bilious attacks brought on by a state of nervous excitement after her recent experiences. It also seems that, after spending time with George Smith without the chaperoning of his mother, she realised that she was developing an emotional attachment to him. She had now been away from Haworth for over five weeks and Ellen's note informing Patrick of her illness caused him great alarm. He immediately wrote to Ellen expressing his concern:

> Notwithstanding your kind letter, is cautiously worded, it gives me considerable uneasiness
> – One thing comforts me, that in you, she will have the kindest and best nurse. It may be
> that she is labouring under one of her usual bilious attacks, and if so, she will, I trust, through
> a merciful providence, speedily recover – Should you see any feverish symptoms, call in the
> ablest Medical advice, for the expenses of which, I will be answerable – And lose no time
> – And write to me, as soon as you can.

And, knowing his own character well, he added:

> Charlotte well knows, that I am rather prone to look at the dark side of things–, and
> cunningly to search out for it, and find it, if it has any existence.

It seems that in her letter Ellen also intimated some of her fears over Charlotte's relationship with George Smith, for Patrick added:

> Tell Charlotte to keep up her spirits – When, once more, she breathes the free exhilarating
> air of Haworth, it will blow the dust and smoke, and impure Malaria of London, out of her
> head and heart.[13]

Soon after her return to Haworth Charlotte wrote to Ellen expressing her annoyance at all the concern over her health which had been felt at home. Patrick had even decided to send John Greenwood, the Haworth stationer, over to Birstall to find out how she was:

> I got home very well – and full glad was I that no insuperable obstacle had deferred my
> return one single day longer. Just at the foot of Bridge-house hill I met John Greenwood
> – staff in hand, – he fortunately saw me in the cab – stopped and informed me he was setting
> off to Brookroyd by Mr Brontë's orders to see how I was – ... I found on my arrival that papa

had worked himself up to a sad state of nervous excitement and alarm – in which Martha and Tabby were but too obviously joining him – I can't deny but I was annoyed; there really being small cause for it all.

It seems clear that Patrick had been considerably disturbed by Ellen's hints about Charlotte's possible romantic attachment to George Smith, for later in her letter Charlotte added:

> I have recently found that Papa's great discomposure had its origin in two sources – the vague fear of my being somehow about to be married to somebody – having "received some overtures" as he expressed himself as well as in apprehension of illness – I have distinctly cleared away the first cause of uneasiness.[14]

Charlotte's annoyance at all the fuss being made at home was a little insensitive. It was not surprising that a father who had lost three of his children in the previous two years should be anxious when hearing of the illness of his sole surviving child, particularly since she had not been home for the previous six weeks.

At the end of July 1850 two boxes arrived at the parsonage. One, addressed to Patrick, contained George Richmond's portrait of Charlotte. The other, for Charlotte, contained a portrait of the Duke of Wellington. Charlotte told Ellen that initially Patrick thought Richmond's portrait made her look too old, although he acknowledged that 'the expression is wonderfully good and life-like'.[15] In a letter to George Smith she said:

> Papa seems much pleased with the portrait, as do the few other persons who have seen it, with one notable exception; viz, our old servant, who tenaciously maintains that it is not like – that it is too old-looking; but as she, with equal tenacity, asserts that the Duke of Wellington's picture is a portrait of 'the Master' (meaning Papa), I am afraid not much weight is to be ascribed to her opinion.[16]

Patrick himself told George Smith that:

> in looking on the picture, which improves upon acquaintance, as all real works of Art do, I fancy I see strong indications, of the Genius, of the author, of "Shirley", and "Jane Eyre".

He was also delighted with the portrait of the Duke of Wellington, which 'comes the nearest to my preconceived idea of that great Man'. Although it was a gift to Charlotte, Patrick seems to have thought that both portraits were intended for him:

> For the sake of the giver, as well as the gift, I will lay the portraits up, for life, amongst my most highly valued Treasures.

And, in a moving reference to those of his family who had recently died, and perhaps especially Branwell, who had set out on a career as a painter, he added:

> I … have only to regret, that some are missing, who, with better taste and skill, than I have, would have fully partaken of my joy.[17]

In mid-August Charlotte was on the move again. She had received an invitation from the Kay-Shuttleworths to join them at Briery Close, the holiday house they had taken for the autumn and winter on the shores of Lake Windermere. Although she did not welcome Sir James' attentions, Charlotte agreed to go, partly on the urging of Patrick. As Charlotte told Ellen on 16 August:

> I consented to go with reluctance – chiefly to please Papa whom a refusal on my part would much have annoyed – but I dislike to leave him – I trust he is not worse – but his complaint is still weakness.

She left home on 19 August and her stay in the Lake District is chiefly memorable for her first meeting with Elizabeth Gaskell, who had also been invited. In a letter to her friend Catherine Winkworth, written a few days later, Mrs Gaskell gave a vivid description of Charlotte, whom she referred to as 'a little lady in a black silk gown':

> She is, (as she calls herself) <u>undeveloped</u>; thin and more than ½ a head shorter than I, soft brown hair not so dark as mine; eyes (very good and expressive looking straight & open at you) of the same colour, a reddish face; large mouth & many teeth gone; altogether <u>plain</u>; the forehead square, broad, and <u>rather</u> overhanging. She has a very sweet voice, rather hesitates in choosing her expressions, but when chosen they seem without an effort, <u>admirable</u> and <u>just</u> befitting the occasion.[18]

Lady Kay-Shuttleworth was ill with a cold during the time they were there and was unable to go out of the house. As a result her two guests spent much time together and became firm friends. Charlotte confided in Mrs Gaskell the story of her early life. She responded warmly to Mrs Gaskell's kind sympathy and, after her return home, she wrote to her saying how much she had enjoyed their meeting:

> Papa and I have just had tea; he is sitting quietly in his room, and I in mine; "storms of rain" are sweeping over the garden and churchyard; as to the moors – they are hidden in thick fog. Though alone – I am not unhappy; I have a thousand things to be thankful for, and – amongst the rest – that this morning I received a letter from you, and that this evening – I have the privilege of answering it.[19]

During their visit Lady Kay-Shuttleworth also gave Mrs Gaskell information about Charlotte's family background and early life, but unfortunately she was relying on the evidence of Martha Wright, the nurse who had assisted in looking after Mrs Brontë in her last illness and had subsequently been dismissed. She passed on to Mrs Gaskell the stories which this 'old woman at Burnley' had told her about 'the strange half mad husband' Mrs Brontë had married, and about his fits of temper during which he sawed off the legs of chairs and burned hearth rugs. Mrs Gaskell felt great sympathy for Charlotte in the loss of her brother and sisters and in her lonely withdrawn situation in Haworth. Since this was the first information about Patrick which she had heard, it made an indelible impression on her mind. In a long letter to Catherine Winkworth, written a few days after her return home, she poured out all the stories which she had heard about Charlotte's family and home background, and especially about Patrick's eccentricity.[20] These stories were later reproduced almost word for word in the first edition of her *Life of Charlotte Brontë*, published in 1857. The success of this biography was so great that her unfavourable picture of Patrick has influenced the public's assessment of him ever since.

In September 1850 Pope Pius IX announced the re-establishment of the Roman Catholic hierarchy in Britain and appointed Nicholas Wiseman as a cardinal and the first Archbishop of Westminster since the Reformation. This action provoked a furious reaction amongst churchmen, who feared that the establishment of the Church of England was now under serious threat. Patrick himself was moved to write a letter to the *Leeds Intelligencer* on 19 October under the title 'A Tract for the Times':

> Though not a tractarian, I wish to write what I would entitle a little tract for the times we live in.[21] ... The whole fabric of our establishment is shaken to its very centre, and threatens to fall. The people no longer took [sic] on our establishment as the bulwark of Protestantism, but as a Romish nursery – whilst true churchmen are overwhelmed with confusion and sorrow. ... Let not Romanists and other dissenters rejoice in this state of things. Let them be assured that the spirit of the age is to pull down not to build up, and that there is a vast majority of the unbelieving and discontented, who, if they can succeed in overthrowing the Church of England, will try to displace true religion everywhere, and substitute on its pedestal, as formerly in France, the Godess [sic] of Reason.

A meeting of the clergy of the archdeaconry of Craven was held in Leeds on 27 November to discuss this matter. Although Patrick was not well enough to make the journey, Arthur Nicholls was one of 250 clergymen who signed a resolution condemning the Pope for dishonouring the Queen, ignoring the existence of the Church of England and sowing the seeds of strife throughout the land.

In December Charlotte was away again, this time on a visit to Harriet Martineau at her home, The Knoll in Ambleside. She left home on 16 December and spent a week with Miss Martineau. On 21 December Charlotte wrote to Patrick reporting on her visit:

I have enjoyed my visit exceedingly. … As to Miss Martineau I admire her and wonder at her more than I can say – her powers of labour – of exercise and social cheerfulness are beyond my comprehension – In spite of the unceasing activity of her colossal intellect – she enjoys robust health – she is a taller, larger and more strongly made woman than I had imagined from that first interview with her. She is very kind though she must think I am a very insignificant person compared to herself. She has just been into the room to shew me a chapter of her History which she is now writing, relating to the Duke of Wellington's character – and his proceedings in the Peninsula – she wanted an opinion on it and I was happy to be able to give a very approving one – she seems to understand and do him justice.

Early in April 1851 James Taylor, the managing clerk of Smith, Elder & Co., called at Haworth on his way south from his home in Scotland. He was about to take up a post as the firm's representative in Bombay, where he expected to be for five years, and he had requested a visit to say farewell. He had, it seems, developed an affection for Charlotte and had some hopes that she might accept his overtures. Up till now their main contact had been almost entirely through correspondence and, although Charlotte found his letters both interesting and amusing, she was physically repelled by his appearance. As she had told Ellen after meeting him in London in December 1849, she had found him:

rigid, despotic and self-willed – He tries to be very kind and even to express sympathy some-times – and he does not manage it – he has a determined dreadful nose in the midd[l]e of his face which when poked into my countenance cuts into my soul like iron – Still he is horribly intelligent, quick, searching, sagacious – and with a memory of relentless tenacity.[22]

It is not clear whether during this visit James Taylor made a firm proposal to Charlotte. A letter to Ellen written on 9 April shows that Charlotte herself had certainly considered the possibility of marriage:

An absence of five years – a dividing expanse of three oceans – the wide difference between a man's active career and a woman's passive existence – these things are almost equivalent to an eternal separation. – But there is another thing which forms a barrier more difficult to pass than any of these. Would Mr. T – and I ever suit –? Could I ever feel for him enough love to accept of him as a husband? Friendship – gratitude – esteem I have – but each moment he came near me – and that I could see his eye fastened on me – my veins ran ice. Now that he is away I feel more gently towards him.

In a later letter Charlotte told Ellen that to her surprise Patrick had spoken in support of James Taylor:

I discover with some surprise that Papa has taken a decided liking to Mr Taylor. The marked kindness of his manner to the little man when he bid him good bye – exhorting him to be "true to himself his Country and his God" and wishing him all good wishes – struck me with some astonishment at the time – and whenever he has alluded to him since it has been with significant eulogy.

It seems that Patrick had had no illusions over the purpose of James Taylor's visit to Haworth. Charlotte's letter continued:

You say Papa has penetration – on this subject I believe he has indeed. I have told him nothing – yet he seems to be au fait to the whole business – I could think at some moments – his guesses go farther than mine. I believe he thinks a prospective union, deferred for 5 years, with such a decorous reliable personage would be a very proper and advisable affair – However I ask no questions and he asks me none.[23]

The prospect of her eventual marriage to a respectable professional man with a decent income held several advantages. He was clearly anxious that some provision should be made for Charlotte's future when he should be dead. He was aware that his health was not good and this was underlined when, on the evening of Mr Taylor's departure from Haworth, he suffered a sudden sickness and had to be put to bed, although he recovered after a few days.

Since 1838 a grant from the evangelical Church Pastoral Aid Society had enabled Patrick to afford the services of a curate. In the early months of 1851, however, he found it necessary to write several letters to the society seeking assurance that his grant would be renewed for the forthcoming year. On 24 February he told the secretary:

Three times have I written, and never once have received an answer, to any one of my letters, nor have I written, without a cause. My salary is so small, that it is utterly impracticable to pay for a Curate out of it, and yet there is so much to do, and My Curate and I do so much.

He was very worried by this matter, because without the assistance of a curate he would not be able to perform all his duties as incumbent. This was all the more essential in view of the fact that a national census held on Sunday 31 March 1851 had revealed that, of those attending services in Haworth that day, 85% had worshipped in nonconformist churches.[24] Eventually, Patrick wrote to the society's district secretary, based in Manchester, the Rev'd A.P. Irvine, requesting him to intervene on his behalf. On 15 April he was glad to be able to thank Mr Irvine for his successful intervention:

I write to thank you kindly, for your friendly interference in my behalf – with the Church Pastoral Aid Society – I have, after long, and painful Suspense, received a letter from them stating that my Grant is renewed.

Patrick also informed him that he had made an additional application to the society for a lay reader to assist in the work of resisting high-church Puseyism in the chapelry. As he told him:

I thoroughly detest it both root and branch, Yea in all its bearings and habits, whether under the pretence of decency it appears in formal dresses ... or whether it, may shew itself in candles or in crosses, or in vigils or in fastings, whatever colour or form it may assume, it is equally odious to me. ... A judicious, pious, Evangelical young man, as a Lay Reader, by entering into every house and doing his best, might, under providence be an instrument of much good, and no evil.

As this letter shows, Patrick had not lost all his indomitable spirit, although he regretted the limitations forced on him by old age:

Now being in the 75th year of my age, I have lost something of the elasticity of youth – I wish to have additional aid, in this, and other pious undertakings – I can, yet, and generally do, take two ... Services on the Sundays – but I am unable to run over these hills, as I once did – and my Curate though an active and diligent young man, cannot do all that ought to be done.

It is not known whether his application for the assistance of a lay reader was successful.

On 28 May 1851 Charlotte left Haworth to pay another visit to London. She arrived at Euston at 10 p.m. and on the next day, realising that Patrick might be anxious about her in view of two recent fatal railway accidents, she dashed off a letter telling him of her safe arrival. During her time in London she paid five visits to the Great Exhibition in the Crystal Palace in Hyde Park and she wrote several other letters to Patrick describing her experiences. On 31 May she told him:

I have now heard one of Mr Thackeray's lectures. ... The lecture was truly good: he has taken pains with the composition, it was finished without being in the least studied – a quiet humour and graphic force enlivened it throughout.

She wrote again on 7 June:

Yesterday I went for the second time to the Crystal Palace – we remained in it about three hours – and I must say I was more struck with it on this occasion tha[n] on my first visit. It is a wonderful place – vast – strange new and impossible to describe. Its grandeur does not consist in <u>one</u> thing but in the unique assemblage of <u>all</u> things – Whatever human industry has created – you find there – from the great compartments filled with Railway Engines and boilers, with Mill machinery in full work – with splendid carriages of all kinds – with harness of every description – to the glass-covered and velvet spread stands loaded with the most gorgeous work of the goldsmith and silversmith – and the carefully guarded caskets full of real diamonds and pearls worth hundreds of thousands of pounds.

And on 17 June she reported on a meeting which she knew he would find of interest:

Yesterday I saw Cardinal Wiseman and heard him speak. It was at a meeting for the Roman Catholic Society of St Vincent de Paul; the Cardinal presided. He is a big portly man something of the shape of Mr Morgan; he has not merely a double but a treble and quadruple chin; he has a very large mouth with oily lips, and looks as if he would relish a good dinner with a bottle of wine after it. He came swimming into the room smiling, simpering, and bowing like a fat old lady, and sat down very demure in his chair and looked the picture of a sleek hypocrite. He was dressed in black like a bishop or dean in plain clothes, but wore scarlet gloves and a brilliant scarlet waistcoat. A bevy of inferior priests surrounded him, many of them very dark-looking and sinister men. The Cardinal spoke in a smooth whining manner, just like a canting Methodist preacher. The audience seemed to look up to him as a god. A spirit of the hottest zeal pervaded the whole meeting. I was told afterwards that except myself and the person who accompanied me there was not a single Protestant present.

Charlotte left London on 27 June and, before going back to Haworth, she took up an invitation to stay for a few days with Mrs Gaskell at her home in Manchester. She returned to the parsonage on 30 June, having been away from home for over a month. In her absence Martha Brown had undertaken a thorough spring-cleaning of the house and Patrick had taken the decision to remove the piano from the parlour which he used as his study into one of the bedrooms upstairs. In one of her letters from London Charlotte had expressed surprise at this action:

I … am quite shocked to hear of the Piano being dragged up into the bed-room – there it must necessarily be absurd – and in the Parlour it looked so well – besides being convenient for your books – I wonder why you do not like it.[25]

It does not seem to have occurred to her that Patrick's grief at the loss of his children ran deep and that the piano would be for ever associated in his mind with Emily and Anne, who had often played on it.

At the end of August 1851 William Morgan paid a visit to the parsonage. In a letter to Ellen Charlotte noted:

Mr Morgan was here last Monday fat – well and hearty – he came to breakfast by nine o'clock – he brought me a lot of tracts as a present.[26]

Charlotte had never been impressed by her father's old friend, although a letter she had written to Ellen in May showed that she had slightly revised her opinion of him after realising his sensitive appreciation of certain portions of her novel *Shirley*:

I enclose a letter of Mr Morgan's to Papa – written just after he had read "Shirley." It is curious to see the latent feeling roused in the old gentleman – I was especially struck by his remark about the chap[ter] entitled "The Valley of the Shadow &c." he must have a true sense of what he read or he could not have made it.[27]

During this visit William Morgan told Patrick that he had decided to end his long ministry in Bradford. He had served there for forty years, thirty-six of them as minister of Christ Church. He was now aged sixty-nine and he felt it was time to hand over to a younger man. This must have been sad news for Patrick. William Morgan was one of his oldest friends. They had known each other since the time, forty-two years earlier, when they had been fellow curates to John Eyton at All Saints' church, Wellington. They were related through their late wives and for almost all their ordained ministry they had worked in neighbouring areas. In some of the happiest and also some of the saddest moments of his life Patrick had been able to turn to him for support. William Morgan had baptised four of Patrick's children and had taken the funeral of Patrick's wife, Maria, and three of his children, Maria, Elizabeth and Branwell. He left Bradford at the end of October to become the rector of the small rural parish of Hullcott in Buckinghamshire.

A month later Patrick had another reminder from the past. In the third week of September Thomas Brontë Branwell, the son of his wife's youngest sister, Charlotte, paid an unexpected visit to the parsonage. He had been born in the same year as Branwell, and his middle name suggests that he may have been Patrick's godson. His visit lasted several days. A few days later Charlotte's former teacher Miss Wooler arrived to stay at the parsonage. Charlotte found her a most pleasant companion and, as she told Ellen, so did Patrick:

Miss Wooler is and has been very pleasant She is like good wine; I think time improves her – and really – whatever she may be in person – in mind she is younger than when at Roe-Head. Papa and She get on extremely well I have just heard Papa walk into the dining-room and pay her a round compliment on her good sense.[28]

Writing to Miss Wooler a few days after her departure, she told her:

> Papa enjoins me to give you his best respects and to say he hopes erelong to see you at
> Haworth again. He would not say this unless he meant it.[29]

Early in January 1852 Patrick himself had an invitation to leave home. Richard
Monckton Milnes, a Yorkshire M.P., had met Charlotte when she attended Thackeray's
lecture in London. Now, in an effort to secure a visit from Charlotte, he wrote
inviting both her and her father to come to stay with him at his home, Fryston Hall at
Ferrybridge. Charlotte had been ill since the beginning of January and a visit was out of
the question. Patrick wrote a polite refusal:

> My Daughter, and myself, beg to offer our acknowledgements for your invitation, for
> which we both feel the implied kindness. Were I in the habit of going from home, there are
> few persons, to whom I would give preference over Yourself, – Such not being the case, you
> will permit me to retain my customary rule, unbroken, And kindly accept my excuse.
> My Daughter, I regret to say, is not well enough to be a visitor anywhere, just now – She has
> been out of health, for some time, and though now better, requires care, And for the present,
> I should wish her to stay at home. She begs me to express the pleasure she felt meeting You in
> London, – as well as her gratitude for the present attention.[30]

At the end of May, Charlotte, who had been in low spirits for some time, decided to go to Filey
for a short holiday. On 2 June she wrote to her father from her lodgings at Cliff House:

> The Sea is very grand. Yesterday it was a somewhat unusually high tide – and I stood about
> an hour on the cliffs yesterday afternoon – watching the tumbling in of great tawny turbid
> waves – that made the whole shore white with foam and filled the air with a sound hollower
> and deeper than thunder.
> On Sunday afternoon I went to a church which I should like Mr Nicholls to see. … At one
> end there is a little gallery for the singers – and when these personages stood up to perform
> – they all turned their backs upon the congregation – and the congregation turned their
> backs on the pulpit and parson – the effect of this manoeuvre was so ludicrous – I could
> hardly help laughing – had Mr Nicholls been there – he certainly would have laughed out.
> Looking up at the gallery and seeing only the broad backs of the singers presented to their
> audience was excessively grotesque. There is a well-meaning but utterly inactive clergyman at
> Filey – and Methodists flourish.

While Charlotte was away from home Martha carried out her annual rigorous spring
clean of the parsonage and Patrick's account book reveals that a local man, John Hudson,
painted all the windows and doors, gates, waterspouts and watertubs.

At the end of July Patrick suffered a minor stroke. As Charlotte reported to Ellen:

He was suddenly attacked with acute inflammation of the eye. Mr Ruddock was sent for and after he had examined him – he called me into another room, and said that Papa's pulse was bounding at 150 per minute – that there was a strong pressure of blood on the brain – that in short the symptoms were decidedly apoplectic –

Active measures were immediately taken – by the next day the pulse was reduced to 90 – Thank God he is now better – though not well – the eye is still a good deal inflamed.[31]

Eight days later she wrote to Ellen again:

Papa is now considered quite out of danger. … I think he gains ground if slowly – surely. There was partial paralysis for two days – but the mind remained clear. … One eye still remains inflamed – and Papa is weak – but all the muscular affection is gone – and the pulse is accurate. One cannot be too thankful that Papa's sight is yet spared – it was the fear of losing that which chiefly distressed him.[32]

Patrick continued to make a steady recovery and by 25 August Charlotte was able to report that:

Papa's convalescence seems now to be quite confirmed. There is scarcely any remainder of the inflammation in his eyes and his general health progresses satisfactorily.[33]

'His union with my Daughter was a happy one'
1852–1854

I am distress'd for Mr. Nicholls, whose grief is very great – His union with My Daughter was a happy one – They were well fitted for each other, and naturally look'd forward, to future scenes of happiness for a long time to come.

Patrick Brontë to the Bishop of Ripon, 10 April 1855

On 13 December 1852 a dramatic event occurred which completely disrupted the quiet and even tenor of life in the parsonage: Patrick's faithful and hard-working curate, Arthur Bell Nicholls, plucked up his courage and made Charlotte a proposal of marriage. Two days later Charlotte wrote to Ellen describing what had happened:

On Monday evening – Mr. N[icholls] – was here to tea. I vaguely felt – without clearly seeing – as without seeing I have felt for some time – the meaning of his constant looks – and strange feverish restraint.

After tea – I withdrew to the dining-room as usual. As usual – Mr. N. sat with Papa till between eight & nine o'clock. I then heard him open the parlour door as if going. I expected the clash of the front door – He stopped in the passage: he tapped: like lightning it flashed on me what was coming. He entered – he stood before me. What his words were – you can guess; his manner – you can hardly realize – nor can I forget it – Shaking from hea[d] to foot, looking deadly pale, speaking low, vehemently yet with difficulty – he made me for the first time feel what it costs a man to declare affection where he doubts response.

The spectacle of one ordinarily so statue-like – thus trembling, stirred and overcome gave me a kind of strange shock. He spoke of sufferings he had borne for months – of sufferings he could endure no longer – and craved leave for some hope. I could only entreat him to leave me then and promise a reply on the morrow. I asked if he had spoken to Papa. He said – he dared not – I think I half-led, half put him out of the room.

As soon as Nicholls had left, Charlotte went across the hall to her father's study and told him what had happened. On hearing the news Patrick fell into a violent rage and seemed to be on the verge of suffering a second stroke:

> Agitation and Anger disproportionate to the occasion ensued – if I had <u>loved</u> Mr. N– and had heard such epithets applied to him as were used – it would have transported me past my patience – as it was – my blood boiled with a sense of injustice – but Papa worked himself into a state not to be trifled with – the veins on his temples started up like whip-cord – and his eyes became suddenly bloodshot – I made haste to promise that Mr. Nicholls should on the morrow have a distinct refusal.[1]

Although it is difficult to give an adequate explanation for Patrick's disproportionate response, his irrational fury seems to have been caused by a combination of several emotions. In the first place he was probably taken aback by the sudden shock of the news. It was late in the evening and he does not seem to have had any previous intimation of what was afoot. It must be remembered that he was a lonely old man who had suffered terribly from the successive tragedies which had befallen his family, stripping him of his wife and five of his children. He was now deeply reliant on his sole surviving daughter to support him in his old age and he could not imagine how he could carry on his ministry in Haworth without her constant help and encouragement.

He also felt highly indignant at his curate's behaviour. In his eyes Arthur Nicholls was seriously lacking in courtesy for not consulting him first before speaking to Charlotte – though Nicholls clearly knew that, had he done so, he would have received short shrift. As Charlotte told Ellen:

> You must understand that a good share of Papa's anger arises from the idea – not altogether groundless – that Mr. N. has behaved with disingenuousness in so long concealing his aims.[2]

He was also very annoyed at Nicholls' presumption in considering himself worthy of marriage with his daughter. Patrick was inordinately proud of Charlotte's literary achievements and of her wide-spread fame. Forgetful of his own humble Irish origins, he was confident that, should she marry, she was worthy of obtaining a superior and far grander husband than his staid Irish curate. As Charlotte told Ellen:

> I am afraid also that Papa thinks a little too much about his want of money; he says the match would be a degradation – that I should be throwing myself away – that he expects me, if I marry at all – to do very differently.[3]

A further reason for Patrick's attitude was probably his fear over Charlotte's state of health. The tragedies which had befallen his family had naturally made him concerned over any illness she might have. As he had written to Ellen Nussey in July 1850:

Charlotte well knows, that I am rather prone to look at the dark side of things, and cunningly to search out for it, and find it, if it has any existence.[4]

He was well aware of her generally weak health and he was probably concerned, rightly as it turned out, that she did not have the strength for childbirth. Martha Brown later recorded that, when in March 1855 Charlotte's illness was pronounced to be hopeless by the specialist, Patrick came down to the kitchen and said, 'I told you, Martha, that there was no sense in Charlotte marrying at all, for she was not strong enough for marriage.'

It seems to have been a combination of all these feelings which brought about Patrick's violent reaction to his daughter's sudden news. Although Charlotte readily acknowledged the injustice of some of Patrick's harsh comments about Arthur Nicholls, she felt that she could not oppose her father's wishes. The unfairness of Patrick's condemnation of Arthur Nicholls' motives and character, however, was the one thing calculated to appeal to her innate sense of justice. As she told Ellen:

Papa's vehement antipathy to the bare thought of any one thinking of me as a wife – and Mr. Nicholls' distress – both give me pain. Attachment to Mr. N- you are aware I never entertained – but the poignant pity inspired by his state on Monday evening – by the hurried revelation of his sufferings for many months – is something galling and irksome. That he cared something for me – and wanted me to care for him – I have long suspected – but I did not know the strength of his feelings.[5]

Faced with Patrick's furious reaction, Arthur Nicholls resigned from his curacy. He also showed the great strain he was under by refusing to eat his meals, much to the concern of his landlady, Martha Brown's mother. When Patrick sent him what Charlotte described as 'a most cruel note' she told Ellen that she felt she must do something to lessen the blow:

I felt that the blow must be parried, and I thought it right to accompany the pitiless despatch by a line to the effect that – while Mr. N. must never expect me to reciprocate the feeling he had expressed – yet at the same time – I wished to disclaim participation in sentiments calculated to give him pain; and I exhorted him to maintain his courage and spirits.[6]

On 2 January Charlotte wrote to Ellen again. Possibly seeing a glimmer of hope in the note she had sent him, Nicholls had asked if he might withdraw his resignation:

A few days since he wrote to Papa requesting permission to withdraw his resignation, Papa answered that he should only do so on condition of giving his written promise never again to broach the obnoxious subject either to him or to me. This he has evaded doing, so the matter remains unsettled.

She felt bound to defend him against the general condemnation to which he was subject:

> I am sorry for one other person whom nobody pities but me. Martha is bitter against him: John Brown says <u>he should like to shoot him</u>. They don't understand the nature of his feelings – but I see now what they are. Mr. N[icholls] is one of those who attach themselves to very few, whose sensations are close and deep – like an underground stream, running strong but in a narrow channel.

Her letter showed that relations between Patrick and Arthur Nicholls remained tense:

> He continues restless and ill – he carefully performs the occasional duty – but does not come near the Church procuring a substitute every Sunday. … Dear Nell – without loving him I don't like to think of him suffering, in solitude, and wish him anywhere so that he were happier. He and Papa have never met or spoken yet.

Unable to do anything to resolve the situation, Charlotte now decided to accept an invitation from Mrs Smith to pay another visit to London. She left Haworth on 5 January 1853 and was away for over a month. During this time her third novel, *Villette*, was published, its publication date (28 January) having been delayed to avoid coming out at the same time as Mrs Gaskell's latest novel, *Ruth*. While Charlotte was in London she received two letters from her father.[7] It was clear that the situation in Haworth had not changed and both letters reveal Patrick's implacable hostility towards Arthur Nicholls.

In his first letter Patrick made it clear that the two were not speaking:

> You may wish to know, how we have all been getting on here, especially in respect to <u>master</u> and <u>man</u>, On yesterday, I preached twice, but my man, was every way, very queer – He shun'd me as if I had been a Cobra de Capello[8] – turning his head from the quarter, where I was, and hustling away amongst the crowd, to avoid contact – It required no Lavater[9] to see, that his countenance was strongly indicative of mortified pride, and malevolent resentment – People have begun to notice these things, and various conjectures are afloat – you thought me too severe – but I was not candid enough – His conduct might have been excus'd by the world, in a confirmed rake – or unprincipled Army officer, but in a <u>Clergyman</u> it is justly chargeable, with base design and inconsistency, – I earnestly wish that he had another and better situation – As I can never trust him any more, in things of importance – I wish him no ill – but rather good, and wish that every woman may avoid him forever, unless she should be determined on her own misery – All the produce of the Australian diggings would not make him and any wife he might have happy.

In his second letter Patrick adopted the persona of the family dog, Flossy:

> Flossy to his much respected And beloved mistress Miss Brontë; My kind Mistress, as, having only paws, I cannot write, but, I can dictate and my good Master, has undertaken to set down what I have to say – He well understands, the dog's Language, which is not very copious, but is nevertheless, significant and quite sufficient for our purposes, and wants which are not many – I fear that my Master, will not do my simple language justice, but will write too much in his own style, which I consider quite out of character, and wrong – You have condescendingly sent your respects to me, for which I am very grateful, and in token of my gratitude, I struck the ground three times with my tail – But let me tell you my affairs, just as they stand at present, in … my little world, little in your opinion, but great in mine. Being old now, my youthful amusements, have lost their former relish, – I no longer enjoy as, formerly, following sheep, and cats, and birds, and I cannot gnaw bones, as I once did – yet, I am still merry and in good health and spirits – As many things are done before me, which would not be done, if I could speak (well for us dogs that we cannot speak) so, I see a good deal of human nature, that is hid from those who have the gift of language. I observe these manuevres [sic] and am permitted to observe many of them, which, if I could speak, would never be done before me – I see people cheating one another, and yet appearing to be friends – many are the disagreeable discoveries, which I make, which you could hardly believe if I were to tell them.

Patrick's opposition to his curate had so distorted his sense of fairness that he even upbraided him for discontinuing his habit of taking Flossy for walks:

> One thing I have lately seen, which I wish to mention – No one takes me Out to walk now, The weather is too cold, or too wet for my master to walk in, and my former travelling companion, has lost all his apparent kindness, scolds me, and looks black upon me – I tell my master all this, by looking grave, and puzzled, hol[d]ing up one side of my head, and one lip, showing my teeth then, looking full in his face and whining, – Ah! My dear Mistress, trust dogs rather than men – They are very selfish, and when they have the power, (which no wise person will readily give them) very tyrannical – that you should act wisely in regard to men, women, and dogs is the sincere wish, of yours most
> Sincerely – Old Flossy

Nicholls was now forced to make plans for his future. His first idea was to offer himself to the Society for the Propagation of the Gospel as a missionary to the Australian colonies of Sydney, Melbourne or Adelaide. On his application form he wrote:

> I have for some time felt a strong inclination to assist in ministering to the thousands of our fellow Countrymen, who by Emigration have been in a great measure deprived of the means of grace.[10]

He listed six referees, including Patrick. Any fears he might have had that he would not do him justice were removed by Patrick's fair and just assessment:

> I shall briefly, plainly, and faithfully answer your questions, respecting the Revd. Arthur Bell Nicholls, A.B. He has been my curate for seven years, and during that time has behaved himself, wisely, soberly, and piously – He has greatly promoted the interest of the National and Sunday Schools; he is a man of good abilities, and strong constitution – He is very discreet, is under no pecuniary embarrassment, that I am aware of, nor is he, I think, likely to be so, since, in all pecuniary and other matters, as far as I have been able to discover, he is wary and prudent – In principles he is sound and orthodox – and would I think, under Providence, make an excellent Missionary.[11]

Nicholls told the Society that he would be leaving his present engagement as curate of Haworth at the end of May.

Patrick took a great interest in the success of Charlotte's latest novel, *Villette*. Whether this was an attempt to compensate for his unbending attitude to Arthur Nicholls and to persuade her to concentrate on her literary career rather than on marriage is not clear. It seems that she had read it to him in manuscript. In her *Life of Charlotte Brontë* Mrs Gaskell tells how Patrick's wishes had influenced the way in which Charlotte had composed the ending:

> Mr Brontë was anxious that the new tale should end well, as he disliked novels which left a melancholy impression upon the mind; and he requested her to make her hero and heroine (like the heroes and heroines in fairy-tales) 'marry and live happily ever after.' But the idea of M. Paul Emmanuel's death at sea was stamped on her imagination till it assumed the distinct form of reality; and she could no more alter her fictitious ending than if they had been facts which she was relating. All she could do in compliance with her father's wish was so to veil the fate in oracular words, as to leave it to the character and discernment of her readers to interpret her meaning.[12]

Patrick read the reviews as they appeared in the London papers and on 7 February wrote to George Smith with a suggestion for further publicity:

> I know not whether you are in the habit of canvassing for your publications – the suffrages of the provincial press. There is, however, one provincial Editor, to whom it might be advisable to send a copy of my daughter's work, "Villette" – viz, Mr Baines, Editor of the "Leeds Mercury", His paper enjoys a wide circulation and considerable influence in the North of England – and as I am an old subscriber, and occasional contributor to the "Mercury", a fair notice, I think of "Villette" might be relied upon.

On the same day he wrote to Mr Baines himself:

> I have this day, written to the publisher of "Vil[l]ette["] my Daughter's last work, request-
> ing him to send you a copy, in order that if you thought proper it might be noticed in the
> "Mercury" – Already, several, able, and just reviews, have appeared in the London papers.

Patrick was unaware that the *Mercury* no longer reviewed works of fiction, but his efforts
show the interest he was taking in Charlotte's work. His manifest pride in her success is
also seen in the letter he wrote on 20 January to his brother Hugh in Ireland, enclosing
a copy of the single-volume edition of *Jane Eyre* which had been recently produced:

> This is the first work, published by my Daughter – under the fictitious name of "Currer
> Bell" – which is the usual way – at first, by Authors, but her real name, is everywhere known
> – She sold the copyright of this, and her other two works for fifteen hundred pounds – so
> that she has to pay for the books she gets, the same as others – Her other two books, are in
> six volumes, and would cost nearly four pounds – This was formerly in three volumes – In
> two years hence, when all shall be published in a cheaper form, if all be well, I may send them
> – You can let my brothers and sisters read this.

At the beginning of March the tense situation in Haworth, with Patrick and his curate
barely on speaking terms, was further complicated by a visit from the diocesan bishop,
Dr Charles Longley, who came to stay one night at the parsonage.[13] When he was on
his travels the bishop had the habit of writing a daily letter to his wife, Caroline, and
his letters on this occasion provide a rare insight into life at the parsonage at this time.
On 2 March the bishop was driven over to Haworth from Thornton where he had been
staying. That night he wrote to his wife to report on his journey:

> I left Thornton at ½ past Eleven, it having just begun to snow again; and it snowed the whole
> way here – becoming a … storm when I got within a mile of this Place – It is a curious spot.
> … I had to cross a great deal of Moor to get to it; The descent to it is just like that from
> Swinton to Bewerley, quite as steep – so much so that I had some difficulty in sitting on my
> seat without tumbling forward – Old Mr Brontè called it "that dismal Hill – that fearful
> Precipice["] but when I got to the bottom of the Hill, I had to climb another for Haworth is
> perched on an Eminence, the Church crowning … the whole – The most remarkable thing
> on the road was the enormous number of Turnpikes. It cost me six shillings in 8 miles.

He also described his arrival at the parsonage:

> In driving up to the Parsonage, I had to go thro' so narrow, Dent-like a Street, that I thought
> the Carriage would have stuck – arrived however at the Parsonage I found Mr Brontè in a

very comfortable Room, & … his sight much restored, cheerful – His daughter appeared soon after – the only surviving child of six – but before I had seen her, I saw a very fine crayon full sized Portrait of her by Richmond, which some one presented to her Father. You have heard her person described – She is small, but with marked features quite [?] but quite self-[?] possessed. … Her conversation is interesting & agreeable and she does not assume the Blue at all – we had a young clergyman at supper here who would talk to her about her Books – but she soon gave him to understand she did [not] like this subject on all occasions.

He was impressed by the remote wildness of Haworth and also by the strange tale he had heard of Mr Redhead's reception when he tried to enter on the incumbency in the autumn of 1819:

The wildness I had heard described on the scenery of this Place is not at all exaggerated – and the people used to be (I will not answer for what they are now) as wild as the place. What think you of the following History of the Predecessor of Mr Bronte who was actually driven out by the people after his 3 first Sundays – and this unhappy victim was no other than old Mr Redhead, whom you may remember as having once staid at the Palace – The Story is this – there is an ancient Feud between Bradford & Haworth about the payment of Church rates from Haworth to the Parish Church at Bradford – this feud is from time to time exasperated by the fact that while the Vicar claims the nomination to the Incumbency of Haworth, the people of Haworth can by the Trust Deed of the living prevent the person appointed by the Vicar from entering the Parsonage or receiving any of the Emoluments, if he does not please them – a former Vicar, Mr Heap exercised his right of appointment, in the case of Mr Redhead the inhabitants exercised their right of resistance & opposition – and to such a point did they carry it, that they actually brought a Donkey into the Church while Mr. R was officiating, & held up its head to stare him in the face – they then laid a plan to crush him to death in the vestry, by pushing a Table against him as he was taking off his surplice and was hanging it up, foiled however in this for some reason or other, they then turned out into the Churchyard where Mr. R. was going to perform a funeral and were determined to thrust him into the grave, bury him alive – getting Information of this however, he called in some constables & better minded people to his assistance & escaped with his life – he determined however to remain no longer among them, & Mr Bronte's appointment satisfied them – this was not above 40 years ago.

The presence of the bishop was an unusual occurrence in Haworth, and he was surprised by the number of people who crowded into the church to hear him:

All I can say of the present generation is that severe and unpromising as the night was, I preached to such a Congregation as Mr. B says never was assembled in the Church on a week day before – he reckoned the number one thousand – and they gave me their deep attention – May God bless the word to their profit![14]

Two days later, writing from Wilsden, near Bingley, he made further comments on his visit. The inaccuracies in his account provide a salutary reminder of the unreliability of many of the details then in circulation about the Brontë family:

> I left Haworth, where as I told you I met with a very warm & cordial reception both in the Parsonage & the church. Old Mr Brontë is a man of a superior cast of mind, and his Children inherit his Talents. His Sons were very clever but wild & dissipated – one of them used to amuse himself with writing Fragments of Novels, which he was wont to carry about in his Pocket & read to his companions – I think the Sister has worked up some of those Fragments into her own earlier works, and this will account for much of what I hear is in Jane Eyre.

His letter is interesting for his description of Charlotte:

> She is not the least like the Miss Barkers – she has none of that … stamp of genius in her countenance which they undoubtedly bear about them – she has none of that mark of inward inspiration (if I may be allowed thus to use the term) which one cannot but read in their expression [–] none of that close reserve, & difficulty of access in conversation which I at any rate found in them – She looks like a clever little boy – well-mannered – ready in conversation – just and sensible in her remarks which indicate thoughts and reflexions, active in her household duties, an excellent daughter, as her Father assured me, without any of the abstractions of genius – without making any fuss, she was exceedingly attentive to my comfort – would go up to my room & stir the fire, & see that all was ready for me before I went up for my morning writing after Breakfast. Her [?] young Clerical Neighbours speak of her as Satirical and I cannot help suspecting that they have a little tournament with her now and then – and that she took her revenge on them in Shirley.

He repeated his description of the wildness of the moors round Haworth and stressed the difficulties which Patrick had to face due to the large number of Dissenters in the parish:

> This place is the acme of Desolation – there is not a tree to be seen up the bare late snow sprinkled hills that surround it and the Church interest is in a most desolate condition. Every single man of influence in the District is a violent Dissenter, they use all their influence as Millowners against the Church – pay money to induce the children in their factories to go [to] the Dissenting Schools.[15]

His visit had been a busy time for Charlotte, who had also had to provide hospitality that same week for an inspector of the Haworth National School. She was, as she told Ellen, greatly impressed by Dr Longley, whose visit had clearly been a success:

The Bishop has been and gone. He is certainly a most charming little man – the most benignant little gentleman that ever put on lawn sleeves – yet stately too, and quite competent to check encroachments – His visit passed capitally well – and at its close, as he was going away, he expressed himself thoroughly gratified with all he had seen.

The house was a good deal put out of its way as you may suppose – All passed however orderly, quietly and well. Martha waited very nicely and I had a person to help her in the kitchen. Papa kept up too full as well as I expected – though I doubt whether he could have borne another day of it. My penalty came on in a strong headache and a bilious attack as soon as the Bishop was fairly gone. How thankful I was that it had politely waited his departure.[16]

The bishop's visit must have been a difficult occasion for Arthur Nicholls. He had been invited to tea and supper along with the other curates, Mr Grant of Oxenhope and Mr Smith of Oakworth, and Charlotte was not pleased at the way he conducted himself:

We had the parsons to supper as well as to tea. Mr. Nicholls demeaned himself not quite pleasantly – I thought he made no effort to struggle with his dejection but gave way to it in a manner to draw notice; the Bishop was obviously puzzled by it.[17]

The bishop did not take long to appreciate the nature of the situation and he reacted with kindness towards Arthur Nicholls, as Charlotte reported a year later in a letter to Miss Wooler:

It seems his penetration discovered the state of things when he was here in Jany. 1853 – while his benevolence sympathized with Mr N – then in sorrow and dejection. I saw him press his hand and speak to him very kindly at parting.[18]

Charlotte, however, was displeased with some aspects of Nicholls' behaviour:

Mr. N– also shewed temper once or twice in speaking to Papa. Martha was beginning to tell me of certain "flaysome" looks also – but I desired not to hear of them. The fact is I shall be most thankful when he is well away – I pity him – but I don't like that dark gloom of his – He dogged me up the lane after the evening service in no pleasant manner – he stopped me also in the passage after the Bishop and the other clergy had gone into the room – and it was because I drew away and went upstairs that he gave that look which filled Martha's soul with horror.[19]

Earlier in the week Nicholls had also earned Charlotte's disapproval by getting into 'a most pertinacious and needless dispute with the Inspector'.

On Easter Day 1853 Mr Cartman came from Skipton to preach the afternoon and evening sermons in the church and on the following day Patrick gave one of the speeches at the annual *soirée* of the Haworth Mechanics' Institute, where the guests were also entertained by the local choral society. Arthur Nicholls had now changed his mind over going as a missionary to Australia and on 1 April he withdrew his application. He seems to have thought that such a move would have been too final a break while he had any hope of winning Charlotte's affection. He now began looking for another curacy. On 6 April Charlotte wrote to Ellen to report on the situation:

> You ask about Mr. N[icholls. ... He & Papa never speak. He seems to pass a desolate life. He has allowed late circumstances so to act on him as to freeze up his manner and overcast his countenance not only to those immediately concerned but to everyone. He sits drearily in his rooms – If Mr. Cartman or Mr. Grant or any other clergyman calls to see and as they think to cheer him – he scarcely speaks. ... He still lets Flossy go to his rooms and takes him to walk – He still goes over to Mr Sowden sometimes – and poor fellow – that is all. He looks ill and miserable. I think and trust in Heaven he will be better as soon as he fairly gets away from Haworth. I pity him inexpressibly. We never meet nor speak – nor dare I look at him – silent pity is just all I can give him – and as he knows nothing about that – it does not comfort. He is now grown so gloomy and reserved – that nobody seems to like him. ... Papa has a perfect antipathy to him – and he – I fear – to papa – Martha hates him – I think he might almost be dying and they would not speak a friendly word to or of him.

She told Ellen that she could not be sure of the genuineness of his feelings for her:

> How much of all this he deserves I can't tell – certainly he never was agreeable or amiable – and is less so now than ever – and alas! I do not know him well enough to be sure that there is truth and true affection – or only rancour and corroding disappointment at the bottom of his chagrin. In this state of things I must be and I am – entirely passive. I may be losing the purest gem – and to me far the most precious – life can give – genuine attachment – or I may be escaping the yoke of a morose temper – In this doubt conscience will not suffer me to take one step in opposition to Papas [*sic*] will – blended as that is with the most bitter and unreasonable prejudices. So I must just leave the matter where we leave all important matters.

Charlotte now felt that, with Nicholls still having another two months of his curacy to serve, she could bear the situation no longer and she accepted an invitation to visit Mrs Gaskell and her family in Manchester. She left Haworth on 22 April and, after spending a week in Manchester, went on to spend a few days with Ellen Nussey at her home in Birstall.

As the time of Arthur Nicholls' departure drew nearer the tense situation in Haworth reached its climax. On 16 May Charlotte reported to Ellen:

Yesterday was a strange sort of day at church. It seems as if I were to be punished for my doubts about the nature and truth of poor Mr. N[icholls'] regard. Having ventured on Whitsunday to stay the sacrament – I got a lesson not to be repeated. He struggled – faltered – then lost command over himself – stood before my eyes and in the sight of all the communicants white, shaking, voiceless – Papa was not there – thank God! Joseph Redman spoke some words to him – he made a great effort – but could only with difficulty whisper and falter through the service. I suppose he thought; this would be the last time; he goes either this week or the next. I heard the women sobbing round – and I could not quite check my own tears.

When the news got back to Patrick he showed no sympathy, merely referring to his curate as an 'unmanly driveller'. Charlotte, however, had been stirred by Nicholls' genuine display of emotion:

I never saw a battle more sternly fought with the feelings than Mr. N– fights with his – and when he yields momentarily – you are almost sickened by the sense of the strain upon him. However he is to go – and I cannot speak to him or look at him or comfort him a whit – and I must submit.

A subscription was organised in the parish to raise a testimonial for Arthur Nicholls. The reason for his going was never made public, although gossip had been rife ever since he had broken down at the communion service. As Charlotte reported to Ellen, the churchwardens felt it necessary to question him over his reason for going:

The Churchwardens recently put the question to him plainly Why was he going? Was it Mr Brontë's fault or his own? His own – he answered. Did he blame Mr Brontë? "No he did not: if anybody was wrong it was himself." Was he willing to go? "No: it gave him great pain."

Although she was critical of her father's unrelenting attitude towards his curate, Charlotte felt bound to comment unfavourably on Nicholls' conduct:

He is not always right. I must be just. He shews a curious mixture of honour and obstinacy; feeling and sullenness. Papa addressed him at the school tea-drinking – with <u>constrained</u> civility, but still with <u>civility</u>. He did not reply civilly: he cut short further words. This sort of treatment offered in public is what Papa never will forget or forgive – it inspires him with a silent bitterness not to be expressed.

Finally she expressed her exasperation at the pair of them:

I am afraid both are unchristian in their mutual feelings: Nor do I know which of them is least accessible to reason or least likely to forgive. It is a dismal state of affairs.[20]

On the evening of 25 May a ceremony was held in the National School room at which Arthur Nicholls was presented with a handsome inscribed watch by Michael Merrall on behalf of the congregation, teachers and scholars of the Sunday school. Patrick was not present. He had been feeling unwell and Charlotte had advised him to stay away. On the following evening Mr Nicholls called at the parsonage to hand over the deeds of the National School, to which he had devoted so much of his time and attention. On the next day Charlotte wrote to Ellen telling her what had transpired:

> Yesterday evening he called to render into Papa's hands the deeds of the National School – and to say good-bye. They were busy cleaning – washing the paint &c. in the dining room so he did not find me there. I would not go into the parlour to speak to him in Papa's presence. He went out thinking he was not to see me – And indeed till the very last moment – I thought it best not – But perceiving that he stayed long before going out at the gate – and remembering his long grief I took courage and went out trembling and miserable. I found him leaning again[st] the garden-door in a paroxysm of anguish – sobbing as women never sob. Of course I went straight to him. Very few words were interchanged – those barely articulate: several things I should have liked to ask him were swept entirely from my memory. Poor fellow! But he wanted such hope and such encouragement as I could not give him. Still I trust he must know now tha[t] I am not cruelly blind and indifferent to his constancy and grief. For a few weeks he goes to the south of England – afterwards he takes a curacy somewhere in Yorkshire but I don't know where.

Arthur Nicholls left Haworth at 6 o'clock the following morning. His successor, George de Renzy, who had already been appointed, performed his first duties two days later on 29 May. It was not until August that Mr Nicholls was appointed to the curacy of Kirk Smeaton, near Pontefract.

Charlotte now decided that the time was right for Mrs Gaskell to pay a long-promised visit to the parsonage. At their first meeting in the Lake District in August 1850 the two writers had developed an instant liking for each other. They had subsequently become firm friends and Charlotte had twice stayed at Mrs Gaskell's home at Plymouth Grove in Manchester. She wrote to Mrs Gaskell on 1 June inviting her to come a week later. The great strain she had been under during the previous weeks, however, now took its toll and she caught a cold which developed into a bad bout of influenza, confining her to bed for ten days. Patrick was forced to write on his daughter's behalf, requesting Mrs Gaskell to postpone her visit.

> I am obliged to act as Amanuensis for my Daughter, who is at present, confined for the most part to her bed, with influenza, and frequent sharp attacks of "Tic Dollhaureux" in the head, which have rendered her utterly unable to entertain you as she could wish. ... As soon as my Daughter shall have got well – which I trust in God will be ere long – she will let you know, and we hope then, to see you, at your earliest convenient opportunity.[21]

A few days later Patrick himself succumbed to the stress he had been under through his dispute with Nicholls, and he suffered a second stroke. Although he remained generally well and did not lose his appetite, he was for a time completely blind. Gradually he recovered some sight, although his vision remained limited for the rest of his life. On 3 July Charlotte reported on his condition to George Smith:

> Thank you for your kind enquiries about my Father: there is no change for the worse in his sight since I wrote last; rather – I think – a tendency to improvement. He says the sort of veil between him and the light appears thinner; his general health has however been lately a good deal affected – and desirable as it might appear in some points of view to adopt your suggestion with reference to seeking 'the best' Medical advice – I fear that at present there would 'be' a serious hazard in undertaking a long journey by rail. He must become stronger than he appears to be just now – less liable to sudden sickness and swimming in the head, before such a step could be thought of.

Two weeks later she wrote again, giving him a further report:

> In June he had a sudden seizure – which without seemimg greatly to affect his general health – brought on for a time total blindness. He could not discern between day and night. I feared the optic nerve was paralyzed, and that he would never see more. Vision has however been partially restored, but it is now very imperfect. ... I think him very patient with the apprehension of what, to him would be the greatest of privations, hanging over his head. I can but earnestly hope that what remains of sight may be spared him to the end.[22]

Patrick was in fact able to read and to write in a reasonably legible hand until a few months before his death and he never became totally blind.

The onset of his stroke caused Patrick to defer a strange scheme that he had formulated to pay a visit to London for a few days that summer. His motives are not clear but he may have been trying to compensate a little to Charlotte for all the trouble he had caused her. His last trip away from the parsonage had been in February 1842, when he had escorted his daughters to Brussels, and this London trip would have been completely contrary to his firm habit of not leaving Haworth. Charlotte explained the situation to George Smith:

> My father's half-formed project of visiting London this summer for a few days – has been rather painfully frustrated. ... He sometimes utters a wish that he could see the camp at Chobham, but that would not be possible under present circumstances.[23]

Patrick had a great interest in military matters and it seems that he wished to visit the experimental camp which was established during the summer of 1853 at Chobham

Common in Surrey to provide young men with military training. This innovation had attracted considerable attention and on 21 June Queen Victoria had visited the camp, riding there on a black charger. George Smith had offered to provide accommodation for Patrick during his visit, but Charlotte had told him that if Patrick came to London he would make his own arrangements:

> Your kind offer of attention in case he should ever come to Town merits and has my best acknowledgments. I know however that my Father's first and last thought would be to give trouble nowhere, and especially to infringe on no precious time. He would, of course, take private lodgings.[24]

In mid-September Mrs Gaskell wrote to say that she was now free to pay her post-poned visit to Haworth and that she intended to come in four days' time. Charlotte was away from home on a short holiday in Ilkley with Miss Wooler, so it fell once again to Patrick to write to Mrs Gaskell on her behalf:

> My daughter having gone from home, for only two or three days – when your letter arrive'd – I deem'd it best to open it, lest it should have required an immediate answer – She will return on Saturday – next – Therefore she will be here to receive you, on the Monday after – … As far as I am able to discover from what my Daughter has told me, and from my perusal of your able, moral, and interesting literary works – I think that you, and she are congenial spirits, and that a little intercourse between You, might … be productive of pleasure and profit to you both – … We can promise you nothing here but a hearty welcome, and peaceful seclusion – nevertheless, this may not be without its use – for a season.[25]

It is interesting to note that Patrick claimed to be familiar with Mrs Gaskell's works. In September 1853 he could have read *Mary Barton* (published October 1848), *Ruth* (January 1853) or possibly *Cranford*, as it appeared in serial form in *Household Words* from December 1851 to May 1853. Charlotte returned home the next day and immediately wrote to Mrs Gaskell to confirm the details:

> I was from home – staying two or three days at Ilkley when your note came – I have just returned, received and read it – and now I only say <u>come</u> – <u>come</u> – on Monday the 19th. At 2h 26m. a Cab shall be waiting at Keighley station to bring you on.[26]

Mrs Gaskell arrived in Haworth on Monday 19 September and stayed till the following Friday. Shortly after her return home she wrote a full account of her visit to a friend (probably John Forster).[27] She began by describing her arrival at the parsonage:

> We turned up a narrow bye lane near the church – past the curate's, the schools, & skirting the pestiferous church yard we arrived at the door into the Parsonage yard. In I went – half-

blown back by the wild vehemence of the wind which swept along the narrow gravel walk
– round the corner of the house into a small plot of grass, enclosed within a low stone wall.[28]
There are two windows on each side the door & steps up to it … in at the door into an
exquisitely clean passage, to the left into a square parlour looking out on the grass plot, the
tall head-stones beyond, the tower end of the church, the village houses, & the brown distant
moors. Miss Brontë gave me the kindest welcome, & the room looked the perfection of
warmth snugness & comfort, crimson predominating in the furniture, which did well with
the bleak cold colours without. … My room was above this parlour, & looking on the same
view, which was really beautiful in certain lights moon-light especially.

She went on to give an account of daily life at the parsonage:

Mr Brontë lives almost entirely in the room on the opposite (right hand side) of the front
door: behind his room is the kitchen, behind the parlour a store room kind of pantry. Mr
Brontë's bedroom is over his sitting room, Miss Brontë's over the kitchen, the servants over
the pantry. …
We dined – she & I together – Mr Brontë having his dinner sent to him in his sitting room
according to his invariable custom; (fancy it! Only they two left,) … Mr Brontë came in at
tea, – an honour to me I believe. Before tea we had a long delicious walk, right against the
wind on Penistone moor which stretches directly behind the Parsonage. …
In the evening Mr Brontë went to his room & smoked a pipe, – a regular clay – & we sat over
the fire & talked, – talked of long ago when that very same room was full of children; & how
one by one they had dropped off into the church yard close to the windows. At ½ past 8 we
went in to prayers, – soon after nine every one was in bed but we two. … Each day – I was 4
there – was the same in outward arrangement – breakfast at 9 in Mr Brontë's room, – which
we left immediately after. What he does with himself through the day I cannot imagine!

Her account is interesting for its a vivid description of the 76-year-old Patrick:

He is a tall fine looking old man, with silver bristles all over his head; nearly blind; speaking
with a strong Scotch accent (he comes from the North of Ireland), raised himself from the
ranks of a poor farmer's son – and was rather intimate with Lord Palmerston at Cambridge,
a pleasant soothing recollection now, in his shut out life. … He was very polite and agreeable
to me; paying rather elaborate old-fashioned compliments, but I was sadly afraid of him in
my inmost soul; for I caught a glare of his stern eyes over his spectacles at Miss Brontë once
or twice which made me know my man; He is very fearless; has taken the part of the men
against the masters, – or vice versa just as he thought fit and right; & is consequently much
respected & to be respected. But he ought never to have married. He did not like children:
& they had six in six years; & the consequent pinching & family disorder – (which can't
be helped), and noise &c made him shut himself up & want no companionship – nay be

positively annoyed by it. He won't let Miss Brontë accompany him in his walks, although he is so nearly blind; goes out in defiance of her gentle attempts to restrain him, 'speaking' as if she thought him in his second childhood; & comes home moaning & tired, having lost his way. "Where is my strength gone?" is his cry then. "I used to walk 40 miles a day &c." ... Moreover to account for my fear, – rather an admiring fear after all of Mr Brontë, please to take into account that though I like the beautiful glittering of bright flashing steel I don't fancy fire-arms at all, at all; and Miss Brontë never remembers her father dressing himself in the morning without putting a loaded pistol in his pocket, just as regularly as he puts on his watch. There was this little deadly pistol sitting down to breakfast with us, kneeling down to prayers at night – to say nothing of a loaded gun hanging up on high ready to pop off on the slightest emergency.

When considering Mrs Gaskell's impression of Patrick it has to be remembered that her visit occurred during the period of his estrangement from his former curate, and at a time when Charlotte was highly critical of her father for his attitude towards Arthur Nicholls. It is unfortunate that having already had her mind coloured by the unfavourable portrait of Patrick given her by Lady Kay-Shuttleworth, Mrs Gaskell visited the parsonage at the only time when Charlotte and her father were in severe disagreement. This may go some way towards accounting for the 'glare of his stern eyes over his spectacles' when glancing at his daughter. It may also explain the passage in *The Life of Charlotte Brontë* where, after describing Patrick as 'a most courteous host', she added:

> He never seemed quite to have lost the feeling that Charlotte was a child to be guided
> and ruled ... and she herself submitted to this with a quiet docility that half amused, half
> astonished me.[29]

During Mrs Gaskell's visit Charlotte told her what had occurred over Mr Nicholls and what her feelings were in the matter, and in the *Life* Mrs Gaskell commented:

> I was aware that she had a great anxiety on her mind at this time; and being acquainted with
> its nature, I could not but admire the patient docility which she displayed in her conduct
> towards her father.[30]

Patrick's habit of loading a pistol every day probably went back to his time at Hartshead, when the unrest caused by the Luddite riots was centred in his parish and his personal security and that of his family was at risk.[31]

Mrs Gaskell persuaded Martha to take her to the church to see the memorial to the dead members of the family and Martha also told her how last thing at night the sisters would walk round and round the table in the parlour discussing their writing:

'For as long as I can remember – Tabby says since they were little bairns – Miss Brontë & Miss Emily & Miss Anne used to put away their sewing after prayers, & walk all three one after the other round the table in the parlour till near eleven o'clock. Miss Emily walked as long as she could; and when she died Miss Anne and Miss Brontë took it up, – and now my heart aches to hear Miss Brontë walking, walking on alone.' And on enquiring I found that after Miss Brontë had seen me to my room, she did come down every night, and begin that slow monotonous incessant walk in which I am sure I should fancy I heard the steps of the dead following me. She says she could not sleep without it – that she & her sisters talked over the plans and projects of their whole lives at such times.

After Mrs Gaskell's departure Charlotte felt increasingly restless and lonely. She was worried over her treatment of Arthur Nicholls and she sympathised with him in his hopelessness and despair. After staying a week with Miss Wooler in Hornsea in early October, she was planning a visit to London when she received news that George Smith was engaged to be married, to Elizabeth Blakeway, the daughter of a wealthy London wine merchant. The removal of any lingering hope she might have had of marriage to Mr Smith caused Charlotte to think again about her attitude towards Arthur Nicholls. Her father's health was always a matter of concern and she realised that if he should die she would be left alone in the world. She now began to question her rejection of the one person who had shown unwavering love for her.

Ellen Nussey came to stay at the parsonage towards the end of June. It appears that during this visit she came to realise that Charlotte was seriously reconsidering her attitude towards Mr Nicholls and that she expressed her strong disapproval of this change of mind. She seems to have felt that Charlotte had a duty to remain a spinster and she also feared that the intimacy of their close friendship would be threatened by Charlotte's marriage. Whatever was said at the time, following this visit Charlotte seems to have ceased her correspondence with Ellen and the two friends became seriously estranged. This break in their relationship lasted until February the following year, when a mutual friend wrote to Ellen saying how glad she was that Ellen had heard from Miss Brontë and that their friendship had been resumed.[32]

It seems that some time in July Arthur Nicholls came to stay with Mr Grant, the curate of Oxenhope. After getting into contact with Charlotte, he persuaded her to enter into correspondence with him. The sequence of events was outlined by Charlotte a year later in a letter to Ellen, in which she brought her up to date on the situation:[33]

Matters have progressed thus since last July. He renewed his visit in Sept[embe]r – but then matters so fell out that I saw little of him. He continued to write. The correspondence pressed on my mind. I grew very miserable in keeping it from Papa. At last sheer pain made me gather courage to break it – I told all. It was very hard and rough work at the time – but the issue after a few days was that I obtained leave to continue the communication.

Faced with Charlotte's determination to continue her correspondence with Nicholls and also to arrange a meeting with him, Patrick accepted the inevitable and reluctantly withdrew his opposition. In January 1854 Arthur Nicholls spent ten days at Oxenhope As Charlotte told Ellen:

> Mr. N. came in Jan[uar]y he was ten days in the neighbourhood. I saw much of him – I had stipulated 'with Papa' for opportunity to become better acquainted – I had it and all I learnt inclined me to esteem and, if not love – at least affection.

During this visit Nicholls came to the parsonage, where he was 'received but not pleasantly'.[34] Although Patrick had agreed to their meeting he was still not reconciled to their marriage and Charlotte told Arthur Nicholls of 'the great obstacles that lay in his way'.

Sometime after his return to Kirk Smeaton Mr Nicholls was visited by Mrs Gaskell's friend, Richard Monckton Milnes, the M.P. for Pontefract, who on her behalf offered him two livings, one in Lancashire and one in Scotland. If he had taken either of them, his financial position, which Mrs Gaskell thought was the main obstacle to their union in Patrick's eyes, would have been greatly improved but, knowing Charlotte's determination to continue to support her father, Nicholls declined to accept either offer.[35]

On Monday 3 April 1854 Arthur Nicholls came over to Haworth to stay at the parsonage, where he remained until the Friday. Patrick himself was far from well, with a troublesome cough and inflammation on the chest. During this stay Arthur obtained Patrick's consent to his marriage to Charlotte. As she reported to Ellen:

> He has persevered – The result of this his last visit is – that Papa's consent is gained – that his respect, I believe, is won – for Mr. Nicholls has in all things proved himself disinterested and forbearing. He has shown too that while his feelings are exquisitely keen – he can freely forgive. Certainly I must respect him – nor can I withhold from him more than mere respect. In fact, dear Ellen, I am engaged.

Charlotte had clearly defined her terms for agreeing to marry Mr Nicholls. He would return to the curacy of Haworth and they would live in the parsonage with Patrick, who would be guaranteed 'his seclusion and convenience uninvaded'. As Charlotte triumphantly reported:

> What seemed at one time – impossible – is now arranged – and Papa begins really to take a pleasure in the prospect.[36]

A week later Charlotte wrote to Miss Wooler describing the agreement which had been reached:

I must tell you … that since I wrote last – Papa's mind has gradually come round to a view very different to that which he once took, and that after some correspondence, and as a result of a visit Mr. Nicholls paid here about a week ago – it was agreed that he is to resume the curacy of Haworth, as soon as Papa's present Assistant is provided with a situation, and in due course of time he is to be received as an inmate into this house.

It gives me unspeakable content to see that – now my Father has once admitted this new view of the case – he dwells on it complacently. In all arrangements his convenience and seclusion will be scrupulously respected. Mr. Nicholls seems deeply to feel the wish to comfort and sustain his declining years. I think – from Mr. N.'s character – I may depend on this not being a mere transitory impulsive feeling, but rather that it will be accepted steadily as a duty – and discharged tenderly as an office of affection. …

It is Mr. N's wish that the marriage should take place this Summer – he urges the month of July – but that seems very soon.[37]

Charlotte was delighted with the change in her father's attitude. As she told Ellen:

Papa's mind seems wholly changed about this matter; and he has said … how much happier he feels since he allowed all to be settled. It is a wonderful relief for me to hear him treat the thing rationally … He is rather anxious that things should get forward now – and takes quite an interest in the arrangement of preliminaries. …

The feeling which had been disappointed in Papa – was ambition – paternal pride, ever a restless feeling.[38]

A few days later she wrote to Mrs Gaskell to give her the news:

You remember – or perhaps you do not remember – what I told you when you were at Haworth. Towards the end of autumn the matter was again brought prominently forward. There was much reluctance and many difficulties to overcome. … Be this as it may – in January last papa gave his sanction for a renewal of acquaintance. … After further visits … I find myself what people call 'engaged'. Mr. Nicholls returns to Haworth. … The Rubicon once passed, papa seems cheerful and satisfied; he says he has been far too stern; he even admits that he was unjust – terribly unjust he certainly was for a time.[39]

At the beginning of May Charlotte travelled to Manchester to spend four days with Mrs Gaskell at Plymouth Grove. During this visit she told her how the matter had been resolved. Later in the month Mrs Gaskell wrote to her friend, John Forster, telling him what she had heard from Charlotte:

To hear her description of the conversation with her father when she quietly insisted on her right to see something more of Mr. Nicholls was really fine. Her father thought she had

the chance of somebody higher or at least farther removed from poverty. She said 'Father I
am not a young girl, not a young woman even – I never was pretty. I now am ugly. At your
death I shall have 300£ besides the little I have earned myself – do you think there are many
men who would serve seven years for me?' And again when he renewed the conversation
and asked her if she would marry a curate? – 'Yes I must marry a curate if I marry at all; not
merely a curate but <u>your</u> curate; not merely <u>your</u> curate but he must live in the house with
you, for I cannot leave you.' The sightless old man stood up & said solemnly 'Never. I will
never have another man in this house', and stalked out of the room. For a week he never
spoke to her. She had not made up her mind to accept Mr. Nicholls, & the worry on both
sides made her ill – then the old servant interfered, and asked him, sitting blind & alone, 'if
he wished to kill his daughter?;' and went up to her and abused Mr. Nicholls for not having
'more brass' [boldness].[40]

Charlotte was still not entirely sure of the rightness of her action. In mid-April she told
Mrs Gaskell:

> I could almost cry sometimes that in this important action in my life I cannot better satisfy
> papa's perhaps natural pride. My destiny will not be brilliant, certainly, but Mr Nicholls
> is conscientious, affectionate, pure in heart and life. He offers a most constant and tried
> attachment – I am very grateful to him. I mean to try and make him happy, and papa too.[41]

She knew, however, that she had fulfilled her obligations to her father. As she told
Ellen:

> My hope is that in the end this arrangement will turn out more truly to Papa's advantage
> – than any other it was in my power to achieve. Mr. N[icholls] only in his last letter – refers
> touchingly to his earnest desire to prove his gratitude to Papa by offering support and
> consolation to his declining age. This will not be mere <u>talk</u> with him – he is no talker – no
> dealer in professions.[42]

The advantage of the proposed arrangement was brought home to Patrick by his
continuing ill health, which for some time had prevented him from preaching. On
Easter Monday 1854 he was too unwell to attend the annual *soirée* of the Haworth
Mechanics' Institute and on 18 April he had to write to his friend, James Cheadle, the
vicar of Bingley, turning down an invitation to meet the bishop:

> It would give me great pleasure to meet our Excellent Bishop, and to see you and other
> friends – but for several years past, I have avoided going abroad to public meetings, or indeed
> any other occasion, I am now, in my seventy eighth year, and at that advanced age, strength
> generally begins to fail, and retirement is best – Through Divine Mercy, I am yet able to

preach twice on the Sundays, and my health is as good, as can be reasonably expected – At
present however, I am but just beginning to recover from an attack of bronchitis, which has
prevented me from going to Church as formerly.

It was particularly disappointing that he was not able to meet the bishop, because, as
Charlotte told Miss Wooler, he had recently had a letter from:

the good and dear Bishop – which has touched and pleased me much. It expresses so cordial
an approbation of Mr. N's return to Haworth (respecting which he was consulted –) and
such kind gratification 'at' the domestic arrangements which are to ensue.[43]

Both Patrick and Arthur Nicholls wanted the wedding to go ahead as soon as possible,
but it was necessary for alterations to be made to the parsonage to accommodate the
new arrangements. The little pantry behind the dining room had to be converted into a
study for Arthur. As Charlotte told Ellen on 22 May:

Since I came home I have been very busy stitching – the new little room is got into order now
and the green and white curtains are up – they exactly suit the papering – and look neat and
clean enough.

Problems were caused, however, by the curate, George de Renzy, when Patrick gave him
legal notice of the termination of his curacy. Mr de Renzy felt aggrieved at Patrick's action
and seemed determined to cause as much difficulty as possible. While remaining 'smooth
and fair-spoken' to Patrick, much to Charlotte's annoyance he had written an unpleasant
letter to Arthur. He had also expressed his grievances to the sexton, John Brown, and to
the Haworth schoolmaster, Edmund Bickall.[44] On 7 June Charlotte reported to Ellen:

That unlucky Mr. de Renzy continues his efforts to give what trouble he can – and I am
obliged to conceal and keep things from Papa's knowledge as well as I can to spare him that
anxiety which hurts him so much. Mr. de R's whole aim is to throw Papa into the dilemma
of being without a curate for some weeks. Papa has every legal right to frustrate this at once
by telling him he must stay until his quarter is up – but this is just the harsh decided sort of
measure which it goes against Papa's nature to adopt and which I can not and will not urge
upon him while he is in delicate health. I feel compelled to throw the burden of the contest
upon Mr. Nicholls who is younger – more pugnacious and can bear it better. The worst of it
is Mr. N. has not Papa's rights to speak and act or he would do it to purpose.

There was also a worry over Arthur Nicholls' health. On 21 May Charlotte wrote to
Ellen to say that she had heard that Nicholls 'was suffering sharply from his rheumatic

affection'. When he arrived at the parsonage on the next day to stay for a week she was frightened by his appearance:

> It was wasted and strange, and his whole manner was nervous. My worst apprehensions – I thought were in the way of being realized. However – inquiry gradually relieved me. In the first place – he could give his ailment no name. He had not one touch of rheumatism – that report was quite groundless – He was going to die, however, or something like it.

This melancholy statement drew a sharp comment from Charlotte:

> I took heart on hearing this – which may seem paradoxical – but you know – dear Nell – when people are really going to die – they don't come a distance of some fifty miles to tell you so.[45]

After making further enquiries Charlotte discovered that Mr Nicholls had consulted the Leeds doctor, Mr Teale, who had informed him that 'he had no manner of complaint whatever except an over-excited mind'. Although the fear over Nicholls' health had proved to be groundless, it transpired that it was one of the reasons for Patrick's opposition to the marriage.[46]

One other factor to be arranged before the wedding was Charlotte's marriage settlement. This was drawn up on 24 May. Her earnings from her writing and from the residue of her railway investments amounted to £1,678 9s 9d (£1,678.49). A clause was inserted in the settlement stating that if she died childless the entire value of the trust would go, not to Arthur Nicholls but to Patrick. This stipulation shows that Charlotte was determined that her father should not lose financially by her marriage. It is a mark of Arthur Nicholls' love for her that he acquiesced in this arrangement.

There were problems fixing the date of the wedding. Cover for the services at Haworth would be required while they were away on their honeymoon and, as Charlotte told Ellen, Mr de Renzy was continuing to be difficult:

> Papa gave him up to three weeks of his quarter – and now he is moving heaven & earth to get a fortnight more – on pretence of wanting a holiday.[47]

A few days later she reported:

> Mr. de Renzy has succeeded in obtaining his holiday – and whereas – his quarter will not be up till the 20th. of August – he leaves on 25th June. This gives rise to much trouble and many difficulties, as you may imagine – and Papa's whole anxiety now is to get the business over – Mr. Nicholls – with his usual trustworthiness – takes all the trouble of providing substitutes on his own shoulders.[48]

It seems that Charlotte was being a little unfair on the unfortunate Mr de Renzy. The registers show that he returned to Haworth to take five baptisms on 16 July and a service on 21 July. Other clergymen whom Mr Nicholls engaged to take services during this period were Thomas Crowther of Cragg Vale, who performed ten baptisms on 23 July and also preached the Sunday school sermons on that day, Joseph Grant of Oxenhope and William Mayne, the incumbent of Ingrow.

The date of the wedding was finally fixed for Thursday 29 June. Eighteen wedding cards announcing the marriage were sent out to friends, but the only guests invited to the ceremony were Ellen Nussey, who was to act as bridesmaid, and Miss Wooler. On the evening of the 28th Margaret Wooler and Ellen Nussey arrived at the parsonage. According to Mrs Gaskell's *Life*, it was just at bedtime that Patrick announced his intention of stopping at home while the others went to church. He had not been well and it seems that at the final moment he was in such a state that his resolution failed him and he felt he could not be present at the ceremony. His illness seems genuine enough, for a month later, on 28 July, Charlotte wrote to Martha Brown from Dublin:

> I feel very anxious about Papa – the idea of his illness has followed me all through my journey and made me miserable sometimes when otherwise I should have been happy enough.

Patrick's announcement caused great consternation to the wedding party. They were worried over who could properly give away the bride in the absence of her father. After recourse to the Prayer Book they found to their relief that the rubric enjoins that the minister shall receive 'the woman from her father's or friend's hands' and that nothing was specified as to the sex of the 'friend'. Miss Wooler volunteered to perform this duty.

Charlotte had wanted the wedding to be as quiet as possible. Arthur had fallen in with this desire and hardly anyone in Haworth was aware of what was happening. Early on the 29th John Robinson, a youth who had had private lessons from Mr Nicholls, was waylaid in Church Lane by the sexton, John Brown. He was informed about the wedding and told to go to the top of the hill and look out for the arrival of three men, Arthur Nicholls, Joseph Grant and Sutcliffe Sowden. As soon as he saw them he was to run to the parsonage to convey the news. After the lad had carried out these instructions he was sent to bring the parish clerk, Joseph Redman, to the church. The marriage ceremony was performed by Sutcliffe Sowden, the vicar of Hebden Bridge and Arthur Nicholls' closest friend, who had provided him with much support and hospitality during the past year. After the short service the party retired to the parsonage for a wedding breakfast. The few Haworth people who saw Charlotte thought she looked like a snowdrop in her white muslin wedding dress with a lace mantle, and white bonnet trimmed with green leaves.

Shortly after breakfast a carriage and pair drove up to the parsonage and took the bridal couple to Keighley station for the start of their journey to Conway, where they

spent a few days touring the North Wales coast before taking the packet steamer to
Dublin. After Arthur had shown Charlotte the sights of Dublin, including his *alma
mater*, Trinity College, they travelled to his former home at Banagher, where they were
warmly received by his aunt, Mrs Bell, at Cuba House. When she saw the grandeur of
the surroundings in which Arthur had spent his childhood, Charlotte was compelled
to revise her opinion of her husband's humble origins. The couple spent a week at
Banagher, and then set out on an extensive tour of the country. After reaching the
west coast, they visited Kilkee, Tarbert, Tralee, Killarney, Glengariff and Cork before
returning to Dublin. They returned to Haworth in the early evening of Tuesday 1
August, having been away almost a month.

'My Daughter is indeed dead'
1854–1855

I thank you for your kind sympathy. My Daughter is indeed dead. … The marriage that took place, seem'd to hold forth, long and bright prospects of happiness, but … all our hopes have ended in disappointment.

Patrick Brontë to Mrs Gaskell, 5 April 1855

Patrick had been unwell for much of the time that Charlotte and Arthur were in Ireland, but with their return he soon recovered and within a few weeks he was able to resume preaching at least once on Sundays. Arthur was as good as his word in giving his support and on 22 August Charlotte was able to report to Margaret Wooler:

Papa has taken no duty since we returned – and each time I see Mr. Nicholls put on gown or surplice – I feel comforted to think that this marriage has secured Papa good aid in his old age.

The couple received so many expressions of good will from the parishioners that they decided to invite all those associated with the church, the scholars and teachers of the Sunday and day schools together with the bellringers and singers, to a tea and supper in the schoolroom. Five hundred were invited and the occasion was a great success:

They seemed to enjoy it much, and it was very pleasant to see their happiness. One of the villagers in proposing my husband's health described him as "a consistent Christian and a kind gentleman." I own the words touched me.[1]

To her surprise Charlotte found that she greatly enjoyed her new married life. She was proud of her husband's work:

Every Morning he is in the National School by nine o'clock; he gives the children religious instruction till ½ past 10. Almost every afternoon he pays visits amongst the poorest

parishioners. Of course he often finds a little work for his wife to do, and I h
sorry to help him.[2]

Married life also seems to have improved Charlotte's health, and in Nove....ber she was able to report to Miss Wooler:

> It is long since I have known such comparative immunity from headache, sickness and indigestion, as during the last three months.
>
> My life is different from what it used to be – May God make me thankful for it! I have a good, kind, attached husband, and every day makes my own attachment to him stronger.[3]

Charlotte's friends Joe and Amelia Taylor and their little daughter 'Tim'[4] called at the parsonage in October and Charlotte's description of their visit provides a brief glimpse of the seventy-eight-year-old Patrick at this time:

> Tim behaved capitally on the whole. She amused Papa very much – chattering away to him very funnily – his white hair took her fancy – she announced a decided preference for it over Arthur's black hair – and coolly advised the latter to "go to the barber, and get his whiskers cut off." Papa says she speaks as I did when I was a child – says the same odd unexpected things.[5]

Such an anecdote would seem to give the lie to the suggestion that Patrick did not like children. Among the other visitors to Haworth at this time was Sir James Kay-Shuttleworth, who came early in November with the suggestion that Arthur should accept the living of the new church he had built near his house in Padiham. The income of £200 would have represented a considerable increase on his present salary, but Arthur remained true to his promise not to leave Haworth.

Despite his wife's literary fame, Arthur Nicholls was very keen on their privacy. Realising how freely Charlotte expressed herself in her letters to Ellen Nussey, he sought an assurance that Ellen would destroy all the letters which she received. This greatly upset Ellen, who had carefully kept all Charlotte's letters over the many years of their friendship. At first she prevaricated, but when Arthur pressed the matter she wrote back promising to destroy Charlotte's letters provided that he pledged himself 'to no censorship in the matter communicated'.[6] Since she was convinced that Nicholls did censor his wife's letters, she then felt herself free of any commitment in the matter.

As the year drew to a close, the news from the Crimean War was very bad. Although the British had repulsed the Russian attacks on Balaclava and Inkerman, they had suffered very heavy casualties and had also failed to take Sebastopol. A National Patriotic Fund was set up to assist the wounded and also to provide benefit for their wives and children. Patrick was anxious to raise local contributions to the fund. On 16 November

..e convened a meeting in the National School to raise a subscription in the township. Since his eyesight remained very poor, Charlotte and her husband wrote the circular letters which were sent in Patrick's name to the leading parishioners requesting their attendance at the meeting.

In the second week of January 1855 Charlotte and Arthur went to stay with Sir James and Lady Kay-Shuttleworth at Gawthorpe Hall for a few days, but on their return Charlotte became unwell. Although she may have been suffering from a cold, the real reason for her illness was that she was pregnant. She wrote to Ellen with a hint of her condition:

> Don't conjecture – dear Nell – for it is too soon yet – though I certainly never before felt as I have done lately. But keep the matter wholly to yourself – for I can come to no decided opinion at present.[7]

At first she was well enough to receive at the parsonage a cousin of Arthur's, the Rev'd James Adamson Bell, who came on a short visit and whom she described as 'a true gentleman by nature and cultivation'. She also planned a visit to Ellen, but was then compelled to take to her bed. On 29 January Arthur Nicholls told Ellen that he had sent for Dr Macturk from Bradford 'as I wish to have better advice than Haworth affords.' Three days later he told her:

> Dr. Macturk saw Charlotte on Tuesday. His opinion was that her illness would be of some duration, – but that there was no immediate danger.[8]

On 3 February Patrick described the situation in a letter to Sir James Kay-Shuttleworth:

> For Several days past, she has been confin'd to her bed, where she Still lies, oppress'd with nausea, sickness, irritation, and a slow feverish feeling – and a consequent want of appetite and digestion. Our Village, surgeon, visits her daily, and we have had a visit from Dr. Mackturk [sic] of Bradford – who, both think her sickness is symptomatic – and that after a few weeks they hope her health, will again return – nevertheless the trying circumstance gives much uneasiness in our little family circle.

Charlotte's condition did not improve, however, and on 17 February she made her will, in which she overturned her marriage settlement and left everything to Arthur Nicholls. The witnesses were Patrick and Martha Brown. The terms of the will provide a striking testimony to the happiness of her marriage and her confidence in Arthur's integrity. She also paid tribute to him in a short note to Ellen, which she pencilled from her bed on or after 21 February:

> I want to give you an assurance which I know will comfort you – and that is that I find in my husband the tenderest nurse, the kindest support – the best earthly comfort that ever woman had. His patience never fails and it is tried by sad days and broken nights.

On the same day that Charlotte made her will, Tabby Aykroyd died at the age of eighty-four. She had been a faithful servant to the family for over thirty years. Arthur Nicholls had the sad task of taking her funeral and burying her in Haworth churchyard.

As the days passed, Charlotte gradually grew weaker and Mrs Gaskell recorded that, when Martha tried to cheer her by telling her to look forward to the baby that was coming, she could only sigh:

> I dare say I shall be glad some time, but I am so ill – so weary.

And, overhearing her husband murmuring some words in prayer that God would spare her, she whispered:

> Oh! I am not going to die am I? He will not separate us, we have been so happy.[9]

Towards the end of March, Arthur Nicholls, who had shown great courage in continuing all his parish duties, asked his old friend Joseph Grant to perform these for him, while he remained at Charlotte's bedside.

As the inevitable outcome became clear, Patrick showed great strength and fortitude. On 30 March, when Arthur Nicholls was too overcome to write a letter, Patrick himself wrote a short, dignified note to Ellen, to give her warning of Charlotte's imminent death:

> My dear Madam,
>
> We are all in great trouble, and Mr Nicholls so much so, that he is not sufficiently strong, and composed as to be able to write – I therefore devote a few moments, to tell You, that my Dear Daughter is very ill, and apparently on the verge of the grave – if she could Speak, she would no doubt dictate to us whilst answering Your kind letter, but we are left to ourselves, to give what answer we can – The Doctors have no hope of her case, and fondly as we along [*sic*] time, cherished hope, that hope is now gone, and we [have] only to look forward to the solemn event, with prayer to God, that he will give us grace and Strength sufficient unto our day – Will you be so kind as to write to Miss Wooler, and Mrs Joe Taylor, and inform them that we requested you to do so – telling them of our present condition.

Charlotte died early the next morning, Saturday 31 March 1855, just three weeks before her thirty-ninth birthday. Mr Ingham, the Haworth surgeon who had attended her throughout her last illness, certified the cause of death as 'Phthisis', a progressive wasting disease. It was her pregnancy and the consequent nausea which she suffered, however, which finally caused her death. Later that day Ellen Nussey arrived in response to Patrick's letter and was invited by Patrick to stay at the parsonage until the burial.

Charlotte's funeral was held on Wednesday 4 April. The church and churchyard were crowded with parishioners. Amongst them, as Patrick later discovered, was a poor blind girl whom Charlotte had supported:

> A poor blind girl, who received an annual donation from [my] Daughter, … after her death requir'd to be led four miles, to be at my daughters funeral, over which she wept many tears of gratitude and sorrow.[10]

The service was taken by Sutcliffe Sowden, who only nine months before had performed Charlotte and Arthur's wedding ceremony, and her body was committed to the family vault. After the service Patrick returned to the parsonage with his son-in-law. A few weeks before her death, Charlotte had written to her friend Amelia Taylor saying how happy she was at their relationship:

> It is an hourly happiness to me dear Amelia to see how well Arthur and my Father get on together now – there has never been a misunderstanding or a wrong word.[11]

Three days after Charlotte's burial, Patrick's old friend William Cartman, the headmaster of Skipton Grammar School, came over from Skipton to preach the memorial sermon. He took as his text Luke 8: 52:

> And all wept, and bewailed her: but he said, Weep not; she is not dead, but sleepeth.

News of Charlotte's death spread gradually during the following days. John Greenwood, the Haworth stationer, took it on himself to inform some of her famous friends, including Mrs Gaskell and Harriet Martineau. Mrs Gaskell, who had not known that Charlotte was ill, wrote at once to Patrick to offer her sympathy. She received a dignified reply:

> I thank you for your kind sympathy – My Daughter, is indeed, dead, and the solemn truth presses upon her worthy, and affectionate Husband and me, with great, and, it may be, with unusual weight – But, others, also, have, or shall have their sorrows, and we feel our own the most – The marriage that took place, seem'd to hold forth, long, and bright prospects of happiness, but in the inscrutable providence of God, all our hopes have ended in disappointment, and our joy in mourning – May we resign to the Will of the most High – After three months of Sickness, a tranquil death closed the scene. But our loss we trust is

her gain – But why Should I trouble you longer with our sorrows. "The heart knoweth its own bitterness" – and we ought to bear with fortitude our own grievances, & not to bring others – into our sufferings.

In a postscript he added:

Excuse this scrawl, I am not fit, at present, to write much – nor to write satisfactorily.[12]

On 20 April George Smith wrote to express his condolences. Patrick wrote an appreciative reply:

I thank you for your kind sympathy. Having heard my Dear Daughter speak So much about you and your family, your letter seem'd to be one from an Old Friend. Her Husband's sorrow And Mine is indeed very great – We mourn the loss of one, whose like, we hope not, ever to see again.[13]

The letter which seems to have moved Patrick most, however, was the one he received from the Bishop of Ripon, Charles Longley, who had stayed at the parsonage two years earlier. Patrick's reply reveals both his deep sense of bereavement and the strong comfort which he derived from his firm Christian belief:

My Lord Bishop,

Amongst the various letters of kind sympathy which we have received, Your Lordships Letter, gives us especial pleasure – It is wort[hy] of One who is justly esteem'd the Father of His Clergy, and I will retain it Amongst my most valued treasures, as long as I shall live. "A word in due season, how good is it!" And most assuredly, if a Season of Sorrow, needs a word of consolation and support, ours is that season. I have lived long enough, to bury a beloved Wife, and six children – all that I had – I greatly enjoyed their conversation and company, and many of them, were well fitted for being companions to the Wisest and best – Now they are all gone – Their image and memory remain, and meet me at every turn – but they, themselves have left me, a bereaved Old man – I hoped and wish'd, that the Lord would spare them, to see me laid in my grave, but the Lord has ordered it otherwise, and I have seen them all laid in that place, "where the wicked cease from troubling and the Weary are at rest" – I have not only my own sorrow to bear, but I am distress'd for Mr. Nicholls, whose grief is very great – His union with My Daughter was a happy one – They were well fitted for each other, and naturally look'd forward, to future scenes of happiness for a long time to come – but the Lord gave, and the Lord took early away – May we both be able from our hearts to say blessed be the name of the Lord. But, I have often found, and find in this last Sad trial, that it is frequently extremely difficult to walk entirely by faith, and sincerely to pray, "Thy will be done on earth, as it is in heaven" – Mr. Nicholls, who is every thing I could desire, to the Church and to me, intends to stay with me, during the brief remainder of my life – May we beg, that Your Lordship, will sometimes, remember us in Your prayers, –

> I remain, My Lord Bishop,
> Your Lordship's most
> Obedient Humble Servant,
> Patrick Brontë.[14]

'No quailing Mrs Gaskell!
No drawing back!'
1855–1857

Mr Brontë ... desirous above all things that her life should be written, and written by me. (His last words were 'No quailing Mrs Gaskell! no drawing back!').

Mrs Gaskell to Ellen Nussey, 24 July 1855

Charlotte died at the beginning of Holy Week. Both Patrick and Arthur were too stricken with grief to perform any duties. Their clerical friends rallied round to give support at this busy time. Sutcliffe Sowden, who had taken Charlotte's funeral, also performed four other burial services. The incumbent of Cullingworth, the Revd J. H. Mitchell, took the services on Easter Day and also carried out Patrick's usual task of addressing the Haworth Mechanics' Institute on the following day. At this meeting a moving tribute was paid by Michael Merrall, the chairman, to 'the Institute's most distinguished member and patroness, 'Currer Bell".[1]

Patrick and Arthur soon resumed their quiet, ordered life in the parsonage. Two weeks after Charlotte's death Patrick noted in his account book a purchase he had made from William Summerscale, the master of the Haworth Free Grammar School, who was also the church organist:

On April 13th. 1855 I bought from Mr. Summerscale, "Cato", then only a year and a half old – for £3-0-0 (£3) He is two thirds, a Newfoundland dog, and one third a retriever, His mother belonged to Mr. Ferrand – My Dr D-t-r Ch.tt, greatly admired him.

It was probably Charlotte's admiration for the dog which motivated Patrick to make this purchase so soon after her death. Two months later he bought a second dog from Mr Summerscale, which he named Plato, describing it as a 'breed from a Newfoundland bitch, and a water spaniel'.

There were also changes in the household. In June Martha Brown was taken ill. The efforts of running the household single-handedly, while also nursing Tabby Aykroyd and Charlotte in their last illnesses, had taken its toll. She could not be cared for at the parsonage and, because her father was terminally ill, there was no room for her at home. She was sent to Mrs Dean's almshouses in Leeds, where she was gradually nursed back to health. Her place at the parsonage was taken by her younger sister, Eliza. Both Patrick and Arthur took a keen interest in Martha's progress and Arthur visited her in Leeds. Patrick wrote to her on 9 June:

> I am glad, Martha that – notwithstanding you do not seem to get much better, you have not got worse – and I think it will be best for you to come home at the time you mention. Eliza says she can stay here till you get well – and are able to do the work of the house, as usual – I am quite satisfied by Eliza's proceedings, She is very steady, and does her work very well. I will tell Mr. Nicholls, that you were very much pleased, and thankful for his calling to see you – Both He, and I, are very desirous of your recovery – ... All your Family, except your Father, are well – He is not worse, than when you saw him last time – but he is not much better. The warm weather may do him some good – but his case is dangerous.
>
> Your Mother – Eliza, and all Your Family, send their love to You –

Martha's father, John Brown, the Haworth sexton, died on 13 August 1855 and his funeral was taken by Arthur Nicholls.

When they heard of Charlotte's death, the former servants at the parsonage, Nancy and Sarah Garrs, renewed contact with Patrick. Nancy paid a visit to Haworth and Sarah (now Mrs Newsome), who had emigrated to the United States after her marriage, wrote to him from Iowa. On 12 June Patrick replied to her letter:

> Since you were with me, many solemn, and important changes have taken place, in my domestic concerns – When You, and your sister Nancy, first came to us at Thornton, My Dear Wife, and all my Dear Children were living – ... They are all now dead – and I bordering, on the age of eighty years, am left Alone – But it is God's will – and to this, it is our duty and wisdom to resign – You probably, little thought, that the children You nursed on your knees, would have been so much noticed by the world – as they have been – Emily and Anne, wrote and published clever books – and Charlotte's writings and fame, are known in all parts where Genius, and learning are held in high esteem. ... My Children and I, often thought and talked of you.

A year later Patrick wrote to their brother, Henry Garrs, who had written to him on the first anniversary of Charlotte's death, enclosing some verses in her memory. Patrick's letter reveals the continuing depth of his grief:

I thank you for your friendly and able letter – your lines are pathetic and good, and I might say much upon them – but my grief is so deep and lasting, that I cannot long dwell on my sad privation – I try to look to God, for consolation, and pray that he will give me grace, and strength equal to my day – and resignation to his will.[2]

It is clear that Patrick and Arthur were now getting on very well together. In his letter to Sarah Newsome, Patrick had described Arthur as 'a very worthy and respectable Clergyman' and he was very grateful for his continued help and support. Patrick's respect for Arthur was made abundantly clear on 20 June 1855 when he made his will. After leaving forty pounds 'to be equally divided amongst all my brothers and sisters', and thirty pounds 'to my servant, Martha Brown, as a token of regard for long and faithful services to me and my children', he left the residue of his personal estate 'to my beloved and esteemed son-in-law, the Rev. Arthur Bell Nicholls, BA.' Nicholls was also made his sole executor. The will was witnessed by Joseph Redman, the parish clerk, and by Eliza Brown.[3]

Tributes to Charlotte were published in a wide range of newspapers and magazines. Many of them based their information on an obituary written by Harriet Martineau in the *Daily News* of 6 April 1855. Drawing on Charlotte's Biographical Notice of her sisters, written for the 1850 edition of their works, on information given her by John Greenwood, the Haworth stationer, and on her own memories of meeting Charlotte, Miss Martineau's portrayal contained many of the half-truths and misunderstandings which would later become part of the accepted myth about the Brontë family. She described Mr Brontë as 'simple and unworldly' and 'too much absorbed in his studies to notice her occupations' and set Charlotte's home 'among the wild Yorkshire hills in a place where newspapers were never seen'.

At the beginning of June an anonymous article appeared in *Sharpe's London Magazine* under the heading 'A Few Words About Jane Eyre'. It contained many misleading statements about Charlotte's life and painted a bleak picture of her isolated home background, 'on the northern side of one of the wildest and bleakest moors of Yorkshire.' It also portrayed her father as:

A man of studious and solitary habits, and of a singular and highly eccentric turn of mind, which together with a very peculiar temper, must have rendered him anything but a suitable guardian to a youthful family.

After reading the article, Ellen Nussey wrote an indignant letter to Arthur Nicholls:

I have been much hurt and pained by the perusal of an article in 'Sharpe' for this month. ... I am sure both you and Mr Brontë will feel acutely the misrepresentations and the malignant spirit which characterises it. Will you suffer the article to pass current without any refutations? The writer merits the contempt of silence, but there will be readers and believers. Shall such be left to imbibe a tissue of malign falsehoods, or shall an attempt be made to do justice to one who so highly deserved justice, whose very name those who best knew her but speak with reverence and affection? Should not her aged father be defended from the reproach the writer coarsely attempts to bring upon him?

She went on to suggest the writer who should be asked to respond:

> I wish Mrs Gaskell, who is every way capable, would undertake a reply, and would give a sound castigation to the writer.

She added that if Mrs Gaskell lacked the necessary information, she herself would supply her with:

> facts sufficient to set aside much that is asserted, if you yourself are not provided with all the information that is needed on the subjects produced.[4]

There is an ironic twist to this situation. A careful study of the article in *Sharpe's London Magazine* reveals that much of its content is taken from a letter which Mrs Gaskell wrote after her first meeting with Charlotte, when they were both guests of Sir James and Lady Kay-Shuttleworth in the Lake District in August 1850. During her stay Mrs Gaskell had heard from Lady Kay-Shuttleworth the details of Charlotte's strange home background and the eccentricities of her father, which she had gleaned from the nurse from Burnley who had worked at the parsonage during Mrs Brontë's last illness. All this information Mrs Gaskell had poured out a few days later in a long letter to her friend, Catherine Winkworth.[5] It is clear that the author of the article in *Sharpe's London Magazine* has incorporated many details from this letter. The similarities, verbatim in places, are far too numerous for this to have happened by coincidence. Although it seems inconceivable that Mrs Gaskell actually wrote the article herself, it is abundantly clear that the information in it is taken from the letter which she wrote at that time.[6]

The author of the article was probably Frank Smedley, a former editor of *Sharpe's London Magazine*. On 5 May 1855 Smedley received a letter from Charles Dickens in which Dickens wrote:

> I cannot reconcile it to my heart to publish these details so soon after Miss Brontë's death. For anything I know they might be saddening and painful to her husband, and I am not at all clear that I have any right to them.

It would appear that Dickens was writing to say that he felt unable to accept an article on Charlotte Brontë which Smedley had submitted for inclusion in Dickens' weekly magazine, *Household Words*. It is probable that Frank Smedley then decided to insert his article in *Sharpe's London Magazine*, to which he was still a regular contributor.

On receiving Ellen's letter, Arthur Nicholls ordered a copy of the magazine so that he and Patrick might see for themselves what had been said. He then wrote to Ellen pointing out that, although there were many mistakes in the article, the writer had not written with any unkind intent, but merely 'to gratify the curiosity of the multitude' over one who 'had made such a sensation in the literary world.' He added that the remarks about Patrick had merely caused him great amusement:

> Indeed, I have not seen him laugh as much for some months as he did while I was reading the article to him.

Arthur thought that it would be best not to reply to the article, 'as by doing so we should have given it an importance which it would not otherwise have obtained.'[7]

It seems that there was then further discussion of this matter at the parsonage. Although Arthur wanted privacy above all things, Patrick seems to have been attracted by the idea that a celebrated author, herself a friend of Charlotte, should be asked to write an authorised biography of his daughter. Only five days after Arthur had written to Ellen rejecting her idea, Patrick himself wrote to Mrs Gaskell a letter which was to have far-reaching consequences:

> My dear Madam,
>
> Finding that a great many scribblers, as well as some clever and truthful writers, have published articles, in Newspapers, and tracts – respecting my Dear Daughter Charlotte, since her death, seeing that many things that have been stated, are true, but more false – and having reason to think that, some may venture to write her life, who will be ill qualified for the undertaking, I can see no better plan, under these circumstances, than to apply to some established Author, to write a brief account of her life – and to make some remarks on her works – You, seem to me, to be the best qualified, for doing what I wish should be done – If, therefore, you will be so kind, as to publish a long or short account of her life and works, just as you may deem expedient & proper – Mr Nicholls, and I, will give you such information, as you may require.[8]

Mrs Gaskell, who herself had already toyed with the idea of writing a memoir about Charlotte, readily agreed to Patrick's request. As she told George Smith:

> I have received most unexpectedly the enclosed letter from Mr Brontë; I have taken some time to consider the request made in it, but I have consented to write it, *as well as I can*. Of course it becomes a much more serious task than the one which, as you know, I was proposing to myself, to put down my personal recollections &c. I shall now have to omit

a good deal of detail as to her home, and the circumstances, which must have had so much to do in forming her character. All these can be merely indicated during the life-time of her father, and to a certain degree in the lifetime of her husband.[9]

Patrick was delighted by Mrs Gaskell's acceptance and on 20 June he wrote to give her some information about his own early life and family background. He also described the lives and education of his children and, in a reference to their writing, said:

> When my daughters were at home, they read their manuscripts to each other, and gave their candid opinions of what was written – I never interfer'd with them at these times – I judged it best to throw them upon their own responsibility, Besides a Clergyman bordering on the age of eighty years, was likely to be too cold and severe a critic of the efforts of buoyant and youthful Genius – Hence it came to pass that I never saw their works till they appear'd in print.

In a postscript, he added:

> Your kind consent – has given Mr. Nicholls, and me great pleasure – it has broken in like a ray of light on our gloomy solitude. We shall have great pleasure to see you here whenever you may choose – But you will see a sad change – You will be so kind as to let us know, a few days before your arrival.

His letter was accompanied by a biographical note giving the dates of some important family events. In subsequent letters Patrick provided Mrs Gaskell with further details about his family.

Mrs Gaskell was not able to fit in a visit to the parsonage until 23 July, when she came to Haworth accompanied by Winkworth. Four days later, in a letter to her daughter Marianne, she gave a brief account of their visit:

> On Monday Katie & I set out in that broiling heat for Haworth, & got there about 1 o'clock. It was a most painful visit. Both Mr Brontë & Mr Nicholls cried sadly. I like Mr Nicholls.[10]

She came away from the parsonage with a dozen of Charlotte's letters, most of them written to Emily, a few to her father and brother, and one to Aunt Branwell, all from the period 1839–1843. Aware that Charlotte's life might appear uneventful and that it might be difficult to extract personal details from Patrick and Arthur, she was determined to get as much information as she could from Charlotte's friends. On the day after her visit to Haworth, she wrote to Ellen Nussey with the request that she should let her see some of the many letters which she had received from Charlotte. She told Ellen that, although both Patrick and Arthur had agreed to her writing Charlotte's life, they had differing attitudes towards the project:

Mr Brontë not perceiving the full extent of the great interest in her personal history felt by strangers, but desirous above all things that her life should be written, and written by me. (His last words were 'No quailing Mrs Gaskell! no drawing back!') Mr Nicholls was far more aware of the kind of particulars which people would look for; and saw how they had snatched at every gossiping account of her, and how desirable it was to have a full authorised history of her life, if it were done at all. His feeling was against it's being written; but he yielded to Mr Brontë's impetuous wish.

A few days later she went to see Ellen at her home in Birstall. At this meeting Ellen handed over some 300 of the 500 letters from Charlotte which she had kept. After carefully reading through them, she had erased some names of persons and places and had arranged them in chronological order. A few weeks later Mrs Gaskell wrote to her telling her how much she valued them:

> They gave me a very beautiful idea of her character. I am sure that the more fully she, Charlotte Brontë – the *friend* the *daughter* the *sister* the *wife*, is known – and known where need be in her own words – the more highly will she be appreciated."

It is clear from this statement that in the biography Mrs Gaskell intended to quote directly from Charlotte's letters. This was not what Arthur Nicholls had anticipated. In a letter to Ellen of 24 July he had written:

> Mrs G. is anxious to see any of her letters – Especially those of any early date – I think I understood you to say that you had some – if so we should feel obliged by your letting us have any that you may think proper – not for publication, but merely to give the writer an insight into her mode of thought.

Mrs Gaskell had, however, come to realise that the direct use of Charlotte's letters would add vigour and interest to the biography. She now sought to obtain more of Charlotte's letters and, after some reluctance on their part, she was given several by Margaret Wooler and George Smith.

On 27 August Patrick wrote to Mrs Gaskell again, to deny certain false statements which he had heard had been made about him:

> I have heard indirectly, that it has been reported that I was opposed on my entrance into this Living – and that my salary was withheld from me, for two years, and that this was mentioned to a Clergyman, by a Lady who was engaged in writing the life of "Currer Bell". As there is misunderstanding here, I wish to say, that I never met with any opposition, and never had any part of my salary kept from me – but on the contrary have always received from the Inhabitants and Patrons friendly and kindly treatment.

He went on to say that he assumed these stories arose from the dispute between the trustees and the vicar of Bradford over the nomination of his predecessor, Samuel Redhead, in which the opposition of the inhabitants had led to his enforced resignation.

Throughout the autumn of 1855 Mrs Gaskell busied herself collecting material about Charlotte from all those who had known her. She was reluctant to pay a second visit to the parsonage, where she felt she would only revive painful memories of Charlotte's death. She was also convinced that Arthur Nicholls would be unwilling to give her any information beyond what he considered absolutely necessary. By December both Patrick and Arthur were disturbed by the fact that they had seen and heard nothing of Mrs Gaskell since her visit in July. On 24 December Arthur wrote to Ellen expressing his concern:

> We have neither heard nor seen anything of Mrs Gaskell – I have every confidence that she will do ample justice to Charlotte – but I am quite sensible that she has undertaken a very difficult task with only slender material.

On 23 January 1856 Patrick wrote in similar vein to Mrs Gaskell:

> Mr Nicholls, and I, often think of what you have so obligingly enter'd on, of what the public, will expect from you, on whatever subject you may write; and of the few facts, and incidents you have of a biographical nature – we so frequently talk over, and meditate on these things, that we are forced at last, to solve the difficulty, by saying that You must draw largely on the resources of your own mind. ... I often think that if you would write a running critique on her works, as well as her life, – it would be highly popular, and render your task easier, by an accession of subject matter.

It is clear from this letter that Patrick thought that, in order to gain enough material for the biography, Mrs Gaskell, in addition to giving an account of Charlotte's life, would find it necessary to evaluate her literary works. What neither he nor Arthur realised was that she now had access to a very large number of Charlotte's letters, which revealed many details of her home and private life, and that it was her intention to include long quotations from these in her biography.

Early in May Mrs Gaskell travelled to Brussels where, although Madame Heger was unwilling to see her, she had a meeting with her husband, Constantin. The two got on very well together and when the biography was published Mrs Gaskell protected Monsieur Heger's reputation (and Charlotte's) by glossing over the reasons for Charlotte's estrangement from Madame Heger which had led to her departure from Brussels in December 1843.

By the late summer of 1856 much of the biography had been written. As the work progressed Mrs Gaskell read passages from her manuscript to both George Smith and

Ellen Nussey. In July Mr Smith wrote to her expressing his concern over certain aspects of her portrayal of Patrick. In some alarm she wrote to Ellen enclosing George Smith's note to her:

> A note of his ... which I enclose for your own *private* reading, makes me rather uncomfortable. See the passage I have marked at the side. I thought I carefully preserved the reader's respect for Mr Brontë, while truth and the desire of doing justice to her compelled me to state the domestic peculiarities of her childhood, which ... contributed so much to make her what she was; yet you see what Mr Smith says, and what reviews, in their desire for smartness and carelessness for scrupulous consideration, would be sure to say, even yet more plainly.[12]

Ellen's reply showed that she too shared some of George Smith's concerns over how readers would react to the portrayal of Mr Brontë:

> Your description of Mr B made an impression on me which I always meant to describe to you when I saw you next – The anecdote of the little coloured shoes produced a mental sting that no time would obliterate and I felt that all commonplace readers would fail to see the Spartan nature of the act unless you plainly pointed it out to them, and I was intending to ask you to make very clear and distinct comments on Mr B.'s character – I do not wish anything you have said suppressed only I think readers will have to be taught to think kindly of Mr B.[13]

Eager to obtain fresh material Mrs Gaskell now decided to pay a second visit to the parsonage, this time in the company of Sir James Kay-Shuttleworth. In order to prepare for her visit, she persuaded her husband to send Patrick a printed copy of a sermon Mr Gaskell had preached in Cross Street Chapel on Sunday 4 May 1856, which had been celebrated as a Day of National Thanksgiving for the peace concluded with Russia at the end of the Crimean War.[14] In this sermon Mr Gaskell had defended both the war and the peace as being honourable. He drew the distinction between 'the peace of mere compulsion', which he termed 'a state of slavery hopeless of all redemption' and 'the peace of the gospel', which he described as 'the fellowship of free agents'. He declared that he did not regard war as the greatest of all evils: 'Fighting assuredly is bad, but national dishonour is worse.' These were sentiments close to Patrick's own heart and on 23 July he wrote to Mr Gaskell expressing his gratitude:

> I thank you for Your Sermon, which I have read carefully over, with pleasure, and I trust with profit. The principles, and practices, which, it so ably advocates, are perfectly in accordance with my, own on the great subjects of war and peace.

And he added:

> We often wonder here, how Mrs Gaskell, is getting on, with Her mournful, but interesting task.

He was not to be kept in ignorance for long. Mrs Gaskell, together with Sir James, arrived at the parsonage on the very next day. Although Patrick was confined to bed with an attack of rheumatism, he got up to receive the visitors. Having caught Patrick and Arthur off guard by their sudden arrival, Sir James had no hesitation in demanding more personal information about Charlotte and he refused to accept Arthur Nicholls' denials. Despite her eagerness to obtain fresh material for her biography, even Mrs Gaskell felt embarrassed by Sir James' behaviour. She reported on her visit to George Smith the next day:

> I have had a very successful visit to Haworth – I went from Gawthrop, accompanied by Sir J
> P. K Shuttleworth, to whom it is evident both Mr Brontë & Mr Nicholls look up. – & who
> is not prevented by the fear of giving pain from asking in a peremptory manner for whatever
> he thinks desirable. He coolly took actual possession of many things while Mr Nicholls was
> saying he could not possibly part with them.[15]

She came away with the unpublished manuscripts of *The Professor* and of *Emma*, the unfinished last story which Charlotte had been writing. She was also given what she described as 'by far the most extraordinary of all':

> A packet about the size of a lady's travelling writing case, full of paper books of different
> sizes ... they are the wildest & most incoherent things, as far as we have examined them, *all*
> purporting to be written, or addressed to some member of the Wellesley family. They give
> one the idea of creative power carried to the verge of insanity.

These were the juvenilia, the little books written by the Brontë children in their childhood.

On 3 November 1856 Patrick wrote again to Mrs Gaskell to warn her of errors and misunderstandings about himself which he had heard were being given publicity. He enclosed with his letter a pamphlet giving information about himself and his family which he described as 'a strange compound of truth and error'. He said that the writer's comments about his marriage were 'in many respects entirely wrong':

> I was never in Penzance, or in Cornwall, the native town and County of my wife – I saw her
> only in Yorkshire – she was then of full age, and so was I – Her parents were dead, and with
> respect to our intended union, we had none to consult. We exercised our own judgment, and
> none, ever express'd any dissatisfaction with our marriage.

He added that he had no great objection to 'the Bookmaking gentry' making him out to be 'a somewhat extraordinary and eccentrick personage', but:

> The truth of the matter is – that I am, in some respects, a kindred likeness to the father of Margaret, in 'North and South' peaceable, feeling, sometimes thoughtful – and generally well-meaning. Yet unlike him in one thing – by occasionally getting into a satirical vein when I am disposed to dissect, and analyze, human character, and human nature '' like a curious surgeon – And being in early life thrown on my own resources – and consequently obliged, under Providence, to depend on my own judgment and exertions, I may not be so redy [sic] as some are, to be a follower of any man, or a worshipper of conventualit[i]es or forms, which may possibly to superficial observers, acquire me the character of a little eccentricity. Thus freely have I spoken to you – in order that in your work, you may insert such facts, as may counteract any false statements, that may have been made, or might be made, respecting me or mine.

It is unfortunate that Patrick's trust in Mrs Gaskell's willingness to examine critically the tales which were circulating was sadly misplaced. When the biography was published she included unaltered the tales about Patrick's supposed eccentricity, which she had first heard from Lady Kay-Shuttleworth in the summer of 1850: how his fits of wild temper caused him to cut up his wife's silk dress, to burn his children's coloured boots, to set fire to a hearth rug and to saw the legs off chairs.

At the conclusion of his letter Patrick added a stipulation which caused Mrs Gaskell some embarrassment. Alarmed by Sir James Kay-Shuttleworth's overbearing conduct on his recent visit to the parsonage and fearing that he might try to influence Mrs Gaskell over what was to be included in the biography, he concluded:

> We begin, now to long for seeing your work in print – And doubt not, you will see the propriety of shewing your manuscript to none, except Mr Gaskell, your Family, and the Publisher, and compositor. Much harm has often been done, by an opposite line of conduct, Authors, have been fetter'd, bias'd, and made to appear in other lights than their own – Genius has often been crush'd, and fame mar'd, by officious Critics, and familiar friends.

Mrs Gaskell, thinking that his comments were aimed at Ellen Nussey, was now placed in a quandary. In gratitude to Ellen for supplying so many of Charlotte's letters, she had promised her that she could read the completed manuscript. After some thought she deftly overcame Patrick's prohibition by inviting Ellen to come to Manchester where she read the manuscript to her.

It had always been Mrs Gaskell's intention to quote extensively from Charlotte's correspondence, but she now received a letter from Henry Chorley, the literary critic of the *Athenaeum*, warning her of the dangers of such action:

> Remember correspondent's permission to publish goes for nothing; the legal power over any
> deceased person's papers lies with the executors; … and thus Mr Nicholls *may*, if he likes turn
> sharp round on you, and not merely protest, but *prohibit*.

In great alarm she immediately contacted George Smith:

> Now I did *not* know all this; and Mr Nicholls is a terribly fickle person to have to do with; if
> I asked him for leave to make large extracts from her letters as I am doing, he would, ten to
> one, refuse it, – if I did not ask him, but went on, as I am doing, I *think* he would sigh and
> submit; but I could not feel sure. I was getting on so beautifully, & feeling or fancying the
> interest growing with every page.[16]

This was potentially a very serious situation. Both George Smith and Mrs Gaskell were
well aware that quotations from Charlotte's letters provided the biography with much
of its life and originality. If these were removed, the quality and impact of the work
would be greatly reduced. Mr Smith decided to send Mr Nicholls what he termed a
'business form of application', which would transfer the copyright of the 'materials of
the biography' into Mrs Gaskell's hands. This was presented to Mr Nicholls as a simple
precaution to prevent any claims being made on the biographer by Charlotte Brontë's
executors. Arthur Nicholls was not deceived, however, and refused to sign:

> not because I have or ever had the slightest intention of making any pecuniary claim on Mrs
> Gaskell on account of the work on which she is engaged; but simply because if I did so, I
> should be thereby precluded from making any further use of the MS referred to.[17]

He pointed out that when he had handed manuscripts over to her he had never had the
intention of parting with 'the exclusive right to them.' In response to Nicholls' refusal,
Mr Smith seems to have accused him of reneging on the agreement which he had made
with Mrs Gaskell. This accusation stung Arthur Nicholls, who in reply vehemently
denied that he had ever made any such agreement:

> I never authorized her to publish a single line of my wife's MS and correspondence. Such a
> thing was never mentioned – in fact until the receipt of your note I was not even aware that
> it was contemplated.[18]

He did, however, agree to sign the document, although in his letter he expressed the
bitterness which he had felt right from the beginning over the whole affair:

> I trust I shall not be required to do anything more in a matter, which from beginning to end
> has been a source of pain and annoyance to me; as I have been dragged into sanctioning a

proceeding utterly repugnant to my feelings – Indeed nothing but an unwillingness to thwart Mr Brontë's wishes could have induced me to acquiesce in a project, which in my eyes is little short of desecration.[19]

The Life of Charlotte Brontë was published on 25 March 1857 and created an immediate sensation similar to that made by the publication of *Jane Eyre*. Mrs Gaskell's decision to vindicate Charlotte by her stark portrayal of her family and their upbringing in the remote moorland village of Haworth was seized on by the critics as explanation for the strange and violent power of their novels. The success of her portrayal is most aptly exemplified by the review in the *Christian Romancer*, which stated:

Charlotte Brontë's small glimpse of the world showed her but an indifferent part of it, her home held a monster whom the strong ties of an inordinate family affection constrained her to love and care for and find excuses for. Whatever extenuation can be found for want of refinement – for grosser outrages on propriety than this expression indicates – the home and the neighbourhood of Charlotte Brontë certainly furnish; she wrote in ignorance of offending public opinion.[20]

On 2 April, in a letter which reflects his indomitable strength of spirit, Patrick wrote to Mrs Gaskell, thanking her for sending him the work and expressing his own opinion:

My dear Madam,

I thank you for the Books you have sent me, containg [sic] the Memoir of my Daughter, I have perused them, with a degree of pleasure and pain, which can be known only to myself. As you will have the opinion of abler Criticks [sic] than myself, I shall not say much in the way of criticism – I shall only make a few remarks in unison with the feelings of my heart.

With a tenacity of purpose, usual with me, in all cases of importance, I was fully determined, that the Biography of my Daughter, should, if possible, be written by one not unworthy of the undertaking. My mind, first turn'd to You – and You kindly acceded to my wishes. Had you refused, I would have applied to the next best – and so on – and had all applications fail'd, as the last resource, though above eighty years of age, and feeble, and unfit for the task, I would, myself, have written, a short though inadequate memoir, rather than have left all, to selfish, hostile or ignorant scribblers. But the work is now done, and done rightly, as I wish'd it to be, and in its completion, has afforded me, more satisfaction, than I have felt, during many years of a life, in which has been exemplified [sic] the saying that "man is born to trouble as the sparks fly upwards."

You have not only given a picture of my Dear Daughter Charlotte, but of my Dear wife, and all my Dear Children, and Such a picture too, as is full of truth and life. The picture of my brilliant and unhappy Son, and his diabolical Seducer, are Masterpieces. Indeed all the pictures in the work have vigorous, truthful, and delicate touches in them, which could have been executed only by a Skillful female hand. There are a few trifling mistakes, which should it be deem'd necessary, may be corrected in the Second Edition.

Patrick's letter shows remarkable forbearance towards Mrs Gaskell after the critical way in which she had depicted him. It is interesting to note the comment that her American friend, Charles Eliot Norton, made in his notebook on 16 April as he was travelling home with her from Italy where they had both been on holiday:

> Mrs Gaskell read to me the letter Mr Brontë wrote to her on receiving the volumes of her memoir of his daughter. It is a fine, strong, strange letter, quite characteristic of him. … He speaks of the mingled pain and pleasure he had had in reading it, not a word of what Mrs. G. had said of himself.

Since Mrs Gaskell was away in Italy at the time when Patrick's letter arrived, it was opened by her husband. William Gaskell was already aware that a storm was brewing over some of the allegations made in the book, and he hastily wrote to Patrick to ask for details of the 'few trifling mistakes' which Patrick had mentioned in his letter. Patrick replied on 7 April. Surprisingly, it was not the unfavourable portrait of himself on which he concentrated, but the statement that he had forbidden his family to eat meat. He singled this out because he considered that it had given some justification to the defenders of the Clergy Daughters' School, who were arguing that it was the weak health of Patrick's children, rather than the bad regime at the school, which had been responsible for their deaths:

> The principal mistake in the memoir – which I wish to mention, is that I laid my Daughters under restriction with regard to their diet, obliging them to live chiefly on vegetable food. This I never did. After their Aunts [*sic*] death, with regard to housekeeping affairs they had all their own way. Thinking their constitutions to be delicate, the advice, I repeatedly gave them was that they should wear flannel, eat as much wholesome animal food as they could digest, take air and exercise in moderation, and not devote too much time to study and composition.
> I should wish this to be mentioned in the Second Edition.

It was only in a postscript that he added:

> The Eccentric Movements ascribed to me, at pages 51 & 52, Vol. 1 – have no foundation [in] fact.

Writing to George Smith two days later, he repeated these denials:

> I never laid my Children, under restriction with respect to animal food, or any other wholesome food, they might have thought proper to use. … I never was subject to those

explosions of passion ascribed to me, and never perpetrated those excentric and ridiculous movements, which I am ashamed to mention.

Patrick's generally charitable attitude towards Mrs Gaskell was all the more noteworthy in view of the fact that in April the local papers drew attention to the unfavourable personal details which she had recounted. A reporter for the *Bradford Observer* paid a visit to the parsonage and commented:

> As we looked at that weatherbeaten house, and thought of the stern old man, left childless and alone, we could not help feeling for his troubles, although they had in a great measure been brought about by his own discipline and mode of life."

In a letter to George Smith, Arthur Nicholls gave a characteristically fair appraisal of the work, despite his repugnance at the disclosure of so many personal details:

> I have read the work with inexpressible pain – Mrs Gaskell has done justice to her subject – she has however fallen into many errors; but fewer perhaps than might have been expected. She has moreover inserted some things which ought never to have been published – It was not without reason that I instinctively shrank from the proposal of a Biography – But I suppose it matters not, provided the curiosity of the Publick be gratified.

Mrs Gaskell was very upset by all the controversy which had arisen. On 16 June she wrote to Ellen Nussey:

> I am in the Hornet's nest with a vengeance. ... I have cried more since I came home tha[n] I ever did in the same space of time before; and never needed kind words so much, – & no one gives me them. *I did so try* to *tell the truth*, and I believe *now* I hit as near the truth as any one *could* do. And I weighed every line with all my whole power & heart, so that every line should go to it's [*sic*] great purpose of making *her* known and valued, as one who had gone through such a terrible life with a brave and faithful heart.

Her letter clearly reveals her overriding motive in writing the biography – to provide a justification for Charlotte's writings in the circumstances of her life and home background. She had explicitly stated this in the biography itself when, after recounting the stories of Patrick's supposed eccentricities, she had commented:

> I have named these instances of eccentricity in the father because I hold the knowledge of them to be necessary for a right understanding of the life of his daughter.

An understanding of this overriding motive is essential if we are to make a fair evaluation of the unfavourable way in which she portrayed Patrick. Despite her generally warm and friendly approach towards him, it is apparent that she never fully appreciated the depths of Patrick's personality. Her sense of mission in seeking to vindicate the character of Charlotte seems to have prevented her from making a true assessment of her father. Long before she met Patrick in person, she had formed an impression of his character based on the gossip purveyed by Lady Kay-Shuttleworth and, despite her further acquaintance with him, she never allowed herself to revise her opinion.

The publication of *The Life of Charlotte Brontë* stirred up a furious controversy over her description of the conditions at the Clergy Daughters' School, which the young Brontë children had attended, and also over her references to Lady Scott (formerly Mrs Robinson), whom she had accused of seducing Branwell. Mrs Gaskell was still away in Italy when Lady Scott threatened to bring a libel action. The publishers immediately made a formal retraction of Mrs Gaskell's statements. This retraction was published in *The Times* on 30 May and all unsold copies of the book (both the first edition and the second identical edition which had been published in May) were recalled.

The storm over the Clergy Daughters' School was not so easily dealt with and the controversy raged for three months. Arthur Nicholls, incensed by the doubts being raised over the veracity of his wife's portrait of the school in *Jane Eyre*, was drawn into the dispute, publishing his replies in the press. After seeing a pamphlet circulated by the Carus Wilson family, refuting the charges made against the school, Patrick and Arthur decided to insert an advertisement in *The Times*, in which Nicholls refuted all the points made by Carus Wilson's son. On 6 June Arthur wrote to George Smith asking him to insert it for them, but in his reply Mr Smith questioned the wisdom of such action. In Arthur's absence, Patrick replied, thanking him for his advice:

> As Mr. Nicholls, is gone to Ireland for two or three weeks, it falls to my lot to answer your kind letter. Owing to what you have Said we have made up our minds not to advetise in the "Times". Enough has been written, to justify "Currer Bells [*sic*]," intimations, in regard to what has been stated, under the garb of fiction, in "Jane Eyre".

Patrick was very anxious, however, that no concessions over what Mrs Gaskell had written about the school should be made in the forthcoming third edition of the biography and he expressed his disappointment over the public retraction of the references to Lady Scott:

> I hope, therefore, that Mrs Gaskell, having strong proofs on her side, will make no <u>concessions</u> to Messrs Shepherd and Wilson, whether they cajole or threaten. There ought to be <u>nomore</u> [*sic*] <u>concessions</u> – Errors may be legitimately corrected, but nothing more should be done by authors.[22]

Six days later he wrote to Mr Smith again, urging him to use his influence over the changes which would be made in the third edition:

> Mrs Gaskell, in her third Edition, of the "Memoir", will require, the full exercise, of her talents, taste and judgment. I hope, that you will put in a word, now and then.[23]

He was so worried over this matter that a month later he wrote a third letter to George Smith, seeking an assurance that no concessions should be made about the Clergy Daughters' School. He also said that he had asked Mrs Gaskell to remove the false statements about himself:

> Several days Since, I wrote to Mrs Gaskell, requesting her, in the next Edition of the Memoir, to expunge those false statements respecting my denying my children the use of animal food, and in passionate explosions, performing various excentric movements, which never had any existence, but in the invention of waggish informants, whose delight it is, to impose on the credulous.[24]

On 30 July Patrick wrote to Mrs Gaskell, thanking her for the letters she had written to him. Once again he expressed his praise for her work and showed his forbearance over her portrayal of him:

> My dear Madam,
>   I thank you, for your own letters, and those of others, which I have received from you this morning, their contents, please me much. I may have been troublesome to you and your amiable daughter, but I was roused a little, by the impertinent remarks, of a set of pennyaliner, hungry, pedantic, and generally ignorant reviewers. ... I do not deny that I am somewhat e<x>ccentrick [sic]. Had I been numbered amongst the calm, sedate, concentric men of the world, I should not have been As I now am, and I should, in all probability, never have had such children as mine have been. I have no objection, whatever to your representing me as a little excentric [sic], since you, and other learned friends will have it so; only dont [sic] set me on, in my fury to burning hearthrugs, sawing the backs off chairs, and tearing my wifes [sic] silk gowns – ...

Then in memorable terms he gave his final, considered assessment of her work:

> I am much pleased with reading the opinions of those in your letters, and other eminent characters, respecting the "Memoir." Before I knew theirs I had formed my own opinion, from which you know I am not easily shaken. And my opinion, and the reading World's opinion of the "Memoir", is, that it is every way worthy of what one Great Woman, should have written of Another, and that it ought to stand, and will stand in the first rank of Biographies, till the end of time.

He also added a timely piece of advice to all those who would write biography:

> Some slips there have been, but they may be remedied. It is dangerous, to give credence
> hastily, to informants – Some may tell the truth, whilst others, from various motives, may
> greedily, invent and propagate falsehoods.

And he concluded:

> I am not in the least offended, at your telling |me| that I have faults I have many – and being
> a Daughter of Eve, I doubt not, that you also have some. Let us both try to be wiser and
> better, as Time recedes, and Eternity advances.

The controversy over *The Life of Charlotte Brontë* was not yet at an end. On 13
August William Dearden, a Keighley schoolmaster and an old friend of Patrick,
wrote to the *Bradford Observer* attacking Mrs Gaskell for her critical portrait of
Mr Brontë, whom he described as 'this venerable clergyman now on the verge
of the grave'. He said that her description was based on 'the malice of an ignorant country gossip'. He criticised her for relying on the evidence of the servant
who had been sacked from the parsonage, instead of listening to the testimony of
Martha Brown and Nancy Garrs, who had given years of faithful service to the
Brontë family. He returned to the attack in the following week, quoting Patrick
himself as saying:

> I did not know that I had an enemy in the world; much less one who would traduce me
> before my death. Everything in that book … which relates to my conduct to my family, is
> either false or distorted.

Patrick was highly embarrassed by Mr Dearden's unsolicited attack on Mrs Gaskell and
he immediately wrote to her expressing his strong disapproval of it:

> An article, in reference to the Memoir – by Mr Dearden of Bradford, has lately appear'd
> in the "Bradford Observer" – and abstracts from it in Some of the country Newspapers
> … with this article I had nothing whatever to do – I knew nothing of it till I saw it
> in print, and was much displeased when I saw it there. Though hard press'd by some
> ruthless Critics, as well as Mr Wilson and his party, I held both my tongue and my pen
> – believing, that you were a friend to my daughter Charlotte, and no enemy to me, and
> feeling confident that whatever you found to be mistakes, you would willingly correct in
> the third Edition.[25]

In a letter to George Smith written on 23 August Mrs Gaskell expressed her gratitude to Patrick for his continued support:

> I only hope Mr Brontë won't be over worried. Hitherto he has acted like a 'brick'. (I hope you understand slang?).

On the same day she also wrote to Maria Martineau:[26]

> I enclose copy of Mr B's first letter; an intermediate letter about the mistakes, dated July 30, & one received *today* by the same post as yours, evidently meaning *very* kindly; and he really has been so steady in his way to me all along, that I would rather let them all go on attacking me, than drag him into any squabble either with me, or the public or any one.

Mrs Gaskell also wrote to Patrick that day, thanking him for his letter and telling him what difficulties she had encountered since the publication of the biography. Struck by the despondent tone in her letter, Patrick wrote an immediate reply in which he tried to provide some comfort:

> I sincerely thank you for your very kind letter which I have received this morning. As you must be nearly overwhelmed with letters, and oppress'd with answering them, I should not have troubled you, with this of mine, were it not, that I think it might divert your attention, from considerations, which may disturb you more than is necessary. Why should you disturb yourself concerning what has been, is, and ever will be the lot of eminent writers? ... Above three thousand Years Since, Solomon Said, "He that increaseth Knowledge, increaseth Sorrow – Much Study is the weariness of the flesh. – So you may find it, and so my Daughter Charlotte found it. You have had and will have much praise, with a little blame. Then drink the mix'd cup, with thankfulness to the great physician of Souls. It will be far more salutary to you in the end.

Feeling that he had been a little forward in addressing such a distinguished author in these forthright terms, he concluded:

> But I am forgetting to whom I am writing this line – and so I must conclude a most ill-written, incoherent scrawl.[27]

Unfortunately, there was now yet another intervention, this time from Harriet Martineau. Having read Mr Dearden's article containing Patrick's alleged criticism of Mrs Gaskell, she wrote to the *Daily News* on 24 August declaring that she had seen two letters of Patrick praising Mrs Gaskell's work in such terms as to make it impossible for him to have changed his mind and to have accused Mrs Gaskell of being an enemy. Miss Martineau then used her letter to make an attack on Mrs Gaskell herself for the account she had given in the biography of her quarrel with Charlotte:

> When I find that, in my own case, scarcely one of Miss Brontë's statements about me is altogether true, I cannot be surprised at her biographer having been misled in other cases of more importance.[28]

Miss Martineau's comments were quoted in the *Bradford Observer* on 27 August and two days later William Dearden called at the parsonage to inform Patrick that he would defend him against her attack. Patrick tried to dissuade him and a few days later wrote urging him to desist:

> I trouble you with a few lines merely to state, that I wish nothing more should be written against Mrs Gaskell, in regard to the "Memoir". She has already encountred [*sic*] very severe trials, which generally falls to the lot of celebrated authors. She has promised to omit, in the third Edition, the erroneous statements, respecting me; which is all, I can now, reasonably expect or desire, as nomore [*sic*] I think, can be … safely or prudently done. As for myself, I wish to live in unnoticed retirement.

In a postscript he added:

> I never thought otherwise of Mrs Gaskell, than that she was a friend of my Daughter, and no enemy to me. In alluding to enemies, I meant false informants, and hostile Critics.[29]

And, on the same day, he wrote to Mrs Gaskell, repeating much of what he had said to Mr Dearden and adding:

> My real, or pretended friends, seem in their gossiping skill, to have combined to paint me not as a single, but a double Janus, looking, and smiling, or frowning with my four faces, in opposite directions, as may best suit my own selfish convenience; They would please me better, by minding their own affairs, and letting mine alone.[30]

Mrs Gaskell had assured Patrick that the false anecdotes about him would be removed from the third edition of the *Life*. In her letter to Maria Martineau she had mentioned the stories which Patrick wished removed:

> Mr Nicholls has sent me a list of omissions which Mr Brontë wishes to have made in this third edition; (refusal of animal food, sawing up chairs, burning hearth rug – all told me on the authority of uneducated Haworth people) and the cutting up of the silk gown.[31]

In a letter written to George Smith on the same day she reported that the reference to the 'pistol shooting' was not included in the list of omissions submitted by Mr Nicholls but said 'I am willing to do anything for a quiet life, – so if you can, please take it out.'[32] It is significant that Patrick had not requested the removal of allusions to his regular shooting of his pistols. Since the days of the Luddite riots in his parish at Hartshead he had adopted the habit of carrying a pistol and its regular discharge was necessary for its efficient maintenance.

At the beginning of September 1857 the third edition of *The Life of Charlotte Brontë*, described as 'Revised and Corrected', was published.[33] Mrs Gaskell had been as good as her word and had removed the offending passages about Patrick, as well as those about Lady Scott, and also the allegations she had made of wastefulness by the servants in the Brontë household. On 9 September Patrick wrote to her giving his verdict:

Though my opinion may be worth little, I wish to say, that I have look'd over the third Edition of the "Memoir," and that it gives me full satisfaction, in all its parts and bearings, and that I ardently wish it may go down, without alteration, augmentation, or diminution, to the latest posterity. With the work as it now stands, all reasonable persons must be satisfied; since in it, there is much to praise, and little or nothing to blame. It has, I think, arrived at a degree of perfection, which was scarcely attainable, in a first, and second Edition.

He went on to express the wish that all controversy might now be at an end:

I hope that I may conclude that after a storm there will now be a calm, and that there will be no faultfinders, unless some one like Miss Martineau should arise, determined to be hostile, and put the worst construction, on the best intentions, both in words and actions.

As Patrick had feared, Miss Martineau continued to complain that Charlotte's statements about her were not true and on 5 November Patrick wrote to her to remonstrate with her privately:

I should not have troubled you with any remarks of mine, had it not been that you have publicly stated, my Daughter Charlotte to have said or written some things of you that were not true. This is a somewhat heavy charge made against one, who has been generally considered, and who, I firmly believe was a woman of candour and veracity, and who if she had been disposed for malevolent misrepresentation, would have placed You among the last she would have misrepresented. I have ever heard her speak of You, in terms of kindness, and veneration, and when anyone spoke of You otherwise, she took your part: and be assur'd, whatever you may think or say to the contrary, your unfortunate Book on Atheism, made you many opponents and enemies, and gave a shock to those who gave you credit for reasoning powers, that would have kept you from descending to say "there is no God". What you have written respecting my Daughter, has, perhaps, been written hastily, and without much regard to conseqences [*sic*]. But even if it were so, it was wrong.

In her reply Harriet Martineau said that, whilst she had no doubt of Charlotte's 'kindly disposition' and even 'personal affection' towards herself:

There is scarcely a statement concerning myself in her letters which is altogether true; & I may add that some of them are more like hallucination than sober statement.

And, after expressing sympathy to Patrick for his family bereavements, she added a postscript:

I ought to add, as I perceive you have not read the Atkinson Letters, that it is not an atheistical book, & that I have never said "there is no God".[34]

She followed up this letter with one to Arthur Nicholls, in which she said she was 'deep in her last illness' (although she was to live for another nineteen years). Patrick replied to her letter on 11 November. After expressing regret that she was unwell and thanking her for her sympathy in his bereavement, which he said made him sensitive to any misrepresentations about Charlotte, he continued:

As far as I myself, may be concern'd, I am not over anxious. My World, is but a little one, my Parish, and Neighbourhood, are the Sphere in which I move, and if I be respected and can do good there, I ought to be satisfied. It is otherwise in the case of my Daughter Charlotte, so far as her chacter [*sic*] may be concern'd.

He went on to say that he had indeed read her book:

I have read it, thought of it & understood its contents, and so have many others; and they, and I have felt convinced, that you maintained there was no God. Hardly anything would give us greater pleasure, except your entire orthodoxy, than that on your own public assertion, to all the world, we were mistaken.

Then, returning to her attack on Charlotte's statements, he said:

What most astonishes me, is the real, or apparent prejudice, you have against her, if I may judge from some things you have written or said. As I well knew, her character for veracity and candour, and had many proofs of her affection, and veneration for you, I entreat You on the grounds of mere justice, to do justice to her, in all you may think, say, or write, and could she speak from the tomb she would ask for no more.

This letter received a conciliatory reply and there was no more correspondence between them.

'I wish to live in unnoticed and quiet retirement' 1857–1861

As for myself, I wish to live in unnoticed and quiet retirement; setting my mind on things above in heaven, and not on things on the earth beneath, and performing my duty to the utmost of my power.

Patrick Brontë to William Dearden, 31 August 1857

One of the chief effects of the publication of *The Life of Charlotte Brontë* was an influx of tourists into Haworth. As Arthur Nicholls told George Smith on 23 May 1857:

Haworth has been inundated with visitors. But with one or two exceptions we have not seen anything of them – It would be a great nuisance if they were to intrude on us.

Some visitors were given a welcome at the parsonage, however. Among them was the Rev'd Thomas Akroyd, who came to Haworth in the spring of 1857. He was a Wesleyan minister from Liverpool who was convalescing in his home area near Halifax after a severe attack of bronchitis. While looking at the tombs in the churchyard he met the parish clerk (Joseph Redman), who showed him round the church. Wishing to test the accuracy of Mrs Gaskell's account of the Brontë family Mr Akroyd said to him:

I suppose we must not believe everything in the book; such things, for instance, as Mr Brontë's being in the habit of firing off his superfluous excitement by a gun from the kitchen door. 'I've 'eeard it hundreds of times' was his matter-of-fact reply.

After taking lunch Mr Akroyd went to the parsonage where he was admitted to see Mr Brontë:

He was a tall, thin man, of rather florid complexion, with weak eyes over which he wore a green shade. His dress was of the orthodox black throughout, and his chin nestled in the capacious folds of an over-affluent neckcloth. He rose to greet me in the most courteous and affable manner, and then something like the following conversation followed:

Mr B. – So you are from Liverpool, I see.

T.A. – I am, Mr Brontë.

Mr B. – You have a church there, I suppose?

T.A. – No, I am a Wesleyan minister.

Mr B. – A what? (putting his hand behind his ear, for he was rather deaf).

T.A. – A Wesleyan minister.

Mr B. – O, indeed? A Wesleyan? Well, I have a great respect for the Wesleyans. I have known several of the ministers of your denomination. Very good men they were, very good men; and names are nothing to me – I care nothing about names. If we are only fighting under the banners of Jehovah – Jesus – that's the great thing. And the work of God is prospering amongst you in Liverpool, I hope?

T.A. – Yes, Mr Brontë. I am happy to say we are not labouring altogether in vain. We have large congregations and some fruit of our work amongst them.

Mr B. – I am very glad to hear it. I rejoice to hear it. I am not able to preach much myself now, but I am thankful to God I can still do a little. I generally preach once every Sunday and am grateful for this.

Mr Akroyd mentioned Mrs Gaskell's *Life* of Charlotte and suggested that not everything she had said about his family should be taken as accurate:

Mr. B. – Well, no. Mrs Gaskell is a novelist, you know, and we must allow her a little romance, eh? It is quite in her line. But the book is substantially true for all that. There are some queer things in it, to be sure – there are some about myself, for instance – but the book is substantially true, sir, substantially true.

Mr Akroyd then felt he had taken enough of Mr Brontë's time and rose to take his leave:

He came with me to the door of the room, and shaking me very heartily by the hand bade me god-speed in my ministerial work.[1]

One distinguished visitor to call at the parsonage was the Duke of Devonshire, who came in August. He spent an hour with Patrick and Arthur and on leaving invited them to visit him at Bolton Abbey in September. Also in August a correspondent of the *Bradford Observer* came over to Haworth accompanied by a friend. They found the village rather different from the description of it given by Mrs Gaskell:

Our previous conceptions of the locality had been formed entirely from Mrs Gaskell's description and the frontispiece to the "Memoirs of Charlotte Brontë;" and we found all our expectations most gloriously disappointed. We had supposed Haworth to be a scattered and straggling hamlet, with a desolate vicarage and a dilapidated church, surrounded and shut out from the world by a wilderness of barren heath, the monotony of the prospect only broken by the tombstones in the adjacent graveyard. Our straggling hamlet we found transformed into a large and flourishing village – not a very enlightened or poetical place certainly, but quaint, compact, and progressive, wherein, by the bye, we observed three large dissenting chapels and two or three well-sized schools.[2]

After taking lunch at the White Lion Inn they managed to secure a short interview with Patrick at the parsonage. They were greatly impressed by his fine physique and his courteous and gentlemanly bearing. Later they asked some of his parishioners what they thought of him and were told that he was held in great affection.

On 25 January 1858 the Revd Edward White Benson (later Archbishop of Canterbury, 1883–1896) came to visit Patrick. He was a cousin of the Sidgwick family of Stonegappe where Charlotte had been a governess. Mr Benson kept a pocket book in which he jotted down some impressions of his visit:

Rode over to Haworth. Today it was a dismal place indeed to see, with a cold east wind blowing and a chill thick damp still obstinately clinging about all. ... Mrs Gaskell was very hasty and inaccurate in the steps she took to gain information, and never consulted Mr Nicholls or old Mr Brontë, as the latter himself told me. They never saw the book till it was in print. He lamented much the 'many unfounded things pertaining to our neighbours' which was therein related, and though he said there were also 'many ridiculous anecdotes about himself which never had existed except in some curious imaginations' this did not seem to move him. He seemed too old and too composed to mind it. ... Mr Brontë thought the 3rd edition more truthful, but he said 'vulgar readers would prefer the 1st'.[3]

In the autumn of 1858 a Mr William Davies spent a weekend in Haworth accompanied by a friend. They also had an interview with Patrick. Mr Davies described him as 'a tall and dignified gentleman of the old school, with easy manners and courteous bearing', although the reliability of his impressions is thrown into doubt by his further comment that he had 'that stamp of breeding which often distinguishes the Englishman of high birth and ancestral surroundings'. On the Sunday they worshipped in the church. At the afternoon service, which was attended by a large congregation, Mr Nicholls officiated and Patrick preached the sermon:

During the reading of the first lesson, with the steps of age, solemn and slow, robed in black gown, Mr Brontë came in and seated himself in the old-fashioned square pew. At the final hymn he went into the pulpit and gave a vigorous and impressive discourse, no word of which was lost upon the listeners. It might have been considered a model sermon in many respects. Yet there was an element of the grotesque in its delivery, though it was without the least affectation or mannerism of any sort. He wore an enormous white cravat, which covered the features up to the level of the ears. When he wished to be particularly impressive, he seemed to emerge from this receptacle and then gradually retire into it. His fingers were long and skinny, almost of the nature of talons, and were displayed on the pulpit cushion. This gave something of an eerie appearance to the preacher, and perhaps added to the impressiveness of his discourse, which in all respects was one to be remembered.[4]

Another visitor about this time was James Hoppin, a professor from Yale University who was on an extensive tour of England,. After attending the morning service he was invited to call on Mr Brontë:

I went through … a small flower-garden (rather run to waste now) and was shown by 'Martha' into Mr Brontë's study. … Mr Brontë met me with real kindness of manner, but with something of the stateliness of the old school. His hair, worn short, was white as the driven snow; his ample cambric cravat completely covered his chin; and his black dress was of the most scrupulous neatness. He has been called handsome, but that he never could have been. He has strong, rugged, even harsh features, with a high, wrinkled forehead, and swarthy complexion; and his eyes are partially closed, for he is almost blind. He said he was induced to invite me to his house, though he saw very little company, because he learned I was an American, and he thought much of America.

Our conversation was chiefly upon religious topics, and he wished to be informed about the great spiritual movements which from time to time pass over America. He thought that revivals in England and Ireland were accompanied by too much animal excitement; yet he believed in their reality. … He spoke of education in England – that was all the fashion just now; but I could not help thinking that the conservative, granite-minded old 'Helston'[5] looked upon a great deal of it as sentimental and superficial. He struck me as being naturally a very social man, with a mind fond of discussion, and feeding eagerly on new ideas, in spite of his reserve. …

He also had the opportunity to hear Patrick preach:

In the afternoon I heard Mr Brontë preach from Job iii 17: 'There the wicked cease from troubling; and there the weary be at rest.' It was the simple extemporaneous talk of an aged pastor to his people, spoken without effort, in short, easy sentences, – and was drawn, it appeared to me, *right out of that old graveyard*, among whose stones his feet had walked, and his imagination had lived so long. In parts it was pathetic, especially where he alluded to the loss of children. He branched off upon the sorrows, convulsions, and troubles then in the world, and he seemed to long for wings like a dove to fly away from this changeful scene, and be at rest. The old church clock, as if echoing the venerable preacher's remarks, had written upon it, 'Time how short – eternity how long!'[6]

Another American who called at this time was Mr H. J. Raymond, who was for many years the editor of the *New York Times*. After sending in his card he was shown into Mr Brontë's study:

The room was small, very plainly furnished, with small bookcases round the walls, the one between the windows containing copies of the Brontë novels. Mr Nicholls soon came in and made me welcome. To my apologies for my intrusion he assured me that while they were under the necessity of declining many visits, both he and his father [-in-law] were always happy to see their friends, and that the words 'New York' upon my card were quite sufficient to ensure me a welcome. Mr Brontë, he said was not up when I called, but had desired him to detain me until he could dress and come down, as he did soon after. I had an exceedingly pleasant conversation of half an hour with them both. … Mr Brontë's personal appearance is striking and peculiar. He is tall, thin, and rather muscular, has a quick energetic manner, and a resolute promptness of movement which indicated marked decision and firmness of character. The extraordinary stories by Mrs Gaskell of his inflammable temper, of his burning silk dresses belonging to his wife which he did not approve of her wearing, of his sawing chairs and tables, and firing off pistols in the back-yard by way of relieving his superfluous anger, find no warrant certainly in his present appearance, and are generally considered exaggerations. I remarked to him that I had been agreeably disappointed in the face of the country and the general aspect of the town, that they were less sombre and repulsive than Mrs Gaskell's descriptions led me to expect. Mr Nicholls and Mr Brontë smiled at each other, and the latter remarked: 'Well, I think Mrs Gaskell tried to make us all appear as bad as she could.' Mr Brontë wears a very wide white neckcloth, and usually sinks his chin so that his mouth is barely visible over it. This gives him a singular expression, which is rendered still more so by spectacles with large round glasses enclosed in broad metallic rims. Though over eighty years old and somewhat infirm, he preaches once every Sunday in his church.[7]

At least one attempt was made to take advantage of the interest of such distinguished visitors in Haworth and the Brontë family. In January 1858 Patrick received a letter from Sir Joseph Paxton,[8] which revealed that an approach had been made to the Duke of Devonshire through Sir Joseph seeking financial assistance towards a public subscription which had been raised in Haworth to pay for the provision of heating in the church and in the schools. On 16 January Patrick wrote to Sir Joseph declaring that he knew nothing of this move:

Your letter which I have received this Morning, gives both to Mr. Nicholls and to me, Great uneasiness. It would seem, that application has been made, to the Duke of Devonshire, for money, to aid the Subscription, in reference to the expense of Apparatus for heating our Church and Schools. This has been done, Without our knowledge, and most assuredly, had we known it, would have met with our strongest opposition. We have no claim on the Duke. His Grace, honour'd us with a Visit, in token of his respect for the memory of the Dead, and His liberality and munificence, are well, and widely known, and the Mercenary, taking an unfair advantage of these circumstances, have taken a Step Which both Mr. Nicholls, and I utterly regret and condemn. In Answer to your query, I may state that the whole expense for both the Schools and the Church, is about one hundred pounds – and that, after what has been and may be subscribed, there May fifty pounds remain as a debt, but this may – and ought to be rais'd by the Inhabitants in the next Year after the depression in trade, shall it is hoped, have pass'd away. I have written to his Grace on the Subject.

One aspect of the publication of Mrs Gaskell's biography of Charlotte that gave great pleasure to Patrick, was the fact that he now received letters from some of his old friends. On 29 August 1857 he wrote to James Cheadle, the vicar of Bingley, to correct a misapprehension which might make it harder for his friends to get in touch:

Revd. & Dear Sir,
Mr Grant has lately informed me, that through mistake you told some Inquirer, that I had been of Trinity College, Dublin, whereas I was of St. John's, Cambridge, and took my Degree there, – You will greatly oblige me, therefore, if you will be so kind, as to correct this mistake, at your early convenience – since the Inquirer may be some old Friend, with whom I should like to revive half-dead associations. At any age, this is pleasant, but at mine, it is especially so – since many I once knew and esteem'd and loved, are now gone, – and but few new ones, have arisen, to take their place.

In February 1858 his old friend and fellow-student at St John's College, John Nunn, now the rector of Thorndon in Suffolk, got in touch. He was five years younger than Patrick, but he was in a poor state of health. He and his wife had clearly been alarmed by Mrs Gaskell's description of life in Haworth parsonage and, on her husband's behalf, Mrs Nunn wrote to Patrick offering to send him a newspaper. On 1 February Patrick wrote to thank her for her offer:

My dear Madam,
I thank you for your kind offer of the excellent newspaper you have mentioned, but there is no necessity of sending to me, since, owing to the newspapers I take, and the various institutions in the village, I can see the "Record", or any other I may choose, daily. And truly, in this changeable and ever-changing world, this state of our probation, we clergymen ought to read and know what is passing, and to discern the signs of the times, so that we may be able to speak a word in season to the people committed to our charge. I have forgotten the age of

my dear old friend Mr Nunn – will you be so kind as to mention it when you next write. I am now in the eighty-first year of my age. I think he must be six or seven years younger; but it appears that his bodily strength has considerably failed him, and that it is now his duty not to exert himself, as formerly, but to be a little cautious, so that by Divine aid his useful life may be spared long for the benefit of the flock of our blessed Lord and Saviour. I preach once every Sabbath afternoon, but I cannot do more. Mr Nicholls joins me in kind regards.[9]

A year later Mrs Nunn wrote again, this time suggesting that Patrick should come and live with them in their large and comfortable rectory. Patrick politely declined the offer:

My Dear Madam,

I thank you for the picture of the Rectory. It is well executed, and shows a very respectable and convenient building, which is, I hope, and believe, only the earnest and forerunner of 'that House, not made with hands, eternal in the Heavens.' But large and commodious as your house is, I think it has no room for a third person as a lodger, who would probably be a discordant string that would spoil your domestic harmony. You inquired whether your parcels and letters cost me anything; they all come free, and I pay for all I send to you. … I hope that you will be able to read this miserable scrawl. My sight is very scanty, and the day is dim. Mr Nicholls joins me in kind regards to you and my dear friend.[10]

Another old friend who now renewed contact was the Revd Robinson Pool, who had been the Dissenting minister of the chapel at Thornton during the time of Patrick's incumbency there. On 18 March 1858 Patrick replied to his letter, saying how pleased he had been to hear from him and recalling their time together over forty years earlier:

Revd and Dear Sir,

I have read your kind letter, with a high degree of interest – and melancholy pleasure, Old times, and old circumstance, which have never escaped my memory, have been brought to view in more lively colours, and I can fancy, almost, that we are still at Thornton, good neighbours, and kind, and Sincere friends, and happy with our wives and children. … You have had Your trials, both sharp and severe, but God has given you grace, and strength Sufficient unto your day – My trials you have heard of – I feard [sic] often, that I should sink under them; but the Lord rememberd mercy in judgment, and I am still living, till I am in the eighty Second year of my age. You I think are considerably Younger. I am still able to preach once on the Lord's day, but, cannot do more. At present, however, I am troubled with an attack of chronic Bronchitis, and a severe cough, but am Something better than I was a few days ago. About eleven years Since, I lost my Sight, through cataract in my eyes, but having undergone a surgical operation, I have through Divine Mercy, been able Since that time, to see to read and write, and find my way without a guide. Mr. Craven gave an account of Your health and circumstances and from what he Said, and what you tell me, I have derived especial pleasure. The Memoir, which you refer to, though in General, well, and ably written, contains some extravagant aneckdotes [*sic*] about me, which are utterly untrue, and without the least foundation.

Amidst this time of renewed friendship Patrick heard the sad news that his old friend William Morgan had died while on a visit to Bath. Since leaving Bradford in 1851 he had been the rector of Hulcott in Buckinghamshire. He was five years younger than Patrick and his passing was a reminder to him that he had now outlived almost all of his old friends. Aware that his own death could not be long delayed he ordered a new memorial tablet for his family in Haworth church. The old one had become so full that the letters towards the bottom had had to be made smaller and when Charlotte died it had been necessary to inscribe her name on a separate plaque. The new tablet was sculpted by Mr Greaves of Halifax. It gave the names, ages and dates of death of Mrs Brontë and her six children, and space was left at the bottom for the insertion of Patrick's own name. William Brown, who had now succeeded his brother John as sexton, was given instructions to break up the old tablet and bury the pieces deep in the parsonage garden to guard against souvenir hunters.

Patrick continued to live a quiet and simple life. He still preached on Sundays but, after a severe attack of bronchitis, he now restricted himself to doing so only once at the afternoon service. One task he gave himself was to send a fragment from one of Charlotte's letters to those, many of them Americans, who wrote asking for Charlotte's autograph. Life in the township was gradually changing. A Haworth Gas Company was established in 1857 to provide lighting for the streets and also for the houses of those wealthier inhabitants who could afford such a luxury. One development must have given Patrick great pleasure. In 1858 a small reservoir was completed in the fields above the Parsonage, which at last provided Haworth with the supply of pure fresh water for which he had campaigned so long.

Throughout these last years Patrick kept in touch with his brothers and sisters in Ireland. Two of his letters to them survive, in both of which he refers to receiving letters from them. On 2 December 1858 he wrote to his younger brother Hugh after hearing that he had been unwell:

Dear Brother,

I hope that you are now in better health than formerly. My sister Mary's letter gave me to understand that you were in a very delicate state of health. I should think that if you cannot manage the farming business rightly my brother James would be able to supply your place. From the newspapers I learn that farmers in Ireland are now doing well, and if they would in Ireland leave off their Bible warning, murdering, and quarrelling with each other, and as rational beings attend to the improvement of their country, owing to its good soil and harbours, mines, and many other peculiar advantages, Ireland, instead of being a degraded country, would be one of the most respectable portions of the globe. Trade here has for a long time been very flat, but it is now something better; nevertheless, vast numbers are out of work, and owing to this and the high price of provisions, there is a great deal of distress, and the poor rates are high; but we hope for better times. God is over all, and the supreme disposer of all events, and He will have mercy on the poor, and send them relief in the best time and manner. Considering my advanced age, I have much reason to be thankful to God that I am yet able to preach once or twice on the Sundays, and to do some duty besides. My son-in-law still continues with me, and is very kind. He generally sees your letters. Hoping you are all well and doing well in reference to time and eternity,

I remain,
Your affectionate brother,
P. Brontë

On 1 February 1859 he wrote to his sister Mary. He had heard that another of his sisters, Sarah, had been unwell and he wanted to help her by sending a small gift of money:

Dear Sister,

I am sorry to learn that my sister Sarah is unwell. May God, for Christ's sake, comfort and support her, and save her with an everlasting salvation. I have herewith sent her £1 in a post office order. It is a small sum, but it will purchase for her some medicine and be useful in other ways. You must go to the post office in Loughbrickland and sign the order, and get the money in your own name. The boyish papers which you sent me remind me of old times. David Cruickshanks, which you mention, must now be an old man. I remember him well. Most of those whom I once knew must now be dead, and Ireland must in many respects be greatly changed from what it was when I resided in it. I am, through divine mercy, as well as can reasonably be expected at my advanced age of more than eighty-one years. I still preach once on Sunday, and Mr Nicholls, who is very obliging and willing, preaches twice. We have still a great many calls from lords and ladies and others, but they do not stop long, as I cannot do with much company. The day is very dark, and my sight is very dim, so you will have some difficulty in reading this letter. I am glad to learn that all my brothers and sisters except one are well.

Your affectionate brother,
P. Brontë

Interest in the Brontë family continued to flourish. In August 1859 Patrick had the pleasure of seeing his pamphlet *The Cottage in the Wood* reprinted by Abraham Holroyd, a Bradford antiquarian. In October that year Arthur Nicholls agreed to a request from George Smith that the two chapters of Charlotte's last unfinished novel should be printed under the title 'The Last Sketch' in the *Cornhill Magazine*, the new periodical which he was starting, and that Charlotte's hero, Thackeray, should be invited to write an introduction to it. Both Arthur and Patrick were thrilled to receive a letter from Thackeray, explaining his new role as editor of the *Cornhill* and his hopes for its future. As Arthur told Mr Smith, 'Mr Brontë was wonderfully pleased with the talent & tact displayed in it.'

'The Last Sketch' appeared in the March 1860 issue, prefaced by a generous and personal tribute from Thackeray. Patrick was very moved by Thackeray's tribute and on 26 March, in one of the last letters he ever wrote, he expressed his gratitude to George Smith:

> My Dear Sir,
>
> Though writing, is to me now Something of a task, I cannot avoid sending you a few lines, to thank you for sending me the Magazines, and for your gentlemanly conduct towards my Daughter Charlotte, in all your transactions with her, from first to last. All the numbers of the Magazines were good; the last, especially, attracted my attention, and excited my admiration. The 'Last Sketch', took full possession of my mind. Mr Thacary [*sic*], in his remarks, in it, has excelled, even Himself; He has written, "Multum in parvo, dignissimum cedro [?]"[11] – And what he has written, does honour both to his head, and heart. Thank him kindly, both in Mr. Nichol'ls [*sic*] name, and Mine. …
>
> If Organless Spirits, see as we see, and feel as we feel, in this material clogging world, my daughter Charlotte's spirit will, receive additional happiness, on scanning the remarks of her Ancient Favourite. In the last letter I received from You, You mentioned that Mrs. Smith was in delicate health; I hope that she is now well – I need scarcely request you to excuse all faults, in this hasty scrawl, since a man in his 84th year generall[y] lets his age, plead his apology.

Patrick's health was now beginning to fail and it was left to Arthur Nicholls to perform virtually all the parochial duties.[12] On 30 October 1859 Patrick preached what proved to be his final sermon in Haworth church. He did however perform one last baptism, in the parsonage itself, on 14 November 1859. There were special reasons for this action. John Greenwood, the Haworth stationer, who was eager to proclaim his friendship with the Brontë family, decided to give his youngest child the name of Brontë. Arthur Nicholls, always eager to maintain the family privacy and angry over John Greenwood's role in acting as Mrs Gaskell's informant, said that he would not christen the baby with that name. When the little boy was nine months old he became seriously ill and it was thought that he would not live. On hearing this Patrick summoned the Greenwoods to the parsonage and baptised the baby privately. When Arthur Nicholls saw the entry in the register he was very angry, until he saw the sense of Patrick's assertion that he would have been in a very difficult position if the boy had died unbaptised.

The winter of 1859 was a very severe one. Patrick suffered from his usual bronchial colds and was confined to the house. He was not seriously ill, however, and writing to George Smith in January 1860, Arthur Nicholls reported that, though he was approaching his eighty-third birthday, Patrick was 'wonderfully well'. In February he reported:

> Mr Brontë continues pretty well – He has been much confined to the house this winter owing to the very severe frost. I hope that with the return of a milder season he will be able to resume his afternoon Sermon.

This was not to be, however, and Patrick never returned to his pulpit again. In August 1860 Dr Robert Bickersteth, who had replaced Charles Longley as Bishop of Ripon in 1857, came to Haworth to conduct a confirmation service. Patrick, confined to his bed and unable to take any part in the proceedings, left all the arrangements to Arthur Nicholls. Before he left the village the bishop came to see Patrick in his bedroom. Patrick's non-appearance at the confirmation ceremony caused rumours to circulate that he was at the point of death. These were quashed, however, in September, when he had recovered sufficiently to walk with Arthur Nicholls' assistance round the garden and to take a short stroll along the footpath leading to the moor. This renewed activity caused the *Bradford Observer* to comment:

> If Mr Brontë continues to improve in the same ratio as he has done of late, he will preach again, an event which no one in Haworth would have considered possible a few weeks ago.[13]

On 25 October Mrs Gaskell, accompanied by her daughter Meta, came to Haworth to visit Patrick. Meta, who had never met Patrick, had told her mother how much she would like to see him. After the visit both mother and daughter wrote letters giving an account of their visit. Mrs Gaskell's description was written two months later in a letter to Mr Williams, the reader at Smith Elder. For such a lively and exuberant correspondent, her account of their meeting is surprisingly brief and insensitive, and seems to underline the fact that she was never willing to make the attempt fully to understand Patrick's character. Her single-minded devotion to the mission of exculpating Charlotte from the accusations of coarseness and insensitivity which had been levelled against her, and her obsession with what she took to be Mr Brontë's selfishness in his unwavering control over Charlotte's life, seem to have made Mrs Gaskell virtually blind to the sterling qualities which he showed. In her letter she told Mr Williams:

> About six weeks ago I paid a visit to Mr Brontë, and sat for about an hour with him. He is completely confined to bed now, but talks hopefully of leaving it again when the summer comes round. I am afraid that [he] will not be leaving it as he plans, poor old man! He is touchingly softened by illness; but still talks in his pompous way, and mingles moral remarks and somewhat stale sentiments with his conversation on ordinary subjects.[14]

That evening Meta wrote a description of their visit in a letter to Emily Shaen, the sister of Catherine Winkworth and a close friend of the family. Her letter reveals a completely different attitude towards Patrick. She began her account by explaining that her mother was at first hesitant over going to Haworth:

> Mama ... fancied he would not like to see her; because so many reviews, letters in newspapers etc., which she knew had reached him, had dwelt on the way in which, while pretending to have been his daughter's friend, she had held up his character to ridicule.

After plucking up courage, however, Mrs Gaskell had written to Patrick to request a visit and:

> this morning there came a few tremulous, feeble lines to say he should be glad to see us.

So mother and daughter rushed to the station, caught an early train to Keighley, where they took a fly, and arrived in Haworth at 11.15 a.m. They were unaware that Patrick was now confined to bed and on arrival at the parsonage they were asked to wait in the parlour for a short while before Martha ushered them up to Mr Brontë's bedroom:

> We were taken into his bedroom; where everything was delicately clean and white, and there he was sitting propped up in bed with a clean nightgown, with a clean towel laid just for his hands to play upon – looking Oh! Very different from the stiff scarred face above the white walls of cravat in the photograph – he had a short soft white growth of beard on his chin; and such a gentle, quiet, sweet, half-pitiful expression on his mouth, a good deal of soft white hair, and spectacles on. He shook hands with us, and we sat down, and then said how glad he was to see Mama – and she said how she had hesitated about coming, – feeling as if he might now have unpleasant associations with her – which never seemed to have entered into his head.

Patrick asked about Meta's engagement (to an Indian Army officer, Captain Hill) and when he was told that it had been broken off:

> He ... turned round and told me that he hoped I would forget the past; and would hope – that we all ought to live on hope.

He repeated his praise for the biography:

> He said to Mama – 'As I told you in my first letter, the <u>Memoir</u> is a book which will hand your name down to posterity' and that there was only one fault he had to find with it.

Meta and her mother thought that he was going to make some allusion to Lady Scott, but it was the supposed ban on meat for his children which he mentioned, because it had been quoted by Mr Carus Wilson and his defenders as being more likely to have caused his children's delicacy than the food at Cowan Bridge:

> He said … his children had always been allowed meat; but … he had chosen not to defend himself at the expense of proving Mama inaccurate: and so giving a handle to those who accused her of mis-statements.

Patrick soon turned the conversation to politics:

> He … asked Mama whether she thought the English ought to interfere in Italian affairs at present, or wait until the Italians asked for help; and seemed very pleased when she said she thought we ought to hold back for the present. 'You see we agree in politics as in everything else.'

He then spoke about himself:

> He alluded to his own 'eccentricity' with a certain pride; and his 'independence' too, of other people's opinion; not but what he valued the opinion of good people – Mama said: 'Yes – I was just telling my daughter as we came up the hill, that I thought you had always done what you thought right.' – 'And so I have,' he said, 'and I appeal to God.' There was something very solemn in the way he said it; and in him altogether – None of the sternness I had fancied.

Eventually Mrs Gaskell felt that it was time to go:

> Mama said something about our not staying too long to tire him and that they were going for me to make a sketch. And he said, 'There are certain circumstances, you see,' looking very knowing, 'which make it desirable that when you leave in 5 minutes of so, we should shake hands – and I give your daughter free leave to make a sketch, or do anything outside the house. Do you understand Latin? Mrs Gaskell does at any rate, well verbum sap. A word to the wise,' and then he chuckled very much; the gist of it was, as Mama saw, and I guessed, that he feared Mr Nicholls' return from the school – and we were to be safely out of the house before that.[15]

Patrick's words have usually been taken to mean that he was in some way under the sway of Arthur Nicholls and that he feared Nicholls' reaction to Mrs Gaskell's presence. It is more likely, however, that he was trying to avoid an embarrassing encounter between the two of them. Arthur Nicholls' dislike of nonconformists was well known and he had been grievously hurt by the revelations about himself and Charlotte which Mrs Gaskell had made.

Unlike her mother's brief, slightly insensitive, summary of the visit, Meta's vivid and lively description of the occasion provides an illuminating and perceptive portrait of Patrick in the last year of his life. Meta's appreciation of the old man's character would seem a more discerning guide to his personality than Mrs Gaskell's unfavourable portrait of him in her biography.

Patrick remained confined to bed throughout the winter. Early in 1861 he suffered a severe relapse and it was thought that he would not recover, but his amazingly tough constitution enabled him to pull through. He was now getting weaker, however, and was in a steady decline. Much of Martha's time was now devoted to attending him and on 1 February the decision was taken to employ once more her younger sister, Eliza, to assist in the running of the house. She was to be paid £10 a year. This decision was recorded by Arthur Nicholls in the little account book which Patrick kept. Patrick himself had continued to make entries in this book until 18 January 1861.

The weather in the early part of 1861 was extremely severe. Heavy falls of snow made the roads between Skipton and Keighley virtually impassable, with deep snow drifts covering the walls. Patrick's friend, Dr Cartman,[16] the headmaster of Skipton Grammar School, showed great determination in getting through to Haworth to celebrate Patrick's eighty-fourth birthday on 17 March 1861. He also preached two sermons in the church on that day. On 4 April Arthur Nicholls was able to report to George Smith:

> Mr Brontë continues pretty well – He has been confined to bed for some months, and seems to lose strength very gradually; his mental faculties however remain quite unimpaired.

Two weeks later Patrick received the sad news that his old friend John Nunn had died at the age of seventy-nine.

The end, however, was drawing near. At about 6 o'clock on the morning of 7 June 1861 Patrick was seized with convulsions and fell into unconsciousness. Arthur and Martha stayed by his side and he died some time between 2 and 3 o'clock in the afternoon. He had been an ordained minister of the Church of England for fifty-five years and had served as incumbent of Haworth for forty-one of them. Many of the people of Haworth had known no other incumbent and they came in their hundreds to pay their last respects at his funeral, which was held on 12 June. Arthur Nicholls followed the coffin as chief mourner, accompanied by Martha Brown, her sister Eliza, their mother and Nancy Garrs. The *Leeds Intelligencer* carried a long report of the ceremony:

> Our correspondent informs us that on his early arrival at the village the shops were universally closed, and the silence and solemnity that reigned around showed the deep estimation in which the venerable incumbent was held. At the time the procession was formed hundreds

of people were congregated in the church-yard from distant villages around, and upon the arrival at the church it was found that every pew and available space within that venerable edifice was occupied by an orderly and well-conducted and apparently sorrow-stricken concourse. The Rev A.B. Nicholls M.A. was chief mourner, followed by his faithful and attached servants, one of whom had been in the family 26 years.

Patrick had expressed the wish that the service should be conducted in complete simplicity and Arthur Nicholls ensured that his instructions were fully carried out:

Not a bell was tolled nor a psalm sung. Everything connected with the funeral was truly simple and unostentatious. The Rev Dr. Burnet[t], vicar of Bradford and the Rev Dr Cartman, of Skipton, preceded the coffin, which was borne from the parsonage to the church and thence to the grave, by the clergymen resident in the immediate district, and close friends of the deceased, viz, the Rev Joseph Grant, incumbent of Oxenhope, the Rev. J.H. Mitchell incumbent of Cullingworth near Bingley, the Rev H. Taylor, incumbent of Newsholme, the Rev Wm. Fawcett incumbent of Morton, the Rev John Smith, incumbent of Oakworth and the Rev W.G. Mayne incumbent of St John's Keighley. The sublime and touching burial service was read amid the audible sobs of the surrounding crowd, by the vicar of Bradford. The Rev A.B. Nicholls appeared to be deeply affected and was supported from the grave to the parsonage by the Rev Dr Cartman whose intimacy with the family commenced in the year 1822, and with but three years intermission has been continued during the long period of 39 years. The day of mourning and woe will be long remembered in Haworth and the surrounding districts.[17]

On 23 June Dr Burnett returned to Haworth to preach Patrick's memorial sermon. The church was packed and Arthur Nicholls was said to have read the prayers 'with great solemnity'.[18]

The report of Patrick's funeral in the *Leeds Intelligencer* had stated that, since the churchyard had been closed in 1856 to any further burials, the authority of the Secretary of State had been obtained to re-open the Brontë family vault and to lay Patrick's body to rest alongside his wife and five of his six children (Anne having been buried at Scarborough). Some time later the memorial tablet recording the deaths of the Brontë family received the following addition:

ALSO OF THE AFOREMENTIONED REVD. P. BRONT Ë, A.B. WHO DIED JUNE 7TH, 1861, IN
THE 85TH YEAR OF HIS AGE, HAVING BEEN INCUMBENT OF HAWORTH
FOR UPWARDS OF 41 YEARS.

The memorial concluded with a quotation from 1 Corinthians 15: 56–57:

The sting of death is sin, and the strength of sin is the law; but thanks be to God, which giveth us the victory through our Lord Jesus Christ.

This was the truth which Patrick had spent his whole life proclaiming. His work was now done and he could rest in peace.

Epilogue

It was generally thought that Arthur Nicholls would be appointed the next incumbent of Haworth and a few days after Patrick's funeral he resumed his parish duties. One sad task he was called upon to perform on 13 August was to take the funeral of his closest friend, Sutcliffe Sowden,[1] the vicar of Hebden Bridge. Mr Sowden had been visiting in his parish and was returning late on a dark and stormy night when he seems to have had a fit and had fallen into the canal and drowned.

When in September the Haworth Church Lands Trustees met to discuss Patrick's successor they unexpectedly decided by seven votes to five to appoint John Wade, the candidate who had the support of the vicar of Bradford. It may be that the trustees were influenced by the fact that John Wade, unlike Arthur, had independent means and would not be dependent on parish funds. A more likely reason for their preference, however, is that given by Juliet Barker:

> The trustees' choice of John Wade in preference to Arthur Nicholls seems attributable chiefly
> to that bloody-mindedness which is characteristic of Yorkshiremen and more especially of
> the people of Haworth. They seem to have wished to assert their own authority in the face of
> a general expectation that they would prefer the curate.[2]

Arthur heard the decision on 18 September and immediately handed in his resignation as curate.

He decided to return to his old home in Ireland. Retaining everything of personal value to him, all the family MSS, their signed books, their writing desks, pictures and some of Charlotte's clothing, he put the rest of the parsonage's contents up for sale at auction on 1 and 2 October. A few days later he quietly left Haworth, accompanied by Martha Brown, and also by Patrick's dogs, Plato and Cato.

Arthur took up residence at Hill House, Banagher, with his aunt, Mrs Bell, and her daughter, Mary Anna. Martha Brown later returned to Haworth, but subsequently paid frequent visits to Banagher. Arthur also wrote to her on many occasions, giving her advice on her railway share dividends and on other practical matters.³ He made no attempt to secure a clerical appointment and lived quietly in genteel poverty as a small farmer.⁴

On 25 August 1864 he married his cousin, Mary Anna. Theirs was a happy marriage, although Mary was under no illusions about his undying devotion to his first wife. When Arthur died on 2 December 1906, aged eighty-seven, she had his coffin placed in the drawing room beneath Richmond's portrait of Charlotte. Mary herself died on 27 February 1915 and was buried next to Arthur in Banagher churchyard.

Notes

Abbreviations

ABN	Arthur Bell Nicholls
Barker	Juliet Barker, *The Brontës*
Borthwick	Borthwick Institute of Historical Research, University of York
BPM	Brontë Parsonage Museum
Bronteana	*The Rev'd Patrick Brontë's Collected Works*, ed. J. Horsfall Turner
BS	*Brontë Studies*
BST	*Brontë Society Transactions*
CB	Charlotte Brontë
CB *Letters*	*The Letters of Charlotte Brontë*, ed. Margaret Smith
ECG	Mrs Elizabeth Cleghorn Gaskell
ECG *Life*	*The Life of Charlotte Brontë*, by Mrs Gaskell
EJB	Emily Jane Brontë
EN	Ellen Nussey
GS	George Smith
Guildhall	Guildhall Library, London
L&D	John Lock & Canon W. T. Dixon, *A Man of Sorrow*
MW	Margaret Wooler
PB	Patrick Brontë
PB *Letters*	*The Letters of the Rev'd Patrick Brontë*, ed. Dudley Green
PBB	Patrick Branwell Brontë (Branwell)
SHB	The Shakespeare Head Brontë
WSW	William Smith Williams
WYAS	West Yorkshire Archive Service

Chapter 1: 'Ireland … Ah "Dulce Domum"'

1. The Latin may be translated 'how sweet is one's home'.
2. The Rev'd John Campbell was the curate of St Peter's, Glenfield. He came from South Carolina, U.S.A., and had been a contemporary of Patrick at Cambridge.
3. PB to ECG, 16 June 1855.
4. PB to ECG, 20 June 1855.
5. *The Belfast Mercury*, April 1855, quoted in SHB *Letters* IV, p. 184.
6. Wright, *The Brontës in Ireland*. Originally published in 1893, it was reissued by the Brontë Society Irish Section in 2004.
7. For this incident see chapter 4.
8. Keeper was the name of Emily Brontë's dog.
9. Chitham, *The Brontës' Irish Background* (Macmillan, 1986), p. 8.

10. Wright, pp. 157–158.
11. The two certificates signed by his father are in the Guildhall Library, London (10326/137).
12. For Patrick's writings see chapter 12.
13. Wright even goes so far as to claim that it was David Harshaw who was responsible for Patrick considering a career as an ordained minister in the Church of England. Harshaw apparently pointed out to Patrick that in the Church of England he would be able to seek ordination after a university course of three or four years, instead of the eight required by the Presbyterian Church.
14. PB to ECG, 20 June 1855.
15. Chitham, p. 78.
16. One possible link with this time is an arithmetic book by Voster, printed in Dublin in 1789, which bears the inscription 'Patrick Prunty's book bought in the year 1795'. This came into the possession of Dr Wright and is now in the Brontë Parsonage Museum. Although the inscription would date the book to Patrick's time at Glascar, it has no established Brontë provenance and the authenticity of the signature has been called into question.
17. PB to editor of the *Halifax Guardian*, 29 July 1843.
18. PB to Hugh Brontë, 20 November 1843.
19. Chitham, p. 90.

Chapter 2: 'I have been educated at Cambridge'

1. Henry Martyn to William Wilberforce, 14 February 1804: Bodleian: Wilberforce d.14, folio 16. Patrick was in fact twenty-five at the time of his entry to St John's.
2. Admissions Register 1802–1835: C4.5, no 1235.
3. Admissions & 1st Residence Book: C27.1.
4. Brotherton: Kirke White, *Remains* I, 180–183.
5. *The Prelude*, Book Third.
6. Examination Book, C15.6.
7. BPM Bonnell: HAOBP bb 207, 208; '*semper*' is the Latin for 'always'.
8. Details are to be found in the Scholars' Admissions Register, C3.5 (pp. 547, 516–519, 747, 610), and in the Exhibition Book SB 9.14.
9. BPM Bonnell: HAOBP bb 54.
10. Henry Martyn to the Rev'd John Sargent, January/February 1804: Bodleian: Wilberforce d.14, folio 16.
11. L&D, p. 18.
12. CB to EN, 3 May and 18 August 1848 (Smith, CB *Letters*, Vol II, pp. 62, 104).
13. Shorter (ed.), *The Brontës: Life & Letters*, I:25, n. 2.
14. ECG *Life*, p. 78. For Patrick's further contact with Lord Palmerston when he was a curate at Dewsbury see chapter 4.
15. Guildhall 10326/137.
16. Guildhall 10326/137.
17. BPM Bonnell: HAOBP bb 54.
18. Guildhall 10326/137.
19. Guildhall 10326/137.
20. Guildhall 10326/137.
21. Guildhall 10326/137.
22. Wright, p. 267 (note).
23. Guildhall 10326/137.

Chapter 3: 'Two Curacies in the South'

1. Lambeth Palace: Visitation Returns, Randolph 1810 SZ 44
2. Dixon, 'Reminiscences of an Essex Country Practitioner a Century Ago,' the *Essex Review*, XIII (1914), p. 195.
3. The '*Si Quis*' (Latin for 'if anyone') was a public notice on behalf of a candidate for ordination. It was issued on three successive Sundays and required anyone who wished to object to the

candidate's ordination to come forward and state their objection. Patrick was required to send to the bishop a statement, signed by his vicar and churchwardens, affirming that the notice had been issued and that no objections had been received.

4. Guildhall 10326/138.
5. Birrell, *Life of Charlotte Brontë*, p. 20.
6. PB to Mary Burder, 1 January 1824.
7. His curacy at Wethersfield was worth only £60 a year.
8. Birrell, pp. 22–23.
9. Mary Burder to PB, 8 August 1823, quoted in SHB *Letters* I, p. 64.
10. Residence Register: C27.1.
11. The Latin means 'love conquers everything'.
12. Shorter (ed.), *The Brontës: Life & Letters* I:25, n. 2.
13. Morgan, *The Parish Priest*, pp. 8–9.
14. James Wood Commonplace Book 180836 (6 Nov. 1809) M1.3 pp. 214, 219, 223 (St John's College, Cambridge).
15. BPM Bonnell: HAOBP bb57.

Chapter 4: 'I came to Yorkshire'

1. Yates, *The Father of the Brontës*, p. 38.
2. Yates, p. 29.
3. Yates, pp. 46–47.
4. Yates, pp. 32–33.
5. Yates, pp. 46–47.
6. Yates, p. 48.
7. Yates, pp. 35–36.
8. Yates, pp. 75–76.
9. *Leeds Mercury*, 15 December 1810.
10. Borthwick: ADM 1810.
11. BPM Bonnell: HAOBP bb11.
12. BPM.

Chapter 5: 'My dear saucy Pat'

1. Patrick's friend William Morgan, who was courting Maria's cousin Jane Branwell, is often jocularly referred to as 'the Doctor' in Maria's correspondence.
2. For Patrick's writings see chapter 12.
3. Yates, p. 86.
4. PB to Joseph Buckle, 31 July 1811.
5. Borthwick: ADM 1811, Institution Act Books: INST.AB.18 p. 25
6. Some indication of the dangers prevalent at that time is given in a letter from John Abbott (who knew both Patrick and Maria), describing a night-time encounter with a band of Luddites, quoted in Barker, p. 53.
7. Minute Book of the Wesleyan Academy, Woodhouse Grove, 19 August 1811, 25 September 1811.
8. Maria would almost certainly have known my great-great-great grandfather, the Revd George Coryton. He was the Master of Penzance Grammar School and curate of St Mary's Church during the time when Maria was in her teens. The church is only a stone's throw away from the Branwell family home.
9. The text of all Maria Branwell's letters is given in SHB I pp. 8–23 (and also in Green, PB *Letters*, Appendix III). The MS of her letter of 18 November 1812 is in the Brotherton Library, Leeds. For the incident when Patrick showed these letters to Charlotte see chapter 19.
10. *Bronteana*, pp. 83–84.
11. Yates, p. 89.

Chapter 6: 'At Thornton ... happy with our wives and children'

1. The Revd Robinson Pool was the Dissenting minister of Kipping Chapel in Thornton during Patrick's ministry there.
2. Assignation of Dues to Bradford, BPM BS 151.
3. Borthwick.
4. PB to Richard Burn, 27 January 1820.
5. Holgate, 'The Brontës at Thornton', *BST* 13, 69, pp. 326–327.
6. Scruton, *Thornton and the Brontës*, pp. 76–78.
7. Firth Papers, Special Collections, University of Sheffield Library.
8. Borthwick: Y/DSR 63.
9. Legh Richmond (1772–1827) was the rector of Turvey in Bedfordshire. He was a well-known evangelical clergyman and became famous for his tract *The Dairyman's Daughter*, which was translated into nineteen languages and sold 4 million copies. This told the story of Elizabeth Wallbridge, a young woman to whom he had ministered while he was the curate of Brading and Yaverland in the Isle of Wight (1797–1805). She had a deep religious faith and had died of consumption at the age of thirty-one.
10. Holgate, pp. 327–328.
11. Holgate, p. 335.
12. Holgate, p. 336.
13. Scruton, p. 59.
14. Churchwardens' Book for the Chapelry of Thornton, 27 December 1819, WYAS, Bradford.

Chapter 7: 'Providence has called me to labour ... at Haworth'

1. PB to Stephen Taylor, 8 July 1819.
2. Michael Stocks to Mr Greenwood, 1 June 1819, BPM: BS, ix, S p. 1.
3. L&D, pp. 210–211.
4. Anthony Moss to the Revd Edward Ramsden, 15 June 1819: MS RMP 392, WYAS Calderdale.
5. Henry Heap to the Archbishop of York, 2 June 1819: MS ADM 1820, Borthwick.
6. *Leeds Intelligencer*, 14 June 1819.
7. Borthwick: ADM 1819
8. PB to Stephen Taylor, 9 October 1819.
9. ECG *Life*, pp. 74–75.
10. *Leeds Intelligencer*, 18 April 1857.
11. *Leeds Intelligencer*, 22 November 1819.
12. Borthwick: ADM 1820.
13. Henry Heap to the Archbishop of York, 9 February 1820, Borthwick: ADM 1820.
14. Borthwick: ADM 1820.
15. BPM: Mildred Christian Documents.
16. PB to the Archbishop of York, 9 February 1820.
17. Borthwick: Institution Act Books: INST.AB.18 p. 329.

Chapter 8: 'The greatest load of sorrows'

1. Benjamin Herschel Babbage, 'Report to the General Board of Health', 1850.
2. Jocelyn Kellett, *Haworth Parsonage: The home of the Brontës*, The Brontë Society, 1977.
3. PB to the Rev'd John Buckworth, 27 November 1821.
4. Isabella Dury to Miss Mariner, 14 February 1823, BS ix D.
5. Mary Burder to PB, 18 August 1823, SHB I p.64.
6. *Leeds Intelligencer*, 4 December 1823.
7. PB to ECG, 20 June 1855.
8. Attendance Register, Cumbria Record Office, Kendal: WDS 38/3.
9. PB and others to the Archbishop of York, 8 April 1820.

10. *Leeds Mercury*, 4 September 1824.
11. *Bronteana*, pp. 209–212.
12. PB to the *Leeds Intelligencer*, 9 September 1824; PB to the *Leeds Mercury*, 16 September 1824.
13. Barker, p. 859, note 63.
14. *Leeds Mercury*, 11 September 1824.
15. Nancy Garrs, *Illustrated Weekly Telegraph*, 10 January 1885.
16. Attendance Register, Cumbria Record Office, Kendal: WDS 38/3.
17. PB to ECG, 30 July 1855.
18. ECG *Life*, p. 109.
19. For a full analysis of the evidence see Sarah Fermi in *BST* 21:6 (1996), pp. 219–231.
20. Barker, p. 857.
21. Carus Wilson, *A Child's First Tales*, p. 47.
22. See *The Life and Works of William Carus Wilson* by Jane M. Ewbank.
23. CB to WSW, 4 January 1848

Chapter 9: 'Always ... at my post'

1. Green, PB *Letters*, pp. 55–57.
2. Green, PB *Letters*, pp. 58–60
3. *Bradford & Wakefield Chronicle*, 24 September 1825.
4. PB, James Greenwood and Thomas Andrew to the Secretary of the British and Foreign Bible Society, 3 October 1825.
5. See Appendix IV, 'Ecclesiastical Census: Sunday 30 March 1851.'
6. BPM: BS 183.5.
7. For a full discussion of Patrick's attitude to the question of Church Rates see chapter 13.
8. Green, PB *Letters*, pp. 84–85.
9. Green, PB *Letters*, pp. 88–89.
10. John Winterbotham to *Leeds Mercury*, 20 September 1834.
11. Green, PB *Letters*, pp. 98–99.
12. Green, PB *Letters*, pp. 103–104, 105–106.
13. PB to Messrs James and Richard Thomas, 13 July 1855, 2 May 1856, 20 August 1860.
14. Green, PB *Letters*, pp. 83–84.
15. Barker, p. 884, notes 59, 60.
16. 'Z' to *Leeds Mercury*, 17 December 1836.
17. William Hodgson to *Leeds Mercury*, 31 December 1836.
18. *Halifax Guardian*, 9 January 1838
19. See PB to *Leeds Intelligencer*, 22 April 1837 and the discussion of this matter in chapter 17.
20. *Leeds Intelligencer*, 1 April 1837.
21. On the death of his father Stephen in December 1831 George Taylor had succeeded him as churchwarden.
22. PB to Mrs Taylor, 19 July 1837.
23. Benjamin Binns in *Bradford Observer*, 17 February 1894.
24. In 1836 Haworth had been transferred from the Archdiocese of York into the newly created Diocese of Ripon. The first Bishop of Ripon was Charles Longley, who later served as Archbishop of Canterbury (1862–1868) and founded the Lambeth Conference.
25. PB to Bishop of Ripon, 30 January 1839.
26. Green, PB *Letters*, Appendix XI.
27. CB to EN, ?7 April 1840
28. CB to EN, ?4 April 1847.

Chapter 10: 'Intelligent companionship and intense family affection'

1. Nancy Wainwright [*née* Garrs], *Illustrated Weekly Telegraph*, 10 January 1885.
2. For further details of Martha Wright see Ann Dinsdale, *The Brontës at Haworth*, pp. 20, 53, 57.
3. ECG *Life*, p. 87.

4. Leyland, *The Brontë Family*, Vol I, pp. 65–66.
5. Sarah Garrs, quoted in Harland, *Charlotte Brontë at Home*, p. 32.
6. Emily and Anne Brontë, Diary Paper, 24 November 1834, BPM: Bonnell 131.
7. CB to EJB, 1 October 1843.
8. PB to the Rev'd William Gaskell, 7 April 1857.
9. Sarah Garrs, quoted in Harland, *Charlotte Brontë at Home*, pp. 17–24.
10. Emily and Anne Brontë, Diary Paper, 24 November 1834, BPM: Bonnell 131.
11. William Dearden, *Bradford Observer*, 27 June 1861.
12. PB to ECG, 24 July 1855.
13. PB to ECG, 30 July 1855.
14. CB, *The History of the Year*, 12 March 1829: BPM Bonnell, 80 (11).
15. CB, *Tales of the Islanders*.
16. PB to ECG, 24 July 1855.
17. CB, *Tales of the Islanders*.
18. CB to BB, 17 May 1832.
19. EJB, fragmentary translations of Virgil's *Aeneid* and notes on Greek tragedy, 13 March 1838: MSS at King's School, Canterbury.
20. William Dearden, *Bradford Observer*, 27 June 1861
21. John Greenwood's Diary, BPM.
22. EN, Reminiscences, MS in the Walpole Collection, the King's School, Canterbury: reprinted in Smith, *CB Letters*, Vol I, pp. 596–601.
23. CB, 'The following strange occurrence', 22 June 1830: MS Harvard, Eng 35.5.
24. PB to Mrs Franks, 28 April 1831.
25. EN, Reminiscences, *Scribner's Monthly*, May 1871: reprinted in Smith, CB *Letters*, Vol I, p. 591.
26. Mary Taylor to ECG, 18 January 1856.
27. PB to Mrs Franks, 6 July 1835.
28. CB, Prefatory Note to *A Selection of Poems by Ellis Bell*, 1850.
29. Barker, pp. 228–229.
30. CB to EN, 29 December 1836.
31. James de la Trobe to William Scruton: quoted in Scruton's 'Reminiscences of the late Miss Ellen Nussey', *BST* 1:8:23 (1898).
32. PB to John Driver, 23 February 1838.
33. CB to EN, 2 October 1838.
34. CB to EN, 15 April 1839.
35. *Agnes Grey*, chapter 1.
36. CB to EN, 21 December 1839.
37. Barker, p. 897, notes 6 and 7.
38. EN, Reminiscences, given as a footnote in SHB I, p. 201.
39. Barker, p. 900, note 63.
40. CB to EN, end of June 1840.
41. CB to EN, ?14 August 1840.
42. CB to EN, ?14 August 1840.

Chapter 11: 'I went to Brussells'

1. BPM: BS 17
2. ECG *Life*, p. 224
3. Binns, *Bradford Observer*, 17 February 1894.
4. *Bronteana*, pp. 252–262. For extracts from this sermon see Green, PB *Letters*, Appendix XIII.
5. PBB to Francis Grundy, 25 October 1842 (SHB I pp. 272–273).
6. PBB to Francis Grundy, 29 October 1842 (SHB I p. 273).
7. Constantin Heger to PB, 5 November 1842 (SHB I pp. 278–280).
8. PB to William Thomas, 1 August 1843, PB to George Taylor, 29 February 1844. For full details of the forgery case see Sarah Fermi and Dorinda Kinghorn, 'The Brontës and the Case of the Beaver Forgery', *BST* 21:1 (1993) pp. 15–24.

9. PB to Hugh Brontë, 20 November 1843.
10. CB to EN, ?10 August 1844.
11. CB to EN, ?29 July 1844.
12. PB to ECG, 2 April 1857.
13. Barker, p. 925, note 55.
14. PBB to Francis Grundy, October 1845 (SHB II p. 65).
15. CB, *Biographical Notice of Ellis and Acton Bell*, pp. 359–360 (reprinted in Smith, CB *Letters*, Vol II, Appendix II, pp. 742–743).
16. CB, *Biographical Notice*, p. 360.
17. ECG *Life*, pp. 324–325.
18. For Patrick's efforts to establish a National School at Haworth see chapter 16.
19. CB to EN, 21 August 1846.
20. Graham, *Modern Domestic Medicine*, BPM HAOBP: bb 210 38, pp. 226–228.
21. ECG, *Life*, p. 90.

Chapter 12: 'Employment ... full of real indescribable pleasure'

1. L&D, p. 56
2. *Bronteana*, pp. 17–67.
3. *Bronteana*, pp. 69–99.
4. For extracts from this poem see chapter 5, p. 34.
5. *Bronteana*, pp. 100–129. *The Cottage in the Wood* also appeared, without the poetry section, in *The Cottage Magazine*, edited by Patrick's former vicar John Buckworth, and it was reprinted in its entirety in a second edition in 1818.
6. SHB I, pp. 24–27.
7. *Bronteana*, pp. 130–200.

Chapter 13: 'An advocate for temperate reform'

1. PB to *Leeds Intelligencer*, 29 January 1829.
2. For CB's description of the scene at the parsonage see pp. 73–74.
3. *The Times*, 27 February 1837.
4. *Bronteana*, pp. 150–151.
5. PB to *Leeds Intelligencer*, 30 January 1841.
6. PB to *Leeds Mercury*, 5 June 1847.
7. The Brontë family had been close friends of Elizabeth Franks (*née* Firth) and her father during their time in Thornton.
8. PB to Dr Outhwaite, 20 September 1844.
9. BPM: Bonnell 131.
10. *Bronteana*, pp. 220–232.

Chapter 14: 'I never was friendly to Church Rates'

1. See the Ecclesiastical Census, Sunday 30 March 1851, printed in Appendix I.
2. PB to *Leeds Intelligencer*, 18 January and 8 February 1834, and to *Leeds Mercury*, 22 February and 8 March 1834; Rev'd John Winterbotham to *Leeds Mercury*, 25 January and 8 March 1834. Both Mr Winterbotham's letters are reprinted in Green, PB *Letters*, Appendix VIII.
3. Barker, p. 884, note 50.
4. *Bradford Observer*, 29 September 1836.
5. *Bradford Observer*, 2 March 1837.
6. *Bradford Observer*, 9 March 1837.
7. 'Miss Celia Amelia' was the affectionate name given to William Weightman by the Brontë sisters.

8. CB to EN, ?7 April 1840.
9. MS in Unsorted Bundle, Scoresby Papers, Whitby.
10. Chadwick, *The Victorian Church*, Pt I, p. 157, note 1.
11. Chadwick, Pt I, pp. 149–150.
12. Chadwick, Pt I, p. 150.
13. John Winterbotham to *Bradford Observer*, 20 May 1841.
14. *Halifax Guardian*, 3 July 1841.
15. *Bradford Observer*, 13 October 1842.

Chapter 15: 'My aim has been ... to preach Christ'

1. The only exceptions were when he was asked to provide a copy of his address, as in the case of the funeral sermon for William Weightman (*Bronteana*, pp. 252–262), or when he considered the occasion sufficiently memorable, as happened in 1824 with the moorland bog-burst on Crow Hill (*Bronteana*, pp. 209–219).
2. Wright, *The Brontës in Ireland*, p. 267.
3. Ellen Nussey, *Reminiscences* (reprinted, Smith, Vol I, p. 600).
4. Scruton, *Thornton and the Brontës*, p. 113 (reprinted Lemon, *Early Visitors to Haworth*, p. 26).
5. Lemon, *Early Visitors to Haworth*, p. 65.
6. The parish clerk was a layman who assisted the minister in the administration of the church and in the performance of minor duties during services, such as leading the singing, reading the Gospel or Epistle, announcing the metrical psalm and making the congregational responses. The clerk was often entrusted with making up the parish registers, although it was unlawful for the priest to delegate this responsibility.
7. ECG, *Life*, p. 90.
8. PB to *Leeds Mercury*, 16 March 1844.
9. Binns in *Bradford Observer*, 17 February 1894.
10. PB to the Rev'd W. J. Kennedy, 3 May 1844.
11. PB to Mr Metcalfe, 30 June 1831.
12. L&D, p. 342.
13. BPM Copy Documents.
14. BPM:BS 175. For railway policemen see *Victorian Raillwaymen* by Dr P. W.Kingsford (Frank Cass, 1970).
15. For a discussion of this case see chapter 11, note 8.
16. PB to Dr McLaw, 27 July 1858.
17. *Bronteana*, p. 256.

Chapter 16: 'Our School has commenced'

1. For the numbers in the various denominational Sunday schools see the Ecclesiastical Census, Sunday 30 March 1851, printed in Appendix I.
2. Church of England Record Centre (National Society Collection).
3. PB to the Revd W. J. Kennedy, 4 December 1843.
4. PB to the Revd W. J. Kennedy, 8 December 1843.
5. PB to the Revd W. J. Kennedy, 12 December 1843.
6. PB to the Revd W. J. Kennedy, 19 January 1844.
7. PB to the Revd W. J. Kennedy, 21 October 1844.
8. PB to the Revd W. J. Kennedy, 26 October 1844.
9. PB to the Revd W. J. Kennedy, 31 March 1845.

Chapter 17: 'There is now a great want of pure water'

1. Petition from the principal Inhabitants of Haworth to the General Board of Health, 28 August 1849 (L&D, p. 432)

2. Benjamin Herschel Babbage, Report to the General board of Health, 1850.
3. L&D, pp. 435–437.
4. PB to the General Board of Health, 8 September 1851
5. L&D, pp. 436–437.

Chapter 18: 'My Son! My Son!'

1. Green, PB *Letters*, Appendix X, p. 356.
2. SHB II, p. 177.
3. ECG, *Life*, p. 284. Branwell's final comment was a reference to Lady Robinson.
4. ECG, *Life*, p. 324.
5. SHB II, p. 223.
6. SHB II, p. 224.
7. Grundy, *Pictures of the Past*, pp. 90–92.
8. Barker, p. 939, note 82.
9. CB to WSW, 6 October 1848.
10. Grundy, *Pictures of the Past*, p. 92.
11. CB, *Biographical Notice of Ellis and Acton Bell* (reprinted in Smith, CB *Letters*, Vol II, Appendix II, p. 746).
12. ECG, *Life*, p. 358, CB to WSW, 25 June 1849, ECG to ?John Forster, September 1853.
13. EN, *Reminiscences*, *BST* VIII: 42 (1932), pp. 21–22.
14. *The Poems of Anne Brontë*, ed. Chitham, pp. 163–164.
15. CB to George Smith, 22 January 1849.
16. AB to EN, 5 April 1849 (Smith, Vol II, p. 195).
17. EN, *A short Account of the Last Days of Dear A.B.*, King's School, Canterbury (reprinted in Smith, CB *Letters*, Vol II, Appendix I, pp. 739–740).

Chapter 19: 'I can, yet ... take two Services on the Sundays'

1. See chapter 17.
2. CB to WSW, 24 August 1849.
3. *Shirley*, chapter 37.
4. PB, 'A Christmas Hymn', *Leeds Intelligencer*, 22 December 1849.
5. CB to EN, ?16 February 1850.
6. CB to EN, ?16 February 1850.
7. CB to George Smith, 22 September 1849.
8. CB to EN, ?11 March 1850.
9. CB to EN, 19 March 1850.
10. CB to EN, 12 April 1850.
11. CB to PB, 4 June 1850.
12. Benjamin Binns in *Bradford Observer*, 17 February 1894.
13. PB to EN, 12 July 1850.
14. CB to EN, 15 July 1850.
15. CB to EN, 1 August 1850.
16. CB to George Smith, 1 August 1850.
17. PB to George Smith, 2 August 1850.
18. ECG to Catherine Winkworth, 25 August 1850.
19. CB to ECG, 27 August 1850.
20. ECG to Catherine Winkworth, 25 August 1850.
21. Patrick is referring to the members of the Oxford Movement whose members were working for the reform of the Church of England. In 1833 the first of a series of Tracts for the Times had appeared, written by men such as John Henry Newman (1801–1890), John Keble (1792–1866), Richard Froude (1803–1836) and Edward Pusey (1800–1882).
22. CB to EN, ?5 December 1849.
23. CB to EN, 5 May 1851.

24. See Appendix I, Ecclesiastical Census, Sunday 30 March 1851.

25. CB to PB, 14 June 1851.

26. CB to EN, 1 September 1851.

27. CB to EN, 5 May 1851.

28. CB to EN, 3 October 1851.

29. CB to Margaret Wooler, 21 October 1851.

30. PB to Richard Monckton Milnes, 16 January 1852.

31. CB to EN, 26 July 1852.

32. CB to EN, 3 August 1852.

33. CB to EN, 25 August 1852.

Chapter 20: 'His union with My Daughter was a happy one'

1. CB to EN, 15 December 1852.

2. CB to EN, 18 December 1852.

3. CB to EN, 18 December 1852.

4. PB to EN, 12 July 1850.

5. CB to EN, 15 December 1852.

6. CB to EN, 18 December 1852.

7. Both Patrick's letters are undated but must have been written before 19 January since Charlotte refers to 'portions of two notes' from her father in her letter to Ellen Nussey of that date.

8. The hooded snake of India. Charlotte had referred to seeing this snake in her letter to her father of 4 June 1850, in which she described her visit to the gardens of the Zoological Society in London.

9. Johann Kaspar Lavater was a Swiss Protestant pastor and the founder of the study of physiognomy. He believed in the interaction of mind and body and he thought that the nature of a person's spirit might be traced from their features. Charlotte was familiar with the practice of physiognomy.

10. ABN to the Society for the Propagation of the Gospel, 28 January 1853.

11. PB to the Rev'd W. J. Bullock, 31 January 1853.

12. ECG, *Life*, p. 484.

13. When the Diocese of Ripon was created in 1836 Charles Longley was consecrated as its first bishop. He went on to be successively Bishop of Durham (1856–1860), Archbishop of York (1860–1862) and Archbishop of Canterbury (1862–1868).

14. Charles Longley to Mrs Longley, 2 March 1853, Lambeth Palace Library MS 4547.

15. Charles Longley to Mrs Longley, 4 March 1853, Lambeth Palace Library MS 4547.

16. CB to EN, 4 March 1853.

17. CB to EN, 4 March 1853.

18. CB to Margaret Wooler, 12 April 1854.

19. CB to EN, 4 March 1853.

20. CB to EN, 19 May 1853.

21. PB to ECG, ?5 or 6 June 1853.

22. CB to GS, 14 July 1853.

23. CB to GS 14 July 1853.

24. CB to GS, 3 July 1853.

25. PB to ECG, 15 September 1853.

26. CB to ECG, 16 September 1853.

27. ECG to ?John Forster, September 1853.

28. Mrs Gaskell also recorded that as she arrived at the parsonage she encountered another visitor, a Mr Francis Bennoch. He had written the previous day to say that he wished to call on Charlotte. Despite Charlotte's unwillingness Patrick insisted on seeing him. When both Charlotte and Mrs Gaskell expressed their displeasure at Mr Bennoch's action, Patrick called them 'a couple of proud minxes'.

29. ECG, *Life*, p. 508.

30. ECG, *Life*, p. 511.

31. Patrick's interest in military weapons is shown by the letters he wrote to the Master-General of the Ordnance suggesting improvements to the musket used by the British Army and recommending a

projectile to be used in naval warfare: PB to Sir George Murray, 19 and 29 November 1841, PB to the Marquess of Anglesey, 4 July 1848. These letters are printed in Appendix X.
32. Mary Hewitt to EN, 21 February 1854 (Smith, Vol III, p. 226).
33. CB to EN, 11 April 1854.
34. CB to EN, 28 March 1854.
35. Richard Monckton Milnes to ECG, 30 January 1854 (Smith, Vol III, p. 223).
36. CB to EN, 11 April 1854.
37. CB to MW, 14 April 1854.
38. CB to EN, 15 April 1854.
39. CB to ECG, ?18 April 1854.
40. ECG to John Forster, 17 May 1854.
41. CB to ECG, ?18 April 1854.
42. CB to EN, 15 April 1854.
43. CB to MW, 12 April 1854.
44. CB to EN, 14 May 1854.
45. CB to EN, 27 May 1854.
46. CB to EN, 21 May 1854.
47. CB to EN, 11 June 1854.
48. CB to EN, 16 June 1854.

Chapter 21: 'My Daughter is indeed dead'

1. CB to MW, 22 August 1854.
2. CB to MW, 19 September 1854.
3. CB to MW, 15 November 1854
4. Emily Martha, the three-year-old daughter of Joe and Amelia Taylor, was affectionately known as 'Tim'.
5. CB to EN ?20 October 1854.
6. EN to ABN, November 1854 (Smith Vol III p. 297).
7. CB to EN, 19 January 1855.
8. ABN to EN, 1 February 1855. (SHB IV, p. 173).
9. ECG, Life, pp. 523–524.
10. PB to ECG, 27 August 1855.
11 CB to Amelia Taylor, ?21 January 1855.
12. PB to ECG, 5 April, 1855.
13. PB to GS, 20 April 1855.
14. PB to the Bishop of Ripon, 10 April 1855, Lambeth Palace Library MS 4545.

Chapter 22: 'No quailing Mrs Gaskell! no drawing back!'

1. *Leeds Mercury*, 12 April 1855.
2. PB to Henry Garrs, 2 April 1856.
3. For Patrick's will see Green, PB *Letters*, Appendix XIV.
4. EN to ABN, 6 June 1855 (SHB IV p.189).
5. ECG to Catherine Winkworth, 25 August 1850. Catherine Winkworth was an accomplished translator of German hymns and a close friend of Mrs Gaskell. Catherine and her sister Susanna had lessons in Greek from William Gaskell.
6. For a detailed study of this matter see John Geoffrey Sharps, *Mrs Gaskell's Observation and Invention*, Appendix III: 'The Ironical Origin of The Life of Charlotte Brontë. For the relevant texts see Appendix VIII.
7. ABN to EN, 11 June 1855 (SHB IV pp.89–190).
8. PB to ECG, 16 June 1855.
9. ECG to GS, 18 June 1855.
10. ECG to Marianne Gaskell, 27 July 1855.
11. ECG to EN, 6 September 1855.

12. ECG to EN, 9 July 1856 (SHB IV p. 203).
13. EN to ECG, July 1856 (SHB IV p. 205).
14. The Revd William Gaskell was the Unitarian minister of Cross Street chapel, Manchester.
15. ECG to GS, 25 July 1856.
16. ECG to GS, *c.* 15 November 1856.
17. ABN to GS, 28 November 1856.
18. ABN to GS, 3 December 1856.
19. ABN to GS, 1 December 1856.
20. *Christian Romancer*, July 1857.
21. *Bradford Observer*, 30 April 1857 (reprinted in Lemon, *Early Visitors to Haworth*, pp 28–34.
22. PB to GS, 9 June 1857.
23. PB to GS, 15 June 1857.
24. PB to GS, 16 July 1857.
25. PB to ECG, 20 August 1857.
26. Harriet Martineau's niece and companion.
27. PB to ECG, 24 August 1857.
28. Charlotte visited Harriet Martineau when she was in London in December 1849 and a year later stayed several days with her at her home in Ambleside. Charlotte broke off their friendship after Miss Martineau's critical review of *Villette* in the *Daily News* (3 February 1853), ECG *Life*, pp 494–495.
29. PB to William Dearden, 31 August 1857.
30. PB to ECG, 31 August 1857. The Roman god Janus was represented with two faces which looked both ways. The month of January was dedicated to him.
31. ECG to Maria Martineau, 23 August 1857.
32. ECG to GS, 23 August 1857.
33. A second edition, merely a reprint of the first, had been published on 22 April (Barker, p. 799).
34. In 1851 Harriet Martineau collaborated with Henry George Atkinson in writing *Letters on the Law of Man's Social Nature*, a work which caused great controversy at the time for its agnostic approach.

Chapter 23: 'I wish to live in unnoticed and quiet retirement'

1. Lemon, *Early Visitors to Haworth*, pp. 36–38.
2. J. W. E., 'A Day at Haworth', *Bradford Observer*, 19 November 1857.
3. Lemon, pp. 40–41.
4. Lemon, p. 59.
5. The Revd Matthewson Helstone was the rector of Briarfield in *Shirley*, a character thought to be based on Patrick's friend the Rev'd Hammond Roberson. In a letter to William Smith Williams (21 September 1849) Charlotte said that as a child she had been struck by Mr Roberson's 'appearance and stern martial air'.
6. Lemon, pp. 63–65.
7. Lemon, p. 67.
8. Sir Joseph Paxton (1801–1865) had designed the Crystal Palace, the building for the Great Exhibition of 1851. In 1826 the Duke of Devonshire had appointed him superintendent of the gardens at Chatsworth. He was the M.P. for Coventry from 1854 until his death in 1865.
9. PB to Mrs Nunn, 1 February 1858.
10. PB to Mrs Nunn, 26 October 1859.
11. The Latin phrase may be roughly translated as 'On a small scale, he has written a great deal, which fully deserves to be preserved.' '*Cedrus*' is the Latin for cedar oil, which was used to preserve books.
12. Patrick performed his last marriage on 24 February 1857, his final baptism in church on 26 April 1857 and took his last funeral on 26 October 1858.
13. *Bradford Observer*, 13 September 1860.
14. ECG to WSW, 20 December 1860. But see also Mrs Gaskell's letter of 1 November 1860 to an unknown correspondent (Chapple & Shelston, *Further Letters of Mrs Gaskell*, p. 215) where she reveals a more sympathetic and sensitive understanding of Mr Brontë.
15. SHB, XIV, pp. 239–241 (reprinted in Green, PB *Letters*, Appendix XV).

16. In 1859 William Cartman had been awarded a Lambeth Doctorate of Divinity by the Archbishop of Canterbury in recognition of his powers as a preacher.
17. *Leeds Intelligencer*, 15 June 1861 (reprinted in Green, PB *Letters*, Appendix XVII).
18. *Halifax Guardian*, 29 June 1861.

Epilogue

1. Sutcliffe Sowden had performed the wedding service for Arthur and Charlotte and had also taken Charlotte's funeral.
2. Barker, p. 824. For a discussion of other alleged reasons see Barker, pp. 822–823.
3. See *Dear Martha: the Letters of Arthur Bell Nicholls to Martha Brown*, transcribed by Geoffrey Palmer (Brontë Society).
4. For details of Arthur Nicholls' life in Ireland see *My Dear Boy: the Life of Arthur Bell Nicholls, B.A.* by Margaret & Robert Cochrane (Highgate Publications).

Patrick Brontë: a Chronology
1777–1861

1777	17 March	Born at Emdale, in the parish of Drumballyroney, County Down, Ireland
1798		Appointed tutor to the sons of the Rev'd Thomas Tighe
1802	1 October	Admitted as a sizar to St John's College, Cambridge
1806	23 April	Graduated as Bachelor of Arts
	10 August	Ordained deacon by the Bishop of London in Fulham Palace Chapel
	12 October	Took first duties as curate of St Mary Magdalene, Wethersfield
1807	21 December	Ordained priest by the Bishop of Salisbury in the Chapel Royal, St James' Palace
1809	early January	Started curacy at All Saints', Wellington, under the Rev'd John Eyton
	5 December	Started curacy at All Saints', Dewsbury, under the Rev'd John Buckworth
1811	end March	His name first appears in the register of St Peter's, Hartshead, as minister
		Cottage Poems published
1812	29 December	Married Maria Branwell
1813	September	*The Rural Minstrel* published
1814	January	Birth of daughter Maria
1815	8 February	Birth of daughter Elizabeth
		The family took up residence in Thornton
		The Cottage in the Wood published
1816	21 April	Birth of daughter Charlotte
		Nancy Garrs (aged thirteen) came to work at the parsonage as a nursemaid
1817	26 June	Birth of son Branwell
1818	April	*The Maid of Killarney* published
	30 July	Birth of daughter Emily
		Sarah Garrs employed at the parsonage as a nursemaid
1820	7 January	Birth of daughter Anne
	8 February	Nominated to Haworth jointly by the vicar of Bradford and the Haworth Trustees
	April	The family moved to Haworth
1821	15 September	Death of his wife Maria (aged thirty-eight)
1824	21 July	Took Maria (aged ten) and Elizabeth (aged nine) to the Clergy Daughters' School, Cowan Bridge
	10 August	Took Charlotte (aged eight) to the Clergy Daughters' School
	25 November	Took Emily (aged six) to the Clergy Daughters' School
	December	Nancy Garrs left the parsonage to be married
1825	January	Tabitha Aykroyd (aged fifty-three) came to the parsonage as cook
	February	Sarah Garrs left the parsonage for employment found by Patrick
	6 May	Death of Maria (aged eleven)
	15 June	Death of Elizabeth (aged ten)
1832	Summer	Opening of the National Church Sunday school in Haworth
1833	July	Ellen Nussey paid her first visit to the parsonage, staying two weeks
1834	23 March	Inauguration of the organ in Haworth church with a performance of Handel's *Messiah*

1834		Bought a cottage piano for the parsonage
1835		Engaged William Robinson to teach painting to Branwell
	22 September	The annual vestry meeting refused to fix a church rate
	December	William Hodgson appointed curate of Haworth.
1836	December	Opened a voluntary subscription to defray church expenses
1837	22 February	Chaired meeting called to petition Parliament against the Poor Law Amendment Act
	May	William Hodgson left to become vicar of Christ Church, Colne
1839	17 January	Death of Henry Heap (vicar of Bradford for twenty-two years)
	February	Bishop of Ripon's proposal to make Haworth a separate parish opposed by the Bradford trustees
	19 August	William Weightman appointed curate of Haworth
	October	The Rev'd Dr William Scoresby appointed as vicar of Bradford
1841		Martha Brown (aged thirteen) became a servant at the parsonage
1842	8–(?)	
	22 February	Escorted Charlotte and Emily to Brussels and visited site of the Battle of Waterloo
	6 September	Death of William Weightman (aged twenty-eight) from cholera
	29 October	Death of Elizabeth Branwell (aged sixty-six)
1843	12 March	James Smith performed his first duties as curate of Haworth
1844	2 February	Opening of the National School in Haworth
	July	Chaired a meeting to discuss the problem of the water supply to Haworth
	October	James Smith left to be the curate of Keighley
1845	25 May	Arthur Bell Nicholls took his first Sunday duties as curate of Haworth
1846	10 March	New peal of bells installed with a ringing competition and dinner at the Black Bull
	May	Publication of *Poems* by Currer, Ellis and Acton Bell
	19 August–	
	28 September	Stayed in Manchester with Charlotte for a cataract operation performed by Mr Wilson
	end December	Resignation of Dr Scoresby from Bradford due to ill health
1847	February	John Burnett appointed vicar of Bradford
	end February	Oxenhope became a separate parish with Joseph Grant as vicar
	19 October	Publication of *Jane Eyre*
	early December	Publication of *Wuthering Heights* and *Agnes Grey*
1848	early July	Publication of *The Tenant of Wildfell Hall*
	24 September	Death of Branwell (aged thirty-one)
	19 December	Death of Emily (aged thirty)
1849	28 May	Death of Anne (aged twenty-nine)
	26 October	Publication of *Shirley*
1850	4 April	Benjamin Herschel Babbage began his enquiries into the water supply at Haworth
1852	13 December	Arthur Nicholls made a proposal of marriage to Charlotte
1853	28 January	Publication of *Villette*
	2–4 March	The Bishop of Ripon, Dr Charles Longley, stayed at the parsonage
	27 May	Arthur Nicholls left Haworth
	29 May	George de Renzy performed his first duties as curate of Haworth
	19–23 September	Mrs Gaskell stayed at the parsonage
1854	3–7 April	Arthur Nicholls stayed at the parsonage – his engagement to Charlotte was agreed
	June	Construction of a main sewer in Main Street, Haworth
	25 June	George de Renzy left Haworth
	29 June	Marriage of Charlotte to Arthur Nicholls
1855	17 February	Death of Tabby Aykroyd (aged eighty-four)
	31 March	Death of Charlotte (aged thirty-eight)
	16 June	Wrote to Mrs Gaskell asking her to write a life of Charlotte

1857	25 March	Publication of *The Life of Charlotte Brontë*
	6 June	Publication of *The Professor*
	22 August	Publication of the third edition of *The Life of Charlotte Brontë*
1858		Completion of a reservoir above Hall Green
1859	30 October	Preached what proved to be his last sermon
1860	August	Visited in his bedroom by the Bishop of Ripon, Dr Robert Bickersteth
	25 October	Visited in his bedroom by Mrs Gaskell and Meta Gaskell
1861	7 June	Died (aged eighty-four)

APPENDICES

Appendix I

The Published Writings of Patrick Brontë

Appendix II

Mrs Brontë's Nurse[1]

The nurse who was employed at the parsonage to assist Mrs Brontë during her last illness was Mrs Martha Wright (*née* Heaton). She was born in Haworth in 1792 and married Joseph Wright, also of Haworth, in 1812. They had one child, a daughter named Mary Ann. Mary Wright's obituary notice in the *Burnley Gazette*, 2 June 1883, said that 'considering the scanty privileges of that period she procured a good education.' It described her as 'a woman of strong mind, sound judgment, and broad sympathies, with a shrewd insight into character'. In view of what she was later to say about Patrick, it is perhaps more significant that she is described as possessing 'a large fund of anecdote and folk-lore'. After Patrick found her to be unsatisfactory and dismissed her from the parsonage, she seems to have borne a grudge against him, although her relations with the rest of the family appear to have been cordial.

After leaving Haworth, Mrs Wright was engaged in business in Burnley 'for about forty years' where she was 'widely known and highly respected'. When her daughter Mary Ann died in 1835 at the age of twenty-two, she was buried in Haworth and her funeral was taken by Patrick. Her husband, Joseph, died in 1853 and was also buried at Haworth. She is said to have visited Gawthorpe Hall at a time when Charlotte was staying with Sir James and Lady Kay-Shuttleworth (which she did in March 1850 and January 1855). At some time prior to Charlotte's meeting with Mrs Gaskell in the Lake District in August 1850, Mrs Wright gave information to Lady Kay-Shuttleworth about the home life of the Brontë family, including the tales of Patrick's eccentricity which later appeared in Mrs Gaskell's biography. She gave up her business in Burnley in 1863 and retired to Dockroyd, near Keighley. She died on 25 May 1883 aged ninety-one and was buried in Haworth Churchyard.

Note

1. I am indebted to Ann Dinsdale for this information. See her article 'Mrs Brontë's Nurse' in *BS*, Vol. 30, November 2005, pp. 258–259.

Appendix III

Three Letters from Patrick Brontë
to the Master-General of the Ordnance

(1)

19 November 1841. The Revd Patrick Brontë to Sir George Murray[1]

On the Muskets

<To the Editor of the Times>[2]

Honourable Sir,

<Hon Sir> Having lately read Mr Greener's able and just remarks on the bad qualities and construction of the musket at present in use, I take the liberty of making a few observations of my own, in the |hope| that if they are judicious, they may reach and influence those in high quarters. In doing this, I shall be as brief as possible, speaking, at the same time, as intelligibly as I can. I should propose, that the new muskets be constructed as follows. That they |should| be at least three inches longer, than those hitherto used, and that they should be a little more than two thirds, as wide in the bore. But what I wish to bring more prominently forward is, the position of the lock, and in some respects its formation. The lock, I conceive, should be placed <u>on the top</u>, as is the case, generally, with pocket pistols, and of course the pipe, or tube on which the percussion cap is to be fixed, on the upper part of the barrel. There should be an aperture, or hole through the cock which when it is raised to the full, ready for firing, should form the sight at the <?> breech, and tend in a proper direction to the sight at the muzzle. This aperture should be wide above, and drawn to a point at the bottom, being only just large enough, for the soldier to take a ready aim. The Line of Aim should pass directly over the percussion cap, to the sight at the muzzle – which sight should have a sufficiently conspicuous knob, raised high enough, to correspond with the elevation of the aperture at the breech, so as to give the proper direction to the bore, at the time of the discharge.

As this plan may be entirely new, it is but right, <?> that I should give my reasons for it, so as to enable the reader to form his <judgmet> judgment with a fair chance of coming to a just conclusion. With the tube on which the percussion cap is placed, at the <top of> upper part of the barrel, in case of destruction the touchhole can be readily and effectually probed – which appears to me to be a matter of vast moment – <and> this facility of probing can never be so great, when, as in the side lock the line of communication, is either angular or curved. Moreover in a lock of my construction, an obstruction, could scarcely ever take place, as must be obvious to every one who duly considers the subject. The sight through the cock is the necessary consequence of having the apparatus on the upper part of the barrel – But, independently of this, the sight thus placed has, I feel confident, its peculiar advantages. It comes at once, to the soldier's eye, and the cock, sights, and object, are all rectilinear, a circumstance of itself calculated to produce, both a scientific and mechanical habit of straight shooting. There are here no lateral objects on the piece to distract the attention, or confuse the vision – All, which, at point-blank distance, is necessary to be done, is to see the <u>under part</u> of the <u>aperture</u> in the Cock, the <u>knob</u> of the sight at the muzzle, and the <u>object</u> in a right line, and this any man, with ordinary powers of vision, and a steady hand might learn to do, in ten minutes, if he had never before, <taken a gun> applied a gun to his shoulder. An achievement, frequently not to be accomplished, <for> according to the present construction of muskets, in as many years. Another argument, might be adduced in favour of my proposed construction. It would altogether give the musket a more agreeable, and lighter appearance. The Instrument would seem of itself, to indicate its projectile avocation, and to invite the Spectator to a trial of its merit and powers. Should the bayonet, be also made three inches longer, than at present, it would be a great improvement. I am fully convinced, that all this might be affected, leaving sufficient strength, – at two pounds less of weight, |than we now have,| admitting due regard was paid, in the construction, to due proportion, as well as the qualities of all the materials. Judging from various experiments which I have seen, I should not hesitate to say, that a scientific gunmaker could turn out a musket <??> of my construction, that would be sufficiently effective, if <?> properly elevated, at the distance of eight or ten hundred yards, and very sure, at two or three hundred, rendering in many instances <the use of> artillery less necessary – and in most cases, the bayonet altogether useless. The plan, if duly carried into effect, would tend powerfully to save our brave men, and give full scope to their unequalled courage and energy – It would also do away with the most torturous and mangling modes of death, in the field of battle, and thus be a kind of mercy in disguise. On these grounds, chiefly, I have been induced to entertain this somewhat appaling [*sic*] subject.

I remain Sir,

Your most obedient servant,

P. Brontë, <perpetual> A.A. –

Perpetual Curate of Haworth, near Bradford, Yorkshire,

Novr 19th: 1841 –

To the
Honourable
General, Sir
George Murray,
Master General of
The Ordnance,
       London.

MS: The National Archives: War Office Records, Ordnance Office Correspondence: W.O.44/621.

Notes

1. General Sir George Murray was the Master-General of the Ordnance, a department of the War Office.
2. It is clear from the deletion at the start of this letter that Patrick had originally intended sending it to the editor of the *Times*. A few days before, on 15 November, he had written to the Duke of Wellington on this subject but had received a rebuff from the Duke, who said that he was not in 'H M's Political Service' and that he would not interfere in matters over which he had no control. The Duke's letter is printed in PB, *Letters*, Appendix XII.

(2)

29 November 1841. The Revd Patrick Brontë to Sir George Murray

Haworth, near
Bradford, Yorkshire,
Novr. 29th: 1841.

Honourable Sir,

    I have just received a kind and attentive Answer to my letter to you, on the subject of muskets. For this answer I would beg leave to thank You, and G.S. Belson Major Rl. Artillery, & Secy. I have no recompense in view, my motives are merely love of queen and Country, and the greatest admiration of the Gentlemen of the Army and Navy. I wish them to be provided with Instruments of War, equal<l> in excellence to their courage, and then, I am sure, they will not meet with their match in the world. I am not a Military man, and never was, but I have had much experience in fire Arms, and have long been an enthusiastic Admirer of them, when rightly constructed – I have also made many scientific experiments with them, in all their possible positions, and I might nearly say, in all their possible forms, – though on a <large> – small scale. You, and the Gentlemen who constitute the Select Committee, are too wise, and considerate, therefore, not duly to examine my plan – Archimedes[1], an Old Mathematician, And no Soldier, was the grand Instrument, through his instructions, of protecting Syracuse, for Several Years against all the Military, <and> Skill, and Power of Rome – But, I wish to be as brief as possible, and consequently, I shall proceed directly, to explain my Plan – which, I beg you will lay before the Honourable Committee, as owing to the Sacredness of my Office, and other considerations, I cannot with propriety attend, since, though humanity, and justice, are at the bottom of my proceedings, I cannot openly appear as an advocate in the Arts and Science of War – I am no draughtsman, and must not call in aid of another – And so I must try in a rude way, to give you something like a representation of my musket, and then, the proper explanation, and my reasons –

A.B. The Musket – C.D. The sight through the Cock, when cocked to the full – E – The sight at the muzzle – C.D.F. The line of aim – I speak only of a percussion Gun – And with the Cock not at the side, but on the top, like ordinary pocket Pistols – I moreover would take the liberty of recommending, that the barrel should be three inches longer, than the barrel of those now used in the Army – and that it should be neither more nor less, than about two thirds as wide in the bore – taking balls of nearly 16 – or 18, to the pound. – My reasons, for this new plan, are as follow[s]. By having the cock, and consequently the pipe for the percussion cap, on the top of the barrel, and not on the side, the communication with the powder in the <?> bore will be direct – & There will be less probability of stoppage – than in an angular, or curved communication, and probing would be , more facile, and speedy – in case of stoppage. The Cock on the top is a necessary consequence of this – but independently, it would be of great utility – because, as the sight through it, which would be correct, when at full cock, and only then, would be a direct guide, to the soldier, when taking his aim over the sight at the muzzle; with but very little instruction, he could be made an excellent shot – The sight, through the cock, ought, I conceive to [be] about this size and form. The upper opening to serve for readily catching a view of the object,

And the under deportment for seeing the lowest portion of the sight through the cock, the knob, or ledge, of the sight at the muzzle, and the object, in a right line – As I have seen from many experiments, a musket thus constructed, and properly charged, would have double the range of the present musket, far greater force and would project the ball, twice as far in nearly a horizontal direction, – And taking duly into consideration, the <for> resistance of the air, the law of Gravitation, and the facility, and almost certainty of the Aim, would as far as I am able to discern, constitute the Achme [sic] of perfection – Of course, it must be evident, that in order to <?> aim over the percussion cap, the sight |must| <would> be raised at the breach [sic] and the sight at the muzzle elevated, in the same proportion – And the handle of the bayonet constructed thus<[rubbed out drawing]> ↘
Or thus 🔧 in order to its being duly fixed –

With every apology for thus troubling you, I remain, Honourable Sir,

To the Honourable
General, Sir George
Murray, Master General
Of the Ordnance,
    London

Your Most obedient Servant,
Patrick Brontë A.B.
Incumbent of Haworth
Near Bradford, Yorkshire.

MS: The National Archives: War Office Records, Ordnance Office Correspondence: W.O.44/621.

Notes

1. The Greek mathematician and inventor who was born at Syracuse in Sicily in 287 B.C.

2. Patrick's proposals were referred to a meeting of the Select Committee held at Woolwich 2 February 1842. The Director-General reported to Sir George Murray the outcome of their discussions as follows:

Woolwich,
$2^{nd.}$ February 1842.

Sir,

I have the honour to report that, agreeably to your Order, the Select Committee have been assembled, for the purpose of considering and reporting upon some Papers relative to the alterations in the Muskuet [sic] at present in use in the Service as proposed by the Rev^d. P. Brontë.

Mr Brontë declined attending, but his Letters having been read, and the Sketches therein of his proposed Muskuet examined by the Committee, it did not appear desirable to them, that his alteration should be adopted into the Service.

I have the honour to be Sir
Your most obedient humble Servant
P [?] Drummond
Director General

General The Right Honble Sir George Murray G.C.B.G.C.

(3)

4 July 1848. The Revd Patrick Brontë to the Marquess of Anglesey[1]

4th July 1848.

My Lord Marquis,

May I request Your Lordship, to consider my explanation of the above figure, and the uses to which I would apply it – Let A-B represent a hollow globe of cast iron – or rather a section of it passing through the centre. – and C-D a strong tube of malleable iron open at both ends – Let it be supposed that the globe is charged, in the manner of a bombshell – and the tube tightly rammed, with ignitible materials, something in the mode of a rocket, and lengthened or shortened, as the case might require – and let this tube be tightly hammered in, and looped over at the orifice at D – so as to be everywhere fire proof, except at the ends – and let it be supposed, that this globe is projected either from a mortar, or a cannon, so as to pass through only one side of a ship and rest in <?> and explode in the interior – or if it did not explode, issue forth, a stream of intense fire, at the orifice at D – Might it not in this way, produce both the effect of a ball, and shell – and being capable of horizontal firing, be extremely destructive to the enemy? – As I know but little of Howitser [sic] practice,[2] or the mode of projecting shells, these notions of mine may, I am aware, be not only crude, but incorrect – However this may be, I cannot submit them, to a better Judge, than Your Lordship – I remain, My Lord Marquis,

> Your Lordship's Most Obedient, Humble Servant,
> Patrick Brontë, A.B –
> Incumbent of Haworth,
> Near Keighley, Yorkshire.

To
The Right Honourable,
The Marquis of Anglesey,
Master General of the Ordnance,
London –

MS: The National Archives: War Office Records, Ordnance Office Correspondence: W.O.44/621.

Notes

1. Henry William Paget (1768–1854), soldier and statesman, was created 1st Marquess of Anglesey for his bravery at the Battle of Waterloo, in which he lost a leg. He was now the Master-General of the Ordnance, a department of the War Office.
2. A gun in general use since the sixteenth century. Its main characterisitic is its high trajectory fire, which enables it to reach targets which are behind cover.
3. As a result of Patrick's letter, the Director-General (Major-General Webber Smith, C.B.) wrote to the Marquess of Anglesey on August 1848:

> Woolwich
> 2nd August 1848

My Lord Marquess

I have the honor to report that in obedience to Your Lordship's orders I have submitted to the consideration of the Select Committee, the letter of the Revd Patrick Brontë A.B. explaining a Projectile, which he considers may produce both the effect of a Ball and of a Shell.

The Committee having attentively read and considered Mr Brontë's Letter beg leave to report, that the object which he proposes, has long been fully accomplished by means of the present Wood Fuse of the Service, applied to Shells, both for Vertical and Horizontal firing from Guns, Howitzers and Mortars in the Naval and Artilery [sic] Services; the mode suggested by Mr Brontë being a crude illustration of the early practice of Shell-firing.

> I have the honor to be My Lord Marquess
> Your Lordships most obedient humble servant
> J Webber Smith
> Dr. Genl.

Field Marshal
The Most Honble The Marquess of Anglesey K>G>

Appendix IV

The Ecclesiastical Census
Sunday 30 March 1851

	Morning	Afternoon	Evening	Total	%
Church Attendance					
West Lane Baptists	171	253	0	424	16
Hall Green Baptists	200	350	350	900	35
West Lane Wesleyan Methodists	95	45	194	334	13
Lower Town Wesleyan Methodists	135	184	103	422	16
Mill Hey Primitive Methodists	0	62	61	123	5
St Michael's Church of England	41	250	92	383	15
Total	**642**	**1,144**	**800**	**2,586**	**100**
Sunday School Scholars					
West Lane Baptists	131	189	0	320	19
Hall Green Baptists	250	250	0	500	30
West Lane Wesleyan Methodists	104	0	0	104	6
Lower Town Wesleyan Methodists	214	222	19	455	27
Mill Hey Primitive Methodists	0	40	0	40	2
St Michael's Church of England	105	139	25	269	16
Total	**804**	**840**	**44**	**1,688**	**100**
Grand Total	**1,446**	**1,984**	**844**	**4,274**	**100**

Reprinted by the kind permission of Robin Greenwood from his *West Lane and Hall Green Baptist Churches in Haworth in West Yorkshire: their Early History and Doctrinal Distinctives* (published by the author, 2005) p. 93. He acknowledges the help of Jean Wilson in providing him with this information.

Notes

1. The figures for church attendance show the number of people (excluding Sunday school scholars) who attended the services on that day. Many people attended all three services.
2. The numbers of West Lane Wesleyan Methodists are considerably understated as many of them attended a special service in Oakworth on that day.
3. These figures show that 85% of those who attended a church service on that Sunday in the township of Haworth were nonconformists.
4. For a discussion of the Church Census see Tom Winnifrith, 'The Church Census and the Brontës', *Brontë Studies*, Vol 32, November 2007, pp. 245–251.

Appendix V

Servants at the Parsonage

Nancy and Sarah Garrs

Nancy Garrs came to the parsonage at Thornton in July 1816 at the age of thirteen to work as a nursemaid. After the birth of Emily in July 1818 she was promoted to the position of cook and assistant housekeeper, and her younger sister Sarah was employed as nursemaid. Both the sisters had been trained at the Bradford School of Industry. Nancy and Sarah remained in the employment of the Brontë family when they moved to Haworth. When Patrick sent his daughters to the Clergy Daughters' School in 1824 he no longer needed to employ the Garrs sisters to look after the children. Nancy left to be married and Patrick assisted Sarah in finding employment. In 1829 Sarah married William Newsome, with whom she later emigrated to the United States.

Tabitha Aykroyd

Tabitha Aykroyd started working at the parsonage in 1824 as a fifty-four-year-old widow and gave thirty years of devoted service to the family, outliving them all except for Charlotte and Patrick. When at Christmas 1836 she fell on some ice and badly broke her leg the Brontë girls, who regarded her as one of the family, insisted on nursing her themselves. Three years later, in December 1839, when her leg became so badly ulcerated that she could no longer work, she retired with her sister to a small house she had bought with her savings. She returned to the parsonage in 1842 and, although her help was of limited value, Patrick continued to employ her until her last illness. She died on 17 February 1855, aged eighty-four, and was buried in Haworth churchyard.

Martha Brown

Martha Brown was the eldest daughter of John Brown, the Haworth sexton. She started working in the parsonage at the age of eleven in December 1839 and she continued in the employment of the Brontë family until Patrick's death. Although at first she was very critical of Arthur Nicholls for proposing to Charlotte, she later came to appreciate his steadfast love for her. Patrick left her £30 in his will and she was one of the chief mourners at his funeral. She accompanied Arthur Nicholls when he returned to Ireland and stayed there for a few months. She later paid several visits to him and they kept up a regular correspondence. She died from cancer in January 1880 and was buried in Haworth churchyard.

Eliza Brown

Eliza Brown was the third daughter of John Brown. She first worked at the parsonage in June 1855 while her sister Martha was unwell and away in Leeds, and on 20 June 1855 she was a witness to Patrick's will. She was again employed at the parsonage during the last months of Patrick's life. She seems to have been an unmarried mother and in 1859 Patrick wrote to her over the death of her baby daughter Jane.

Appendix VI

Patrick Brontë's Curates

The Revd James Bardsley (nominated but did not serve)

James Bardsley was nominated in July 1833 to be Patrick's first curate at Haworth, but on the day before his ordination the Archbishop of York decided to appoint him to Keighley instead. Mr Bardsley remained a close friend of the Brontë family and regularly came with his wife to the parsonage for tea on Sunday afternoons. He later became the rector of St Anne's, Manchester. His elder son John was the Bishop of Carlisle (1892–1905).

The Revd William Hodgson (December 1835–May 1837)

William Hodgson arrived in Haworth in December 1835, but does not seem to have been formally appointed as curate until April 1836, when Patrick received a grant of £50 from the Church Pastoral Aid Society towards the cost of a curate's salary. He was a strong supporter of the established Church and vigorously denounced Dissenters from the pulpit over the question of church rates. In May 1837 he left to become the first vicar of Christ Church, Colne.

The Revd William Wightman (August 1839–September 1842)

William Weightman was a graduate of Durham University and came to Haworth at the age of twenty-six. He was a handsome young man with an attractive personality and he became a friend of the Brontë family. He sent the girls Valentine cards and took them as his guests when he gave a lecture at the Keighley Mechanics' Institute. Charlotte made a pencil drawing of him and frequently mentioned him in her letters to Ellen Nussey. He was a vigorous opponent of Dissenters and in March 1840 preached a fiery sermon against them. He was a diligent visitor in the parish and died of cholera in September 1842 at the age of twenty-eight. It is thought that Anne was particularly upset by his death and may have been in love with him. Patrick was very fond of him and in his funeral sermon he said that their relationship had been 'like father and son'.

The Revd James William Smith (March 1843–October 1844)

James Smith was a graduate of Trinity College, Dublin. Patrick seems to have found him a fiery and intemperate man and Mr Maloney, the curate of Briarfield in *Shirley*, is said to be based on him. Patrick told Charlotte to warn Ellen Nussey about him when he seemed to be paying too much attention to her and said that money would be the main consideration with him in marrying. In October 1844 he left Haworth to be the curate of Keighley and after his departure the accounts of the National School which he had kept could not be found. In 1848 he absconded to Canada, leaving numerous debts behind him.

The Revd Joseph Brett Grant (July 1844–March 1847)

Joseph Grant was a graduate of Emmanuel College, Cambridge. In July 1844 he was appointed the headmaster of the Free Grammar School near Oxenhope and for some time he also acted as Patrick's curate. Joseph Donne, the curate of Whinbury in *Shirley*, is said to be based on him. In 1845 he was given responsibility for the district of Oxenhope and he was appointed its first incumbent when it was made a separate parish in March 1847. He was a friend of Arthur Nicholls who stayed at his vicarage on three occasions during the period of his estrangement from Patrick. He came with Mr Nicholls to Haworth on the day of his wedding. He was one of six clerical pall-bearers at Patrick's funeral.

The Revd Arthur Bell Nicholls (May 1845–May 1853 and August 1854–September 1861)

Arthur Nicholls was born near Belfast in January 1819. His father was a farmer of limited means and he was brought up by his uncle, Dr Alan Bell, the headmaster of the Royal School at Banagher in the south of Ireland. He was educated at Trinity College, Dublin, and, after ordination in Ripon Cathedral, he performed his first duties for Patrick on Sunday 25 May 1845. Because of Patrick's failing eyesight he soon assumed responsibility for almost all the clerical duties in the parish, and especially the running of the Haworth National School. Mr Macarthey, the curate of Briarfield in *Shirley* (who succeeded Mr Malone), is said to be based on him. He preached the sermon at Branwell's memorial service and he conducted Emily's funeral. After the rejection of his proposal of marriage to Charlotte he left Haworth at the end of May 1853 and became the curate of Kirk Smeaton, near Pontefract. He kept in touch through correspondence with Charlotte, who eventually secured a reconciliation with her father. They were married on 29 June 1854. After a honeymoon in southern Ireland they enjoyed nine months of happily married life before Charlotte died on 31 March 1855. Arthur Nicholls remained in the parsonage and continued to take virtually all the parochial duties until Patrick's death on 7 June 1861. When he was not appointed as incumbent of Haworth he returned to his home town of Banagher. He never sought another clerical position, preferring to live as a small country farmer. In August 1864 he married his cousin, Mary Bell. He died on 2 December 1906 at the age of eighty-seven and was buried in Banagher churchyard.

The Revd George de Renzy (May 1853–June 1854)
George de Renzy, a graduate of Trinity College, Dublin, performed his first duties at Haworth on 29 May 1853. In May the following year he married Emily Mackley from Wilsden. Patrick seems to have found him to be an unsatisfactory curate and his employment was terminated after Arthur Nicholls returned to Haworth.

Appendix VII

Two Letters of Patrick Brontë which have Recently come to Light

1. To the Bishop of Ripon, 10 April 1855
2. To Mary Jessup Docwra, 23 September 1858

(1)

10 April 1855. The Rev'd Patrick Brontë to the Bishop of Ripon[1]

Haworth,
N' Keighley
April 10th. 1855

My Lord Bishop,

Amongst the various letters of kind sympathy which we have received, Your Lordships [*sic*] Letter, gives us especial pleasure – It is wort[hy] of One who is justly esteem'd the Father of His Clergy, and I will retain it Amongst my most valued treasures, as long as I shall live. "A word in due season, how good is it!" And most assuredly, if a Season of Sorrow, needs a word of consolation and support, ours is that season. I have lived long enough, to bury a beloved Wife, and six children – all that I had – I greatly enjoyed their conversation and company, and many of them, were well fitted for being companions to the Wisest and best – Now they are all gone – Their image and memory remain, and meet me at every turn – but they, themselves have left me, a bereaved Old man – I hoped and <?and> wish'd, that the Lord would spare them, to see me laid in my grave, but the Lord has ordered it otherwise, and I have seen them all laid in that place, "where the wicked cease from troubling and the Weary are at rest" – I have not only my own sorrow to bear, but I am distress'd for Mr. Nicholls, whose grief is very great – His union with My Daughter was a happy one – They were well fitted for each other, and naturally look'd forward, to future scenes of happiness for a long time to come – but the Lord gave, and the Lord took early away – May we both be able from our hearts to say blessed be the name of the Lord. But, I have often found, and find in this last Sad trial, that it is <often>, frequently extremely difficult to walk entirely by faith, and sincerely to pray, "Thy will be done on earth, as it is in heaven" – Mr. Nicholls, who is every thing I could desire, to the Church and to me, intends to stay with me, during the brief remainder of my life – May we beg, that Your Lordship, will sometimes, remember us in Your prayers, –

I remain, My Lord Bishop,
Your Lordship's most
Obedient Humble Servant,
Patrick Brontë.

To
The Right Reveren'd
The Lord Bishop of Ripon,
Palace, Ripon

MS: Lambeth Palace Library, Longley Papers 4545 ff 208–209

Note

1. Dr Charles Longley (1794–1868) was the first Bishop of Ripon (1836–1857). He subsequently became Bishop of Durham (1856–1860), Archbishop of York (1860–1862) and Archbishop of Canterbury (1862–1868).

(2)

23 September 1858. The Rev'd Patrick Brontë to Mary Jesup Docwra[1]

Haworth
N[r] Keighley,
Septr 23rd 1858

Dear Madam

The enclosed[2] is all I can spare of My dear Daughter Charlotte's handwriting –

Yours very respectfully,
P. Brontë.

MS: BPM

Notes

1. In 1858 Mary Jesup Docwra, who lived at Kelvedon in Essex, began an autograph album in which she inserted samples of the handwriting of famous people, especially writers.

2. Patrick's letter is pasted into Mary Docwra's autograph album. Attached to the top right-hand corner is a snippet of Charlotte's handwriting, taken from a letter written on black-bordered mourrnng paper, which reads:

> '... my book – no one ...
> ... ious than I am to ...'

Five other letters of Patrick survive in which he sent scraps of Charlotte's handwriting to people who had requested it: to Miss Jenkins (9 July 1857), to unidentified (10 November 1858), to Franklin Bacheller (22 December 1858), to Mrs Abba Woolson (16 July 1859) and to Miss Wrigly (4 June 1860).

Appendix VIII

The Article in *Sharpe's London Magazine*, June 1855

Sharpe's London Magazine
Vol VI, New Series, June 1855

A Few Words about "Jane Eyre"

Extract

… As the mystery which attended this lady's public debut has in some degree enshrouded her, even to the moment when the thousands to whom she has afforded pleasurable interest and excitement are lamenting her untimely decease, we imagine the following particulars, obtained from a private and we believe authentic source, though we do not pledge ourselves to their accuracy, may not prove unacceptable to our readers.

On the northern side of one of the wildest and bleakest moors of Yorkshire, stands the little village of Haworth, consisting of a church and a few grey stone cottages. One of these, scarcely superior to its fellows, and distinguished only by a sort of court-yard surrounded by a low stone wall, and overgrown with grass (shrubs and flowers refusing to vegetate in so ungenial an atmosphere), is the parsonage. The architecture is of the simplest description – a straight walk leads up to the front door, on either side of which appears a window, that of the sitting-room looking into the church-yard, well filled with gravestones. On this parsonage, until within a few months since, not a touch of paint, nor an article of new furniture, had been expended for thirty years, the period which has elapsed since the death of Miss Brontë's mother. Some six or seven years antecedent to that date, an Irish clergyman, the Rev. Patrick Brontë, then resident at Penzance, espoused a young lady, contrary to the wishes of her relations, who refused to hold any further intercourse with her after her marriage. Her husband, obtaining the perpetual curacy of Haworth, took his bride to his new residence, where she spent the remainder of her days, dying in a rapid consumption after the birth of her sixth child, Charlotte. Mr Brontë, who though advanced in years, is still alive, is described as a man of studious and solitary habits, and of a singular and highly eccentric turn of mind, which together with a very peculiar temper, must have rendered him anything but a suitable guardian to a youthful family. Nor can we wonder at the dying mother's exclamation, "What will become of my poor children?" Engrossed by his own pursuits, the father never even dined with his family nor taught them anything, and the children learned to write and read from servants only. When Charlotte was twelve years old she (even then of an original and self-reliant nature) asked and obtained her father's permission, that her sisters and herself should be placed at the clergy-school at Cowan Bridge. This, as it then existed, she has described to the life in 'Jane Eyre'. Two of her sisters died of the fever which at one time devastated the school: the two others, and probably Charlotte herself, quitted it with the seed of consumption in their constitutions, fostered by the cruel privations they underwent. The food was horrible, and of it, bad as it was, they obtained so little that often they were literally half starved. Frequently has she "crept under the table to pick up the crumbs others had dropped." At the time of the fever the doctor examined the food, he put some in his mouth, and hastily rejected it, protesting it was not fit for dogs. "So hungry was I," said Charlotte, "that I could have eaten what he threw away." The three survivors returned to Haworth with broken health; but there fresh trials awaited them. "At nineteen," continued Charlotte, "I should have been thankful for a penny a-week. I asked my father; but he said, 'What do women want with money?'" She was yet only nineteen when she advertised for and obtained a situation as teacher in a school: not finding it turn out as she had hoped, she waited until she had saved money enough to pay her passage to Brussels, where she had secured a position as school-teacher – she started alone, never having previously quitted Yorkshire. When she arrived in London it was night; she became alarmed, and, not knowing where to go, and fearing to trust herself with strangers, she took a cab, drove to the Tower stairs, hired a boat, and was conveyed to the Ostend packet. At first the officer in command refused to take her on board till the next morning, but on learning her desolate situation recalled his prohibition. In Brussels, she remained two years; her experiences there are detailed in "Villette." The character of Adèle, in particular, is drawn from life. On her return she found that the health of her two remaining sisters was declining, and that her father's eyesight was becoming affected, and she considered it her duty to remain at home. She tried various ways of increasing their income, but failed in all. Without mentioning her project to her father, she wrote Jane Eyre, a work of which Messrs. Smith and Elder had the good sense to perceive the merits, and were courageous enough to publish it, in spite of its peculiarities, which might have alarmed any but a really spirited publisher. About three months after the appearance of her novel, and when its success was no longer doubtful, Miss Brontë resolved to screw up her courage, and inform her father of the step she had taken. Mr. Brontë, it appears, did not then join his family, even at meal-times. At dinner, Charlotte announced her intention to her sisters, adding, that she would put it into execution before tea! Accordingly, she marched into his study with a copy of her work, wrapped up in a Review of it, which she had received, and the following conversation ensured: –

"Papa, I have been writing a book!"

"Have you, my dear?" (He went on reading.)

"But, papa, I want you to look at it."

"I can't be troubled to read manuscript."

"But it is printed."

"I hope you've not been involving yourself in any such silly expense!"

"I think I shall gain some money by it; may I read you some reviews of it?"

She read the reviews, and again asked him if he would look over the book; he said she might leave it and he would see – later on that same evening he sent his daughters an invitation to drink tea with him. When the meal was nearly concluded, he said – "Children, Charlotte has been writing a book, and I think it is a better one than I expected." For some years he never mentioned the subject again.

A lady, who afterwards became intimate with Miss Brontë, thus describes her first introduction to her. "I arrived late at the house of a mutual friend, tea was on the table, and behind it sat a little wee dark person, dressed in black, who scarcely spoke, so I had time for a good look at her. She had soft lightish brown hair, eyes of the same tint, looking straight at you, and very good and expressive; a reddish complexion, a wide mouth – altogether plain; the forehead square, broad, and rather overhanging. Her hands are like birds' claws, and she is so short-sighted that she cannot see your face unless you are close to her. She is said to be frightfully shy, and almost cries at the thought of going amongst strangers."

Such are a few particulars concerning this remarkable woman; with the broader features of her history, especially her marriage with Mr. Nicol, her father's curate, and her melancholy death six months after she (probably for the first time in her strange eventful life) knew what it was to enjoy domestic happiness – the daily press has already made everyone familiar. That she has been taken from among us in the full vigor of her intellect, ere the sunshine of a happy home had fostered and developed the brighter and more genial portion of her nature, must ever be a source of regret to those who, admiring as we admire the works she has left as her lasting memorial, hoped for yet nobler proofs of her remarkable powers of invention, when time and an increased knowledge of life should have corrected the eccentricity, without lessening the originality, of her genius.

(pp. 341–342)

Mrs Gaskell to Catherine Winkworth

25 August 1850

Extracts

Dark when I got to Windermere station; a drive along the level road to Low-wood, then a regular clamber up a steep lane; then a stoppage at a pretty house, and then a pretty drawing room much like the South End one, in which were Sir James and Lady K S, and a little lady in black silk gown, whom I could not see at first for the dazzle in the room; she came up and shook hands with me at once – I went up to unbonnet &c, came down to tea, the little lady worked away and hardly spoke; but I had time for a good look at her. She is, (as she calls herself) undeveloped; thin and more than ½ a head shorter than I, soft brown hair not so dark as mine; eyes (very good and expressive looking straight and open at you) of the same colour, a reddish face; large mouth & many teeth gone; altogether plain; the forehead square, broad, and *rather* overhanging. She has a very sweet voice, rather hesitates in choosing her expressions, but when chosen they seem without an effort, admirable and just befitting the occasion. There is nothing overstrained but perfectly simple.

Such a life as Miss B's I never heard of before Lady K S described her home to me as in a village of a few grey stone houses perched up on the north side of a bleak moor looking over sweeps of bleak moors. There is a court of turf & a stone wall, – no flowers or shrubs will grow there) a straight walk, & you come to the parsonage door, with a window on each side of it. The parsonage has never had a touch of paint, or an article of new furniture for 30 years; never since Miss B's mother died. She was a pretty young creature brought from Penzance in Cornwall by the Irish Curate, who got this moorland living. Her friends disowned her at her marriage. She had 6 children as fast as could be; & what with that, & the climate, & the strange half mad husband she has chosen she died at the end of 9 years. An old woman at Burnley who nursed her at last, says she used to lie crying in bed, and saying 'Oh God my poor children – oh God my poor children!' continually. ... The sitting room at the Parsonage looks into the Church-yard filled with graves. Mr B has never taken a meal with his children since his wife's death, unless he invites them to tea, *never* to dinner. And he has only once left home since to come to Manchester to be operated upon by Mr Wilson for Cataract; at which time they lodged in Boundary St. Well! These 5 daughters and one son grew older, their father never taught the girls anything – only the servant taught them to read & write. But I suppose they laid their heads together, for at 12 Charlotte (this one) presented a request to the father that they might go to school; so they were sent to Cowan-Bridge (the place where the daughters of the Clergy were before they were removed to Casterton). There the 2 elder died in that fever. Miss B says that the pain she suffered from hunger was not to be told & her two younger sisters laid the foundation of the consumption of which they are now dead. They all came home ill. But the poverty of home was very great ('At 19 I should have been thankful for an allowance of 1d a week. I asked my father, but he said What did women want with money'). So at 19 she advertised and got a teacher's place in a school, (where she did not say, only said it was preferable to the governess's place she got afterwards) but she saved up enough to pay for her journey to a school in Brussels. She had never been out of Yorkshire before; & was so frightened when she got to London – she took a cab, it was night and drove down to the Tower Stairs, & got a boat & went to the Ostend packet, and they refused to take her in; but at last they did. She was in this school at Brussels two years without a holiday except one week with one of her Belgian schoolfellows. Then she came home & her sisters were ill, & her father going blind – so she thought she ought to stay at home. She tried to teach herself drawing & to be an artist but she cd not – and yet her own health independently of the home calls upon her wd not allow of her going out again as a governess. She had always wished to write & believed that she could; at 16 she had sent some poems to Southey, & had 'kind, stringent' answers from him. So she and her sisters tried. They kept their initials and took names that would do either for a man or a woman. They used to read to each other when they had written so much. Their father never knew a word about it. He had never heard of Jane Eyre when 3 months after its publication she promised her sisters one day at dinner she would tell him before tea. So she marched into his study with a copy wrapped up & the reviews. She said (I think I can remember the exact words) –'Papa I've been writing a book.' 'Have you my dear?' and he went on reading. 'But papa I want you to look at it.' 'I can't be troubled to read MS.'

'But it is printed.' 'I hope you have not been involving yourself in any such silly expense.' 'I think I shall gain some money by it. May I read you some reviews.' So she read them; and then she asked him if he would read the book. He said she might leave it, and he would see. But he sent them an invitation to tea that night, and towards the end of tea he said, 'Children, Charlotte has been writing a book – and I think it is a better one than I expected.' He never spoke about it again till about a month ago, & they never dared tell him of the books her sisters wrote.

Charles Dickens to Frank Smedley

5 May 1855

Extract

I cannot reconcile it to my heart to publish these details so soon after Miss Brontë's death. For anything I know they might be saddening and painful to her husband, and I am not at all clear that I have any right to them. I have a particular objection to that kind of interest in a great mind, which prompts a visitor to take "a good look" at the moral habiliments in which it is arranged, and afterwards to catalogue them, like an auctioneer. I have no sympathy whatever with the staring curiosity that it gratifies.

And beyond the husband and even the father of this lady, I cannot help going to herself. It seems that she would have shrunk from this account of her trials, and that such as she wanted given, she has given herself, and that for the present there is enough said about them.

The subject does not present itself to you in this light, I quite understand; nor do I seek to convert you to my opinions. I state them plainly merely as my sole reason for not retaining the paper.

Appendix IX

Mrs Gaskell's Portrayal of Patrick Brontë

Extracts from *The Life of Charlotte Brontë*

The Rev. Patrick Brontë is a native of the County Down in Ireland. His father, Hugh Brontë, was left an orphan at an early stage. He came from the south to the north of the island, and settled in the parish of Ahaderg, near Loughbrickland. There was some family tradition that, humble as Hugh Brontë's circumstances were, he was the descendant of an ancient family. But about this neither he nor his descendants have cared to inquire. He made an early marriage, and reared and educated ten children on the proceeds of the few acres of land which he farmed. This large family were remarkable for great physical strength, and much personal beauty. Even in his old age, Mr Brontë is a striking-looking man, above the common height, with a nobly-shaped head, and erect carriage. In his youth he must have been unusually handsome.

He was born on Patrickmas Day (March 17), 1777, and early gave tokens of extraordinary quickness and intelligence. He had also his full share of ambition; and of his strong sense and forethought there is proof in the fact, that, knowing that his father could afford him no pecuniary aid, and that he must depend upon his own exertions, he opened a public school at the early age of sixteen; and this mode of living he continued to follow for five or six years. He then became a tutor in the family of the Rev. Mr Tighe, rector of Drumgooland parish. Thence he proceeded to St John's College, Cambridge, where he was entered in July 1802, being at the time five-and-twenty years of age. After nearly four years' residence, he obtained his B.A. degree, and was ordained to a curacy in Essex, whence he removed into Yorkshire.[1] The course of life of which this is the outline, shows a powerful and remarkable character, originating and pursuing a purpose in a resolute and independent manner. Here is a youth – a boy of sixteen – separating himself from his family, and determining to maintain himself; and that, not in the hereditary manner by agricultural pursuits, but by the labour of his brain.

I suppose, from what I have heard, that Mr Tighe became strongly interested in his children's tutor, and may have aided him, not only in the direction of his studies, but in the suggestion of an English university education, and in advice as to the mode in which he should obtain entrance there. Mr Brontë has now no trace of his Irish origin remaining in his speech; he never could have shown his Celtic descent in the straight Greek lines and long oval of his face; but at five-and-twenty, fresh from the only life he had ever known, to present himself at the gates of St John's proved no little determination of will, and scorn of ridicule. While at Cambridge, he became one of a corps of volunteers, who were then being called out all over the country to resist the apprehended invasion by the French. I have heard him allude, in late years, to Lord Palmerston as one who had often been associated with him then in the mimic military duties which they had to perform.

We take him up now settled as a curate at Hartshead, in Yorkshire – far removed from his birth-place and all his Irish connections; with whom, indeed, he cared little to keep up any intercourse, and whom he never, I believe, re-visited after becoming a student at Cambridge.[2] Hartshead is a very small village, lying to the east of Huddersfield and Halifax; and, from its high situation – on a mound, as it were, surrounded by a circular basin – commanding a magnificent view. Mr Brontë resided here for five years; and, while the incumbent of Hartshead, he wooed and married Maria Branwell. She was the third daughter of Mr Thomas Branwell, merchant, of Penzance. Her mother's maiden name was Carne: and, both on father's and mother's side, the Branwell family were sufficiently well descended to enable them to mix in the best society that Penzance then afforded.

[There follows a lengthy passage on the life and customs of Penzance at that time, based on an account written by Dr John Davy in a memoir of his brother, Sir Humphrey Davy.]

I have given this extract because I conceive it bears some reference to the life of Miss Brontë, whose strong mind and vivid imagination must have received their first impressions either from the servants (in that simple household, almost friendly companions during the greater part of the day) retailing the traditions or the news of Haworth village; or from Mr Brontë, whose intercourse with his children appears to have been considerably restrained, and whose life, both in Ireland and at Cambridge, had been spent under peculiar circumstances; or from her aunt, Miss Branwell, who came to the parsonage, when Charlotte was only six or seven years old, to take charge of her dead sister's family. ...

Mr Branwell, the father, according to his descendants' account, was a man of musical talent. He and his wife lived to see all their children grown up, and died within a year of each other – he in 1808, she in 1809, when their daughter Maria was twenty-five or twenty-six years of age. I have been permitted to look over a series of nine letters, which were addressed by her to Mr Brontë, during the brief term of their engagement in 1812. They are full of tender grace of expression, and feminine modesty; pervaded by the deep piety to which I have alluded as a family characteristic. I shall make one or two extracts from them, to show what sort of person was the mother of Charlotte Brontë: but first I must state the circumstances under which this Cornish lady met the scholar from Ahaderg, near Loughbrickland.

In the early summer of 1812, when she would be twenty-nine, she came to visit her uncle, the Reverend John Fennel,[3] who was at that time a clergyman of the Church of England, living near Leeds, but who had previously been a Methodist minister. Mr Brontë was the incumbent of Hartshead; and had the reputation in the neighbourhood of being a very handsome fellow, full of Irish enthusiasm, and with something of an Irishman's capability of falling easily in love. Miss Branwell was extremely small in person; not pretty, but very elegant, and always dressed with a quiet simplicity of taste, which accorded well with her general character, and of which some of the details call to mind the style of dress preferred by her daughter for her favourite heroines. Mr Brontë was soon captivated by the little gentle creature, and this time declared that it was for life. ...

There was no opposition on the part of any of her friends to their engagement. Mr and Mrs Fennel sanctioned it, and her brother and sisters in far-away Penzance appear fully to have approved of it. ... The journey from Penzance to Leeds in those days was both very long and very expensive; the lovers had not much money to spend in unnecessary travelling, and, as Miss Branwell had neither father nor mother living, it appeared both a discreet and seemly arrangement that the marriage should take place from her uncle's house. There was no reason either why the engagement should be prolonged. They were past their first youth; they had means sufficient for their unambitious wants; the living of Hartshead is rated in the Clergy List as 202*l.* per annum, and she was in receipt of a small annuity (50*l.* I have been told) by the will of her father. ... She was married, from her uncle's house, in Yorkshire on the 29th of December, 1812; the same day was also the wedding day of her younger sister, Charlotte Branwell, in distant Penzance.

Mr Brontë remained for five years at Hartshead in the parish of Dewsbury. There he was married and his two children, Maria and Elizabeth, were born. At the expiration of that period, he had the living of Thornton, in Bradford parish. ... Here, at Thornton, Charlotte Brontë was born, on 21st of April, 1816. Fast on her heels followed Patrick Branwell, Emily Jane and Anne. After the birth of this last daughter, Mrs Brontë's health began to decline. ... Maria Brontë, the eldest of six, could only have been a few months more than six years old, when Mr Brontë removed to Haworth, on February 25th, 1820.[4] Those who knew her then, describe her as grave, thoughtful, and quiet, to a degree far beyond her years. ... Little Maria Brontë was delicate and small in appearance, which seemed to give greater effect to her wonderful precocity of intellect. She must have been her mother's companion and helpmate in many a household and nursery experience, for Mr Brontë was, of course, much engaged in his study; and besides, he was not naturally fond of children, and felt their frequent appearance on the scene as a drag both on his wife's strength, and as an interruption to the comfort of the household.

Haworth parsonage is an oblong stone house, facing down the hill on which the village stands. ... The house consists of four rooms on each floor, and is two stories high. When the Brontës took possession, they made the larger parlour, to the left of the entrance, the family sitting-room, while that on the right was appropriated to Mr Brontë as a study. ... The people in Haworth were none of them very poor. Many of them were employed in the neighbouring worsted mills; a few were mill-owners and manufacturers in a small way; there were also some shopkeepers for the humbler and every-day wants; but for medical advice, for stationery, books, law, dress or dainties, the inhabitants had to go to Keighley.[5] There were several Sunday-schools; the Baptists had taken the lead in instituting them, the Wesleyans had followed, the Church of England had brought up the rear. Good Mr Grimshaw, Wesley's friend, had built a humble Methodist chapel, but it stood close to the road leading on to the moor; the Baptists then raised a place of worship, with the distinction of being a few yards back from the highway; and the Methodists have since thought it well to erect another and a larger chapel, still more retired from the road. Mr Brontë was ever on kind and friendly terms with each denomination as a body; but from individuals in the village the family stood aloof, unless some direct service was required, from the first. 'They kept themselves very close,' is the account given by those who remember Mr and Mrs Brontë's coming amongst them. I believe many of the Yorkshiremen would object to the system of parochial visiting; their surly independence would revolt from the idea of any one having a right, from his office, to inquire, to counsel, or to admonish them. ... I asked an inhabitant of a district close to Haworth, what sort of a clergyman they had at the church he attended: 'A rare good one,' said he: 'he minds his own business, and ne'er troubles himself with ours.' Mr Brontë was faithful in visiting the sick, and all those who sent for him, and diligent in attendance at the schools; and so was his daughter Charlotte too; but cherishing and valuing privacy themselves, they were perhaps over-delicate in not intruding on the privacy of others.

From their first going to Haworth, their walks were directed rather out towards the heathery moors, sloping upwards behind the parsonage, than towards the long descending village street. A good old woman, who came to nurse Mrs Brontë in the illness – an internal cancer – which grew and gathered upon her, not many months after her arrival at Haworth, tells me that at that time the six little creatures used to walk out, hand in hand, towards the glorious wild moors, which in after days they loved so passionately; the elder ones taking thoughtful care for the toddling wee things. They were grave and silent beyond their years; subdued, probably, by the presence of serious illness in the house; for, at the time which my informant speaks of, Mrs Brontë was confined to the bed-room from which she never came forth alive. 'You would not have known there was a child in the house, they were such still, noiseless, good little creatures. Maria would shut herself up' (Maria, but seven!) 'in the children's study with a newspaper, and be able to tell one everything when she came out; debates in parliament, and I don't know what all. She was as good as a mother to her sisters and brother. But there never were such good children. I used to think them spiritless, they were so different to any children I had ever seen. In part, I set it down to a fancy Mr Brontë had of not letting them have flesh-meat to eat.[6] It was from no wish for saving, for there was plenty and even waste in the house, with young servants and no mistress to see after them,[7] but he thought that the children should be brought up simply and hardily: so they had nothing but potatoes for their dinner; but they never seemed to wish for anything else; they were good little creatures. Emily was the prettiest.

Mrs Brontë was the same patient, cheerful person as we have seen her formerly; very ill, suffering great pain, but seldom if ever complaining; at her better times begging her nurse to raise her in bed to let her see her clean the grate, 'because she did it as it was done in Cornwall;' devotedly fond of her husband, who warmly repaid her affection, and suffered no one else to take the night-nursing; but, according to my informant, the mother was not very anxious to see much of her children, probably because the sight of them, knowing how soon they were to be left motherless, would have agitated her too much. So the little things clung quietly together, for their father was busy in his study and in his parish, or with their mother, and they took their meals alone; sat reading, or whispering low, in the 'children's study,' or wandered out on the hill-side, hand in hand.

The ideas of Rousseau and Mr Day on education[8] had filtered down through many classes, and spread themselves widely out. I imagine Mr Brontë must have formed some of his opinions on the management of children from these two theorists. ... Mr Brontë wished to make his children hardy, and indifferent to the pleasures of eating and dress. In the latter he succeeded, as far as regarded his daughters; but he went at his object with unsparing earnestness of purpose. Mrs Brontë's nurse told me that one day when the children had been out on the moors, and rain had come on, she thought their feet would be wet, and accordingly she rummaged out some coloured boots which had been given them by a friend – the Mr Morgan, who married 'Cousin Jane,' she believes. These little pairs she ranged round the kitchen fire to warm; but, when the children came back, the boots were nowhere to be found; only a very strong odour of burnt leather was perceived. Mr Brontë had come in and seen them; they were too gay and luxurious for his children, and would foster a love of dress; so he had put them into the fire. He spared nothing that offended his antique simplicity. Long before this, some one had given Mrs Brontë a silk gown; either the make, the colour, or the material, was not according to his notions of consistent propriety, and Mrs Brontë in consequence never wore it. But, for all that, she kept it treasured up in her drawers, which were generally locked. One day, however, while in the kitchen, she remembered that she had left the key in her drawer, and hearing Mr Brontë upstairs, she augured some ill to her dress, and running up in haste, she found it cut to shreds.

His strong, passionate, Irish nature was, in general, compressed down with resolute stoicism; but it was there notwithstanding all his philosophic calm and dignity of demeanour. He did not speak when he was annoyed or displeased, but worked off his volcanic wrath by firing pistols out of the back-door in rapid succession. Mrs Brontë, lying in bed up-stairs, would hear the quick explosions, and know that something had gone wrong; but her sweet nature thought invariably of the bright side, and she would say, 'Ought I not to be thankful that he never gave me an angry word?' Now and then his anger took a different form, but still was speechless. Once he got the hearth-rug, and stuffing it up the grate, deliberately set it on fire, and remained in the room in spite of the stench, until it had smouldered and shrivelled away into uselessness. Another time he took some chairs, and sawed away at the backs till they were reduced to the condition of stools.

He was an active walker, stretching away over the moors for many miles, noting in his mind all natural signs of wind and weather, and keenly observing all the wild creatures that came and went in the loneliest sweeps of the hills. He has seen eagles stooping low in search of food for their young; no eagle is ever seen on those mountain slopes now. He fearlessly took whatever side in local or national politics appeared to him right. In the days of the Luddites, he had been for the peremptory interference of the law, at a time when no magistrate could be found to act, and all the property of the West Riding was in terrible danger. He became unpopular there among the mill-workers, and he esteemed his life unsafe if he took his long and lonely walks unarmed; so he began the habit, which has continued to this day, of invariably carrying a loaded pistol about with him. It lay on his dressing-table with his watch; with his watch it was put on in the morning; with his watch it was taken off at night. Many years later, during his residence at Haworth, there was a strike; the hands in the neighbourhood felt themselves aggrieved by the masters, and refused to work; Mr Brontë thought that they had been unjustly and unfairly treated, and he assisted them by all the means in his power to 'keep the wolf from their doors,' and avoid the incubus of debt. Several of the more influential inhabitants of Haworth and the neighbourhood were mill-owners; they remonstrated pretty sharply with him, but he believed his conduct was right, and persevered in it.

His opinions might be often both wild and erroneous, his principles of action eccentric and strange, his views of life partial, and almost misanthropical; but not one opinion that he held could be stirred or modified by any worldly motive; he acted up to his principles of action; and, if any touch of misanthropy mingled with his view of mankind in general, his conduct to the individuals who came in personal contact with him did not agree with such view. It is true that he had strong and vehement prejudices, and was obstinate in maintaining them, and that he was not dramatic enough in his perceptions to see how miserable others might be in a life that to him was all-sufficient. But I do not pretend to be able to harmonize points of character, and account for them, and bring them all into one consistent and intelligible whole. The family with whom I have now to do shot their roots down deeper than I can penetrate. I cannot measure them, much less is it for me to judge them. I have named these instances of eccentricity in the father because I hold the knowledge of them to be necessary for a right understanding of the life of his daughter. ...

Owing to some illness of the digestive organs, Mr Brontë was obliged to be very careful about his diet; and in order to avoid temptation, and possibly to have the quiet necessary for digestion, he had begun, before his wife's death, to take his dinner alone, a habit which he always retained.[9] He did not require companionship, therefore he did not seek it, either in his walks, or in his daily life. The quiet regularity of his domestic hours was only broken in upon by churchwardens, and visitors on parochial business; and sometimes by a neighbouring clergyman, who came down from the hills, across the moors, to mount up again to Haworth Parsonage, and spend the evening there. But, owing to Mrs Brontë's death so soon after her husband had removed into the district, and also to the distances, and the bleak country to be traversed, the wives of these clerical friends did not accompany their husbands; and the daughters grew up out of childhood into girlhood bereft, in a singular manner, of all such society as would have been natural to their age, sex, and station. ...

But the children did not want society. To small infantine gaieties they were unaccustomed. They were all in all to each other. I do not suppose that there ever were a family more tenderly bound to each other. Maria read the newspapers, and reported intelligence to her younger sisters which it is wonderful they could take an interest in. But I suspect that they had no 'children's books,' and that their eager minds 'browzed undisturbed among the wholesome pasturage of English literature,' as Charles Lamb expresses it. The servants of the household appear to have been impressed with the little Brontës' extraordinary cleverness. In a letter which I had from him on this subject, their father writes: 'The servants often said that they had never seen such a clever child' (as Charlotte), 'and that they were obliged to be on their guard as to what they said and did before her. Yet she and the servants always lived on good terms with each other.' These servants are yet alive; elderly women residing in Bradford.[10] They retain a faithful and fond recollection of Charlotte. … One of these former servants went over from Bradford to Haworth on purpose to see Mr Brontë, and offer him her true sympathy, when his last child died. There might not be many to regard the Brontës with affection, but those who once loved them, loved them long and well.

[Here Mrs Gaskell recounts Patrick's story of questioning his children under cover of a mask.]

The strange and quaint simplicity of the mode taken by the father to ascertain the hidden characters of his children, and the tone and character of these questions and answers, show the curious education which was made by the circumstances surrounding the Brontës. They knew no other children. They knew no other modes of thought than what were suggested to them by the fragments of clerical conversation which they overheard in the parlour, or the subjects of village and local interest which they heard discussed in the kitchen. Each had their own strong characteristic flavour. They took a vivid interest in the public characters, and the local and foreign politics discussed in the newspapers. Long before Maria Brontë died, at the age of eleven, her father used to say he could converse with her on any of the leading topics of the day with as much freedom and pleasure as with any grown-up person.

Penguin Edition, edited by Alan Shelston (1975), pp. 77–95. This follows the text of the first edition.

Notes

1. Mrs Gaskell makes no mention of Patrick's curacy at Wellington in Shropshire.
2. Patrick's sister Alice said that Patrick did return home shortly after his ordination.
3. Mrs Gaskell has misspelt his name, which was Fennell.
4. The family's move to Haworth is usually dated to sometime between 10 and 20 April.
5. There was at least one surgeon in Haworth and John Greenwood sold stationery to the Brontë girls.
6. A charge Patrick always denied. See also the reference to 'Dinner Boiled Beef' in Emily and Anne's Diary Paper, 24 November 1834.
7. Nancy and Sarah Garrs vigorously denied this charge. See the testimonial which Patrick wrote for them, dated 17 August 1857.
8. Thomas Day (1748–1789) was an educational theorist and a disciple of Rousseau, who believed in a return to the simplicity of nature.
9. This statement is contradicted by Sarah Garrs, who many years later stated that the children dined at two o'clock with their father.
10. Nancy Garrs (who worked for the Brontë family, 1816–1824), and her sister Sarah (1818–1825). It was Nancy who visited Haworth in 1855. Sarah had emigrated with her husband to the United States.

Select Bibliography

Addison, William, *The English Country Parson*, Dent, 1947.
Alexander, Christine & Smith, Margaret, *The Oxford Companion to the Brontës*, Oxford, 2003.
Barker Juliet, *Sixty Treasures in the Brontë Parsonage Museum*, Brontë Society, 1988.
Barker, Juliet, *The Brontës*, Weidenfeld & Nicolson, 1994.
Barnard, Robert and Louise, *A Brontë Encyclopedia*, Blackwell, 2007.
Beeson, Trevor, *The Bishops*, SCM Press, 2002.
Bentley, Phyllis, *The Brontës and their world*, Thames & Hudson, 1969.
Bull, Angela, *The Machine Breakers: The Story of the Luddites*, Collins, 1980.
Burgess, Henry James, *Enterprise in Education*, The National Society & SPCK, 1958.
Carpenter, S. C., *Church and People, 1789–1889*, SPCK, 1933.
Crowe, W Haughton, *The Brontës of Ballynaskeagh*, Dundalgan Press ,1978.
Cannon, John, *The Road to Haworth*, Weidenfeld & Nicolson, 1980.
Chadwick, Owen, *The Victorian Church, Part I 1829–1859*, A. & C. Black, 1966.
Chapple, J. A. V. & Pollard, Arthur (edd), *The Letters of Mrs Gaskell*, Manchester University Press, 1966.
Chapple, John & Shelston, Alan (edd), *Further Letters of Mrs Gaskell*, Manchester University Press, 2000.
Chitham, Edward, *The Brontës' Irish Background*, Macmillan, 1986.
Chitham, *A Brontë Family Chronology*, Palgrave Macmillan, 2003.
Cochrane, Margaret & Robert, *My Dear Boy: The Life of Arthur Bell Nicholls*, Highgate Publications, 1999.
Colloms, Brenda, *Victorian Country Parsons*, Constable, 1977.
Cook, Faith, *William Grimshaw of Haworth*, Banner of Truth Trust, 1997.
Cragg, George W., *Grimshaw of Haworth*, The Canterbury Press, 1947.
Delafield, E.M., *The Brontës*, Hogarth Press, 1935 (reprinted Ian Hodgkins, 1979).
Dinsdale, Ann, *Old Haworth*, Hendon Publishing Co., 1999.
Dinsdale, Ann, *The Brontës at Haworth* (photographs by Simon Warner), Frances Lincoln, 2006.
Dinsdale, Ann, *The Brontë Connection*, Hendon Publishiong Co., 2007.
Emsley, Kenneth, *Historic Haworth Today*, Bradford Libraries, 1995.
Ewbank, Jane M., *The Life and Works of William Carus Wilson*, Titus Wilson, Kendal 1960.
Ferrett, Mabel, *A Short History of Hartshead Church*, 1993.
Flintoff, Eddie, *In the Steps of the Brontës*, Countryside books, 1993.
Fraser, Rebecca, *Charlotte Brontë*, Methuen, 1988.
Friar, Stephen, *A Companion to the English Parish Church*, Bramley Books, 1996.
Gardiner, *The Brontës at Haworth*, Collins & Brown, 1992.
Gaskell, Elizabeth, *The Life of Charlotte Brontë*, ed. Alan Shelston, Penguin Books, 1975.
Gérin, Winifred, *Charlotte Brontë: The Evolution of Genius*, Oxford, 1967.
Green, Dudley (ed.), *The Letters of the Reverend Patrick Brontë*, Nonsuch Publishing, 2005.
Grundy, Francis H., *Pictures of the Past* , Griffith & Farrar, 1879.
Hart, A Tindal, *The Curate's Lot*, John Baker, 1970.
Hinton, Michael, *The Anglican Parochial Clergy*, SCM Press, 1994.
Hopkins, Annette B., *The Father of the Brontës*, Johns Hopkins Press, 1958.
Howse, Ernest Marshall, *Saints in Politics: The 'Clapham Sect' and the Growth of Freedom*, Allen & Unwin, 1953.
Kellett, Jocelyn, *Haworth Parsonage*, Brontë Society, 1977.
Lane, Margaret, *The Brontë Story*, Heinemann, 1953.
Lemon, Charles, *Early Visitors to Haworth*, Brontë Society, 1996.
Leyland, Francis A., *The Brontë Family*, Hurst & Blackett, 2 vols, 1886.
Lloyd Evans, Barbara & Gareth, *Everyman's Companion to the Brontës*, Dent, 1982.

Lock, John & Dixon, W. T., *A Man of Sorrow, The Life, Letters and Times of the Rev Patrick Brontë*, Nelson, 1965.

May, Trevor, *The Victorian Clergyman*, Shire Publications, 2006.

Miller, Lucasta, *The Brontë Myth*, Jonathan Cape, 2001.

Moorman, J. R. H., *A History of the Church of England*, A. & C. Black, 1953.

Muir, Douglas N., *Postal Reform and the Penny Black*, National Postal Museum, 1990.

Neill, Stephen, *Anglicanism*, Penguin Books, 1958.

Palmer, Geoffrey, *Dear Martha …: The Letters of Arthur Bell Nicholls to Martha Brown*, The Brontë Society, 2004.

Peters, Margot, *Unquiet Soul: A Biography of Charlotte Brontë*, Hodder & Stoughton, 1975.

Pinion, F. B., *A Brontë Companion*, Macmillan, 1975.

Raymond, Ernest, *In the Steps of the Brontës*, Rich & Cowan, 1948.

Reid, T. Wemyss, *Charlotte Brontë*, Scribner Armstrong, 1877.

Russell, Anthony, *The Clerical Profession*, SPCK, 1980.

Russell, Anthony, *The Country Parish*, SPCK, 1986.

Scruton, William, *Thornton and the Brontës*, John Dale & Co., Bradford, 1898.

Shorter, Clement K., *Charlotte Brontë and her Circle*, Hodder & Stoughton, 1896.

Smith, Margaret (ed.), *The Letters of Charlotte Brontë*, Oxford, 3 vols, 1995, 2000, 2004.

Sowden, George, *Recollections of the Brontës*, ed. Ian & Catherine Emberson, Angria Press, 2005.

Steed, Michael, *A Brontë Diary*, Dalesman Books, 1990.

Sumner, Chris, *Reflections on the Brontës in Spen Valley & District*, 1973.

Tate, W. E., *The Parish Chest*, Cambridge, 1946.

Trodd, Valentine, *Banagher on the Shannon*, printed by subscription, 1985

Turner, Coreen, *Dear Saucy Pat*, The Book Guild, 2003.

Turner, J. Horsfall, (ed.), *Brontëana: The Rev. Patrick Brontë, A.B.: His Collected Works and Life*, T. Harrison & Sons, Bingley, 1898.

Turner, Whitely, *A Spring-Time Saunter: Round and About Brontë-Land*, Halifax Courier, 1913.

Vidler, Alec R., *The Church in an Age of Revolution*, Penguin Books, 1961.

Virgin, Peter, *The Church in an Age of Negligence*, James Clarke, 1989.

Walker, Arthur, *The Correspondence of the Brontë Family: A Guide*, E. J. Morten, 1982.

Whitehead, Barbara, *Charlotte Brontë and her 'dearest Nell'*, Smith Settle, 1993.

Whitehead, S. R., *The Brontës' Haworth*, Ashmount Press, 2006.

Wilks, *The Brontës*, Hamlyn, 1975.

Wilson, A. N., *The Victorians*, Hutchinson, 2002.

Wise, Thomas J. & Symington, J. Alexander, *The Brontës: Their Lives, friendships & Correspondence*, Blackwell (The Shakespeare Head), 4 vols, 1933.

Wood, Steven, *Haworth: 'A strange uncivilized little place'*, Tempus, 2005.

Woodward, Sir Llewellyn, *The Age of Reform 1815–1870*, Oxford, 1938.

Wright, Dr William, *The Brontës in Ireland*, Hodder & Stoughton, 1893 (reprinted Brontë Society Irish Section, 2004).

Wright, Uel, *The Rev. Dr. William Wright 1837–1899*, Presbyterian Historical Society of Ireland, 1986.

Yates, W. W., *The Father of the Brontës: His Life and work at Dewsbury and Hartshead*, Fred R Spark & Son, Leeds, 1897 (reprinted Imelda Marsden, 2006).

Index